BRITISH TRADE WITH SPANISH AMERICA,
1763-1808

VALUE OF X to WEST INDIES on AVG 4 years ending in
JAN 1796 £ 3.900.000 (1810 Bullion rept p 26 MR IRVING)

P108 APPX Repts Lords 1797   BILL DRAWN on the TREASURY

STO DOMINGO 296 029.6.10 (1794)   Leeward Island (893.16.1)

772.916.7.3 (1795)   51043.4.2

                                 St. Vincent & Grenada 64402.11.3

2241068.14.1. (1796)   Leeward   713 384.12.1

                       ST Vincent Grenada   74151.1.5

Liverpool Latin American Studies

Series Editors: Professor Catherine Davies, *University of Nottingham* and
Professor Allan J. Kuethe, *Texas Tech. University*
Emeritus Series Editor: Professor John Fisher

Liverpool Latin American Studies, New Series 9

British Trade with Spanish America, 1763–1808

Adrian J. Pearce

LIVERPOOL UNIVERSITY PRESS

First published 2007 by
Liverpool University Press
4 Cambridge Street
Liverpool L69 7ZU

This paperback edition published 2014

British Library Cataloguing-in-Publication data
A British Library CIP record is available

ISBN 978-1-84631-113-0 cased
978-1-78138-006-2 paperback

Typeset by XL Publishing Services, Exmouth
Printed and bound by CPI Group (UK) Ltd, Croydon, CR0 4YY

This work is dedicated to my parents,
Cliff and Jackie Pearce,
with love, admiration, and gratitude

Contents

List of Tables and Maps

Preface

I shall endeavour to approach as near to the probable truth as I am able; though it cannot be expected that, on a subject so complicated in its nature, and indeed so abstruse, by reason of the many intricate channels by which trade is conducted, and the utter impossibility there is of obtaining clear information on several points; I say, it cannot be expected, that anything more can be formed than a notional estimate.

—Long, *History of Jamaica*, 1:499–500

This book is conceived as a study of what might be called 'commercial flows'. Soon after I began in March 1999, the work came to centre around the question of how goods and produce moved from Britain to Spanish America, and from Spanish America to Britain, and in what quantities. This theme involved broader issues, including the factors (geographical, political, institutional, and purely mercantile) which affected this trade, and how they affected it; what commodities were traded on either side; and how much it was all worth. (The latter question seemed particularly important to me, as well as particularly difficult to answer; though at successive conferences and seminars in recent years, I have become aware of the scant importance most scholars now attach to this issue.) Seven years down the line (the last three of them combined with teaching at the universities of Warwick and Nottingham Trent), this book represents close to the best answer I am able to give to these questions. And while many aspects remain unclear or insufficiently explained, I think there is enough evidence here to demonstrate that the foregoing quotation by Edward Long, the eighteenth-century Jamaican historian, while an attractive way to open the study, is essentially misleading. It is misleading to the degree that it exaggerates the 'unknowability' of British trade with Spanish America, of which considerably more can be formed than merely 'a notional estimate'.

The work is intended as a survey of British trade with the Spanish colonies in its entirety, but I am acutely aware that one subject is inadequately discussed in these pages. This is the British slave trade with Spanish America. My book is, first and foremost, a study of the (non-human) commodities trade between Britain and the Spanish colonies. Within that framework, I discuss the trade in enslaved Africans frequently, drawing for the most part on the same body of literature as provides the basis for the rest of my account. But I do not discuss it as fully as I could have wished, nor do I venture very far into the specialist literature devoted to the slave trade. The reason for this emphasis was partly simply practical: there is a limit to how much material any scholar can read and digest effectively in the time available, and this is an ambitious and challenging study as it stands. But it is also true that the slave trade has been analysed in far greater depth than the commodities trade, and that several excellent and up-to-date studies are already available. Historians, including David Eltis, Herbert Klein, and Joseph Inikori, among others, have transformed our understanding of the slave trade in general, and the British slave trade in particular, in recent years.[1] I refer scholars to this body of literature to complement my own study of the commodities trade – a subject which has been far less studied in recent times, and is far less well understood in the details of its operation (and, indeed, in its general outline).

One issue relating to the slave trade requires specific comment, or clarification. The British trade in slaves with the Spanish colonies was overwhelmingly an indirect one; that is to say, only a small minority of Africans were shipped by the British direct from Africa to Spanish-American ports. Most were taken to the British colonies in the West Indies (above all Jamaica, but also Barbados, Dominica, Grenada, and others) for subsequent re-shipment to the Spanish colonies. This was true even during the era of the British-held *Asiento de negros* in 1713–39, when the British had their own factories in the Spanish colonies, and yet shipped only 16 per cent of slaves direct from Africa,[2] and it remained true throughout the late eighteenth century. Slaves formed part of broader exports from the British West Indies to the Spanish colonies, then, and in principle they were included in estimates of the value of that export trade. In principle, but not always in practice; there are occasions when it is unclear whether estimates given by British observers include the value of slaves along with non-human exports. Where slaves were expressly included in contemporary estimates of value, I have indicated this throughout the text, but in some cases a degree of ambiguity remains. Some of the estimates I report may not include the slave trade, while elsewhere some (probably small) proportion of slaves were exported direct from Africa or from other regions (especially the United States) and are likely to have slipped under my radar. I do not think that occasional instances of possible non-inclusion of the slave trade are likely to affect my estimates for the value of British exports more than marginally. This is particularly true of the period of warfare which began in 1796, when British slavers were barred from Spanish colonial ports (where they had been welcome since 1789), and slaves were even excluded from the list of permitted exports from the British free ports in the West Indies.[3] Nevertheless, for these reasons, it may be that some part of the full contribution of the slave trade to British commerce with the Spanish colonies has eluded me.

A further point worth emphasising is that, although intended as a survey of the commodities trade as a whole, the work focuses principally upon British trade which was routed via entrepôts in the West Indies: on the goods sent out from Britain to Jamaica, Trinidad, or the Bahamas, and sent on from there to Mexico, Cuba, or Venezuela. This focus was determined by practical considerations, since the other great branch of trade with Spanish America, routed via ports in the Iberian Peninsula and above all in Andalusia, is far harder to trace. That trade awaits really detailed study, though I have attempted to present a synthesis of current knowledge regarding it, drawn principally from the rather slim number of relevant secondary sources. After a survey of the origins of British trade with the Spanish colonies (in Chapter 1), the work focuses above all on the period 1763–1808. In his Introductory Essay, John Fisher explains the broad reasons behind the selection of this period; but in a narrower sense, the start date of 1763 is for the Peace of Paris, whose impact on British trade through the expansion of British colonies in the West Indies is explored in Chapter 2, and which came only a few years before the first free ports in the British islands. The end date, by contrast, shifted as the work progressed, from 1824 at a very early date, to 1810 much later; it eventually reached 1808, once I became aware that the Anglo-Spanish peace of July that year, with the onset of Spanish-American Independence over the following two years, clearly marked a new epoch in Anglo-Spanish American commercial relations.

A couple of points on terminology: I use 'British' and 'Britain' throughout the text to refer to events post-dating the Act of Union of 1707. These terms thus stand as the translation for *inglés / ingleses / Inglaterra* from Spanish documents referring to the same period, which not only seems technically correct, but also recognises the fact that 'British' has never taken root in the Hispanic world, where *inglés* is still standard usage for British even today. Secondly, in the interests of accesibility to Anglophone scholars unfamiliar with the Spanish-American context, I have used the modern rather than the colonial names of the various regions discussed. Thus, 'Mexico' is used in place of 'New Spain', 'Venezuela' rather than 'Caracas', and so forth. The exception to this rule is the use throughout of the name 'New Granada', since – unlike, I think, with the other regions – recourse to the name 'Colombia' would have been too clearly anachronistic. Additionally, and anticipating the interest of Latin American scholars in the impact of British trade in their own countries, I have kept the sections of each chapter devoted to them as discrete, and so as easy to locate, as possible; in fact, they are usually discussed in the repeating pattern Mexico / Cuba / New Granada / Venezuela and, where appropriate, Puerto Rico and Santo Domingo.

The study of British trade with Spanish America tends to advance by small steps, separated by lengthy periods of relative inaction. In recent years, this slow progress may have occurred in part because – like much economic or economically oriented history – the subject has fallen out of favour, and attracts less interest than once it did. The broader reason, nevertheless, derives from the fact that it was a contraband trade throughout most of its existence, and a secretive one even after its practical legalisation in the second half of the eighteenth century. This in turn renders it a thankless subject of study. It is perfectly possible to spend weeks of diligent labour in the National Archives in London, or the Archivo General de Indias in Seville – as I did – and come away with only a few scraps of information, of apparently modest significance; a thoroughly demoralising process. This may be why the book I regard as the most direct predecessor to this work, Frances Armytage's *The Free Port System in the British West Indies*, was published over fifty years ago (in 1953). And similarly, it may be that no-one attempts another book-length study of this subject for some time. To the next scholar to undertake what can often be a daunting task, then, I say this: take heart. There is little question that abundant information still lies undetected among the mass of documentation held in archives, particularly in London, but also in Seville and elsewhere.

It is customary in prefaces to express gratitude to the staff of the archives and libraries consulted throughout the life of the project. I have to say that my experience of archivists and librarians has not been one of universal welcome or efficiency. But I certainly found both at the National Archives and the British Library in London, and the Sheffield Archives and Staffordshire Record Office; the Archivo Histórico Nacional in Madrid and the Archivo General de Simancas, outside Valladolid; the Archivo General de la Nación in Mexico, Archivo Nacional de Cuba in Havana, and especially the Archivo General de la Nación in Colombia; and the National Archives and Library of Congress in Washington. I also enjoyed and benefited hugely from access to Senate House Library and the Library of the West India Committee (at the Institute of Commonwealth Studies), both in London; the Sydney Jones Library of the University of Liverpool, and John Rylands University Library of Manchester; the library of the Escuela de Estudios Hispano-Americanos, the library of the Universidad Hispalense, and the Biblioteca de la Región Militar Sur, all in Seville, the Biblioteca Nacional, the library of the Colegio de México, and the library of the Instituto Mora, all in Mexico City, the Biblioteca Nacional José Martí in Havana, and the Biblioteca Nacional and Biblioteca Luis Angel Arango in Bogotá.

I have many other people I wish to thank. Special gratitude is due to my former supervisor, and colleague on this project, Professor John Fisher, who has supplied an extremely generous Introductory Essay to the work. John had the vision to perceive that a study such as this was both necessary and feasible, when many would have doubted this, and he secured the funding which made it possible. This book would neither have been commenced, nor carried to conclusion, without his influence. I am very grateful to the Arts and Humanities Research Council for funding the study. The AHRC grant was generous enough to facilitate not only stays of over a year each in London and Seville, but also research visits to Madrid, Washington, Mexico City, Havana, and Bogotá (Caracas eluded me!) without which this study would have been subject to serious limitations. The investment which the grant represented has so far yielded this book, two articles, an edited document, and nine conference and seminar papers, while a further two articles, an edited collection of primary sources, and another book are planned. I would also like to thank Robin Bloxsidge and Anthony Cond, successive editors at Liverpool University Press, for not only accepting my typescript for publication, but also being unusually generous with the word limit.

Several friends and scholars read sections of the work as it progressed. Lorna Scott Fox read part of Chapter 2, and Matt Adams the part of Chapter 4 which was subsequently published as an article in the *Journal of Latin American Studies*. Rebecca Earle not only read complete drafts of Chapters 2–6 of the manuscript, but spent several hours discussing her perceptive and provocative comments with me. This was beyond any reasonable call of duty, but amply reflected her generous and constructive attitude towards colleagues, friends, and students alike. Rory Miller and James Dunkerley similarly offered valuable and generous advice on draft articles or conference papers.

In Seville, Antonio García-Baquero González and Justina Sarabia Viejo were free with time and advice. The group of friends who gathered around the café Las Meninas near the Archivo de Indias and the 'café de las once' (our name for it) and the bar Dos de Mayo near the Escuela de Estudios Hispano-Americanos expanded and contracted over time, as the community of scholars in Seville does. My group at different times included Delphine Tempère, Takeshi Fushimi, Berndt Hausberger, José-Mari Aguiler, and Montse Cachero, as well as Leticia Magallanes, Juani Barrios, and 'Juana de Pamplona' (not her real name). Sergio Rodríguez Lorenzo shared his vast knowledge of Spanish Atlantic trade and provided assistance with naval terminology. Ascensión Baeza Martín shares an earlier obsession, with early Bourbon viceroys. Cynthia Milton preferred the bars behind the Macarena wall, and shared a strange adventure in the Sierra Norte de Sevilla, while Leo Garofalo gave insight into the workings of the US academy. Gloria Borrego Gamito and Miguel Sánchez Esandi provided the homes in which I lived in Seville (in the Macarena and San Lorenzo) on and off between 2000 and 2003. Johannes Zimmerman gave me a non-historical perspective and one extraordinary day in the hills of Cadiz, while Jeff Singer and Andy Kennard provided inspiration and inebriation on a memorable visit in 2003. Chuck Walker supplied great conversation, professional insights, and even references when they were needed, while George Lovell knows the bars of Seville better than anyone and is their noblest guide.

Away from Seville, my cousin Marion Lewis, her husband Reg Ellwood, and their son Tom were warmly hospitable during the year I lived in Chiswick in London in 1999–2000. Jill Lane, Manuel Barcia, and José Ortega enlightened and enlivened my research trip to Havana in May 2001, and Jill put me up in her home in New York during my visit to the United States later the same year.

Tony McFarlane was generous enough to invite me to teach for two years at the School of Comparative American Studies of the University of Warwick in 2003–05, when the funding from my post-doctoral award was already exhausted. Tony and his wife Angela were unstintingly welcoming and supportive, both profesionally and personally, during that time, and his popular course on Pre-Columbian and Spanish America has proved influential in my teaching since. Working at CAS was a wonderful experience, amid one of the UK's strongest collections of Americanist expertise, and I'd like to thank all my colleagues there, particularly Guy Thomson, John King, Gad Heuman, Chris Clark, Roger Fagge, David Nye, and Rebecca Earle, for proving so welcoming. Again, my colleagues at Nottingham Trent since July 2005 have been marvellously supportive and welcoming. My thanks to all, and especially to Ian Inkster and Siobhan Lambert-Hurley, my co-teachers on 'World History since 1500', and Kevin Gould, who gave several days of his time and of his great expertise in the preparation of the maps. Particularly warm thanks are due to Angela Brown, the head of History and Heritage, for so arranging my timetable as to make it possible for me to crack on with the writing even during my first year at NTU.

Outside of my field and immediate working environment, the *cuatro magníficos*, John Croose, Paul Heggarty, Tim Marr, and John Dawe, provided assistance of a different kind, based on advice, humour, enthusiasm, and affection, over many years and in countless venues. The same sentiments apply in still greater measure to my sister Katherine Tansley and her husband Robert, my niece Lucy and nephew Edward, and my twin brother Martin Pearce and his partner Margaret. This work is dedicated to my parents, Cliff and Jackie Pearce.

Lastly, all my love to my son, Chilam, who will be almost two by the time this book is published.

Puebla
11 August 2006

Notes

[1] For a small sample of this work, see Herbert S. Klein, *The Atlantic Slave Trade* (Cambridge: Cambridge University Press, 1999); David Eltis, *The Rise of African Slavery in the Americas* (New York: Cambridge University Press, 2000); Joseph E. Inikori, *Africans and the Industrial Revolution in England: A Study in International Trade and Economic Development* (Cambridge: Cambridge University Press, 2002); and David Eltis *et al.* (eds.), *The Trans-Atlantic Slave Trade: A Database on CD-ROM* (Cambridge and New York: Cambridge University Press, 1999).

[2] P. 19 below.

[3] P. 123; for the Peace of Amiens (1802–04), see p. 132.

List of Abbreviations

Archive Collections

A.G.I.	Archivo General de Indias, Seville
A.G.N.C.	Archivo General de la Nación, Colombia
A.G.N.M.	Archivo General de la Nación, Mexico
A.G.S.	Archivo General de Simancas, Simancas, Spain
A.H.N.	Archivo Histórico Nacional, Madrid
A.M.N.	Archivo del Museo Naval, Madrid
A.N.C.	Archivo Nacional de Cuba, Havana
B.L.	British Library, London
N.A.W.	National Archives, Washington
N.A.	National Archives, London
S.A., W.W.M., R.	Sheffield Archives, Wentworth Woodhouse Muniments, Rockingham Papers
S.R.O., D. (W.)	Staffordshire Record Office, Dartmouth Papers

Sections of the National Archives, London

ADM.	Admiralty
B.T.	Board of Trade
C.O.	Colonial Office
Cust.	Papers of H.M. Customs
F.O.	Foreign Office
P.C.	Privy Council
PRO.	Public Record Office
S.P.	State Papers, Foreign
T.	Treasury

Note on Exchange Rates and Values

The rate of exchange applied by the British to the Spanish-American *peso fuerte* or *peso duro* was calculated at a remarkably precise £1 sterling = 4.44 pesos throughout the period covered by this book. This rate is applied in the text in all cases of conversion between the two currencies. For general purposes, at least during the Napoleonic wars, the rate was sometimes rounded in contemporary sources to £1 = 5 pesos. The Spanish-American peso and the US dollar were held to be at par throughout these years. The exchange rate of the Spanish-American peso against the French franc was generally calculated at 1 peso = 5 francs.

Among the most important problems facing students of British foreign trade before the late nineteenth century is the use of official values accorded commodities in government statistics. In the principal statistical series, the records of the Inspector-General of Imports and Exports, these values were fixed by the early eighteenth century and remained in use until well after 1800. The statistical data available may thus be used with caution to measure volumes and general trends of exports, but they are extremely problematic as sources for the value of trade.[1]

This book presents values for British trade with Spanish America via all its major routes: via the Iberian peninsula, entrepôts in the West Indies, and (after 1796) the neutral powers of Europe and the United States. It is to be emphasised that all such values are understood to be *current at the time they were given*, in pounds sterling. There are many disadvantages to working with a trade which was contraband during much of its existence, and secretive and little recorded thereafter. But one advantage is that the lack of formal statistical series freed expert observers (whether government ministers, West Indian governors, customs officers, or merchants) from reliance on obsolete official values. When these observers enquired after or estimated the value of trade via Cadiz, or Jamaica, or the United States, they necessarily did so in terms of the values current at the time. There are certainly many problems with the sorts of estimates available from such sources, and these are discussed in detail hereafter,[2] but they do at least cut the Gordian knot of fossilised official values.

Lastly, the only detailed official series describing a major branch of British trade with the Spanish colonies, which came to light for the first time during the course of the current research, and is discussed at length in Chapter 3, also avoids the problem of official values. The unique series in the 'States of Navigation and Commerce' for 1792–95, prepared by Inspector-General of Imports and Exports Thomas Irving, gives values which were current at the beginning of the series (that is to say, in 1792), though they remained constant thereafter. These current values, prepared by an official with unusual expertise in American trade and prices, make this series unique among eighteenth-century British records of foreign trade, and an unusually important source for British commercial relations with the Spanish colonies.

Notes

1   See p. 98 below.
2   See esp. pp. 238–9 below.

Introductory Essay

Professor John R. Fisher
Professor of Latin American History
University of Liverpool

The distant and indirect origins of this book lie in my research on Spanish colonial trade, undertaken over more than two decades between the late 1970s and the late 1990s. This saga began with what was intended to be a relatively limited sojourn in the Archivo General de Simancas in 1977, which aimed to get to the bottom of one of the most significant and complex debates of modern Spanish-American historiography: that which concerns Spain's Atlantic trade and the results of the Bourbon monarchy's attempts to reform it, especially from 1765 onwards, through the gradual introduction of 'free trade'. This process reached its first peak in 1778, when the publication by the crown of the *Reglamento para el comercio libre* (Regulation of Free Trade) formally abolished the monopoly of colonial trade enjoyed by the port of Cádiz, by enfranchising twelve additional Spanish ports to trade directly with the principal ports of Spanish America, although a further eleven years would pass before lingering restrictions on trade with Venezuela and the Mexican port of Veracruz were lifted.

The plan in 1977 was to spend several weeks in Simancas analysing the contents of the fourteen boxes (*legajos*) of documents located there that deal specifically with the recording of shipping movements in each direction between Spain and America in 1778–88, and related ministerial correspondence, with a view to settling once and for all the question of whether trade doubled in value in this period (as some scholars asserted), or multiplied sevenfold (as others claimed), or fell somewhere between these two extremes. However, it rapidly became clear as the research progressed that the annual summaries of shipping held in Simancas were incomplete, and entirely lacking for the principal peninsular port of Cádiz. Faced with the choice of abandoning the enterprise or of resorting to the reading and analysis of the thousands of registers of the individual ships, mostly untouched by previous researchers, held in the Archivo General de Indias (A.G.I.) of Sevilla, I opted (perhaps unwisely, I sometimes thought, as I laboured year after year during the next decade in the heat of Andalucía) for the latter course. It also soon became clear that the most sensible terminal point for the initial phase of research was not 1788 (the year when Charles III died after twenty-nine years on the throne, and his prime minister, the Conde de Floridablanca attempted to evaluate for his successor, Charles IV, the significance of his father's imperial policies) but 1796 when Spain again went to war with Britain, with disastrous commercial consequences. I ended up scrutinising nearly 7,000 shipping registers, of which 2,812 were of vessels sailing for America, and 4,012 for those arriving in Spain. In the vast majority of cases, the register records the ship's name and alias, those of its captain and owner(s) – sometimes the same – its destination(s) and intended date of departure, and a detailed inventory of its cargo, valued according to the requirements of the 1778 legislation, together with details of the duties levied by customs officials. I subsequently undertook a follow-up investigation of exports from Spain to Spanish America in 1797–1820, which involved reading a further 2,582 registers, before deciding that enough was enough. The missing piece of the jigsaw, insofar as Spain is concerned, is the value of imports from America in the post-1796 period: in my view the fragmentary nature of the documentation available makes it impossible to undertake this task satisfactorily. Moreover, as Chapters 4–6 of this book demonstrate with remarkable clarity and precision, after 1796 exports from Spanish America to Spain were of steadily diminishing importance in relation to direct Spanish-American trade with neutrals and, remarkably, with the enemy.

The context for the work outlined in the above paragraph was, as is well known, the fact that after the brilliant early years of the Spanish-American silver-mining boom that had reached its peak around 1600, an extended process of decline had affected Spain's colonial trade, whose dramatic effects – principally, the declining frequency of transatlantic fleets, lower returns to the crown in commercial taxation as a consequence of both a genuine downturn in trade and increased expenditure of royal revenues on defence in America, the stark absence of a national manufacturing sector, and pervasive penetration of the commercial monopoly by foreign rivals, to select only the most salient aspects – could no longer be ignored by the eighteenth century.[1] On the accession of Philip V to the throne of Spain in 1700, the new Bourbon dynasty soon began to tinker with the trading system inherited from its Habsburg predecessors. However, despite some significant innovations in the first half of the century (including the abolition of convoys to the isthmus of Panama in favour of supplying the viceroyalty of Peru by individual register ships sailing directly into the Pacific) it was only from 1765 (following the dramatic and symbolic loss of Havana to the British during the Seven Years War), and particularly from 1778, that a programme of reforms was implemented which, if it did not pretend to alter the essential monopoly character of colonial trade – that was too far a step to contemplate for any but a handful of unusually economically enlightened Spaniards – nevertheless brought about by far the most wide-ranging reorganisation of Spanish colonial commerce since the creation of the fleet system in the late 1560s. This programme of reforms is known collectively to historians of the Hispanic world as 'free trade', since – its essentially conservative nature notwithstanding – its central feature was not only the aforementioned enfranchisement between 1765 and 1789 of the principal ports of Spain and Spanish America to trade freely with each other, but also the erosion of the monopolies of receiving, distributing and supplying merchandise hitherto enjoyed by the members of the merchant guilds of Cádiz, Lima, and Mexico, thereby opening the commercial door to peripheral merchant groups excluded from trade under the former regime.

My work on this 'free trade', developed in three monographs and over twenty essays and journal articles published in the period 1979–98, studied in depth both the process of the reforms and their repercussions. My conclusions emphasise the broad success of the programme: the value of exports from Spain to Spanish America increased no less than fourfold across the period 1778–96, while that of imports from the colonies to Spain grew more than tenfold in the same years. These figures, especially those for imports, continue to provoke scholarly debate as to their accuracy: one possible criticism is that the base year, 1778, was untypical, since merchants on both sides of the Atlantic kept their ships in port in anticipation of Spain's entry into the War of American Independence, knowing that this would put them at risk of seizures by the British navy; another is that the figures for the value of imports into Spain from America for that year produced by the officials of the crown's Dirección General de Rentas (General Direction of Taxes) did not include the value of bullion hastily shipped to the peninsula aboard warships, again in anticipation of the outbreak of hostilities, whereas such shipments were included in the shipping registers for 1782–96 (there was virtually no movement of shipping in 1779–81 because of the war), thereby exaggerating the post-war increase in the value of imports. Despite these caveats, it is highly likely that my findings actually understate the real value of the boom in Spanish Atlantic trade in the late eighteenth century, at least until it was brought to an abrupt conclusion by the outbreak of war with Britain in 1796.[2] One reason for this view is that a reliance on individual shipping registers, although unavoidable, takes no account of those that have disappeared for whatever reason. Another, which might actually be seen as a benefit rather than a drawback for the historian, is that the registers, drawn up by customs officers in the ports of Spain for both departing and arriving vessels, recorded the official values of commodities as prescribed by the *arancel* (list of tariffs) appended to the 1778 Regulation. This laid down with precision the official values of a comprehensive list of products, and specified the duties to be charged in each case upon those of 'national' origin as opposed to those imported from other countries for re-export. A hundredweight of imported *bacalao* (salt cod), for example, usually of Portuguese origin, was declared to be worth 60 *reales de vellón* (the equivalent of three *pesos fuertes,* or less than £1 sterling, using the ratio of £1 sterling:4.44 pesos suggested by Pearce in his discussion of exchange rates), and the duty payable on it was four-and-one-fifth *reales*: even in Cádiz its wholesale value was probably about 15 per cent higher, and its real value would have multiplied many times once it reached the kitchen of a rich resident of Mexico City where then, as now, it represented an indispensable ingredient for dinner on Christmas Eve (at least for those who could/can afford it). It would have been washed down with a flagon of wine from Málaga or Jerez, again ridiculously undervalued at ten *reales* per *arroba:* the real values of items such as these, like the vast majority of agricultural and viticultural products exported in increasing quantities to the colonies in the post-1778 period, were determined not by the price of fish in Veracruz or of maize and beans in places like Oaxaca and Guanajuato, but by the ostentatious insistence of the colonial elites in preserving peninsular traditions that enabled them to remain different from the Indian and mixed-race masses who consumed native products. The key point is that official values understate market values, but they have the advantage of enabling us to compare like with like in different years, irrespective of fluctuations either way in the marketplace.

With this cycle of research largely complete by the late 1990s, subject to the omission, noted above, of a comprehensive study of imports into Spain from Spanish America after 1796 (in my view impossible to undertake on a comprehensive basis because of the fragmentary nature of the surviving documentation, and, as Pearce demonstrates in this volume, of less interest than what happened up to 1796 because thereafter so much trade was conducted outside of traditional routes), there remained a major loose end still to be tied: the role of foreign intervention in Spanish Atlantic commerce during the 'free trade' era, and particularly the role of the British in the erosion of Spain's nominal monopoly of commercial intercourse with its American possessions. Foreign penetration of this monopoly was apparent from an early date, with expeditions of trade and plunder by the French and English already under way by the late sixteenth century and increasing rapidly in the seventeenth. In its maturity, this penetration took two forms, following two quite distinct routes. First, foreign merchants sought to infiltrate the formal Spanish trading system by establishing themselves in the sole Spanish port granted the monopoly of trade with the Indies: first, Seville in the sixteenth and seventeenth centuries, and thereafter Cádiz, following the formal transfer there in 1717 of both the merchant guild of Seville and the Casa de la Contratación (House of Trade), the official body, founded in Sevilla in 1503, with responsibility for the regulation of trade until its abolition in 1790 in the wake of the 1778/89 legislation which made it redundant. Thus, foreign merchants traded in these ports, using a variety of mechanisms (summarised by Pearce in Chapter 1) whose goal was the despatch of manufactures from Britain, France, Germany, and elsewhere in the trade fleets, their sale in the Spanish colonies, and repatriation of the profits to the foreign merchant communities. Secondly, rival nations short-circuited the commercial monopoly entirely by trading directly with the Spanish colonies in the Americas in frank disregard of the law; in short, by smuggling. British, French and Dutch merchants ventured to the Caribbean and the adjacent continent – the 'Spanish Main' of pirate tales – and even further afield, to the River

Plate and, less frequently, the Pacific, to trade, under the benign gaze of compliant local officials, with Spanish merchants only too eager to compensate for the high prices and inadequate supplies which were all but inevitable by-products of the monopoly system. This direct contraband trade – itself a rival to trade by foreigners out of Seville or Cádiz – flourished especially after Spain's competitors established their first permanent bases, or colonial possessions, in the Caribbean in the early seventeenth century: the Dutch at Curaçao, the French at St Domingue (modern Haiti) and Guadeloupe, and the British at (initially) St Kitts, Barbados and Jamaica. These islands, initially the havens of pirates (useful occasionally to their nominal masters as privateers during times of war with Spain) became the chief platforms for systematic assault on the commercial monopoly in the Spanish colonies themselves, as in the late seventeenth and early eighteenth centuries the navies of Spain's rivals themselves gradually rooted out their lawless elements in order to encourage both a regulated trade and the production of plantation crops for the international market.

Throughout the seventeenth century, and well into the eighteenth, the share of trade with Spanish America that the British enjoyed was simply one among many. In the re-export trade out of Seville, and thereafter Cádiz, British exports played a perhaps surprisingly distant second fiddle to those of French, Italian, Dutch, and other merchants. The French above all dominated the trade throughout much of the 1600s, and had achieved a probable new peak of influence after the turn of the century, underpinned by not only a powerful textiles industry and merchant class, but also by the close – albeit occasionally fractious – Franco-Spanish alliance inaugurated with the Bourbon succession in Spain in 1700. Only around the mid-eighteenth century do the British appear to have begun to draw even with the French in re-exports from the Iberian Peninsula, and even then it remains doubtful whether they ever displaced them as the leading foreign traders. Since the re-export trade remained the foremost platform for foreign penetration of Spanish Atlantic commerce until the last few years of the eighteenth century – as Pearce argues below[3] – this might have mitigated Spanish animosity over British commercial penetration of the colonial monopoly. But a secondary share possessed by an enemy weighed more heavily than a dominant one possessed by an ally, besides which – in frank but typical disregard for economic realities – the re-export trade figured less prominently in the preoccupations of Spanish economists and politicians than did that perennial *bête noire* (and principal focus of Pearce's monograph), contraband trade in the Americas.

Even among foreign smugglers in the Caribbean, the British were long obliged to content themselves with the minority share left them by commercial rivals at least as powerful as themselves. The leading smugglers throughout much of the seventeenth century were probably the Dutch, particularly after they acquired their major bases at Curaçao and St Eustatius – islands claimed but undefended by Spain – in the 1630s. The Dutch, indeed, retained a major share in smuggling along the northern coast of South America – particularly with Venezuela, but also as far as the coasts of Central America south of Yucatán – throughout the 1700s, only to be finally eclipsed by the British after 1800. During the eighteenth century, nevertheless, Britain's greatest rivals were the French, who took formal possession of their own major base – at St Domingue, the western third of Hispaniola – by the Treaty of Ryswick in 1697. A crumb of comfort for the beleaguered advisers of the feeble Charles II of Spain, the last of its Hapsburg kings, was that Louis XIV fulfilled the promise that, in return, French buccaneers based in Tortuga and other islands – used most recently by his navy to support the lucrative capture in 1697 of Cartagena de Indias (the principal Caribbean port of New Granada – modern Colombia) would be offered the choice of becoming planters or being hunted down as pirates by French forces. The richest of all the plantation economies, St Domingue was also a major trading colony, which competed successfully with Jamaica in several Spanish-American markets until its immolation in the great slave revolt of 1791, when the island's 500,000 slaves massacred most of its 40,000 whites and free coloureds, with those who survived fleeing to Cuba and Venezuela. As Pearce shows throughout the study which follows, the volume and value of British contraband grew rapidly following the creation of free ports in Jamaica – captured from Spain in 1655 on the orders of Oliver Cromwell by a force largely recruited from indentured servants in Barbados, which, despite their poor training, easily overcame the island's 1,500 Spanish inhabitants – and Dominica in difficult commercial circumstances in the early 1760s. In the last third of the century, the British were clearly the leading 'smuggling power' throughout the region. But it was only in the dying years, and especially from the onset of the Napoleonic wars in the 1790s, that this dominance became absolute.

Such a chronology of the construction of British commercial hegemony in the West Indies – more persuasive and fine-grained than anything available to date – would merely have confirmed long-standing Spanish fears and prejudices. Throughout the Bourbon era, as Stanley Stein and Barbara Stein have recently put it, 'in the three-cornered struggle in the Atlantic over empire in America, Spaniards saw England as the aggressor state'[4] – hardly surprising, given the Bourbon alliance with the third player, France. Spanish paranoia over British commercial depredations in the Americas runs as an unbroken thread through the commercial and political correspondence of the eighteenth century. In 1767, British meddling in the Falkland Islands (and supposedly also Paraguay) prompted Spain's ambassador to London to 'infer that the intention of this Government is to take for itself the Commerce of all the Nations'.[5] In 1776–1777, with Britain distracted by events in North America, Charles III and his advisors sought to curb this perceived threat by going on the offensive in the River Plate region, where a 10,000-strong expeditionary force drove Portuguese intruders from Brazil out of the Banda Oriental (modern Uruguay) and established the new viceroyalty of the Río de la Plata, with its capital in Buenos Aires, in an attempt to bolster defences in this exposed flank of empire. In 1792, a later Spanish ambassador to Britain, the Marqués del Campo, predicted with some foresight that the European war then imminent – in which Spain would fight briefly (1793-1795) alongside Britain against France – 'must be the height of happy felicity [*de contento felicidad*] for the British Nation. Certainly its Flag will draw unto itself all of our Trade and navigation, since it will be the most respected in the World'.[6] Britain's clear aim in the Americas, in short, could be characterised as to 'expand its trade, oppose that of other powers, and then invade their colonies'.[7] No scholar working on Spanish Atlantic trade during this period can be unaware of this concern, at times bordering on obsession, with British interloping, in the Caribbean and elsewhere; but it is much more difficult to gain a sense of the reality behind the rhetoric. Just how serious a commercial threat did the British represent? How much of this threat was real, and how much was merely conjured up by over-excited ministerial imaginations? How did British trade affect Spanish Atlantic commerce, and how did Spanish commercial reforms impact upon the business of the British? What was the real worth, to the degree that it is possible to determine such a thing, of British trade with Spanish America during the era of 'free trade'? All these were questions to which the existing literature offered only partial and limited responses.

Despite my interest in this topic – and also despite its manifest importance to students of British economic as well as imperial history, in addition to historians of the Spanish colonies – other research commitments, and my administrative workload as Director of the Institute of Latin American Studies in Liverpool, meant it was unlikely I would have time to devote to it myself. Happily, there remained the alternative of delegating the work to someone else. In 1998, Adrian Pearce completed a doctoral thesis under my direction on Spanish rule in the viceroyalty of Peru during the early Bourbon period (1700–59).[8] My association with Pearce went back some years earlier, to 1993, when he began an MA in Latin American Studies at the Institute, which was awarded with distinction the following year, and led to the commencement of his PhD (funded by a British Academy studentship) in 1994. Pearce's doctorate – which took me back to my first area of expertise as a Peruvianist, albeit of a slightly later period – was a model of incisive scholarship which has since produced two seminal articles published in leading Americanist journals.[9] Moreover, it was very much his own work, a product of his brilliance as a researcher and the benign form of supervision that used to be permitted in the best universities before the quality assurance maniacs were let loose and research 'training', often delivered by failed researchers, began to eat up the time previously devoted to real research. In the summer of 1998, I secured an award from the University of Liverpool's Research Development Fund for Pearce to explore the feasibility of a project on British trade with the Hispanic world during the era of Spanish 'free trade'. As the recipient of this grant, he spent six weeks in the University library and the

National Archives (at that time still the Public Record Office), assessing the range and quality of published and primary source material available for such a study. This preliminary research led to submission to the Arts and Humanities Research Board (now the Arts and Humanities Research Council) of an application for a major grant for a project then titled 'British Trade with the Hispanic World, 1763–1824'. This application was successful – indeed, it enjoyed (I believe) the distinction of being one of the first awards made nationally by the AHRB, then of recent creation – resulting in an initial grant of £39,000 for one year, while the Board found its feet in spending hitherto unheard-of sums for the support of research in the humanities, eventually increasing to £126,000 over three years. With hindsight, I should have asked for more over a longer period, although this did not become immediately clear. The funds provided proved sufficient, nevertheless, for the appointment of Pearce to a research fellowship for the period 1 March 1999–31 August 2002, the last six months of which were funded by the overhead paid by the AHRB to the University of Liverpool (another example of the more relaxed regime that operated in HEIs before the advent of Full Economic Costing, Time Allocation Schedules, and all that jazz).[10] The current monograph – some years down the line, and with a rather narrower focus than was originally (and with hindsight, over-ambitiously) envisaged – is the product of that grant; and I here add my gratitude to that already expressed by Pearce to the AHRB/AHRC in his Preface, for its foresight in financing the project.

That foresight has been richly rewarded, in my view. The present monograph presents the first major, broad-based treatment of British trade with Spanish America in fifty years. Pearce states that he regards Frances Armytage's *The Free Port System in the British West Indies*, published in 1953, as the most direct predecessor to this book.[11] But in fact, his work goes much further than that of Armytage, and not only because it offers an updated and immeasurably more detailed study of trade at the free ports. Pearce's work also describes major branches barely touched on elsewhere – above all British trade which was routed via North America – and also (in summary fashion) ongoing trade via ports in Iberia. In its breadth of focus, indeed, in my view this book is almost without precedent. The only previous full-length study I am aware of which discusses all branches of British trade with the Spanish colonies is Olga Pantaleão's *A penetração comercial de Inglaterra na América espanhola*, published in Portuguese in 1946.[12] Of course, a great many books, articles, and essays directly or indirectly concerned with this topic have been published in recent decades, as the bibliography to this work (itself a significant work of scholarship) attests. Much of this historiography has been of high quality and sheds strong light on major aspects of the trade. But it tends to be fragmented thematically or (especially) geographically, discussing only particular aspects of the trade or its operation in particular Spanish-American regions. (The latter comment applies above all to work produced in Latin America, which – albeit with some significant exceptions – on the whole tends to concentrate upon a national or sub-national, rather than any broader perspective.) There has also often been a sharp division between the Anglophone and Hispanic historiographies, which, again with honourable exceptions, have too often existed in substantial ignorance of each other: too few historians of the British Caribbean (seem to) have a command of Spanish, and too many of the Spaniards who specialise in colonial history are either unfamiliar with works published in English and/or peer at America around the blinkers imposed by a traditional historiography that concentrates upon imperial policy rather than American responses to it. Not the least merit of Pearce's work – which, it should be emphasised, is based overwhelmingly on *primary* source material – is that it draws on this extensive and disparate literature, to present a new synthesis; a genuine *estado de la cuestión* (state of the question), c. 2007. Given this broad-based character, and the narrower focus of most of the previous work produced on this topic, it seems likely that future scholars writing on Anglo-Spanish commercial relations in the Americas will take this book as their starting point, and will be required to place their conclusions within the context set forth in its pages.

The general merits of Pearce's work – its tight structure, careful dating, close engagement with debates concerning all aspects of the trade, and above all its strong interpretative power – I leave to readers to discover for themselves. The lucidity of Pearce's discussion should not obscure the extreme complexity of the subject matter, nor the skill with which he has unravelled and presented it. The remainder of this Introductory Essay will simply draw attention to what I consider to be the chief fresh conclusions arising from Pearce's work. To provide a basis for this discussion, I first wish to quote, at some length, from an account of a smuggling expedition to the Isthmus of Panama and Cartagena de Indias in the early eighteenth century. Nathaniel Uring's description is among the most detailed and evocative available, and it provides an excellent view of the trade during the period before Pearce's account begins:

> In the beginning of the year 1711, I went over [from Jamaica] in a sloop, well mann'd and arm'd, to trade on the coast of New Spain; and we carried with us a great quantity of dry goods, and about 150 Negroes. We first touched at Portobello, but being war-time [N.B. the closing years of the War of the Spanish Succession], we used to go to the Grout within Monkey-Key, which is a very good harbour, and is about four or five miles from the harbour and town of Portobello. As soon as we arrived there, our custom was to send one of our people, who could speak Spanish, into the town with letters to the merchants, to give them notice of our arrival; and they appointed the time and place, where and when our canow should wait for them, to bring them on board, in order to traffick with us; and when they had agreed for so many Negroes, and such a quantity of goods as they wanted, they returned to the town, and the next day brought their money on board and received them.

We lay at this place trading six weeks, in which time the Spanish merchants at Panama had notice of our being there, and they came over the Isthmus to trade with us. These merchants frequently travelled in the habits of peasants, and had their mules with them, on which they brought their money in jarrs, which they fill'd up with meal; and if any of the King's Officers met them, nothing appeared but meal, and pretended they were poor people going to Portobello to buy some trifles; but they for the most part went through the woods, and not in the road, in order to prevent their being discovered by the Royal Officers. When they had bought as many Negroes, and such a quantity of dry goods as their money would purchase, they us'd to proportion and make them up in little packs, fit for one man to carry, and we supplied them with as much provisions as was necessary for their journey cross the Isthmus to the South Sea; and thus they pass'd together through the woods in the most secret manner.

While we lay at the Grout the first voyage, a Spaniard agreed with us for seventy slaves, and a good quantity of dry goods, which we delivered between Chagre and Porto Nova; the signal agreed upon being made from the castle of Chagre, we anchored about two miles from it, and sent our canow on shore, where we found the Spaniards with several asses and mules laden with gold and silver, which we carried on board; and when the money was found to be right, and all things were adjusted, we landed the Negroes and dry goods, providing them with necessaries for their journey over to the South Sea, and then sailed again for the Grout; but not being able to dispose of all our cargoe there, we set sail for Cartagena and by the way touched at Tolue, where we furnished ourselves with a good number of poultry, which are reckon'd the best upon the Main. When we arrived at the Brew, which is the place where we lay to trade with the merchants of Cartagena, we gave notice of it to some of the people of that island, who sent word into the city of our being there: several merchants came from thence to trade with us, and when we had sold what we could, we returned to Jamaica... I was several voyages to the Spanish coast, trading in this manner.[13]

This account is not only a valuable and evocative description of smuggling. It also exemplifies, particularly neatly, major characteristics of the trade both at the moment it describes, and also as it has been perceived in the bulk of the historical literature. These characteristics may be summarised in three main points: (1) British trade with the Spanish colonies was indirect, rather than operating directly from Britain. This point has already been addressed: all British trade passed through third ports, whether British entrepôts in the Caribbean (as in Uring's account), or monopoly ports in Spain (Seville or Cádiz), or Lisbon and Portuguese Brazil (as Pearce notes below).[14] (This, incidentally, along with its clandestine nature, is the reason why the trade has proved so difficult to study, since almost all British commercial records deal only with direct trade with Britain.) (2) The second point is that the trade was illegal; it was an archetypal smugglers' trade. All foreign commerce with Spanish America was prohibited under Spain's close colonial monopoly. It was also formally illegal under British law, after the passing in the mid-seventeenth century of the Navigation Acts, which barred British colonies from trading other than with the metropolis. Hence Uring's furtive dealings in secluded ports and on deserted beaches; hence the clandestine signals between ship and shore, and the Spaniards' passage 'through the woods in the most secret manner'. (3) Third and last, trade was undertaken by British merchants in the Spanish colonies, and not the other way round. We note here that Uring and his companions sail from Jamaica to the Isthmus of Panama and New Granada, and trade there with Spanish merchants; the Spaniards do not sail to Jamaica or Barbados to deal with the British in their own territories. These three points, then (and particularly the last two – the trade's illegality and its principally British agency) represent major salient characteristics of British trade in both the early eighteenth century, and as it is commonly perceived in the literature. They provide a basis from which to draw attention to several of the major fresh findings of Pearce's work; findings which, in turn, may be discussed under four headings: 'Legal status'; 'Ownership of the trade'; 'The United States as a major carrier'; and last, but not least, 'Value of the trade'.

Legal Status

The first major finding concerns the legal status of commerce. As we have seen, direct British trade with the Spanish colonies was illegal from its origins in the sixteenth century and for well over 200 years thereafter, except, partially, during the period 1713–50 (in practice 1713–39), following the transfer by the Treaty of Utrecht to the newly formed South Sea Company of the coveted contract, the *asiento de negros,* to supply African slaves to specified ports in Spanish America. More important still was the associated permission for an 'annual ship' to attend each of the trade fairs held at Porto Bello and Veracruz upon the arrival there of convoyed fleets from Cádiz, a privilege which provided enormous scope for contraband activity behind a veneer of legality. This, indeed, remains the common perception of Anglo-Spanish trade in the Americas, which for the most part continues to be described in the literature in terms of a classic contraband commerce. Pearce demonstrates, however, that this situation changed during the closing decades of the eighteenth century. Scholars already knew that from the mid-1760s the British opened free ports in the West Indies, with the express intention of facilitating and promoting trade by Spaniards – a category that includes, of course, those born in America (the creoles) as well as those from the peninsula – and other foreign merchants. Sixteen of these ports were established by 1805, in a dozen British islands throughout the region.[15] The striking success of this measure (as traced by Pearce in detail) has been much less widely recognised, however; while its implications have been missed practically altogether. The British free ports came to host the overwhelming majority of all trade with Spaniards in the West Indies, as was hardly surprising; after all, they now offered the only legal (and thus entirely safe) venue for Anglo-Spanish commercial relations in the Caribbean. And this dominance of the free ports within all trade with Spaniards, in turn, meant that the majority of the trade now became legal for the first time. For practical purposes, because it was undertaken in the free ports, most Anglo-Spanish trade in the Americas ceased to be contraband from the late 1760s onwards, at least from the British perspective.

There turns out to be more to this question than simply the story of the free ports. Much less well known than the establishment of the free ports is a parallel process of partial legalisation of trade with foreigners which also occurred at this time in the Spanish colonies. This was based not on the establishment of free ports, but rather on the licensing of Spanish merchants to trade on a large scale in the British and other foreign islands. This licensing was done at the local level, by the Spanish governors rather than directly from Madrid, although some initiatives from the centre (including the promulgation of free trade in slaves throughout the Spanish empire in 1789) tended towards the same result. The resulting *comercio de colonias extranjeras* (or 'foreign colonies trade') acquired real economic significance in some regions, fuelling substantial legal trade between particular Spanish colonies and the British and other islands, despite the persistence of the formal colonial commercial monopoly still proclaimed from Madrid, where the political and financial influence of the merchant guild of Cádiz put a brake on proposals for more substantial liberalisation of trade.[16] This process meant that not only was trade by Spaniards at the British free ports legal from the British standpoint, but that in many cases even the voyages of Spaniards to the free ports ceased to be illicit in the eyes of viceroys, governors and other senior Spanish colonial officials during this same period.

Of course, whether all this really constituted the 'legalisation' of the trade is a moot point. The existence of the free ports and licensing of Spanish merchants by their governors for trade with the British notwithstanding, this commerce was probably still contraband in international law; certainly, Spain continued to regard it as such. But in an obvious sense that is really neither here nor there. The key point is that during this period, Anglo-Spanish trade in the Caribbean was *treated* as legal at the principal point of exchange in the British free ports. From the 1760s onwards, Spaniards could trade completely openly in the free ports: in their own ships, under their own flags, and without any serious interference from the British customs officers (who, frustratingly for the historian, even came to regard taking detailed records of trade by Spaniards as too delicate a matter, and ceased for the most part to trouble to do so). Where the *comercio de colonias* took root, Spanish vessels trading with the British free ports did not even have to conceal their intentions from their own authorities, or to run the gauntlet of the much feared *guardacostas* (coastguard). This, then, ceased in any sense closely to resemble a smugglers' trade.

There are a number of interesting things about this. For historians of the Spanish empire and of Spanish imperial trade it underlines the surprisingly modern, pragmatic approach the British took to commercial affairs at this time. Not for nothing have the free ports been called 'the first significant attempt to launch an experiment in free trade and a portentous, if small, breach in the old imperial system'.[17] The same historians will find it less surprising to learn that Spanish governors in the colonies ignored imperial rules and encouraged trade with the British through the *comercio de colonias*. The real significance of this point, nevertheless, surely lies – as Pearce himself has indicated already elsewhere – in helping to explain the strong growth of the trade during this period. If British trade grew steadily and strongly throughout these years, then there can be little doubt that this effective legalisation was a key factor in that growth.[18]

'Ownership' of the Trade

A second major finding is closely related to the first, and concerns the 'ownership' of the trade: that is to say, which national merchant group carried it on locally in the Caribbean. In its classic form, as we have seen, this trade was carried on principally by British merchants trading in the Spanish colonies, out of island bases in the British West Indies. In fact, and as Pearce shows, British merchants by no means carried all the trade – in the late seventeenth century, for example, it may be that a more or less even split developed between British and Spanish traders. In wartime, however – notably during the War of the Spanish Succession of 1702–13, and the Wars of Jenkins' Ear and the Austrian Succession in 1739–48 – and also during the era of the British ownership of the *asiento de negros* in the early eighteenth century, British merchants clearly dominated. The stock image of the trade, as one undertaken by British smugglers like Nathaniel Uring, especially from Jamaica, on deserted stretches of coast on the Spanish Main, held essentially true until the mid-eighteenth century.

But, once again, this situation changed during the second half of the century. It now became American Spaniards who undertook most Anglo-Spanish trade in the Caribbean. Spaniards now sailed to the British colonies rather than the other way round: the traditional pattern was inverted. Why this change took place is not entirely clear; it seems to have happened around 1750, and the most likely explanation appears to relate to commercial turbulence following the war of 1739–48, linked to termination of the British *asiento* around the same time. But whatever the cause, the opening of free ports in the British islands in the 1760s, where Spaniards could trade quite freely, naturally set the seal on the model. Pearce's work suggests that by the early 1790s, around 80 per cent of Anglo-Spanish trade in the Caribbean by volume, and over 95 per cent by value, was undertaken by Spanish rather than British merchants.[19]

How significant is this point? In an obvious sense, it could be argued that it scarcely mattered who carried on the trade. Nevertheless, so striking a shift does seem significant. On the British side, it again underlines the sort of pragmatic, flexible approach the British took in this regard: the fact that they were willing to sacrifice the carrying trade to the Spanish colonies in the Caribbean if by this means they could boost exports and access to Spanish-American markets. On the Spanish side, when Pearce has made oral presentations of this work to Hispanic scholars, this point – the fact that Spaniards themselves now undertook the majority of trade with the British – has tended to be what they have found most striking.[20] This is likely to be because we are accustomed to think of the foreign trade of the Spanish colonies, and certainly of trade with the British, in essentially passive terms; of Spanish Americans as passive receivers of goods from foreign sellers, rather than rather entrepreneurial people who took the risks of the trade upon themselves. I would not want to push this point too far, and certainly Spanish control of the trade locally in the Caribbean probably says little about any new entrepreneurial spirit abroad among the Spaniards. But this remains unquestionably a major shift in our traditional view of Anglo-Spanish trade relations in the Americas.

The United States as a Major Carrier

The third major contribution of Pearce's work lies in its description of the transformations in the operation of Anglo-Spanish trade in the Caribbean under the impact of warfare between 1796 and the definitive Anglo-Spanish peace of July 1808. The transformations occurring in the pattern of Anglo-Spanish trade during these years took various forms. One arose from the capture of Trinidad, conveniently located very close to the coast of Venezuela, from Spain in 1797, to be followed in 1800 by those of St Thomas and Curaçao from the Danes and the Dutch respectively. Trinidad was developed instantaneously as a platform for British trade second only to Jamaica, following the immediate decision to grant licences protecting Spanish vessels from seizure by British warships, hostilities notwithstanding, an example soon followed in other British islands. Surely the most impressive aspect of the changes, however, was the major – and substantially novel – role which now came to be played in Anglo-Spanish commerce by the merchants of the United States.

From 1797, as Pearce demonstrates, the United States became a carrier of British goods to the Spanish colonies on a very large scale. The reasons for this were relatively straightforward: during the war Spain was forced to throw the ports in its colonies open to neutral traders (including, in practice, British merchants flying the flag of the *angloamericanos* [English Americans], as Spanish colonial officials were wont to describe US traders), there being no other means to keep Atlantic channels of trade and communication open in the face of the British maritime blockade. By the late eighteenth century, the United States was far and away the leading neutral power in a position to exploit this opportunity. But, although already a major commercial power, the United States had not yet developed a strong industrial base, and was obliged to import many of the goods for trade from Britain and other European nations. The result was that a major trade with Spanish America developed from 1797 in British goods routed via the United States. This trade was based in the classic colonial ports of the Atlantic seaboard (Boston, New York, Philadelphia, Charleston, and others) and also in New Orleans on the Gulf of Mexico. Some idea of its great value may be gained from the fact that the single US firm which came to be most closely involved with it, Robert Oliver of Baltimore, claimed to have exported some $2,000,000 worth of British manufactures to the Spanish colonies in the year to September 1807. And Pearce demonstrates in Chapter 6 that the total value of British goods shipped to Spanish America via the United States by 1807 or thereabouts was at least £1,000,000 sterling, and may have been considerably higher than this figure.

These exports of British goods to the Spanish colonies were closely bound up with the so-called 'Hope–Barings contract'; thus, for example, Robert Oliver was a partner to Hope-Barings' agent in Philadelphia. The Hope–Barings contract stood behind not only the lion's share of British exports of manufactures to the Spanish colonies via the United States during these years, but also a parallel series of purely financial transactions which brought about the exportation of very large sums of Spanish royal bullion from Spanish-American ports (above all Veracruz). Some sense of the extreme murkiness of these transactions may be gained by the fact that most of the bullion exported from Veracruz – some of it in a British warship during open war with Spain – was destined for no less than the coffers of Napoleon Bonaparte. Pearce's research on this highly complex subject constitutes a further major contribution of his work as a whole. The relevant section of Chapter 6 necessarily provides only a summary; a much more extensive discussion will appear separately in the near future.[21]

The fact that British goods were shipped to the Spanish colonies via the United States perhaps comes as no great surprise to scholars of Atlantic trade during this period. This trade is here traced in some detail perhaps for the first time, however, and its sheer scale will, I think, appear striking to many. The ultimate significance of trade in British goods via the United States, once more, lies in helping scholars to understand how it was possible for Anglo-Spanish American trade to grow so strongly throughout this period. Here we witness a major new branch, or new vehicle, for British trade with the Spanish colonies; a branch which, among other attributes, compensated almost entirely for the collapse of the British re-export trade via Spain at this time as a further consequence of the wars.

Value of the Trade

The fourth, and final, major conclusion advanced by Pearce, especially in Chapter 3 and the interwoven Chapters 4–6, is that the value of trade between

Spanish America and Britain, both before and after the commencement of hostilities in 1796, has been substantially underestimated by previous scholars. There were, of course, ups and downs – from year to year, from island to island – but by the early 1790s the value of trade with Spanish America via the Caribbean (worth c. £700,000 in 1792, and rising to more than £1,000,000 by 1795) indicates that the traditional system of supplying Spanish America with British goods by re-exports via Spanish ports was already being eclipsed by direct trade before the re-export trade collapsed in the aftermath of the renewal of hostilities between Britain and Spain in 1796. To put this into context it is relevant to recall that my findings on the values of exports from peninsular ports in the period 1782–1796, published in 1981/1998 (see note 2 for details), established that their average annual value was 15,000,000 *pesos fuertes*: some £3,400,000, using Pearce's exchange rate of £1 sterling:4.44 *pesos*. The best year was 1792 (22,000,000 *pesos*/ £4,955,000), following which they fell to 15,365,000 *pesos* (£3,461,000) in 1793 and to an unimpressive 7,941,409 *pesos* (£1,789,000) in 1794, as war with France cut off the supply of French manufactures for re-export. A partial recovery in 1795 to 14,100,000 pesos (£3,176,000) fell back in 1796 to 12,594,000 *pesos* (£2,836,000), but the real crisis came in 1797 as the British blockade of Cádiz – which on average still shipped 76 per cent by value of all exports to Spanish America – resulted in the value of exports plummeting to a mere 550,000 *pesos* (£124,000). Although the pause in hostilities in 1802–04 ushered in an impressive recovery, averaging 15,900,000 pesos (£3,581,000) over the three years, their resumption ushered in a second, more definitive, downward spiral, to 2,550,000 *pesos* (£574,000) in 1805, 1,300,000 (£293,000) in 1806, and a mere 700,000 (£158,000) in 1807. The reversal of alliances with Britain in 1808 brought a brief respite, with exports rising to an average of 1,265,000 pesos (£285,000) in 1809–1810, before the onset of a terminal collapse caused by the French occupation of Spain and the onset of the Spanish-American Wars of Independence.

Throughout the period 1782–96 almost half (49 per cent) of the value of the merchandise exported from Spain to Spanish America consisted of re-exports, while in 1797–1820 their share (in any case of a virtually insignificant trade) fell to 37 per cent. Although it is impossible to calculate with precision the share enjoyed by British goods in these re-exports (in part because the customs officials of Cádiz gave global values in the ships' registers, rather than breaking the figures down), Pearce's suggestion that they might have been worth up to £1,000,000 a year prior to 1796 is very plausible. What is even more evident is that thereafter British merchants largely bypassed peninsular ports in favour of supplying Spanish America either through the free ports or via intermediaries, mainly in the United States, with such success that by 1807 the value of their exports had virtually quadrupled.

The above-mentioned points, sketched in this introduction in summary form, represent in my view the most significant fresh findings arising from

Pearce's monograph. But they only hint at the richness of a work which – to risk the hyperbole of the sponsoring scholar – throws up an exceptionally wide range of new issues and interpretations. To give the briefest of samples, at the loftier end of the scale stands the discovery of 'the only detailed statistical survey of a major branch of British trade with the Spanish colonies which exists for any period', already analysed in article form and presented here in full as a Statistical Appendix. Pearce's discussion of the Hope–Barings affair is followed by analysis of the equally remarkable (and still less well known, outside a narrow circle of Americanists) contract held by the Cádiz-based merchant house of Gordon and Murphy during the same years, and by the topic of the 'secret trade' undertaken between Britain and Spanish America under neutral permit; the latter commerce, too, has been little studied to date, and barely at all in its implications for British trade. The first chapter of the work constitutes a valuable contribution in its own right, in the form of a succinct survey of the history of the trade in its first two and a half centuries, while the opening section of Chapter 2 presents by far the most detailed account to date of the establishment of the free ports in the British West Indies. In Chapter 4, again, Pearce presents the first detailed discussion of the commercial role played by *rescates* (ransom permits), in a section which was considered sufficiently significant as to merit separate publication as an article in the *Journal of Latin American Studies*. And at a more modest level, there are countless eyebrow-raisers scattered throughout the text: the discussion of trade undertaken by British merchants in Spanish colonial ports under false American and other neutral papers, for example; or that of US merchants trading directly between Spanish and British colonies during wartime, notably between Cuba and Jamaica;[22] or the case of hapless Grenada, made a free port in 1787, which experienced an explosive commercial boom for a single decade, until its trade shifted almost entirely to Trinidad after its capture by the British in 1797;[23] or the Barry/Baker & Dawson slave-trading contracts of the 1780s, almost entirely unknown and yet described in Chapter 3 as 'a partial renewal of the famous Asiento contract' for the supply of the Spanish colonies. Those wishing to pursue these subjects further will find a comprehensive survey of the available literature in the bibliography, covering the four principal research languages (English, Spanish, Portuguese, and French).

To conclude, my principal contribution to this book was to see that such a study was both necessary and likely to be fruitful, and then to secure the funding which made it possible. A certain defeatism tends to attach to research on Anglo-Spanish trade in the Americas, based above all on the notion that the sources are either too meagre or too unreliable.[24] On the other hand, and paradoxically, the sheer volume of publications directly or tangentially concerned with contraband and foreign trade (see the twenty plus pages of the bibliography) can give the impression that all possible benefit has already been extracted from the subject, and that further research is futile. Pearce's work – to reiterate, the first major study of British trade with Spanish

America in fifty years – amply proves the potential of such research to alter fundamentally our understanding of its basic attributes, and (in this case) to multiply by a factor of from three to four our best estimates for its value. Given the particular circumstances of its genesis, this work focuses upon the last half-century of the colonial era, which – as Pearce notes in his own concluding comments – may be regarded as the true onset of a British commercial hegemony which would reach its peak in the mid-nineteenth century, and which endured in some regions (above all Argentina) until the mid-twentieth. I will close with the suggestion that the example set by Pearce might profitably be taken up for other periods and other regions of Anglo-Spanish commercial relations in the Americas. The time is long overdue for a study similar to this one, but which embraces the period covered in Chapter I (from the sixteenth century to 1763). Again, the practical obstacles in studying trade routed via the Iberian Peninsula and above all via Seville and Cádiz (principally the extreme laboriousness of working with the notarial records most likely to yield meaningful information) must be overcome at some stage, perhaps through a collaborative project between several scholars. Lastly, I have no doubt that a study which picks up the story of British trade with the Hispanic Caribbean where this one leaves off and carries it through to c. 1860 has the potential to yield rich fruit. This period, after all, for all its turbulence, probably marked the high point of British influence, and while good studies exist for particular countries, no major work has yet been undertaken which surveys the whole of the region. Pearce and I, indeed, planned to undertake such a project ourselves, drawing on the expertise acquired over the past seven years; but, in the light of the unwillingness of the AHRC to finance such an enterprise, the task must now fall to another scholar or scholars.[25]

It is a privilege for me to have the opportunity to present this book as a major contribution to the new series of Liverpool Latin American Studies.

John Fisher
Liverpool
5 January 2007

Notes

1   I present an accessible survey of these themes in John R. Fisher, *The Economic Aspects of Spanish Imperialism in America, 1492–1810* (Liverpool: Liverpool University Press, 1997), chap. 6.

2   My major conclusions were presented in a series of articles published in the *Journal of Latin American Studies*: 'Imperial "Free Trade" and the Hispanic Economy, 1778–1796', *JLAS*, 13 (1981), pp. 21–56; 'The Imperial Response to "Free Trade": Spanish Imports from Spanish America, 1778–1796', *JLAS*, 17 (1985), pp. 35–78; 'Commerce and Imperial Decline: Spanish Trade with Spanish America, 1797–1820', *JLAS*, 30 (1998), pp. 459–79. A valuable commentary upon the significance of these findings is provided by Antonio García-Baquero González, *El comercio*

colonial en la época del absolutismo ilustrado: problemas y debates (Granada: Editorial Universidad de Granada, 2003). See in particular the chapter 'Los resultados del libre comercio y "el punto de vista": una revision desde la estadística', pp. 187–216.

3   Chap. 3, passim.

4   Stanley J. Stein and Barbara H. Stein, *Apogee of Empire: Spain and New Spain in the Age of Charles III, 1759–1789* (Baltimore and London: The Johns Hopkins University Press, 2003), p. 49.

5   Ambassador to Marqués de Grimaldi, London, 24 Aug. 1767, Archivo Histórico Nacional (cited hereafter as A.H.N.), Estado, 4269.

6   Del Campo to Conde de Aranda, London, 8 Nov. 1792, A.H.N., Estado, 4252.

7   'Anonymous mémoire prepared after 1747', cited in Stein and Stein, *Apogee of Empire*, p. 49; for comparable views from high-ranking Spanish officials, see pp. 59–60, 295–6.

8   Adrian J. Pearce, 'Early Bourbon Government in the Viceroyalty of Peru, 1700–1759' (unpublished PhD diss., University of Liverpool, 1998).

9   Adrian J. Pearce, 'Huancavelica 1700–1759: Administrative Reform of the Mercury Industry in Early Bourbon Peru', *Hispanic American Historical Review*, 79 (1999), pp. 669–702, and 'The Peruvian Population Census of 1725–1740', *Latin American Research Review*, 36 (2001), pp. 69–104. The latter article was published in Spanish translation as 'El censo demográfico peruano de 1725–1740', in Paulo Drinot and Leo Garofalo (eds.), *Más allá de la dominación y la resistencia: Ensayos de historia peruana, siglos xvi-xx* (Lima: Instituto de Estudios Peruanos, 2005), pp. 136–80.

10   AHRB reference AH/RG/AN1128/APN8282.

11   Frances Armytage, *The Free Port System in the British West Indies. A Study in Commercial Policy, 1766-1822* (London: Longmans, Green & Co., 1953).

12   *A penetração comercial de Inglaterra na América espanhola (1713–1783)* (São Paulo: n.p., 1946). Pantaleão's study was hampered by wartime conditions which prevented her from consulting any archival material; but within this severe limitation, it is well-researched, detailed, and offers information not readily available elsewhere.

13   Nathaniel Uring, *A History of the Voyages and Travels of Capt. Nathaniel Uring ...*, 2nd edn (London: John Clarke, 1727), pp. 164–6. The paragraph divisions here are my own; the original text is continuous.

14   See, in particular, chap. 1.

15   Full details are provided in chap. 4.

16   On the *comercio de colonias* see in particular chap. 3.

17   See chap. 2.

18   See Adrian J. Pearce, '*Rescates* and Anglo-Spanish Trade in the Caribbean during the French Revolutionary Wars, ca. 1797–1804', *Journal of Latin American Studies*, 38 (2006), pp. 607–24.

19   Appendix, tables 4-5; see also Adrian J. Pearce, 'British Trade with the Spanish Colonies, 1788–1795', *Bulletin of Latin American Research*, 20 (2001), pp. 242–3. The best analysis of how the *asiento de negros* functioned and why it was formally terminated in 1750 remains Geoffrey J. Walker, *Spanish Politics and Imperial Trade, 1700–1789* (London and Basingstoke: Macmillan, 1979).

20   Pearce presented his conclusions to predominantly Hispanic scholars in three papers in 2002–03: 'Comercio británico con las colonias españolas del Caribe, 1763–1810: avance de una investigación', Escuela de Estudios Hispano-Americanos, Seville, 18 June 2002; 'Comercio británico con México y Cuba, 1796–1808', 13th International Conference of the European Association of Historians of Latin America [AHILA], Ponta Delgada, Azores, 4 Sept. 2002; 'El ocaso del monopolio: el comercio británico con la América española, 1763–1810', conference on 500 Años de la Fundación de

la Casa de la Contratación de Sevilla (1503–2003), Real Alcázar de Sevilla, Seville, 15 Jan. 2003.

21   A 30-page typescript titled 'The Hope-Barings Contract: Finance and Trade between Europe and the Americas, 1805–1808' has already been completed. The first of a projected series of papers on this subject was recently given in Liverpool: 'The Hope-Barings Contract: Finance and Trade between Europe and the Americas, 1805–1808', symposium 'Rethinking the Iberian Atlantic, 1500–1800', School of History, University of Liverpool, 21 Apr. 2006.

22   See chaps. 5–6.

23   See chaps. 2–4.

24   See, for example, Miguel Izard, 'Algunas notas sobre el comercio colonial atlántico: Los intercambios del Reino Unido con América, 1772–1808', *Revista de Indias*, 40 (1980), pp. 425–39. Izard concludes: 'The product of these notes is rather modest. Limitless dissembling (*la desmesurada ocultación*) both in America and in the United Kingdom have not in the least favoured the initial intention of this work, which was to obtain a general idea of the value of British contraband with the Indies' (p. 432). This article is based on the same documentary series (N.A., Customs 17, 1–30) which yielded the detailed statistical series analysed by Pearce in chap. 3.

25   Our follow-up application to the AHRC in 2002 for a project on British trade with Hispanic America from 1808 to 1860 narrowly missed financing (it was awarded the dreaded 'A' – 'an application of high quality to be funded as a matter of priority' – but was not funded), possibly because one of the referees, although generally very positive towards the project, questioned whether much really new was likely to be gained by it. I think that the present book indicates the risks inherent to speculation of this kind, especially when protected by the cloak of anonymity. The invitation was to resubmit in the following round, but this was not taken up because of the need for Pearce to earn a living and establish himself more firmly in a proper academic post.

CHAPTER ONE

The Origins of British Trade
with the Spanish Colonies,
Sixteenth Century to 1763

Dating the onset of British trade with the Americas precisely is problematic. In principle, English wares may have featured among the arms, foodstuffs, tools, and 'several coffers of trade goods and merchandise to be given away to the Indians' taken by Columbus on his first voyage in 1492, though this is necessarily speculation.[1] The first attested presence of English traders in the West Indies was at Santo Domingo, in the island of Hispaniola, in 1527–28, although the details are vague.[2] English merchants were active in Brazil at a very early period (in 1530–42), and were probably so again in the Caribbean, even before John Hawkins's far more celebrated activities of the 1560s.[3] It is Hawkins's voyages, and those of his contemporary and sometime partner Francis Drake, however, which have claimed most attention. In 1562, Hawkins made a 'relatively pacific attempt' to supply slaves and other goods to the early Spanish settlements in the Caribbean, efforts which culminated in a disastrous clash with Spanish warships at the Mexican port of Veracruz in 1567.[4] The English then undertook a number of raids on settlements on the Isthmus of Panama which endured until the late 1570s, before shifting their attention further south, 'beyond the equinoctial' to the River Plate and the lower coasts of South America. In 1574, Sir Richard Grenville made an expedition to the River Plate, while in 1577–78 Drake spent several months on the Atlantic and Pacific coasts, before returning to England via the second circumnavigation of the world.[5] Drake later returned to the Caribbean, and died off Portobelo four years before the century's close, though by this time, his efforts and those of his fellows were aimed more at plunder than at commerce.

Hawkins and Drake dominate popular perceptions of early English interaction with the Spanish colonies, but a little-known article by G. Connell-Smith suggests that to an important extent this is misleading. Connell-Smith demonstrates the surprising vitality of Anglo-Spanish American trade at a very early date, via Spain. Thus, English merchants established in or operating through Spain traded with most of the Spanish colonies in the Caribbean from the early 1500s. At least as early as 1509, Thomas Malliard supplied goods for Santo Domingo from Britain via Seville.

In 1522, Roger Barlow contracted to send wine to Santo Domingo with the Spanish ship's captain Diego Rodríguez Pepino, and seems to have maintained an agent in Hispaniola. Perhaps the leading English merchant was Robert Thorne, who shipped 40 tons of merchandise to Santo Domingo, Cuba or New Spain with Captain Pedro de Agustín in 1525. In the same year, he sent flour and other foodstuffs, candles, soap, tin, iron goods and esparto, valued at 455,000 *maravedís*, with Juan de Murcia for sale in Puerto Rico or Hispaniola. Thorne also invested in Cabot's voyage to the River Plate in 1526, while his brother Nicholas sent 22,318 maravedís worth of English cloth for sale in Cubagua in Venezuela in 1527. The London draper Thomas Howell also traded to the New World at this time, and similarly maintained a factor in Santo Domingo to handle sales. What is striking about these merchants is that they dwelt and traded openly in Spain, and were not limited to clandestine trade through Spanish intermediaries as in later years. English as well as Spanish factors (including Thomas Tison, Nicholas Arnote, and John Martin) even lived and moved relatively freely around the Spanish Caribbean on behalf of their corresponding houses. This degree of commercial liberty was the product of unusually favourable treaty rights for the English in Spanish trade; it also reflected the absence of tension over religious matters prior to the English Reformation, as well as the lax administrative structures governing Spanish Atlantic trade in its earliest years.[6]

The Reformation and the attendant political circumstances during the later years of the reign of Henry VIII (1509–47) brought about a serious deterioration in conditions, even overt persecution, for these English merchants. For some years, Anglo-Spanish hostilities at sea led to a virtual interruption of trade; and though there was some recovery in the 1550s, it seems that English merchants in Spain were obliged increasingly to become 'to most intents and purposes naturalised Spaniards'.[7] The final rupture, and transition to conditions in which English and other foreign merchants were strictly excluded from trade with the Spanish colonies, came during the reign of Philip II from 1559. Connell-Smith concludes that 'when John Hawkins came to challenge the Spanish monopoly … his protest was thus not against a monopoly which had hitherto excluded English merchants from the New World, but against the stoppage of a legitimate trade long enjoyed by his fellow countrymen in two previous generations'.[8] There followed a half-century of political hostility in Anglo-Spanish relations during which English trade with the Spanish colonies displayed little order and was subject to frequent disruption.[9]

Roughly coincident with Hawkins's voyages, the 1560s witnessed the organisation of Spanish Atlantic trade into the form which it maintained almost throughout the colonial period. The system developed at this time for commercial relations with the colonies has been described many times, and will be summarised here only briefly.[10] Its fundamental principle was a close commercial monopoly, in which trade was strictly limited to Spaniards and all intercourse by foreigners was prohibited. Seville, on the Guadalquivir river in Andalusia, was the sole Spanish port permitted to trade with the colonies, as well as the seat of the commercial bureaucracy (though both functions passed to Cadiz in the early 1700s). Most trade was organised into great commercial fleets, subsequently placed under naval escort, which, in theory, left Seville twice every year. One fleet (the *flota*) supplied Mexico and Central America through a rich trade fair held at Veracruz; the other (the *galeones*) supplied South America through a fair held at Portobelo, whence goods were transported over the Isthmus to Panama and down the Pacific coast to Peru and all points south. A smaller fair was also held at Cartagena de Indias, supplying New Granada (the modern Colombia), while less privileged regions (including Hispaniola, Puerto Rico, and Venezuela) were supplied only erratically by small numbers of registered vessels. All this commerce was limited not only to Spaniards, but to members of the powerful merchant guilds (*Consulados*) of Seville, Mexico City, and Lima, which came to play a key role in the formulation and defence of commercial policy.[11] This remarkable commercial system – known as the *Carrera de Indias*, or 'Indies run' – had some advantages and many drawbacks, but over the long term it served imperial economic interests poorly. It became associated with the under-development of many American regions and the under-exploitation of the empire as a whole. It brought little wider development in the metropolis, which proved unable to supply the colonies adequately, while the commercial monopoly was rapidly undermined by foreign penetration. And especially from the mid-seventeenth century, the system of fleets and fairs itself was subject to decline, evident in a slowing of the rhythm of departures from Seville and in growing problems at the trade fairs.[12]

For all its idiosyncrasies, the formal structure of Spanish Atlantic trade provided the context to British commercial relations with Spanish America from the late sixteenth century until independence in the early 1800s. From this time onwards, English and other foreign merchants were obliged to come to terms with a commercial system from which they were formally excluded and which they could penetrate only by illicit and clandestine means. Although there were further attempts at direct trade, like that of Hawkins, for the most part the methods employed were two. Firstly, the English traded with Spanish America via the formal commercial monopoly centred in Andalusia. Thus, English goods were imported to Seville and later Cadiz and re-exported to the colonies, not openly as in the early 1500s, but clandestinely through Spanish intermediaries and smuggling. (In fact, this was an 'Iberian' rather than a purely Spanish re-export trade, since – as is described hereafter – goods were also routed to the Spanish colonies via Lisbon and Portuguese Brazil.) Secondly, once England acquired colonies of its own in the Caribbean from the early seventeenth century, these were used as bases for contraband trade with the Spanish possessions. By this route, such islands as Barbados and Jamaica came to serve as entrepôts or local platforms articulating smuggling between Britain and Mexico, Cuba, New Granada and other regions. These two great routes: via re-exports through the Iberian Peninsula, and via British entrepôts in the Caribbean, came to account for the vast majority of all Anglo-Spanish American trade up until the long wars and commercial upheaval of the years around 1800. The latter branch of trade (via the Caribbean) forms the major focus of the present monograph. The former branch (re-exports via Spain) was actually both the first to develop and the richest of the two routes, though it is also the hardest to know. This branch is thus discussed in the following section in brief summary, while the remainder of the chapter discusses at greater length the development of the entrepôt trade in the Caribbean between the early seventeenth century and the end of the Seven Years War in 1763.

The Iberian Re-export Trade to 1763

The Spanish monopoly of colonial trade, with its exclusive ports and merchant guilds, trade fleets and commercial fairs, was formalised by the mid-sixteenth century. For some years, this system may have functioned largely as intended, with the bulk of trade and profits reserved for Spaniards. But by the early seventeenth century, it was already severely undermined by foreign rivals.[13] As we have seen, foreign merchants, including the English, imported goods to Seville (later Cadiz), re-exported them to the Spanish colonies in the *flota* and *galeones*, and repatriated most of the profits abroad. The bulk of the returns from colonial trade thus passed through Spain, but only en route for France, Italy, the Low Countries, England, and elsewhere, a system characterised memorably in the phrase 'Spain kept the cow and the rest of Europe drank the milk'.[14]

All trade with the Indies by non-Spaniards was illegal, and foreigners were obliged to find ways to circumvent or subvert the monopoly, a task to which they devoted themselves with extraordinary ingenuity and energy. Several volumes could be written on the methodologies of contraband between Spain and the Indies, but a brief summary must suffice. The least illicit methods were naturalisation, which turned foreigners into Spaniards and so made them fit for trade, and outright sales of foreign goods to Spanish merchants in Seville or Cadiz, who exported them to America on their own account.[15] The latter method placed the onus for breaking the law onto Spanish shoulders, but it also yielded lower profits and involved greater risks, and fell out of favour in the course of the seventeenth century.[16] It was replaced by ever-greater use of Spanish cover-men (*prestanombres*), who shipped goods in their own names on behalf of foreign merchants, in return for a commission. By the late 1600s, the majority of all foreign re-exports via Andalusia were handled by cover-men in this way. There still remained the problem of how to ship foreign goods on the trade fleets. In many cases, foreign wares (especially textiles) were stamped in their country of origin with false seals so as to make them appear Spanish, or factories were established near the ports whose sole task was to re-mark foreign manufactures as national wares. The bulk of all re-exports never passed through Spanish Customs at all, but were smuggled on board ship directly, a practice which increased markedly once trade shifted to Cadiz (with its vast bay, impossible to police effectively). A powerful ring of dedicated smugglers – the *metedores* – handled the loading of goods and the landing of bullion in return. And all of this only hints at the full range of mechanisms employed, which also included transfer of goods on the high seas, bribes to Spanish Customs officers and guards, the use of false or dual registers, and even the construction of merchant shipping with secret compartments or false decks.[17]

The ability of the English to re-export goods from Andalusia to the Spanish colonies naturally depended on their ability first to import those goods to Spain. This in turn depended on treaty rights governing Anglo-Spanish commerce, which thus acquired crucial significance. Major commercial concessions were made to English merchants in Spain throughout the seventeenth century, especially in 1645, but the key breakthrough came in a first great commercial treaty of 1667, which granted England the equivalent of 'most-favoured-nation' status. The privileges acquired were then consolidated under a series of private agreements made before 1680 with the leading tax-farmer in Cadiz.[18] By the late seventeenth century the English thus enjoyed extensive privileges in Spanish trade, which were regarded by jealous rivals as fundamental to their commercial success.[19] Whether for this or for other reasons, the re-export trade in English goods began early and prospered rapidly. As early as 1622, 80 per cent of English exports to the Mediterranean already went to Spain, of which over three-quarters were re-exported to the colonies; 'in other words, almost two-thirds of England's exports to the Mediterranean were fed into the Spanish transatlantic pipeline'.[20] By 1628, the Seville merchant guild estimated the value of all foreign re-exports at 6,000,000 ducats per year, and frankly acknowledged that trade was dependant upon them.[21] And between 1630 and the Treaty of Westphalia in 1648, English trade enjoyed an early boom due to neutral status during the Spanish wars with the Dutch Republic and France. English merchants handled both Spanish bullion transfers to the army in Flanders, and imports of prohibited French manufactures to Spain, and they also participated in shipping between Seville and the Caribbean by offering freight rates many times lower than Spanish rates.[22]

The evidence regarding foreign re-exports to the colonies via Spain is scarce at best for all periods; we know with certainty that the trade was a rich one, but we know little more.[23] Data are particularly hard to come by for the late seventeenth century, when we are obliged to rely on fragmentary and indirect evidence. One set of data accords the English 11 per cent of the total re-export trade during this period, well behind the French (25 per cent), Genoese (22 per cent) and Dutch (20 per cent), and identical to the share of Flemish merchants.[24] An alternative account suggests that 18.5 per cent of foreign goods imported to Cadiz in 1685–86 and 1691 were of English origin, compared with 38.4 per cent for France, 16.5 per cent for Genoa, and 9.9

per cent for Holland.[25] The English share may occasionally have risen higher; the consul in Cadiz thought that British wares accounted for the majority of the returns of the trade fleet of 1692.[26] By the late 1680s, no less than 94 per cent by value of cargoes shipped to America from Cadiz consisted of re-exports of European manufactures, bleak testimony to the utter marginalisation of Spanish producers by this date.[27] Again, probably at least 50 per cent of returns in bullion came as contraband.[28] Textiles dominated trade with Spanish America throughout the colonial period, and at this time the English shipped mainly woollens of different sorts, along with silks, stockings, hats, toys, clocks and watches, salt fish, and salt meats from Ireland.[29] One source suggests that profits on re-exports via Andalusia could reach as high as 100 per cent, and the Dutch appear to have expected returns of at least 40–75 per cent. The English economist John Cary, by contrast, writing in the 1690s, put profits at just 20 per cent, with the figure of 100 per cent reserved for exports via English entrepôts in the Caribbean.[30] So far as value is concerned, already by 1670 Andalusia received English goods worth some £368,000, representing around 18 per cent of the total value of exports from London. By 1700, the value of English trade with Spain stood at around £400,000, representing 20 per cent of English foreign trade earnings, the majority derived from re-exports to Spanish America.[31]

The War for the Spanish Succession between Habsburg and Bourbon, which began in 1702, marked a hiatus for English merchants, whose trade was prohibited and many of whom were expelled from Spain. The war witnessed a great boom in French trade with the Spanish colonies, although also an increase in British smuggling through the Caribbean (discussed below). The British backed the losing candidate, the Habsburg Archduke Charles of Austria; in 1707, at the height of the war, they extorted from him a treaty which envisaged extensive trade with the colonies in British vessels under British naval escort, as well as a joint Anglo-Spanish trading company to exploit American resources after the war, among other privileges.[32] This treaty illustrates the depth of British interest in Spanish-American trade, although it became a dead letter in 1713 when the Treaty of Utrecht ended the war and recognised the Bourbon succession in Spain.

It nevertheless remains true, as one scholar has remarked, that the War of Succession 'marked an epoch in the relations between Britain and Spanish America'.[33] This was largely because the Treaty granted Britain the exclusive slave-trading contract for the Spanish colonies (the *Asiento de negros*). Most British merchants had traditionally favoured trade via Andalusia over smuggling via the Caribbean – the other great branch – either because they regarded contraband as hazardous and unreliable, or simply because it was harder for them to penetrate.[34] But concession of the Asiento raised the stakes, by providing legal access for British merchandise shipped via the Caribbean for the first time. The terms of Utrecht, indeed, have been interpreted as implying that London interests involved in smuggling via the West Indies now enjoyed 'more political clout' than merchants trading via

Andalusia. This seems questionable,[35] but certainly there developed a bitter war of words between advocates of either branch, championed on the 'Spanish' side by none other than the writer Daniel Defoe, himself a participant. Defoe called trade via the Caribbean a 'Thieving Roguing Trade', and the Jamaicans a 'Crew of Peace-breakers, Thieves and Pyratical Traders' who 'deserve the Gallows'. He regarded interloping via the West Indies as both irregular and unreliable, and actively harmful to the extent that it undercut the long-established and far richer trade undertaken via ports in Spain.[36]

Utrecht, and a supplementary commercial treaty of 1715, reconfirmed all the British privileges in Spain, so that a return to the prosperous conditions of the late seventeenth century appeared imminent.[37] In fact, there is little agreement among scholars as to the course of British re-exports to Spanish America during the eighteenth century. Olga Pantaleão suggests that a decline occurred in the first half of the century, caused by a range of factors: Spanish obstructionism through non-observance of treaties and attempts to foster domestic industry and commerce, and competition from foreign rivals (especially the French and Dutch). Most important was the factor indicated by Defoe: greater competition from British exports routed via the new legal framework of the Asiento in the Caribbean.[38] Jean McLachlan similarly observes a decline in British trade via Andalusia, related above all to French competition and to British disillusionment over increasingly irregular departure of the trade fleets and high rates of taxation. She disagrees that the decline was related to British exercise of the Asiento, however, and notes that Cadiz remained 'the richest and most important of British factories in Spain' (with Irish Catholics now making much of the trade).[39] It is true that conditions for the British might be expected to deteriorate in the eighteenth century, with the shift to almost constant Anglo-Spanish tension and frequent conflicts after the generally amicable relations of the late 1600s. Nevertheless, and in contrast to the other authors here cited, Allan Christelow suggests that the British began to gain ground after 1700 on the French, who were clearly dominant until this time.[40]

The most detailed study of British trade via Andalusia after 1713 is that of Lucy Horsfall, covering the period up to 1739. Horsfall describes a trade which raised considerable expectations, but which was subject to repeated frustrations and interruptions due to factors both commercial and political. Throughout much of the 1710s, business remained depressed as a result of French interloping in the Americas and the virtual suspension of the American trade fleets. Spanish plans for commercial revitalisation then provoked renewed optimism, and by September 1718 there were said to be twenty British ships lying at Cadiz. The War of the Quadruple Alliance in 1718–19 again shattered these hopes, but the early 1720s witnessed a warming of Anglo-Spanish relations, as well as more vigorous attempts at commercial reform by Spain. For a brief period, the fleets sailed virtually every year, while a cooler policy towards France left the British 'masters of the field'. In July 1722, there were twenty-one British ships at Cadiz, and until

1725 the British remained upbeat as to their prospects. Political circumstances, and above all a further brief Anglo-Spanish war in 1727–28, then
dealt the trade a further blow. It was described as at a standstill by mid-1726,
and in early 1727 British property at Cadiz was confiscated. After the war,
the British remained broadly pessimistic throughout the 1730s, complaining
at both French competition and the obstructionism of the Spanish authorities.[41] At least as seriously, Spanish Atlantic trade was itself in crisis
throughout the 1730s, in part due to the impact of smuggling in the West
Indies. Nevertheless, one observer in 1738 stated that there were 120 British
ships at Cadiz, and suggested the number was rarely less than 100.[42] Despite
all their tribulations, the British factory at Cadiz remained committed to the
trade throughout these decades (perhaps because, as one consul put it, 'they
know not where to employ their money better'), and dreaded the long war
which eventually broke out in 1739.[43] Horsfall demonstrates conclusively that
the British government, too, consistently gave priority to trade via Spain over
smuggling in the Caribbean, at times directly to the detriment of the latter; a
rational choice, given the respective value of either branch.[44]

The Wars of Jenkins' Ear and the Austrian Succession (1739–48) proved
as disastrous for the merchants in Spain as they predicted. This was not only
because their trade was once more prohibited. Vigorous British naval action
in the Atlantic forced Spain to suspend the trade fleets altogether, and to use
individual registered vessels instead. The French actively exploited both this
system and the temporary discomfort of the British to secure a new boom in
their own trade. French merchants at Cadiz even sent home 'samples of …
English and Dutch woollens of considerable consumption in Spain and the
Indies, to have them produce the same quality, to fold and package them the
way the English and Dutch do, in order to sell them to Spain and the Indies
at the same price'.[45] The result was that the two decades after 1740 witnessed
the peak of French legal and contraband trade with Spain and the Americas,
according to a recent study.[46] It should be emphasised, indeed, that however
rich the trade via Spain, the British were never the leading participants. That
distinction was probably held by the Dutch until the second half of the seventeenth century, when they were increasingly displaced by the French.[47]
France lacked strategically located colonies in the Caribbean until just before
1700, and concentrated heavily on re-exports via Spain.[48] It won major treaty
rights in Spain in 1659, before the English, and had a highly developed textiles
sector, especially in linens. France came to depend on trade to Spanish-
American markets, in fact, so that 'sales of linens, woollens, and silks at Cadiz
… directly impinged upon employment levels and earnings in France's textile
centres'. By 1716, one-third of French manufactured exports went to Spain,
and the country acquired almost all of its silver via the same route.[49] The
result was that on average, between 1724 and 1778, about sixty main French
merchant houses operated in Cadiz, where they were described as 'very
opulent'.[50] Re-exports of French linens alone were estimated to be worth
£300,000 per year by the late 1730s, while Horace Walpole thought that the

French contributed from one-half to two-thirds of the cargoes of the Spanish trade fleets.[51]

The wars of 1739–48 thus brought a temporary crisis in British trade via Spain, although (as we will see) this decline was at least partly compensated for by contraband in the Caribbean. The end of the wars witnessed a sharp increase in British trade via Andalusia, attributed by one scholar to the end of the British Asiento in 1750 and so of legal British access to the Spanish colonies.[52] In 1749, merchants with interests in Cadiz claimed that re-exports yielded profits of from 90 per cent to 107 per cent, and cited instances of registered vessels in which British manufactures made up between one-third and more than two-fifths of the cargo.[53] In these circumstances, it is hardly surprising that British merchants welcomed the re-establishment of the Spanish trade fleets to Mexico (but not to Panama and Peru) in 1754.[54] Writing in 1757, Malachy Postlethwayt observed the huge volume of trade via Spain when he stated that from 300–500 foreign vessels might be seen in Spanish ports at any one time, and as many as 200 British vessels in Cadiz alone.[55] By this time, even French merchants acknowledged the British advantages in the trade, based not only on strong quality control and efforts to supply the goods wanted by the Spaniards, but also on more extensive credit facilities and a reliable banking system.[56] British re-exports thus reached the Seven Years War (1756–63) in some health; and if conditions for British merchants became less favourable over the following two decades, later chapters will demonstrate that until the end of the century, this probably remained the richest route by which British goods were transferred to consumers in the Spanish colonies.[57]

What was the scale of British re-exports to Spanish America by way of Andalusia during the eighteenth century? Foreign re-exports to the Indies were worth an estimated 15–20,000,000 pesos per year in the early 1700s (c. £3,400,000 – £4,500,000). A figure of 15,000,000 pesos was confirmed for the early 1720s by the eminent Spanish economic theorist Gerónymo de Ustáriz. Some five-sixths of the silver received in Spain from the colonies was remitted abroad in payment for these goods.[58] Data are scarce for the 1730s and 1740s, but in the decade following 1757, foreign textiles alone made up an average of 84 per cent of outbound cargoes of Spanish fleets.[59] Spanish producers were thus again utterly marginalised, with Spain 'relegated to the role of simple staging post for the riches of the Indies, which in their great majority served to foment the economic take-off of other countries'.[60] By the early 1760s, the British factory at Cadiz numbered thirty merchants, representing just under 20 per cent of all the foreign traders. Some of the richest of all the foreign merchants were British, surpassed only by a few of the French. Spanish experts estimated the British share of the profits from trade with the Indies as 15 per cent in 1753–54, and marginally more in 1762.[61] In terms of hard figures, Sir Charles Whitworth gave data for British exports to Spain which suggest steady growth throughout these years: from £600,000 in 1722, to £630,000 in 1725, £770,000 in 1730, and £820,000 in 1732.[62] In

1741, a British writer estimated the value of returns from the Indies at some 38,000,000 pesos per year, and accorded the British a share in this bullion of 4,500,000 (c. £1,000,000).[63] Lastly, in 1761, on the eve of the Peace of Paris, which ended the Seven Years War, and which marks the true start date of this study, the British share in re-exports via Cadiz was estimated at some £1,090,000. At this time the French still held a significant advantage, with a trade worth some £1,250,000.[64]

Before concluding this section, it is important to note that re-exports of British goods to Spanish America took place not only via Spain, but also by way of Portugal and Brazil. As already noted, the re-export trade was thus strictly an Iberian rather than a purely Spanish one, since British goods were routed to the Spanish colonies via Lisbon as well as via Seville or Cadiz. Interestingly, Christelow suggests that by the eighteenth century British merchants regarded the trades via Cadiz and Lisbon 'not as two wholly separate trades but rather as a single complex'. Many merchants operated via both places, and goods shipped to Lisbon might be forwarded to Cadiz if circumstances so dictated.[65] The British enjoyed far greater treaty rights in Portugal than in Spain, dating from the 1650s and which were consolidated in the Methuen Treaty of 1703. They were permitted to participate openly and in their own shipping in the Portuguese fleets, and could even maintain factors in Brazil if they wished.[66] They acquired a dominant position in the trade of foreigners with Brazil, and this position was further exploited to develop trade with the adjacent Spanish territories to the south and west. By this route, British goods were imported to Lisbon and re-exported to Brazil, whence some were dispatched onwards to the Spaniards across the River Plate. This trade was thus

> carried on and encouraged by the cheapness with which the Spaniards were supplied with English goods sent from Lisbon in the Rio de Janeiro fleet and from thence transported by sea to the Nova Colonia do Sacramento whither the Spaniards resorted to purchase these goods which were mostly paid in dollars.[67]

The tiny port of Colonia do Sacramento, founded on the north shore of the River Plate in 1680, became the major centre for this trade, despite frequent Spanish assaults.[68] Most British goods reached Sacramento in Brazilian coasting vessels from further north, though some British ships entered there directly; one such, captured by the Spaniards in the early 1740s, had a cargo worth some £40,000.[69] From Sacramento, goods were shipped across the river to Spanish buyers, or (during the Asiento years, 1713–39) to the factors of the South Sea Company resident at Buenos Aires.[70] Some made their way on to the rich mining provinces of Upper Peru (in modern Bolivia), while the same route was also used to remit large sums of money back to Europe.[71] Trade in British goods via Sacramento was described as 'considerable' during the war of 1739–48, and one observer thought that 'had the war lasted a few years longer, we should by this inlet have supply'd with English goods the greatest part of the Spanish settlements in South America'.[72] In 1761, 'the produce of the trade at Nova Colonia in the river of Plate' was reportedly worth fully 40 per cent of the value of all trade with Brazil (4,000,000 and 10,000,000 *cruzadas* respectively).[73] In 1762, a Spanish raid found no fewer than twenty-seven British vessels lying at Sacramento, and the value of the trade was estimated at £200,000 annually.[74]

Contraband Trade in the Caribbean, 1620s–1713

In the Caribbean, British contraband with Spanish America commenced in earnest only some time after 1600, the early voyages of the sixteenth century discussed above notwithstanding. Trade via the Caribbean was destined to become the second great vehicle for Anglo-Spanish American trade, and the dominant one for a quarter-century from the 1790s. It developed once Britain acquired territories of its own in the region for the first time, providing the key bases from which to launch a commercial assault on the Spanish colonies. Between 1624 and 1632 several small islands in the Lesser Antilles were occupied, most importantly (for the present purposes) Barbados, which was established as a British colony in 1627.[75] Smuggling between Barbados and the Spanish Main began at least as early as the 1640s, and was probably never so significant (in relative terms) as during the following two decades.[76] During this period the island was by far the most prosperous of the British Caribbean colonies, while the Acts of Navigation of 1651 and 1660 – which prohibited trade by British colonies outside the imperial system – were yet to be fully enforced. Barbados now imported bullion, cacao, indigo, dyewoods, and drugs, such as sarsaparilla from the Spanish colonies, presumably shipping mainly slaves and some manufactures in return.[77] The newly established Company of Royal Adventurers Trading into Africa established a supply base in Barbados, while Spaniards purchasing slaves there were exempted from the provisions of the Navigation Acts. The right to supply slaves to the Spanish empire was bound up in the celebrated *Asiento de Negros*, the contract which would play a key role in British trade with Spanish America after 1713. From 1663, the holders of the Asiento were permitted to source their slaves from any nation not at war with Spain, and the Genoese merchants possessing the contract arranged to purchase slaves from the British, at Barbados and elsewhere.[78] There followed several years of increased sales of slaves to Spaniards at Barbados, although also bitter disputes between private contraband traders and the Company of Royal Adventurers, which rapidly came to dominate the trade.[79]

Around the end of the 1660s, leadership in trade with the Spanish colonies moved away from Barbados and towards Jamaica, prefiguring the broader shift in economic weight between the two colonies over the following decades.[80] The capture of Jamaica in 1655 as part of Oliver Cromwell's 'Western Design' has been called 'perhaps England's most strategic territorial acquisition in the seventeenth century', due largely to its potential for trade with the Spanish colonies.[81] Jamaica was uniquely well placed for such trade (far more so than Dutch Curaçao, until this time the greatest smuggling centre in the Caribbean).[82] It was initially this strategic location which rendered the island such a valuable possession, and 'as great an eyesore to the creole Spaniards as Gibraltar is to the European'.[83] Trade with Spaniards at Jamaica began almost immediately, a fact attributed by later British observers in part to the agency of Spaniards expelled from the island or who stayed on there after the conquest.[84] The first recorded trade involved a sale of slaves by Governor D'Oyley in 1661, and the following year Governor Lord Windsor was formally instructed to seek 'a good Correspondence & a free Commerce' with the Spaniards in the region.[85] The greatest hopes at this time centred upon the slave trade, again through agreement by the Company of Royal Adventurers to supply the Genoese holders of the Spanish Asiento with Africans from a base established in Jamaica. This trade began in earnest in 1665, with the delivery of 1,600 slaves to the Asiento agents. The late 1660s were a turbulent period, however, and the Company of Adventurers promptly all but collapsed in the context of the second Anglo-Dutch war.[86] In the West Indies, meanwhile, this was the great age of British privateering, with raids launched from Jamaica on Cuba in 1662 and 1668, and (by Henry Morgan) on Portobelo, Maracaibo, and Panama in 1668–71. These assaults brought immediate economic rewards in the form of plunder, but necessarily precluded the creation of stable commercial relations, making these years something of a false start for the Spanish trade out of Jamaica.

Nevertheless, this same era (c. 1670) brought crucial changes which altered the conditions for trade at Jamaica and ushered in an era of great commercial prosperity. The first and surely the most important change resulted from commercial treaties agreed between Britain and Spain in 1667 and 1670. By the Treaty of 1667, Madrid formally recognised British rights to territory already held in the Americas, necessarily including the right of free navigation to and from those territories.[87] By the Treaty of 1670 (known to the British as the 'American Treaty') this concession was confirmed, while trade between British and Spanish colonies in the New World was explicitly prohibited. But provision was also made (in articles eight and nine) both for the licensing of such trade by either monarch in the future, and for entry of the ships of either nation to the ports of the other in case of bad weather or danger of shipwreck. These two clauses provided a loophole amply sufficient for the British to exploit to undertake trade with the Spanish empire.[88] The second major change was the suppression of the buccaneers in the British West Indies. Some scholars have attributed this process to the hopes of commercial gain excited among the British by the 'American Treaty', while others regard it more loosely as 'a matter of expediency and circumstance', albeit one still closely related both to hopes for the Spanish trade and to the rise of the plantation economy in Jamaica.[89] Suppression was not straightforward: although Governor Sir Thomas Modyford, 'the privateers' patron', was recalled in 1671, Morgan was granted a pardon in 1675 and became

Lieutenant Governor of the island. He headed a pro-privateering faction which continued to contest power with the fair trade party of Governor Thomas Lynch for several more years.[90] Nevertheless, by the mid-1670s, the great age of the state-sponsored privateer was over, and the way clear for a more regular commercial system.

Commercial treaties and the suppression of the buccaneers came in the context of Spain's long wars against France and the Dutch Republic, which made peace with England at this time politically and economically imperative.[91] These circumstances, together with ongoing decline in the rhythm of the Spanish trade fleets, conspired from around 1670 to produce a first great florescence of commerce with Spaniards out of Jamaica.[92] Jamaica's Spanish trade may be discussed under the dual headings of, firstly, contraband undertaken by private merchants and, secondly, the slave trade centred in the Royal African Company. We are exceptionally well informed with regard to both branches due above all to the seminal work of Nuala Zahedieh and of Stephen Fortune, published in the mid-1980s.[93] Smuggling at Jamaica now came to engage the energies of much of the population, including 'merchants, shop-keepers, petty traders, factors and agents, governors, customs officials, captains in the navy, and foreigners'.[94] Governor Lynch himself was 'heavily involved' in contraband trade, as was a large proportion of Jamaica's mercantile community. Many of these merchants had previous experience of the re-export trade with Spanish America via Seville and Cadiz, and not all were British nationals. Jewish merchants became particularly prominent, a feature which then endured throughout the eighteenth century. Already by 1672 thirteen Jews held patents of naturalisation permitting them to trade; these men exploited extensive commercial and financial networks throughout Europe and the Americas, arousing the envy and enmity of rivals.[95]

Part of the contraband trade was undertaken in Jamaica's own shipping, for the most part island-built sloops of only around twenty tons. On the back of trade with Spaniards, the Jamaican fleet of such vessels rose from 40 in 1670 to about 100 in 1688, despite many losses. Cargoes shipped in craft such as these were generally worth about £2,000, and voyages were mounted either by shipmasters themselves, or by merchants who freighted the vessels in Port Royal. Another part of the trade was undertaken by English shipping which stopped over at Port Royal before proceeding to the Spanish coasts. Such voyages were generally organised by agents resident in the island, who played a crucial role in selecting cargoes and crews and procuring intelligence as to the state of the markets in the Spanish colonies. Although official records are at best fragmentary, Zahedieh concludes that between 47 per cent and 71 per cent of all the shipping entering Port Royal between 1686 and 1688 was likely to have gone on to trade with the Spaniards.[96] Island-built and English vessels alike hovered off isolated bays and harbours on the Spanish coasts, and dealt with Spanish smugglers either at sea or in brief expeditions on shore. They also entered some of the smaller and poorer Spanish colonial ports directly, exploiting such loopholes as those offered by the 'American

Treaty', while some captains were said to trade in the roadsteads immediately outside. Major ports and administrative centres, such as Veracruz or Cartagena de Indias, generally proved more difficult to penetrate, however.[97] It should be noted that some part of British trade with Spanish America at this time also passed through non-British entrepôts, such as Dutch Curaçao.[98] The prevailing peace with Spain notwithstanding, British smugglers were often seized by Spanish anti-contraband ships, at a rate in the 1670s of between ten and twenty ships per year; for this reason, insuring these voyages seems to have been impossible, and smuggling vessels were usually heavily manned and armed so as to defend themselves.[99] British exports to the Spanish colonies consisted mainly of linen and silk manufactures, ironware, and liquor, supplemented by North American flour and some Jamaican produce; imports consisted mainly of bullion, along with precious stones, indigo, cacao, cattle, and hides.

The second major branch of trade with the Spaniards out of Jamaica – at this time, as for well over a century – was in African slaves. We have seen that a false start was made in the British slave trade with the Spanish colonies when the Company of Royal Adventurers Trading into Africa all but collapsed in the late 1660s. This enterprise was refounded by 1672 as the Royal African Company, which then engrossed the major part of the slave trade of the British West Indies.[100] Supply of slaves to the Spanish colonies depended crucially upon agreement with whatever merchant group possessed the *Asiento de Negros*, the exclusive contract for trade in slaves with the Spanish empire. The merchants holding the Asiento purchased their slaves not only directly from Africa, but wherever they were cheapest and most abundant, which from the late seventeenth century increasingly meant the plantation colonies in the British West Indies. Thus, holders of the Asiento, who, during this period, tended to be Portuguese or Italian merchants, albeit often fronting for Dutch interests, purchased slaves in the British colonies for resale to Spanish Americans in fulfilment of their contract.[101] This practice breached both the Spanish colonial monopoly and the British Navigation Acts, but such was its economic significance that it was condoned, and even actively promoted, by both sides.

By 1677, fresh agreement was reached between Britain and Spain for supply of slaves to the Spanish colonies from the British West Indies.[102] Slaves were imported by the Royal African Company and in principle were sold to agents of the Asiento settled in Jamaica and Barbados. Merchants from the Spanish colonies sailed to Port Royal or Bridgetown, under permit both from their own government and the British, there to purchase slaves from the Asiento factors.[103] In practice, the trade was rather more complex than this, in part because of contraband in slaves direct from Africa to the British West Indies by smugglers who ignored the Royal African Company's monopoly rights, and in part because West Indian planters and other slave-owners themselves resold slaves to Spaniards purchased at first hand from the Company.[104] Under whatever form, a brisk trade developed as Spanish merchants from Portobelo, Cartagena, and Havana travelled to Jamaica for slaves. Successive governors in both Jamaica and Barbados promoted the trade, appreciating its potential as a vehicle for broader commercial inter-course with Spaniards, and indeed themselves participated in it.[105] By the 1680s the Royal African Company was selling between 25 per cent and 50 per cent of the slaves it imported to the West Indies to Spaniards, and it was often claimed that many more could have been sold had the Company been able to procure them. There exists abundant evidence regarding both the slave voyages undertaken during these years, and the frustration of colonial authorities unable to sell still more Africans to the Spaniards. The price of these slaves in the British West Indies varied between £17 and £22 per head, and in early 1688 a single ship was said to have arrived in Jamaica on Asiento business with £126,000 sterling on board. Total recorded exports may have surpassed 4,000 people in 1680–1700, though this seems likely to be only a fraction of the true figure.[106]

Not all Spaniards were willing to run the sea risks (of piracy as well as ship-wreck) involved in shipping bullion from the Spanish coasts to Jamaica to buy slaves. A solution to this problem was offered by the Royal African Company's factor in the island, together with a group of merchants including Governor Lynch himself. These merchants bought slaves from the Company and resold them to Spaniards in Jamaica (as did other merchants), but accepted payment in Spanish ports rather than on the spot. Spaniards could thus make the crossing to Jamaica without bullion, and Lynch and his colleagues even provided convoys for the return voyage – all in exchange for a 35 per cent mark-up on the price of the slaves. This system proved highly popular, attracting many Spanish merchants and quickly making large profits for the Jamaicans concerned; indeed, Zahedieh has noted that while the Royal African Company's overall profits were modest, 'merchants in Jamaica who cornered the '35% trade' did very well'.[107] Such success bred jealousy among less fortunate traders, and the concentration of trade in the hands of the Royal African Company and the holders of the Asiento provoked serious discon-tent among Jamaican merchants and planters. Jamaican smugglers in the Spanish colonies, too, protested at their marginalisation by the privileged access the slavers enjoyed to Spanish colonial ports. These interests combined to fight a strong rear-guard action against the African Company and Asiento, which was often articulated through the island Assembly, and whose tactics ranged from imposition of duties on the slave trade, to seizure of Spanish vessels or even personal harassment of Spanish merchants.[108] This dispute thus foreshadowed the still more serious conflict between island inter-ests and the South Sea Company once Britain itself acquired the Asiento after 1713.

The year 1702 witnessed the outbreak of the War of the Spanish Succession, for many contemporaries a war fought explicitly for control of Spanish-American trade. Circumstances appeared to conspire to make this an unusually opulent sub-period for contraband in the Caribbean. For one thing, the Spanish trade fleets now all but ceased altogether; only a single full trade fair was held at Portobelo between 1696 and 1722 (in 1706), and the *flotas* for Mexico were often sadly under-weight affairs.[109] The consequent near-total disruption of re-exports of European manufactures via the Iberian Peninsula could be expected to redirect British mercantile energies 'with increased force to the Main'.[110] Some of the best-known and most evocative of all descriptions of British smuggling in the Spanish colonies date from the War of Succession, and Frances Armytage has pointed out that these descriptions then continued to be applied throughout much of the rest of the century.[111] One of the best-informed accounts, that of Robert Allen, noted that in the context of the collapse of formal Spanish trade during the war, until 1706 'Jamaica flourished & abounded more in Spanish gold & silver than it ever did before'.[112] Even the slave trade, more vulnerable to wartime disruption than smuggling, seems to have thrived; at least 18,180 slaves were exported from Jamaica in 1702–14, most of them to the Spanish colonies, and total British sales of Africans to Spaniards have been estimated at from 1,500 to 3,000 per year.[113]

Not all was commercial plain sailing during the War of Succession. At the outset, Britain forbade its merchants to trade with the enemy, including Spaniards in the Americas, though the ban was lifted in 1704–06 following protests from merchants.[114] Naval escorts were provided for smugglers sailing to the Spanish coasts, although there were frequent complaints both at the excessive fees demanded by naval captains, and at their own participation in contraband, to the exclusion of private traders.[115] In 1708, a further attempt was made to protect the trade when an Act of Parliament actually created a zone of sanctuary along the coast of Tierra Firme from the Isthmus of Panama to Río de la Hacha, within which Spanish vessels were declared immune from seizure by British privateers.[116] Privateering remained a serious problem, nevertheless, with a great many Spanish vessels captured and consequent disruption to trade.[117] The chief threat to the prosperity of British smuggling during the war, however, arose from commercial competition from Dutch merchants, and particularly from the French. French traders (especially from Saint-Malo in Brittany) exploited France's wartime alliance with Spain to conduct an extraordinarily rich contraband trade both in the Gulf of Mexico and the Pacific. In 1700–25, more than 150 French vessels traded on the Pacific coasts of South America alone, while total returns to France in bullion may have reached 99,000,000 pesos (or more than £20,000,000).[118] Contemporary complaints to the effect that this commerce seriously damaged Britain's own Spanish trade are frequent and thus difficult to ignore, although the figures for value discussed hereafter belie the more febrile claims made at this time of commercial crisis.[119]

Assessing the value of British contraband with the Spanish colonies is difficult, for this as for later periods, since no formal statistical series have been found to record what remained (with the partial exception of the slave trade) an illegal commerce. Smugglers in the Caribbean enjoyed a clear cost advantage over merchants trading through Spain, deriving from lower taxes and shipping expenses, quicker returns, and lower levels of state inference; though both contemporaries and modern scholars have struggled to put precise figures on this advantage.[120] Contraband seems to have begun at a low level, with the value of Jamaica's Spanish trade recorded as only about £20,000 in the sixteen months to March 1679.[121] By 1690, however, a fleet from Jamaica carried £100,000 sterling in bullion to England, almost all of it unquestionably the product of trade with Spaniards.[122] On the eve of the War of Succession, in 1700–02, several observers put the value of the trade at between £150,000 and £200,000 per year, in my view credible figures for this period.[123] Figures of between £100,000 and £200,000 per year continued to be cited for exports of manufactures to the Spanish colonies from Jamaica, or for bullion shipped from Jamaica to England, throughout much of the war, with the highest figure (of £275,000 in merchandise exported) given for the year to August 1707.[124] Such figures, which should only be regarded as indicative, suggest irregular but noteworthy growth in the trade from the 1670s to the end of the War of Succession. They may also suggest that the impact of French wartime competition was felt more in terms of potential market loss than in absolute value. Nevertheless, it is important to emphasise that Britain remained merely one among several major foreign rivals for dominance in Spanish-American markets. Until the late seventeenth century, the Dutch were probably dominant in Caribbean markets; in the early eighteenth century, the French were certainly so in several regions. Not until the period after 1763 – the core focus of this monograph – would the British finally establish a clear commercial superiority.

By the turn of the century, the broader impact of British trade with Spanish America was already considerable. On the one hand, it is now clear that smuggling played a major role in the early economic development of the British West Indies. Zahedieh has argued that it was the Spanish trade, along with buccaneering, which provided the bulk of the capital for the development of the Jamaican plantation economy, in contrast to the traditional view that such capital was imported from the metropolis.[125] Fortune similarly argues for a direct connection between the 'external stimuli' of smuggling and buccaneering and the development of plantation agriculture at Barbados.[126] In this sense, it may be relevant to note that trade similarly preceded agriculture in the subsequent development of the richest of the French plantation colonies, at St Domingue.[127] This point was well known to contemporaries; Daniel Defoe wrote in 1714 that

> it is certain, that this secret Trade to Spain [for Spanish America] is the real and only Occasion of the great Concourse of People ... to the Island of Jamaica ... Has it not been by these Things and their private clandestine Trade with Spain that these Men have been made Rich and Great?[128]

For well over a century, extra-agricultural trade remained a major activity at Jamaica, setting it apart from the majority of the British plantation economies.

Its importance to the development of the West Indies aside, at the broadest level the significance to Britain of trade with the Spanish colonies was as a source of bullion with which to develop commerce with the East Indies. Like the other European powers, Britain had little to sell to the rich Asian economies in return for silks, spices, and other prized commodities, and was obliged to purchase them with silver.[129] Spanish America constituted by far the richest source of silver bullion available to Britain or its European rivals; a figure of £100,000 per year, for example, would suggest that by the 1690s the Spanish trade in the Caribbean already furnished one-quarter of the bullion required to sustain British trade with Asia.[130] When re-exports via Spain (worth at least £300,000 in the same period) are included, it appears that by the late seventeenth century Britain already drew all the silver it needed for trade with Asia from Spanish America. Such was the British share in the great windfall of the 'Columbian exchange', the flow of precious metals from the Americas via Europe to the East which is regarded by many scholars as the single greatest consequence for global history of the discovery of the Americas.[131] Throughout the period covered by this book, Britain's strategic interest in trade with the Spanish colonies remained closely linked to the need for bullion to re-export to Asia.

Trade and Contraband in the Caribbean, 1713–39: The *Asiento* Years

British trade with the Spanish colonies between the end of the War of the Spanish Succession and the onset of the War of Jenkins' Ear in 1739 was dominated by the Asiento contract, which was granted to Britain by the Treaty of Utrecht of 1713. The Asiento, as we have seen, embodied the exclusive right to supply the Spanish colonies with African slaves, a concession valued both on its own terms and for the scope it afforded for contraband. It was wrung from Spain as part of the price of peace with Britain, along with permanent cession of Gibraltar, and like Gibraltar it constituted a serious problem for Spanish statesmen.[132] The Asiento was awarded to the newly formed South Sea Company, the latest of the British privileged companies, which was also granted the British monopoly on trade with South America.[133] The contract was to last for thirty years, and provided for imports of 4,800 *piezas de Indias* (or prime African slaves) to Spanish America each year.[134] The British Asiento was unique in further incorporating a right to send a trading vessel (the 'Annual Ship') to the Spanish-American trade fairs held at Portobelo and Veracruz. It thus offered greater scope than ever for commercial penetration of the Spanish empire, and was regarded as a major prize by both the British and their rivals.[135] To insist, then: what made British trade with the Spanish colonies special under the Asiento was the entirely unprecedented *legal* access the British gained to Spanish-American ports, whether through the slave trade itself, or the 'Annual Ships'. Unsurprisingly, the Asiento era has attracted a richer historiography than any other aspect of British trade with the Spanish colonies, and can be discussed here only in brief summary. The following discussion focuses on four principal themes: the slave trade of the South Sea Company under the Asiento; its 'Annual Ship' trade; contraband undertaken under cover of the Asiento; and smuggling by private merchants in competition with the activities of the Company.

The chief purpose of the South Sea Company's Asiento – ostensibly, at least – was to supply the Spanish colonies with African slaves. In the mid-1710s, an infrastructure was rapidly created to enable the Company to manage this supply, which depended crucially on privileges granted by Spain. Three organising centres were established, at Jamaica, Barbados, and Buenos Aires on the River Plate (although the Barbados centre was effectively abandoned after only a few years).[136] A larger number of factories was established to handle sales of slaves in the different Spanish colonies, at Cartagena de Indias, Veracruz, Havana, and Panama, in addition to Buenos Aires. Sub-factories were established at Portobelo and Santiago de Cuba, while Company agents resided further afield, in Mexico City, Lima, Arequipa, Potosí and Santiago de Chile.[137] In the beginning, the Company obtained all its slaves by monopoly agreement with the Royal African Company, albeit in its own vessels. From the 1720s, however, slaves began to be procured by private traders and by the South Sea Company itself, while over time the Company came to purchase an ever-greater proportion of slaves outright in the British West Indies.[138] Thus, over the life of the British Asiento, only about 16 per cent of Company slaves were shipped to the Spanish colonies direct from Africa (most of them to the River Plate); almost 60 per cent were shipped from Jamaica, with Barbados and St Kitts supplying a further 19 per cent.[139] In the Caribbean, the Company's agents in Jamaica oversaw all aspects of the trade, from the procurement of cargoes for the slave vessels to the purchase or receipt of Africans. Newly-arrived slaves were held in Kingston for about a month for emergency medical care so as to get them into shape before onward shipment to the Spaniards.[140] The majority of slaving voyages to the Spanish colonies were undertaken in vessels owned or rented by the South Sea Company, but for more remote regions where the Company had no factories a licensing system was employed. Thus, private merchants bought licences entitling them to supply slaves to regions such as Santo Domingo, Puerto Rico, Nicaragua, Río de la Hacha or Santa Marta. In some years, as many as a fifth of the slaves supplied by the South Sea Company were delivered by private merchants under licence in this way.[141]

The factory maintained by the South Sea Company at Buenos Aires merits special mention. The Buenos Aires station was unique in being not only a factory like the others scattered throughout the Spanish colonies, but also a main organising centre. This circumstance was imposed by its isolation far to the south on the River Plate, and the same circumstance meant that Buenos Aires received most of its slaves direct from Africa (particularly from Angola). The Company was entitled to send 1,200 *piezas de Indias* per year to the River Plate out of its total 'quota' of 4,800. Like the other South Sea Company factories, that at Buenos Aires was furnished with buildings to house both slaves and stores, and with adjacent land to produce food for the Africans. But unlike them, at Buenos Aires the Company was further entitled to store any goods left over from its trading for slaves on the African coast.[142] From 1725, it also enjoyed the right to export slaves left unsold in Buenos Aires inland to Upper and Lower Peru (modern Bolivia and Peru) and Chile, a practice termed *internación*. This permit led to large caravans of slaves, consisting of up to 400 men accompanied by one or two Britons and some Spanish and African assistants, making the months-long journey across the pampas and up into the Andes to their final destination. Both the Company storehouses and right of *internación* gave particularly rich scope for contraband, which was rife on the River Plate. Returns of goods were mainly in cattle hides, already the region's staple export.[143]

Over the life of the Asiento until its effective termination in 1739, estimates of the total number of slaves sold by the South Sea Company in Spanish America vary from a low of 63,206, to a high of 66,860 people. Almost one-third of these people (about 30 per cent) were sold through the factories on the Isthmus of Panama, at Portobelo or at Panama itself, whence they were reshipped for Peru by their Spanish owners. A further quarter were sold through the factory at Buenos Aires. Next in significance as markets were Cartagena de Indias (in modern-day Colombia), with some 16 per cent, and Cuba, with about 11 per cent; Caracas in Venezuela and Veracruz in Mexico headed the list of the lesser markets. A total figure for exports of Africans of around 65,000 in 1713-39 would imply that the South Sea Company sold only about half of its permitted quota of 4,800 *piezas de Indias* per year, although it has been suggested that contraband (and so unregistered) exports of slaves may have amounted to one-third or one-half of the registered figure.[144] Taken together, slaves exported by the South Sea Company and by British smugglers may have accounted for *four-fifths of all slaves* landed in Spanish America during the period of the British Asiento, and represented between a third and a quarter of all the slaves taken to the New World by the British. A leading authority has thus reasonably concluded that 'clearly, the asiento engendered a major expansion in England's share of the international slave trade'.[145] The value of the South Sea Company's trade is discussed in the conclusion to this section; suffice here to note that the profitability of the slave trade may have varied from a low of less than 2 per cent, to a high of over 68 per cent, according to markets and conditions.[146]

The Treaty of Utrecht granted the British more than the slave trade contract or Asiento alone. It also granted the right to send a single 500-ton ship to each of the great trade fairs held at Portobelo and Veracruz.[147] These trade fairs, it will be recalled, in principle supplied the whole of Mexico and Peru with European goods, and (again in principle, though rarely in practice) were held on an annual basis. In a supplementary treaty signed in May 1716, the tonnage of what (rather misleadingly) is often called the South Sea Company's 'Annual Ship' was raised to 650 tons, and provision was made for it to trade alone in the Americas in the event that no Spanish fleet sailed in a given year.[148] This 'Annual Ship' attracted greater attention and enthusiasm than any other aspect of Britain's new-found trading rights in the Spanish colonies. The Asiento, after all, gave the South Sea Company the right to establish factories in the colonies, and to trade in slaves; but the Annual Ship conferred the right to trade openly in manufactured goods, at the very heart of the Spanish colonial trading system. This was a concession quite without precedent, and it contributed powerfully in 1713 to the sense that the way was clear for British penetration of Spanish-American markets on a vastly increased scale.

In practice, these hopes proved partly illusory. All South Sea Company trade in Spanish America necessarily depended on Spanish goodwill if formal treaty stipulations were not to be frustrated by informal obstructionism or simple bureaucratic delay. At times of tension between Britain and Spain, or in the hands of capable ministers, tactics such as these were employed to hinder both the Company's slave trade and its Annual Ships. At different times, for example, limits were placed on the movements of Company factors in the Americas, or Spanish-American merchant guilds were granted rights of inspection and control over Company activities at the trade fairs. The restrictions appear to have been stepped up in the 1730s, when they included the temporary closure of the Panama factory, and imposition of a minimum quota of slaves to be imported on each ship (an anti-contraband measure).[149] Throughout the life of the British Asiento, Spanish ministers used whatever pretext was at hand to deny the Company the necessary permit to send an Annual Ship at all, preventing the trade altogether in given years.[150] The most important of all the interruptions to the trade came during the periods of outright hostility between Britain and Spain which punctuated these years. In 1718–19, and again in the late 1720s, brief wars led to the enforced suspension of the Company's trade and to reprisals against the Annual Ships. Most seriously, the long war which began in 1739 resulted in permanent suspension of the British Asiento.[151]

Nevertheless, the economic significance of the Annual Ships should not be under-estimated. Between 1717 and 1733, the South Sea Company sent seven ships to trade at Portobelo and Veracruz. These vessels gloried in such names as *Royal Prince, Prince Frederick,* or *Royal Caroline,* reflecting the strong regal interest in the Company. The cargo of the *Royal George,* trading at the Portobelo fair of 1723, had a registered value of over £250,000 and consisted principally of textiles, along with stockings, hats, mirrors, iron, paper, and miscellaneous items including '2 Cases Jews Harps'.[152] The total value of registered cargoes exported in all seven vessels (and in two licensed ships which went with them) was just over £2,100,000 'based on the actual cost of the merchandise purchased by the Company'.[153] When contraband goods carried alongside the registered cargoes are taken into account, the real value of the Annual Ships may be supposed to have been much higher. These voyages, and the Company's trade as a whole, proved less profitable than might have been expected, as we shall see in a moment. But they still had a catastrophic (for the Spaniards) impact on the majority of the trade fairs they attended. The goods imported were often superior to those offered by Spanish merchants, and were far cheaper; as a result, the Annual Ships took the first and richest part of the fairs' trade. At Portobelo in 1722, the Annual Ship and British smugglers 'were almost entirely to blame for the eventual failure of the fair'; at Veracruz in 1723–24, the *Royal Prince* unloaded over 1,000 tons of merchandise, equivalent to 'half the volume of the whole of the Spanish *flota*'. Similar situations recurred at all the fairs held during these years; only when means could be found to frustrate the activity of the Company ship (as occurred at Veracruz in 1725–26) could a relatively healthy fair be staged.[154]

The slave trade and Annual Ships provided legal access for the British to Spanish-American markets; that, of course, was what made the Asiento era distinctive. But this very legal access also provided rich scope for contraband. As Richard Pares put it, 'everybody could see that the Assiento and the Annual Ship would lead to smuggling'; indeed, 'some clauses of the treaty were almost useless except as a pretext for it'.[155] Very extensive smuggling operations thus developed under cover of the Asiento, attracting the gaze of contemporaries and historians alike.[156] Probably the richest scope for smuggling – the more spectacular nature of the Annual Ships notwithstanding – derived from the slave trade. After all, the Asiento implied the establishment of British factories in major Spanish-American ports, and also many voyages per year by Company vessels with legal access to those ports. Often only a few slaves were carried on each ship so as to generate the greatest number of voyages possible, while contraband goods might be carried on board which exceeded the value of the slaves many times over. In some cases no slaves were carried at all; in others, white sailors were said to have been disguised as Africans so as to justify voyages.[157] Under the terms of its contract, the Company was further permitted to send a ship of 150 tons each year to supply its factories with provisions, and these vessels too provided ideal vehicles for smuggling.[158] Alongside enslaved Africans, in these ways the Company exported 'manufactured goods like cottons, woollens, and ironware, plus flour, tar, pitch, beef, pork, mercury, brass, canvas, mules, shoes, and nails'.[159] The slave trade provided such rich scope for smuggling, indeed, that George Nelson concluded that by the 1730s 'it was in the Negro ships, rather than in the annual ships, that the major share – at least ninety percent ... – of the illicit goods was transported under the Asiento'.[160] We have already seen that smuggling was particularly vigorous through the Buenos Aires factory, strategically situated on the River Plate.

While probably correct in its general assertion of the primacy of the slave trade, Nelson's estimate may exaggerate its dominance in smuggling, since there can be little doubt that the Annual Ships also generated a significant volume of contraband. These vessels, too, enjoyed legal access to Spanish-American ports and trade fairs, and this access too could be exploited for both fair trade and foul. Smuggling strategies focused upon the carriage and sale of far more goods than those permitted under the Asiento. False measurement of cargo space, over-loading, and replenishment of the hold by small craft ostensibly bringing foodstuffs and water were all used to boost the volume of goods far beyond the 650 tons permitted. Such practices might easily have been detected, but Company officers proved expert in distributing bribes which ensured the acquiescence or active collaboration of Spanish officialdom. To cite a single example, in 1727 it was alleged that the viceroy of Mexico was given rich gifts, including a diamond-encrusted sword worth 25,000 pesos and a musical clock ('rare and unknown in those parts'), in return for assisting the voyage of the *Prince Frederick*.[161] As a result of these and comparable practices, Nelson further suggested that contraband goods accounted for half as much volume again as legal cargo in the Annual Ships despatched in 1730 and 1733 (the respective figures were £620,000 legal goods and £350,000 contraband). The same author indicated a total value of contraband in all seven Annual Ships and two licensed vessels of 'only about £570,000'.[162] But this and similar calculations are complicated by the fact that very extensive smuggling was undertaken by South Sea Company officials and employees in large part unbeknownst even to the Company itself. Thus, sailors on packet boats carried private consignments for Jamaican merchants, while 'the officers of the ships were more afraid of the company's representatives becoming cognisant of the true extent of their operations than they were of the Spanish customs officials'.[163] In 1728, a Spanish diplomat bought off a former factor at Portobelo and Cartagena, along with the South Sea Company's secretary and principal accountant, and acquired papers from both men which gave some indication of the full extent of smuggling under the Asiento and briefly caused the British some embarrassment.[164]

While greeted with jubilation in Britain, paradoxically the award of the Asiento to the South Sea Company was regarded as a catastrophe by many in Jamaica. We saw in the previous section that a rich contraband trade with the Spanish colonies had developed in Jamaica, especially from c. 1670, which continued throughout the War of Succession. The concession of exclusive trading rights to the South Sea Company in 1713 appeared to threaten this trade. On the one hand, the Company's legal access to Spanish-American markets and strong royal backing gave it enormous competitive advantage over private smugglers. On the other, the Asiento itself was conditional upon the British eliminating all clandestine trade.[165] These factors led Jamaicans to fear for their own participation in smuggling; as early as December 1713, the Assembly predicted that

> this island [is] now likely to become the meanest of all your Majesty's colonies in America, since we have lost the benefits of sending dry goods, the manufactures of Great Britain, and the produce of your Majesty's northern colonies, as well as negroes to the subjects of Spain in America by the Asiento lately settled ...[166]

Throughout the life of the British Asiento, Jamaicans continued to lament the loss of private contraband trade or to criticise its concentration in the hands of the South Sea Company. There was a broader economic dimension to these concerns, too, based on the notion that the Company diverted the best slaves to Spanish markets, to the detriment of Jamaica's plantation economy. The result was a major controversy, played out through both the Assembly and a rich pamphlet literature, in which supporters of the Company responded by deriding Jamaican claims and emphasising the economic advantages supposed to accrue to Britain from the Asiento. Nor was this merely a war of words: the Jamaica Assembly repeatedly sought to attack the Company's trade by imposing irregular duties on slaves exported from the island, while the Company exerted its influence in the Spanish colonies to attempt to have contraband slaves confiscated.[167]

In broad terms, the British government supported the interests of the South Sea Company over those of private traders, so that the Company held the upper hand.[168] Until its suspension in 1739, there seems little doubt that the bulk of British contraband passed through channels controlled by the Asiento. But it was by no means the case that private smuggling out of Jamaica ceased altogether during the Asiento era. It continued at some level throughout these years, and it boomed during periods when the Company's trade was suspended due to hostilities, permitting the smugglers to regain their old primacy. Thus, during the brief war of 1718–19, a Spaniard in Jamaica recorded the voyages of more than 250 vessels whose known or probable destination was the Spanish colonies. Fully two-thirds of these vessels were bound for Cuba, while small fleets of smugglers also traded with the Portobelo coast.[169] Contraband on this scale ceased once more with the end of hostilities, and the early 1720s witnessed a particularly vigorous Spanish campaign against smuggling in the Americas.[170] But a similar boom occurred during a further short war in the late 1720s, when a British naval expedition under Admiral Hosier neutralised all Spanish anti-contraband measures.[171] Nor was smuggling limited solely to these periods of warfare; at the Portobelo trade fair of 1722, for example, the impact of the Annual Ship, though considerable, was 'small compared with that of the smugglers' who massed in the bays nearby.[172] It is interesting to note that at least part of this trade was still carried on by vessels whose voyages originated in Britain and which merely touched at Jamaica or Barbados. A further important branch was undertaken by the captains of Royal Naval vessels assigned to protect Jamaican shipping, since 'trading with the Spanish colonists was even carried on from the decks of warships' – a subject of frequent reports and complaints.[173] In short, some private smuggling continued throughout these years, beyond the reach of the South Sea Company and in open competition with it.

Spanish actions against British smugglers persisted throughout the Asiento years, and it has been calculated that no fewer than 77 British vessels were seized by Spaniards during the period 1713–31. The intensity of anti-contraband operations varied over time, so that half the British ships were taken between 1727 and 1731.[174] The seizures became the source of serious dispute between the two nations only in the late 1730s, however. Nine British craft were taken by Spaniards in 1735, and eleven in 1737; and these 'depredations' were exploited as a *casus belli* by a mercantile faction in Britain already straining for war. The best efforts of Prime Minister Walpole and others notwithstanding, events spiralled out of control, and war was finally declared in October 1739.[175] The outbreak of war brought about the immediate suspension of the Asiento, and so of the South Sea Company's trade in the West Indies, which was never restored thereafter. Although some moves were made to recommence operations after the peace in 1748, little was achieved, and the British Asiento, secured with such fanfare in 1713, was formally terminated by mutual accord in 1750.[176]

It seems surprising that estimates of the value of British trade with Spanish America during the Asiento years – when, after all, a good part of it was legal and managed by a registered British company – should be as vague and problematic as for other periods. And yet estimates of the value of trade under the Asiento vary enormously. They include figures which are surely inflated; thus, the Spanish-American writer Dionisio de Alcedo y Herrera suggested that the British extracted 224,000,000 pesos from Spanish America in 1713–39 (perhaps £50,000,000 in total, or almost £2,000,000 per year), a frankly incredible figure.[177] Nelson thought that licit and illicit trade in slaves and the Annual Ships was worth an average of £600,000 per year in 1730–39, or £6,000,000 for the decade, on the basis of rather dubious calculations. He attributed £5,000,000 of these profits to the slave trade, with £1,000,000 generated by two Annual Ships.[178] In my view the most credible estimates for the value of all British trade with the Spanish colonies – the South Sea Company's legal and illegal trade and private contraband combined – are more conservative, at a minimum of £300,000 per year in 1713–39 (though there are lower estimates).[179] Such figures cannot be regarded as more than approximate, but nevertheless imply a substantial increase over the average of £100,000 to £200,000 suggested for the period c. 1670–1713. A recent doctoral thesis has suggested that whatever the value of sales, the South Sea Company's trade was 'not particularly profitable', largely because it was ineptly managed and subject to frequent interruptions by warfare and seizures.[180] An earlier study even concluded that possession of the Asiento actually harmed British interests, leading to a loss of ground in trade with the Spanish colonies in favour of the French.[181] But mediocre returns to Company shareholders did not, of course, preclude profits to individual manufacturers, merchants, ships' captains, and Company officials. Spanish observers and government ministers were in no doubt that the Asiento years marked a further stage in Britain's commercial penetration of the empire, one which gave the British invaluable expertise and intelligence of Spanish-American markets.[182]

Contraband Trade in the Caribbean, 1739–63

The War of Jenkins' Ear which began in 1739 later merged into the broader European conflict over the Austrian Succession, and finally petered out only in 1748. With the collapse of the South Sea Company's legal commerce, the Spanish trade now reverted to a purely contraband activity, undertaken by private merchants based in Jamaica and elsewhere. While undertaken throughout the region, some authors suggest that it was concentrated above all in Central America from Campeche to Costa Rica, and in Cuba and Santo Domingo.[183] During the war, one striking feature of the trade was the degree of protection afforded to it by the Royal Navy. On the one hand, convoys were granted to smugglers trading in ports near Cartagena de Indias or on the south coast of Cuba. On the other, when Admiral Vernon captured Portobelo in late 1739 he not only demolished its fortifications, in part so as to assist the smugglers, but also spared the town and issued a proclamation inviting Spaniards to 'a free trade with all His Majesty's subjects'.[184] Between 1742 and 1748, the small island of Roatán off the north coast of Honduras was also occupied, providing a further active base for smuggling.[185] In these circumstances, it seems that trade flourished; the Jamaica Assembly remarked that during the war 'a very successful trade was carried on with the Spanish Dominions in America; by which goods of English growth and manufacture to a vast amount, were exported and a great influx of money poured into their island, much the greatest part whereof ultimately center'd in Great Britain'.[186] Smuggling expeditions were typically undertaken in sloops and brigs of from 50 to 120 tons, with cargoes of manufactures and provisions, and returns mainly in bullion. One detailed account suggested that profits on a venture of £12,000 might amount to £1,725 (just under 15 per cent) after all expenses, but this figure almost certainly under-estimates typical profitability.[187] Trade seems to have boomed especially during the first few years of the war, and perhaps fell off to some extent from around 1743.[188] It was reported to be particularly strong in New Granada, where one estimate suggested that more than 7,000,000 pesos in contraband goods were confiscated in 1739–49 in Cartagena alone.[189] Credible estimates for its value are lacking for the wartime years; suffice to note that British smuggling and naval action conspired to bring about the permanent suspension of the Spanish trade fleets to Portobelo and Panama, after almost two centuries.[190]

Two histories of British trade with the Spanish colonies in the mid-eighteenth century offer rich information as to its general characteristics and operation.[191] The British sold a wide range of goods in Spanish-American markets. Textiles were the most important, among which woollens still headed the list, while cottons were hampered by legislative restrictions at home (although large quantities of East India cottons were sold). Linen textiles also now made rapid progress. Most of these textiles were un-made up, although a range of manufactures also featured, including stockings, thread, ribbon, lace, hats (both felt and beaver), and worked leather goods (including shoes). A further significant category was metal manufactures, embracing a wide range of tools, cutlery, locks, hinges, knives, lamps, clocks, and other wares. Miscellaneous manufactures included glass and earthenware (plates and cups, coffee- and teapots, cookware and storage jars), furniture (desks, chairs, wardrobes, and trunks), jewellery, books, paper, candles and candle wax, soap, cards, grindstones, and ships' goods, such as cordage and sailcloth. Several of these items (for example the furniture and glassware) comprehended luxury goods. Foodstuffs also occupied a prominent place among British exports, and included flour, biscuits, salt pork and beef, bottled alcohols, cheese, butter, salt fish, and East India spices. Flour (often produced in North America) was particularly significant, and much trade for foodstuffs was carried on under licence from governors in the Spanish colonies.[192] Enslaved Africans formed a category apart, and we have seen that some 65,000 slaves were sold in the Spanish colonies in 1713–39; one estimate suggests that between 1700 and 1786, a total of 160,000 Africans were exported from Jamaica (representing over a quarter of those imported into the island).[193] The character of return cargoes from the Spanish colonies varied little over time, consisting of silver bullion, dyes and dyewoods, drugs, livestock for the British plantations, foodstuffs, and some miscellaneous products; these items, and their relative significance, are discussed at length in Chapter 3 below.

The mechanisms now used by the British to sell their goods were typical of smuggling in the Caribbean since its origins. They included clandestine trade on isolated stretches of coastline, ruses to gain access to Spanish ports (including pretence of distress and carrying dispatches from the British governors), and the apparently extensive use of fishing as a cover for contraband. Héctor Ramos has attempted a curious character sketch of the typical smuggler, which emphasises the 'desperado' element, but this may represent only part of a group which also included perfectly respectable British merchants.[194] Members of the Jewish community in Jamaica seem to have continued to exercise a disproportionately influential role.[195] Smugglers generally employed small craft, such as sloops and schooners, and sometimes even simple launches; when larger vessels were used, they were often heavily armed.[196] Most sales to Spaniards were made in return for hard cash or (where circumstances obliged) through barter, but the British also offered credit, an innovation which Pantaleão suggests was frequent and had the effect of tying Spanish merchants to the British.[197] Complaints at non-payment of debts by Spanish Americans were frequent, however. It is important to note that in addition to purely commercial transactions, the British also carried large sums of bullion back to Europe on Spanish-American account. Thus, Spaniards gave their money in exchange for letters of credit guaranteeing payment in Spain; in this way they avoided the heavy taxation, and even risk of confiscation, inherent in dispatch of funds via the formal Spanish trading system. The British charged a fee of from 6 to 10 per cent for this service, but it included 'a special all-risks insurance premium' and was highly popular.[198]

Jamaica remained overwhelmingly the most important base for British contraband in the mid-eighteenth century; indeed, until the Peace of Paris in 1763 it had few rivals. Jamaica's sphere of commercial influence covered most of the Caribbean, including the whole of the coast of South America as far east as the mouths of the Orinoco, and Central America from Panama up into Mexico as far north as Tampico. It was particularly strong in Cuba, and further extended to Florida and Santo Domingo (though not, apparently, Puerto Rico). A second smaller base for smuggling was situated among the scattered and shifting British settlements on the Bay of Honduras and Mosquito Shore, which had been founded in the seventeenth century principally by cutters of logwood and other dye-producing trees. These settlements traded with the Spaniards of Guatemala and Nicaragua, and possibly on occasion as far north as Veracruz.[199] The small British islands in the Lesser Antilles, including Barbados, dealt with Puerto Rico and with Trinidad and eastern Venezuela, but only at low levels. Lastly, some trade was still carried on direct from Britain rather than through Caribbean entrepôts, but this was unusual. The Spanish Secretary of State José de Carvajal y Lancaster remarked in 1753 that 'it is very rare for a ship to be loaded on the Thames to sail direct to our coasts. The normal thing is to go to their colonies, sell to the colonists there, and these undertake the contraband with those goods in our Dominions'.[200] During this period, the British continued to face stiff competition from foreign rivals in several Spanish-American markets: from the Dutch in Venezuela and as far west as Santa Marta, and from the French in Santo Domingo (where they dominated) and in Cuba (where they competed vigorously with Jamaica).[201]

The end of the war in 1748 and the return to peacetime conditions was accompanied by a depression in Anglo-Spanish trade in the Caribbean. By 1752, the Jamaica Assembly declared that 'not a fourth part of the money was brought in since the war as was before it, & not a twentieth part of what was brought in during the same'.[202] The Governor of Jamaica confirmed that 'a marked falling off' took place in trade with Spaniards, with only a little business carried on with Río de la Hacha for mules.[203] The depression may have begun slightly earlier, since some British merchants 'ordered their Factors to send their goods back to England, & great quantities were actually so returned, from the year 1746 to 1748'.[204] The evidence for a crisis at this time is not, in fact, unambiguous; the Jamaican historian Edward Long estimated the value of slave exports at £112,500 c. 1750, with exports of merchandise worth about the same.[205] To the degree that there was a slump, observers attributed it to aggressive anti-contraband activity by the Spaniards, or (more convincingly) simply to a glut of the market.[206] Interestingly, still others blamed Spanish wartime reforms, which suspended the trade fleets for South America, substituted them with register ships sailing under individual permit, and opened the route into the Pacific via Cape Horn for the first time since the 1500s.[207] A decade later it was remarked that Jamaica's trade had 'greatly decreased, owing to the kingdoms of Peru, Sta. Fee etc being now supplied with European commodities by ships that go thither from Cadiz round Cape Horn directly'.[208] Tony McFarlane has observed that 'contemporaries believed that the register ships had ended the flagrant breaches of the Spanish monopoly that were common in the first half of the eighteenth century', and certainly seizures of contraband in Cartagena de Indias fell dramatically in the 1750s. This point should not be over-emphasised, however, since any effect on smuggling proved short-lived.[209]

The immediate post-war years also witnessed a major alteration in the operation of Anglo-Spanish trade, which would have far-reaching consequences. From this time, Spaniards began to trade in large numbers in the British colonies, particularly in Jamaica, while British smuggling in Spanish America declined sharply. This shift away from British vessels and towards Spaniards was amply attested by British observers. One writer noted that from 1751, Spaniards 'began to come in their own Vessels, and brought money and mules into almost every port round the island [of Jamaica], carrying off the manufactures of Great Britain'.[210] Another commented in 1764 that 'we have for some time had scarcely any direct importation of bullion in return for the manufactures of this kingdom, but what the Spaniards have risqued in bottoms of their own to Jamaica'.[211] Two legal officers of the Crown observed that Spanish anti-contraband action had 'driven the Spaniards (in the same course of clandestine trade) to bring Bullion to the colonies, and deterred the English from seeking it on the Spanish Coasts'.[212] These views were not unanimous; a different witness claimed that British smugglers still carried the greater part of the trade, and also that 'many vessels pass between both states on short trips, who dextrously manage to belong to each nation, as it suits them best'.[213] By and large, however, the British were convinced that a major change had occurred in the way trade with the Spanish colonies operated.

We have already seen that this was by no means the first time Spaniards traded in the British islands. In the late seventeenth century, business may have been divided almost equally with Spanish merchants, who were encouraged to come to British ports especially to trade for African slaves. But after 1700, the British clearly held the upper hand, either through private smuggling during two major wars in 1702–13 and 1739–48, or through the South Sea Company's Asiento from 1713 to 1739, when the British enjoyed legal access to Spanish ports and naturally predominated.[214] Only around 1750 did trade by Spaniards in the British colonies become widespread, to the degree that from this time onwards, they carried the bulk of it.[215] It is by no means clear what brought about this significant shift in trading relations. Some contemporaries blamed tougher action against contraband in the Spanish colonies, though given the general inefficacy of such action this seems unpersuasive. The change may have arisen out of broader shifts caused by the Spanish commercial reforms, which may also have provoked the

simultaneous depression in Anglo-Spanish trade, although again it is difficult to imagine how such a causal link would operate. The most likely scenario
combines the onset of peace in 1748, and so a decline in British smuggling,
with the termination of the Asiento in 1750, which barred the British from
legal access to Spanish colonial ports.[216] One can speculate that the commercial crisis of c. 1748–52 was a further factor acting to depress trade by the
British and encourage that by Spaniards. But whatever its cause, the shift to
Spanish vessels proved crucial to the development of the trade well into the
nineteenth century. In 1766, as we will see in Chapter 2, the British opened
free ports in the West Indies above all to cater for Spanish merchants, and
these free ports then proved the single most influential factor in the rapid
growth of Anglo-Spanish trade over the following decades.

The peace which began in 1748 lasted a mere eight years, until the outbreak
of the Seven Years War with France in 1756. This period, embracing both
the peace and the war which followed, has been called 'the golden age of
contraband', though this seems at best questionable.[217] After the post-war
depression, trade appears to have remained modest throughout the early
1750s. It is true that a Spanish report of 1753 noted that contraband in Cuba
went on all along the coast 'without hindrance and abundantly, via ports,
anchorages and beaches'. Havana and Santiago de Cuba were smuggling hot
spots, while Puerto Príncipe was devoted almost exclusively to contraband.[218]
In the same vein, the Governor of Jamaica stated of this period that 'the
Spaniards used to come to this island and bring large sums of money ... also
they used to run over from Cuba to the north side of this island in small boats
with mules and cattle for which they carried off dry goods'. But the same official described what seemed a frankly limited trade: 'There were between
fifteen and twenty vessels employed in the Spanish coast trade to Aruba, and
Río de la Hacha who carried off some rum & dry goods and in return
imported about 2,000 mules & horned cattle annually.'[219] A French observer
estimated the value of bullion exports from Jamaica to Britain, derived from
trade with Spaniards, at just 300,000 pesos, or about £67,500, in a work
published in 1758 – the lowest such estimate for the whole of the eighteenth
century.[220] In 1759, in an attempt to prevent Spain from joining the war, the
British ordered their governors in the West Indies to take action to prevent
smuggling; and by 1760, there was a notable decrease in circulating currency
in Jamaica, in part because of interruption to the Spanish commerce.[221]

After remaining neutral throughout the first five years, Spain finally
entered the war as an ally of France and enemy to Britain in January 1762.
Most scholars agree that trade was a major factor in this fateful and (as was
soon proved) disastrous decision. Charles III told the French ambassador
several times in 1760–61 that 'he was determined to end this illicit trade of
the British, which he considered one of the worst dangers to the security of
his empire'.[222] This aim extended not only to the Caribbean, but also to
contraband via Spain, which Charles hoped to thwart by abrogating and
renegotiating the commercial treaties which benefited the British.[223] Spanish

entry to the war briefly dealt a further blow to trade, as Spanish vessels were seized by the Royal Navy and privateers. But there followed a rapid recovery, and a further boom in 1761–63. One Spanish ship's captain now claimed to have witnessed 400 smuggling vessels at work along the coasts of Mexico.[224] A British admiral later claimed that before the passing of the Free Port Act in 1766, Jamaica 'had near an hundred sail of sloops belonging thereto employed in carrying the manufactures of Great Britain to the Spanish Main and to the Spanish and French islands'; returns were 'generally mules and silver'.[225]

By the far the most significant commercial consequences of the war derived from rapid British victories, and especially the seizure of Havana in Cuba and Manila in the Philippines. Havana was one of the great strategic centres of the Spanish empire; its loss was a stunning blow, which is usually regarded as a key turning point and catalyst for the Spanish imperial reforms of the late eighteenth century.[226] During the ten months of the British occupation (August 1762 – June 1763) a great boom in trade took place, reflecting the pent-up commercial energies of a port and hinterland chronically under-supplied by its metropolis. Some 96 British vessels flooded into Havana, contrasting with a handful of Spanish ships in a typical year.[227] A group of some two dozen British and Anglo-American merchants set up in the city, either as factors or partners of houses in Britain and Jamaica. One John Kennion was granted the monopoly slave trade with British-controlled Cuba, and the trade thrived. A minimum of 3,262 Africans were imported, in contrast to a figure of just a few hundred in a typical year. Very large quantities of spirits were also imported, mostly from Jamaica, along with cloth and clothing and North American foodstuffs.[228] And the impact of the occupation was felt further afield, since Spanish refugee voyages to other colonies provided useful cover for smuggling. The British welcomed Spanish vessels into Havana to trade, and in February 1763 a British warship and two merchantmen from Cuba arrived in Veracruz, where they succeeded in landing a contraband cargo consisting of cacao, textiles, and iron.[229]

To conclude this introductory survey of British trade with Spanish America since its origins: what was the value of trade via the Caribbean on the eve of the Peace of Paris of 1763? A Spanish investigation later concluded that losses to contraband in bullion and other products amounted to some 12,000,000 pesos in 1747–61.[230] The British accounted for the majority of this sum, equivalent to about £2,700,000, or a little under £200,000 per year. (Confusingly, elsewhere the same figure is cited, apparently from the same source, but for the period 1757–61).[231] A subsequent British report gave a comparable figure, of 'not less than a million of dollars annually' (c. £225,000), apparently referring to the period prior to 1761.[232] A further estimate for the value of British trade is £175,000 in 1761, considered 'a very poor year'.[233] A much-cited Spanish estimate for the same year, of 6,000,000 pesos, or c. £1,350,000, is certainly an exaggeration unless it also includes trade which went via ports in Spain.[234] Very tentatively, then, we might conclude that the British sold merchandise in Spanish America to the value of around £200,000 annually between the War of the Austrian Succession and the Peace of Paris. Exports of bullion from Jamaica to Britain averaged about £140,000 per year in 1748–65, which might support the notion of a trade worth c. £200,000 once money which stayed in the island or was exported elsewhere is taken into account.[235] These figures do not include trade undertaken with Cuba during the British occupation, which was worth no less than £250,000 sterling in its major year of 1763.[236] Many of these exports were shipped to Cuba direct from Britain, once news of the conquest became widespread there.

Notes

1   From a quotation by Las Casas, in Deagan and Cruxent, *Columbus's Outpost among the Tainos*, p. 20.
2   Wright, 'Rescates: With Special Reference to Cuba, 1599–1610', p. 335.
3   Andrews, 'Beyond the Equinoctial', p. 5.
4   Fisher, *Economic Aspects of Spanish Imperialism*, p. 77.
5   Andrews, 'Beyond the Equinoctial', *passim*.
6   Connell-Smith, 'Trading to the New World', *passim*.
7   Connell-Smith, 'Trading to the New World', pp. 63–5.
8   Connell-Smith, 'Trading to the New World', pp. 65–6.
9   Andrews, *The Spanish Caribbean*.
10 See e.g. Fisher, *Economic Aspects of Spanish Imperialism*, pp. 46–56.
11 Further Consulados were established later, notably in Veracruz and Havana. Stein and Stein, *Silver, Trade, and War* and *Apogee of Empire*, trace the development and context of commercial policy in great detail.
12 García Fuentes, *Comercio español con América*; Walker, *Spanish Politics and Imperial Trade*.
13 Lynch, *The Hispanic World*, pp. 233, 248, suggests that serious penetration dated from the 1620s; see also García Fuentes, *Comercio español con América*, p. 44.
14 Christelow, 'Great Britain and the Trades', p. 3, for which Anon., 'Considerations on the Laws ... so far as they relate to the bullion trade' [c. 1765], B.L., Add. Mss. 35,911, ff. 109–15v, may be the source.
15 On naturalisation, see Lynch, *The Hispanic World*, pp. 245–6; Stein and Stein, *Silver, Trade, and War*, p. 73. Very few Englishmen were naturalised during the 1600s and 1700s.
16 Stein and Stein, *Silver, Trade, and War*, p. 82.
17 On the methodology of smuggling in Spanish Atlantic trade, see esp. Stein and Stein, *Silver, Trade, and War*, pp. 77–82; same authors, *Apogee of Empire*, pp. 198–99; García-Baquero, *Cádiz y el Atlántico*, 1:216–23.
18 The Treaty of 1667 is reproduced in full in Postlethwayt, *Universal Dictionary of Trade*, 2:754–8. On English treaty rights in Spanish trade, see Stein and Stein, *Silver, Trade, and War*, pp. 60–3, 68–71.
19 Christelow, 'Great Britain and the Trades', pp. 5–7. The principal studies of Anglo-Spanish trade, by Nadal Farreras and García Fernández, relate to the eighteenth century.
20 Stein and Stein, *Silver, Trade, and War*, pp. 61–2.
21 Lynch, *The Hispanic World in Crisis and Change*, p. 248.

22 Stein and Stein, *Silver, Trade, and War*, p. 62.

23 Antonio García-Baquero, a leading authority on Spanish Atlantic trade, advised me that the best sources for the subject are those held in Cadiz notarial archives (personal communication, Nov. 2000). This is born out by Connell-Smith, whose article draws on notarial records; however, profitable use of these sources at monographic level lies beyond the scope of a single scholar in the course of a typical research project.

24 García Fuentes, *Comercio español con América*, p. 45; see also Gómez Molleda, 'El contrabando inglés en America', p. 337, who suggests a value for English trade of £6–7,000,000, equivalent to 12.3 per cent of the total. The sterling figure certainly exaggerates the real value many times over.

25 Cited in Stein and Stein, *Silver, Trade, and War*, p. 286 n. 92.

26 McLachlan, *Trade and Peace*, p. 37; Horsfall, 'British Relations', pp. 19–20.

27 Horsfall, 'British Relations with the Spanish Colonies', p. 71; Fisher, *Economic Aspects of Spanish Imperialism*, pp. 74–5.

28 Stein and Stein, *Silver, Trade, and War*, pp. 81, 92.

29 Stein and Stein, *Silver, Trade, and* War, pp. 77–8; McLachlan, *Trade and Peace*, pp. 12–13; for a good primary survey see Savary de Bruslons, *Dictionnaire universel du commerce*, 1:931.

30 McLachlan, *Trade and Peace*, p. 14 (referring to the period 1748–53); Zahedieh, 'Merchants of Port Royal', pp. 573, 587–8; Stein and Stein, *Silver, Trade, and War*, pp. 83–4.

31 Stein and Stein, *Silver, Trade, and War*, pp. 294–5 n. 69; Zahedieh, 'Merchants of Port Royal', pp. 572, 584; Savary de Bruslons, *Dictionnaire universel du commerce*, 1:931.

32 Stein and Stein, *Silver, Trade, and War*, pp. 131–2.

33 Langnas, 'Great Britain's Relations with Spanish America', chap. 1, pp. 4–6.

34 See e.g. McLachlan, *Trade and Peace*, p. 15.

35 Stein and Stein, *Silver, Trade, and War*, p. 140. In fact, there is little evidence that the merchants behind the *Asiento* were the same as those engaged in smuggling via the Caribbean; indeed, these two groups were often in hostile competition with each other (see pp. 23–4 below).

36 Defoe advanced these arguments at least as early as 1698, and until at least as late as 1728; *Interests of the Several Princes and States*, pp. 25–7, and *Plan of the English Commerce*, pp. 325–6. The key sequence appears in *Mercator*, nos. 169–74 (19 June–3 July 1714). I became aware of these references through the article by Novak on 'Colonel Jack's "Thieving Roguing" Trade to Mexico'.

37 On the Treaty of 1715, see Stein and Stein, *Silver, Trade, and War*, p. 140; Horsfall, 'British Relations', p. 73.

38 Pantaleão, *Penetração comercial*, pp. 83–6.

39 McLachlan, *Trade and Peace with Old Spain*, pp. 24–5.

40 Christelow, 'Great Britain and the Trades', pp. 3–4; also Savary, *Dictionnaire universel*, 1:935–6.

41 This paragraph draws on Horsfall, 'British Relations', esp. pp. 47, 55–6, 88–92, 117–19, 134–9, 142–4, 150, 156, 179–84, 234–40.

42 Cited in Pantaleão, *Penetração comercial*, p. 79.

43 Horsfall, 'British Relations', p. 183.

44 Horsfall, 'British Relations with the Spanish Colonies', esp. pp. 93–4, 101–19; also Christelow, 'Great Britain and the Trades', p. 8.

45 Cited in Stein and Stein, *Apogee of Empire*, p. 315.

46 Stein and Stein, *Apogee of Empire*, pp. 232–3.

47 Stein and Stein, *Silver, Trade, and War*, p. 75; Savary de Bruslons, *Dictionnaire*

universel, 1:927-30.

48 Stein and Stein, *Silver, Trade, and War*, p. 66; also Horsfall, 'British Relations', pp. 126–8.

49 Stein and Stein, *Silver, Trade, and War*, pp. 143, 306–7, 312, 317–18.

50 Stein and Stein, *Apogee of Empire*, p. 305.

51 Horsfall, 'British Relations', pp. 235–6; [Horace Walpole], 'Points, to be Consider'd with regard to the Depredations of Spain', Jan. 1738, B.L., Add. Mss. 9,131, ff. 199-250v, see ff. 235–7.

52 Pantaleão, *Penetração comercial*, pp. 85–7.

53 Pantaleão, *Penetração comercial*, pp. 103–4, 200–4.

54 Christelow, 'Great Britain and the Trades', p. 8.

55 Cited in Muller, 'British Business and Spanish America', p. 13.

56 Christelow, 'Great Britain and the Trades', pp. 18–20.

57 See esp. pp. 108–10.

58 McLachlan, *Trade and Peace*, p. 12; Stein and Stein, *Silver, Trade, and War*, pp. 175–6; Jones, 'Historical Study', p. 18.

59 Stein and Stein, *Apogee of Empire*, pp. 126, 377 n. 39.

60 García-Baquero, *Cádiz y el Atlántico*, 1:496–7.

61 García-Baquero, *Cádiz y el Atlántico*, 1:492–6.

62 Data cited in McLachlan, *Trade and Peace*, p. 177 n. 78.

63 J. Campbell, *A Concise History of Spanish America* (1741), cited in McLachlan, *Trade and Peace*, p. 12.

64 Christelow, 'Great Britain and the Trades', pp. 3–4; Temperley, 'Relations of England with Spanish America', p. 235.

65 Christelow, 'Great Britain and the Trades', pp. 4–5.

66 Christelow, 'Great Britain and the Trades', p. 4.

67 'The Memorial of Sr Harry Frankland Bart …', Lisbon, 6 , pp. 1760, N.A., C.O. 388 / 53, n.f.

68 Villalobos, *Comercio y contrabando*, chap. 2 ('Sacramento, bastión del contrabando').

69 175,713 pesos; Pantaleão, *Penetração comercial*, pp. 158–60, also 141.

70 Nelson, 'Contraband Trade', pp. 60–1.

71 Barba, 'Sobre el contrabando de la Colonia del Sacramento', p. 68.

72 'The Memorial of Sr Harry Frankland Bart …', Lisbon, 6 June 1760, N.A., C.O. 388 / 53, n.f.

73 The British Minister Hay, quoted in Christelow, 'Great Britain and the Trades', p. 5.

74 Miller, *Britain and Latin America*, p. 29.

75 Beckles, 'The 'Hub of Empire'', p. 221.

76 Fortune, *Merchants and Jews*, pp. 108–9.

77 Fortune, *Merchants and Jews*, pp. 105–6; Thornton, 'Spanish Slave-Ships', pp. 378–9.

78 On the *Asiento* of Domingo Grillo and Ambrosio Lamolini (or Lomelin), see Stein and Stein, *Silver, Trade, and War*, p. 108; Thornton, 'Spanish Slave-Ships', p. 379; Fortune, *Merchants and Jews*, p. 110.

79 Fortune, *Merchants and Jews*, p. 108.

80 Fortune, *Merchants and Jews*, pp. 111–13.

81 Stein and Stein, *Silver, Trade, and War*, p. 66, also pp. 106–7.

82 Zahedieh, 'Merchants of Port Royal', pp. 574, 592–3, who notes that 'transport costs were at least 20 per cent lower from Jamaica to Cartagena [in New Granada] than from Curaçao'; also Armytage, *Free Port System*, p. 16.

83 'Queries relative to the state of … Jamaica with answers thereto in 1774', N.A., C. O. 137 / 70, ff. 88-98v.

84 Defoe, *Plan of the English Commerce*, pp. 310–11; [Thomas Irving?], 'Observations

on the trade ... between the British West Indies and the Spanish colonies ...', [1785-86], B.L., Add. Mss. 38,345, ff. 208-13v.

85 Thornton, 'Spanish Slave-Ships', pp. 377–78; Zahedieh, 'Merchants of Port Royal', p. 575.

86 Zahedieh, 'Merchants of Port Royal', p. 589.

87 For the Treaty of 1667, see p. 5 above; also Jones, 'Historical Study', pp. 6–7.

88 Reproduced in Postlethwayt, *Universal Dictionary of Trade*, 2:761–62; see also Zahedieh, 'Merchants of Port Royal', p. 574; Brown, 'Anglo-Spanish Relations in America', pp. 375–6; Stein and Stein, *Silver, Trade, and War*, pp. 63–4 and n. 34, p.283.

89 Zahedieh, 'Merchants of Port Royal', pp. 574–5; Fortune, *Merchants and Jews*, p. 114.

90 Fisher, *Economic Aspects of Spanish Imperialism*, pp. 82–83; Pares, *War and Trade in the West Indies*, pp. 6–7.

91 'War with everyone but peace with England'; Stein and Stein, *Silver, Trade, and War*, p. 111.

92 See e.g. the comments of [Horace Walpole], 'Points, to be Consider'd with regard to the Depredations of Spain', Jan. 1738, B.L., Add. Mss. 9,131, ff. 199–250v, esp. ff. 232v–3; also [Hall], *Importance of the British Plantations*, p. 41.

93 See esp. Zahedieh, 'Merchants of Port Royal', which may be consulted for all information in the following paragraphs not cited from other sources. This article, with the same author's 'Trade, Plunder and Economic Development in Early English Jamaica', in my view constitutes the most significant work published in English on British trade with the Spanish colonies since the mid-1950s.

94 Fortune, *Merchants and Jews*, pp. 113–14.

95 Zahedieh, 'Merchants of Port Royal', pp. 579–80; Fortune, *Merchants and Jews*, pp. 41, 97–8 (for Barbados).

96 Zahedieh, 'Merchants of Port Royal', pp. 576–8.

97 Stein and Stein, *Silver, Trade, and War*, p. 83.

98 Pitman, *Development of the British West Indies*, pp. 195–6.

99 Zahedieh, 'Merchants of Port Royal', pp. 585–6; Fortune, *Merchants and Jews*, pp. 114–15.

100 Davies, *Royal African Company*, is the standard work.

101 On the *Asiento* and its successive holders, see Scelle, *La traite negrière aux Indes de Castille*.

102 Zahedieh, 'Merchants of Port Royal', p. 590; Thornton, 'Spanish Slave-Ships', pp. 381–2.

103 On perhaps the best known of these agents, who arrived in 1684 and became a leading Port Royal citizen, see Osborne, 'James Castillo'.

104 Thornton, 'Spanish Slave-Ships', p. 375; Zahedieh, 'Merchants of Port Royal', pp. 590–1.

105 Thornton, 'Spanish Slave-Ships', pp. 382–4.

106 Nettels, 'England and the Spanish American Trade', pp.3–5 n. 4.

107 Zahedieh, 'Merchants of Port Royal', p. 591; also Nettels, 'England and the Spanish American Trade', p. 4.

108 This key source for this dispute is Nettels, 'England and the Spanish American Trade', pp. 4–17.

109 Walker, *Spanish Politics and Imperial Trade*, appendix 1, table 2.

110 Jones, 'Historical Study', p. 30.

111 See esp. Uring, *History of the Voyages*, pp. 164–6, describing a smuggling expedition in 1711; this is closely mirrored by Postlethwayt, *Universal Dictionary*, 1:77; Defoe,

Mercator, no. 169 (19–22 June 1714), follows an earlier ms. cited by Zahedieh, 'Merchants of Port Royal', p. 582 n. 74. See also Armytage, *Free Port System*, pp. 18–19.

112 [Robert Allen,] 'An Essay on the Nature and Methods of Carrying on a Trade to the South Seas', [1712], B.L., Add. Mss. 28,140, ff. 20–8, f. 24v.

113 Palmer, *Human Cargoes*, pp. 97–8; see also Nettels, 'England and the Spanish American Trade', p. 29.

114 Atkins, *Voyage to ... the West Indies*, pp. 247; Nettels, 'England and the Spanish American Trade', pp. 19–20; Pitman, *Development of the British West Indies*, pp. 148–89; Jones, 'Historical Study', p. 31.

115 Nettels, 'England and the Spanish American Trade', pp. 26–7; Fortune, *Merchants and Jews*, pp. 115–16.

116 6 Anne I cap. 37; discussed in Anon., 'Considerations on the Laws ... so far as they relate to the bullion trade', n.p., n.d., B.L., Add. Mss. 35,911, ff. 109–15v.

117 McLachlan, *Trade and Peace*, p. 85.

118 For French contraband in the Pacific, see Dahlgren, *Les relations commerciales*; Malamud Rikles, *Cádiz y Saint Malo* (which is less satisfactory); Villalobos, *Comercio y contrabando*, chap. 3; for the figure of 99,000,000 pesos, Stein and Stein, *Silver, Trade, and War*, p. 113.

119 See esp. [Allen,] 'An Essay on the Nature', B.L., Add. Mss. 28,140, ff. 20–8, ff. 25–v; Pitman, *Development of the British West Indies*, pp. 149–50.

120 Defoe, *Interests of the Several Princes and States of Europe*, pp. 25–7; the most sensitive modern attempt is Zahedieh, 'Merchants of Port Royal', pp. 587–8.

121 Jones, 'Historical Study', p. 12.

122 Zahedieh, 'Merchants of Port Royal', p. 584; Jones, 'Historical Study', p. 8. [Hall], *Importance of the British Plantations*, p. 41, gives the unusually high figure of '250 to 300 Thousand Pounds a Year' in c. 1670–1702.

123 Gov. Beeston to Board of Trade, 14 Mar. 1700, quoted in Pitman, *Development of the British West Indies*, p. 148 (£150,000); 'Estimate of the Exports from Jamaica to England', 20 Jan. 1704, in Headlam, *Calendar of State Papers ... 1704–1705*, 19, no. 36 (£200,000); Atkins, *Voyage to ... the West Indies*, p. 247 (same). A figure of £1,500,000, first given by Edwards, *History*, 1:236–7, and repeated among others by Renny, *History*, pp. 119–21, and Pitman, *Development of the British West Indies*, pp. 137–8, is certainly an error (perhaps arising from a mis-transcription?).

124 See esp. Nettels, 'England', pp. 28–32; Jones, 'Historical Study', pp. 31–2; also Pantaleão, *Penetração*, pp. 163–9.

125 Zahedieh, 'Trade, Plunder, and Economic Development', esp. pp. 215–20; also Fortune, *Merchants and Jews*, p. 115.

126 Fortune, *Merchants and Jews*, pp. 108–9.

127 See Stein and Stein, *Silver, Trade, and War*, pp. 113–14.

128 Defoe, *Mercator*, nos. 171–3, 24 June–1 July 1714; see also the comments in Reynal, *Philosophical and Political History*, 3:488; Saavedra, *Journal*, pp. 67–8.

129 About 70 per cent of all British exports of bullion in 1665–75 went to the East Indies; Fortune, *Merchants*, p. 28.

130 Zahedieh, 'Merchants of Port Royal', pp. 583–4; Nettels, 'England and the Spanish-American Trade', pp. 7–8.

131 For a pugnacious account of the role of American precious metals in world history, see Frank, *ReOrient*, esp. part 3.

132 On the negotiations regarding commercial matters which preceded the Treaty of Utrecht, see Horsfall, 'British Relations', pp. 28–45.

133 Palmer, *Human Cargoes*, p. 10.

134 On the important distinction between *piezas de Indias* and 'slaves', see Palmer, *Human Cargoes*, pp. 98–100.

135 For general descriptions of the British Asiento, see Stein and Stein, *Silver, Trade, and War*, pp. 137–8; Aiton, 'The Asiento Treaty', pp. 167–8; Palmer, *Human Cargoes*, p. 9.

136 Palmer, *Human Cargoes*, pp. 59–60; but see also Nelson, 'Contraband Trade', p. 60.

137 On the territorial organisation of the trade, see Palmer, *Human Cargoes*, p. 60; Gómez Molleda, 'El contrabando inglés en América', pp. 345–6; Nelson, 'Contraband Trade', p. 57.

138 Penson, 'The West Indies and the Spanish-American Trade', pp. 336–8.

139 Palmer, *Human Cargoes*, table 9, p. 99.

140 Nelson, 'Contraband Trade', p. 57; Palmer, *Human Cargoes*, pp. 61–2.

141 For this licensed trade, which was banned by Spain in 1733, see Palmer, *Human Cargoes*, pp. 73–9.

142 Pares, *War and Trade in the West Indies*, p. 12.

143 On the South Sea Company's trade at Buenos Aires, see esp. Villalobos, *Comercio y contrabando*, chap. 4, and Palmer, *Human Cargoes*, pp. 70–2.

144 Palmer, *Human Cargoes*, pp. 110–11, table 20; also Sorsby, 'British Trade with Spanish America', pp. 426–7.

145 Palmer, *Human Cargoes*, p. 159.

146 Palmer, *Human Cargoes*, chap. 9 (where these figures are described as 'provisional and ... advanced with some trepidation').

147 Walker, *Spanish Politics and Imperial Trade*, pp. 71–2; Stein and Stein, *Silver, Trade, and War*, pp. 138–9.

148 For 'Bubb's Treaty' of 26 May 1716, see esp. Walker, *Spanish Politics and Imperial Trade*, pp. 85–6.

149 Nelson, 'Contraband Trade', pp. 62–3.

150 See also Pearce, 'Early Bourbon Government in the Viceroyalty of Peru, 1700–1759', pp. 76–7.

151 For a general discussion, see Palmer, *Human Cargoes*, chap. 8 ('Stresses and Strains, 1714–39'). Sorsby, 'British Trade with Spanish America', *passim*, provides the most detailed survey.

152 Walker, *Spanish Politics and Imperial Trade*, pp. 243–4, appendix IV. The single most valuable item was 'Colchester Bays', of which the *Royal George* carried over £33,000.

153 Sorsby, 'British Trade with Spanish America', pp. 424–5.

154 For the three fairs mentioned here, see Walker, *Spanish Politics and Imperial Trade*, pp. 143–7, 131, 135–6.

155 Pares, *War and Trade in the West Indies*, p. 11.

156 For general discussions, see the articles by Brown ('The South Sea Company and Contraband Trade' and 'Contraband Trade'); Nelson, 'Contraband Trade'; and Pantaleão, *Penetração comercial*, pp. 106–16.

157 Nelson, 'Contraband Trade', p. 59.

158 Palmer, *Human Cargoes*, p. 136.

159 Fortune, *Merchants and Jews*, p. 123.

160 Nelson, 'Contraband Trade', pp. 64–5.

161 Brown, 'The South Sea Company and Contraband Trade', pp. 665–6, which may be compared with Baeza Martín, 'La acusación contra el virrey Casafuerte', p. 19.

162 Nelson, 'Contraband Trade', p. 65 n. 68.

163 Brown, 'The South Sea Company and Contraband Trade', pp. 671–2.

164 These papers were discovered by Vera Lee Brown, and are discussed in 'The South Sea Company and Contraband Trade'; they are also analysed in Gómez Molleda, 'El

contrabando inglés en América'.

165 Horsfall, 'British Relations', pp. 61–2.

166 Quoted in McLachlan, *Trade and Peace with Old Spain*, p. 62.

167 On this controversy, see Pitman, *Development of the British West Indies*, pp. 79–84; Palmer, *Human Cargoes*, pp. 65–8; Pantaleão, *Penetração comercial*, pp. 169–74; and Horsfall, 'British Relations', esp. pp. 53–4, 61–2, 77, 131, 172–7, 227–8.

168 Horsfall, 'British Relations', provides the most detailed study of official British attitudes towards trade with Spanish America during the early eighteenth century.

169 Brown, 'Contraband Trade', pp. 181–3; see also Horsfall, 'British Relations', pp. 95–7.

170 Pearce, 'Early Bourbon Government in the Viceroyalty of Peru', pp. 74–7.

171 Horsfall, 'British Relations', pp. 144–9, 157–8; Walker, *Spanish Politics and Imperial Trade*, p. 155.

172 Walker, *Spanish Politics and Imperial Trade*, p. 146.

173 Nelson, 'Contraband Trade', p. 60; see also Brown, 'The South Sea Company and Contraband Trade', pp. 672–3; Horsfall, 'British Relations', p. 130; Palmer, *Human Cargoes*, pp. 84–5.

174 Horsfall, 'British Relations', pp. 202–3.

175 See the classic article by Temperley, 'The Causes of the War of Jenkins' Ear'; also Hildner, 'The Rôle of the South Sea Company in the Diplomacy leading to the War of Jenkins' Ear'.

176 Aiton, 'The Asiento Treaty', p. 177; for this final period (1739–50), see Batcheler, 'The South Sea Company and the Assiento', chap. 11.

177 Quoted in Pantaleão, *Penetraçao comercial*, pp. 200–4, who actually thinks this figure may be conservative.

178 Nelson, 'Contraband Trade', pp. 63–4.

179 Fortune, *Merchants and Jews*, p. 148; Brown, 'Contraband Trade', pp. 183–4; also Burnard, '"Prodigious Riches"', pp. 511–12. McLachlan, *Trade and Peace*, p. 177 n. 78, cites figures from Whitworth, *State of the Trade of Great Britain*, which appear to show exports from Britain (by the South Sea Company?) worth from £200,000 to £240,000 in 1722–32.

180 Sorsby, 'British Trade with Spanish America'; Pantaleão, *Penetração comercial*, pp. 92–3, had already reached a similar conclusion.

181 Penson, 'The West Indies and the Spanish-American Trade', pp. 344–5.

182 Stein and Stein, *Apogee of Empire*, pp. 59–60, 295–6.

183 Brown, 'Contraband Trade', p. 184; Jones, 'Historical Study', p. 42.

184 Pares, *War and Trade in the West Indies*, pp. 115–18; Metcalf, *Royal Government*, pp. 75–6.

185 Pantaleão, *Penetração comercial*, pp. 150–3.

186 See J. Robarts, 'Observations upon the Trade in General, and upon the Trade with the Spanish West Indies in particular', n.p., 1766 or 1767, S.R.O., D. (W.) 1778, II, no. 253, ff. 8–v.

187 [James Kerr?], 'Remarks on the Spanish Trade at Jamaica from the breaking out of the War with Spain in 1739 ...', n.p., 1765, S.R.O., D. (W.) 1778, II, no. 2112; further copy in S.A., W.W.M., R. 35 / 1.

188 Pares, *War and Trade in the West Indies*, pp. 120–1.

189 McFarlane, *Colombia before Independence*, pp. 116–17. On smuggling in New Granada to 1763, see Grahn, 'An Irresoluble Dilemma' and *The Political Economy of Smuggling*.

190 Stein and Stein, *Silver, Trade, and War*, p. 198. For (generally rather dubious) evidence for the value of the trade during the war, see Stein and Stein, *Silver, Trade, and War*, p. 196; Romano, *Moneda, seudomonedas y circulación*, p. 67; and Ramos,

Contrabando inglés, p. 13, who cites the frankly absurd figure of £25,625,000 sterling in 1739!

191 The following is based above all on Pantaleão, *Penetração comercial*, and Ramos, *Contrabando inglés*. Of these two studies, Pantaleão is by far the better organised, with the greater explanatory power, though it is based entirely on secondary sources. Ramos draws on a rich primary source base, from a wide range of archives, particularly in Spain and Britain, but suffers from poor structure and a relatively weak analysis. For a detailed Spanish primary account covering this period, see Juan and Ulloa, *Noticias secretas*, pp. 197–229.

192 On the products sold by the British, see Pantaleão, *Penetração comercial*, pp. 181–93; Ramos, *Contrabando inglés*, chap. 8.

193 Gardner, *History of Jamaica*, p. 153; Romano, *Moneda, seudomonedas y circulación*, pp. 65–7.

194 Ramos, *Contrabando inglés*, pp. 35–45, 61–5, 84–8, 91–2; character sketch, pp. 122–35.

195 Fortune, *Merchants and Jews*, esp. pp. 131–7, 148–50.

196 For a typology of smuggling vessels, see Ramos, *Contrabando inglés*, pp. 77–9.

197 Pantaleão, *Penetração comercial*, p. 204.

198 Pantaleão, *Penetração comercial*, pp. 206–8; Walker, *Spanish Politics and Imperial Trade*, pp. 146–7.

199 See esp. *Penetração comercial*, pp. 144–50; Dawson, 'William Pitt's Settlement', *passim*.

200 Quoted in Ramos, *Contrabando inglés*, p. 367. This survey of the spheres of commercial influence of the British colonies draws on Ramos, *Contrabando inglés*, pp. 367–73.

201 Pantaleão, *Penetração comercial*, pp. 156–7.

202 J. Robarts, 'Observations upon the Trade in General, and upon the Trade with the Spanish West Indies in particular', n.p., 1766 or 1767, S.R.O., D. (W.) 1778, II, no. 253, ff. 8–v.

203 Governor Trelawny to Board of Trade, Jamaica, 15 Aug. 1752, in Armytage, *Free Port System*, p. 22.

204 [James Kerr?], 'Remarks on the Spanish Trade at Jamaica ...', n.p., 1765, S.R.O., D. (W.) 1778, II, no. 2112; further copy in S.A., W.W.M., R. 35 / 1.

205 Pitman, *Development of the British West Indies*, pp. 152–4.

206 Joseph Salvador to unknown correspondent, London, 28 Jan. 1766, B.L., Add. Mss. 38,339, ff. 225–6.

207 On these reforms see e.g. Lynch, *Bourbon Spain*, pp. 153–6; Fisher, *Commercial Relations*, p. 12; Villalobos, *Comercio y contrabando*, pp. 41–4.

208 Anon., 'Observations on the Commerce of our Colonies with those of Spain ...', n.d. [c. 1764], B.L., Add. Mss. 35,911, ff. 116–27; further copy in S.R.O., D (W) 1778, II, 136a; see also Ward, 'The British West Indies', p. 423; Jones, 'Historical Study', pp. 43–6.

209 McFarlane, *Colombia before Independence*, pp. 117–18.

210 'Mr Kerr's Reasons for Opening the Port of Lucea, under Restrictions, in preference to Montego Bay, Answered, with Observations thereon', n.p., n.d., S.A., W.W.M., R. 35 / 24.

211 Anon., 'Observations on the Commerce ...', n.d. [c. 1764], B.L., Add. Mss. 35,911, ff. 116–27.

212 Attorney & Sollicitor General to Board of Treasury, 11 Nov. 1765, B.L., Add. Mss. 35,911, ff. 88–9v.

213 Untitled interrogatory, n.p., marked 1763 but certainly Jan. 1766, B.L., Add. Mss. 38,373, ff. 130–1v.

214 Ramos, *Contrabando inglés*, pp. 159–60; Pantaleão, *Penetração comercial*, pp. 129–35; Nelson, 'Contraband Trade', p. 57.

215 Armytage, *Free Port System*, pp. 22–3; Ramos, *Contrabando inglés*, p. 32; also Pantaleão, *Penetração comercial*, p. 175; Williams, 'Mercados británicos', p. 96.

216 Ramos, *Contrabando inglés*, pp. 173–5.

217 Langnas, 'Great Britain's Relations with Spanish America', chap. 1, p. 7; Rydjord, *Foreign Interest*, p. 52.

218 Quoted in Pantaleão, *Penetração comercial*, pp. 156–7.

219 'Report of the State of the Island of Jamaica Anno 1763 ...', N.A., C.O. 137 / 33, ff. 56–65v; cited at length in Pitman, *Development of the British West Indies*, pp. 152–4.

220 Georges Butel-Dumont, *Histoire et Commerce des Antilles Angloises* (Paris: 1758), p. 17, cited in Fortune, *Merchants and Jews*, p. 119; this seems likely to be the source of a similar figure given by Reynal, *Philosophical and Political History*, 3:491.

221 Temperley, 'Peace of Paris', pp. 487–8; Pitman, *Development of the British West Indies*, pp. 152–4.

222 Christelow, 'Contraband Trade', p. 313 (citing French archival sources).

223 Christelow, 'Great Britain and the Trades', pp. 9–10; on the circumstances of Spanish entry into the Seven Years War, see also Stein and Stein, *Apogee of Empire*, pp. 11–12; Domínguez Ortiz, *Sociedad y Estado*, pp. 300–1.

224 Rydjord, *Foreign Interest in the Independence of New Spain*, p. 52.

225 Admiral Sir George Rodney to Philip Stephens, *Portland*, Port Royal Harbour, 12 Mar. 1774, N.A., ADM. 1 / 239, n.f.; also Armytage, *Free Port System*, pp. 23–4.

226 Brading, 'Bourbon Spain and its American Empire', pp. 122–3.

227 Christelow, 'Contraband Trade', p. 314 n.11.

228 See esp. Böttcher, 'Trade, War and Empire', pp. 175–9; Stein and Stein, *Apogee of Empire*, pp. 51–5, 67–8.

229 Mateu y Llopis, 'Navíos ingleses en el puerto de Veracruz en 1763'.

230 Kuethe, 'El fin del monopolio', pp. 63–4.

231 Stein and Stein, *Apogee of Empire*, p. 153.

232 [Thomas Irving?] 'Observations on the trade carried on between the British West Indies and the Spanish colonies in America ...', [1785 or 1786?] B.L., Add. Mss. 38,345, ff. 208–13v.

233 Fortune, *Merchants and Jews*, p. 148.

234 Christelow, 'Contraband Trade', p. 313; Ramos, *Contrabando inglés*, 175; Stein and Stein, *Silver, Trade, and War*, p. 309 n. 79; and see chap. 7, p. 241.

235 'An Account of Bullion imported from Jamaica and the other West India islands from 1748 to 1765', S.A., W.W.M., R. 34 / 5c.

236 Böttcher, 'Trade, War and Empire', p. 162, citing data from Whitworth, *State of the Trade*.

CHAPTER TWO

The 'Spanish Trade', 1763–83:
Geographical Expansion and the Free Ports

The treaty which ended the Seven Years War, signed in Paris in February 1763, substantially expanded British imperial holdings in the Americas. In the Caribbean, it gave Britain the French islands of Dominica, Grenada and St Vincent, as well as full rights to Tobago, hitherto neutral and unoccupied. From Spain Britain gained East and West Florida, as well as formal treaty rights to cut dyewoods on the coast of Honduras. The wartime captures of Martinique, Marie-Galante, St Lucia and Guadeloupe were returned to France, the latter cession a victory for West Indian planter interests threatened by Guadeloupe's rich plantation economy.[1] Havana was returned to Spain in exchange for the Floridas, a contentious decision but one which probably simply acknowledged the practical obstacles to retaining such a key Spanish port. In a parallel cession, Spain acquired Louisiana from France in compensation for its losses elsewhere.[2] This 'Peace of Paris' had its critics; the always acute Abbé Reynal thought that by its terms, presumably specifically by the return of Havana, Britain lost a unique opportunity for outright dominion of Mexico.[3] Most observers, however, immediately recognised that the prospects for British commercial intercourse with Spanish America had been immeasurably enhanced. Settlers, officials and speculators in the 'Ceded Islands' looked to contraband trade for future prosperity, and proposals were drawn up for free ports in Dominica, Grenada, the Grenadines and Tobago to facilitate the trade.[4] The attitude of Governor Johnstone of West Florida was typical: 'Nature seems to have intended to place the seat of commerce on this bay; within a few days sail of the richest cities in the world (the Havannah, Merida, Campeachy, La Vera Cruz and Mexico) Pensacola bids fair for a considerable share in their commerce.'[5] Spanish officials, too, quickly recognised that the new territorial disposition brought fresh threats; the Intendant of Havana wrote that 'since the English now navigate the Gulf of Mexico to go to their ports in Florida … it is almost impossible to verify the illicit trade of these two Nations'.[6] There seemed, in short, every reason to believe that conditions were ripe for British trade with the Spanish colonies to enter a new, expansive phase.

In the event, the years following the Peace were indeed crucial to the subsequent development of British trade with Spanish America, although not in ways many would have anticipated. First of all, the Spanish trade entered a slump following the war which lasted for at least a number of years, and in the case of Jamaica perhaps even for a decade or longer. Partly in response to this crisis, but also due to a much broader range of economic and political circumstances not foreseeable in 1763, in 1766 free ports were opened in Jamaica and Dominica, in an unprecedented break with earlier British commercial policy overseas. The ports in Jamaica were designed to counter the post-war decline in the Spanish trade, but they also represented a pragmatic British response to the dominance of Spanish vessels of the trade in recent years. After rather uncertain beginnings, the free ports proved richly successful in fomenting, protecting, and expanding British intercourse with the Spaniards. The system was extended in later decades until it covered most of the British West Indies, and British trade with Spanish America centred on it until the beginning of the nineteenth century.[7] For these reasons, the first part of this chapter reviews the origins of the free port system in some depth. It then sketches the broader development of British trade with the Spanish colonies in the period through to the end of the American Revolutionary War.

The Origins of the Free Port System, 1763–66

The essential context to the events described in the following pages was a severe crisis affecting British commerce during these years. The crisis lay in Britain's Atlantic trade, especially (since it made up by far the most important branch) British trade with the Thirteen Colonies in North America. Its causes were to be found in innovations in British colonial policy which were born out of the stresses of the late war and which culminated little more than a decade later in the rupture of the American Revolution. These events cannot be traced here in any detail, but two principal points of controversy must be mentioned very briefly. First, the Sugar Act of 1764 imposed heavy duties on foreign sugars and molasses imported into North America, and was accompanied by vigorous anti-smuggling measures designed to prevent contraband with the French colonies in the Caribbean.[8] The Act was a product of British anger at American trade with the French islands during the war, but it was also clearly a revenue measure. Both for this reason and because it threatened the important French trade, it was deeply unpopular in the colonies, and aggravated the post-war depression there. Second, the Stamp Act of 1765 required that all public documents (from legal transactions to newspapers) be printed on special stamped paper sold by government agents. The Stamp Act was a further revenue measure, designed to make the colonies shoulder more of the burden of their future defence. It was still more unpopular than the Sugar Act, and its consequences were far more serious, provoking a wave of disturbances in Boston, New York, Philadelphia and elsewhere.[9] Merchants played a leading part in the protests, and many simply refused to order further goods from Britain until the Act was repealed. The effect of these protests was immediately felt in Britain, where the post-war years were a period of notable economic stress and crisis in mercantile and manufacturing towns. It was this crisis, at base, which fuelled the intense discussion of commercial affairs and commercial reforms which characterised these same years.

Secondary to the north Atlantic crisis, but closely linked to it and still of real importance, was a slump in the Spanish trade in the Caribbean. As we shall see, the reasons for this decline are a matter of debate, but one factor arose out of an Act of Parliament passed early in 1763 under the auspices of Prime Minister George Grenville. Grenville was responsible for a vigorous campaign against contraband trade both at home and overseas,[10] and the Act of 1763, known as the Hovering Act, extended earlier British anti-contraband legislation to the colonies in America.[11] Its most striking provision vested naval captains with powers from the Customs for seizing and condemning vessels found contravening the Navigation Acts. On 9 July 1763 Secretary of State the Earl of Egremont despatched copies of the Act to the colonial Governors, who were ordered to use their 'utmost Endeavours' to enforce the Navigation system; corresponding orders were sent to the customs officers the following November.[12] The Hovering Act was really aimed at illicit trade with the French, especially in North America, but colonial officials could only interpret its provisions as embracing *all* trade with foreigners throughout the colonies – including trade with Spaniards in the Caribbean. Thus Governor Lyttleton of Jamaica expressed grave misgivings at meddling with the valuable Spanish trade; but 'as the orders I have received, do not appear to me, to admit of any latitude of interpretation, this particular trade stands prohibited'. On 4 January 1764 Lyttleton instructed naval, military, and customs officers to implement the Hovering Act strictly, an action whose impact fell principally upon Spanish traders.[13] Later the same year, an important clause of the Sugar Act incorporated further stringent anti-contraband provisions, including seizure of any foreign vessel found hovering off British coasts for longer than forty-eight hours after being ordered to leave by the Customs.[14] Contrary to what is sometimes asserted, the Sugar Act appears to have been less influential in the crisis affecting the Spanish trade during these years than the Hovering Act – though it certainly did not help matters.

The consequences of implementation of the Hovering Act were swift and predictable: '... the Spanish vessels bringing dollars into our ports, were unexpectedly, & contrary to usage and former allowance, seized upon & prosecuted'. Protests at the measure in Jamaica, the great centre of the trade, began almost immediately. On 1 February 1764, Lloyd, Boston & Co. wrote from Kingston that by implementation of the Act 'our trade will be intirely destroyed and the ruin of our credit may from this time take its date'.[15] On 7 April another correspondent wrote that 'payments are very backward and money very scarce here at present & is likely to be more so, the Law for extending the Hovering Act to the colonies & appointing Captains of Men of War Custom House Officers has hurt us much'.[16] An anonymous letter from the island, dated 5 May and published in a London periodical, read:

> The commercial concerns in this part of the world were never known so bad as since the peace was concluded; for that part of trade which was the support of this island, and its credit at home, is entirely subsided, by orders from home, to suppress all commerce with the Spaniards... Not a Spanish vessel can now come with money to this island, but what is seized by officers either under the Admiral or Governor.[17]

On 30 May the Jamaica Customs officers themselves wrote to their superiors in London 'stating, the bad consequences of the late Regulations', a course of action replicated by at least one naval officer, Captain Lee of the *Dreadnought*. A parallel series of protests flowed from West Florida, where the Spanish trade was yet negligible but was thought crucial to the success of the new colony. The governor wrote that the settlers were 'in a deplorable situation, being in the utmost want of every necessity, and no cash circulating amongst them', since local naval captains prevented Spanish vessels from entering even with bullion.[18] Still in October 1765, Governor Johnstone wrote that 'we have lived here for some time past as in a town besieged by our own fleet', while a merchant trading to Pensacola wrote plaintively, 'If no relief is had I know not what will become of us ... our hands tyed and what can we do.'[19] As far afield as New York, merchants reported that 'the English vessels won't allow the Spanish vessels to come in to us'.[20]

In an influential article published in 1942, Allan Christelow argued that the Hovering and Sugar Acts were not significant factors behind the slump in the Spanish trade during the years following the Peace. Christelow noted that the mercantile allegations were vague and possibly interested, that action against Spanish traders lasted only about six months before it was tempered by new instructions, and that effective disruption of the trade may have been minimal. In short, the 'wild rumours' of seizures of Spanish vessels were 'quite untrue', and it may be that the Spanish trade went on 'pretty much as usual'.[21] It is true that the relevant letters from Jamaica are mostly imprecise on the question of seizures, for example giving no names of ships or cargoes involved – though for Florida there is more specific evidence of Spanish vessels prevented from trading by the navy in mid-1764. One expert observer asserted that British exports to Jamaica in 1765 fell short of the figure for 1763 by some £168,000 sterling because of the naval interference;[22] other estimates that 'near a million of dollars' or 'two millions of dollars' were prevented from entering British colonial ports seem clearly exaggerated.[23] Figures for imports of bullion to Britain from Jamaica suggest a measured decline of about one-quarter in 1763–65.[24] The lack of reliable data makes the broader crisis in the Spanish trade itself hard to measure or even substantiate. Bourgoing's estimate for the total value of British contraband 'après la paix de 1763' of 20,000,000 pesos per year appears grossly inflated and was already questioned by Humboldt.[25] One writer thought that the trade placed in jeopardy by the Hovering Act was worth £200,000–£300,000 per year to the British, which we have seen may represent from 100–150 per cent of the real figure.[26] The lowest contemporary estimate is that of Reynal, who stated that Jamaica's Spanish trade was worth less than £70,000 per annum on the eve of the establishment of the free ports (though this figure may date to c. 1758).[27]

Christelow was certainly right to identify and emphasize other factors beyond the Acts contributing to and sustaining the slump during these years. Some of these factors seem trivial or improbable: the actions of a corrupt Customs officer, for example, or ongoing Spanish pique at the occupation of Havana. More credible is a glutting of Spanish-American markets during the occupation, a hypothesis supported moreover by evidence from Spanish sources, though no such glut should last more than a year or two.[28] The well-informed merchant Joseph Salvador gave a sophisticated explanation for the scarcity of specie in the colonies related principally to hang-over effects from the war.[29] The most convincing explanation appears to relate to the post-war boom in exports from Spain to the colonies, leading into the general post-war depression of 1764–69, 'one of the worst of the whole eighteenth century'. It seems that this general depression, albeit aggravated by more limited factors, was what kept trading conditions in the British islands depressed throughout the mid-1760s. None of this, however, diminishes the impact of the Hovering and Sugar Acts and the events of 1764 on the subsequent development of the Spanish trade. There do not now appear to be grounds to doubt that some real short-term disruption of the trade occurred as a result of the Acts.[30] Most importantly, given the decline in the Spanish trade, and always in the context of the broader contemporary commercial crisis, the protests now raised provided a focus for serious reflection on the Spanish trade and its problems in government circles. The letters from Jamaica, Florida and elsewhere, besides protesting specifically at the consequences of Grenville's regulations, almost uniformly emphasized two key issues: the importance and legal status of imports of bullion by Spaniards at British ports, and the danger that the Spanish trade would be permanently diverted to French and Dutch ports and lost to the British. These issues defined ministerial reflections on trade during the next two years.

The effects of Grenville's anti-contraband measures, once known, provoked widespread alarm in mercantile circles in London; anger at the Ministry was patent.[31] Early in May 1764 a mercantile deputation headed by the Chairman of the West India Committee petitioned Secretary of State the Earl of Halifax about the matter. Halifax disclaimed all knowledge of the disruptive orders, noting that 'no Government could hurt that trade and something should be done'. At the Treasury, Grenville himself professed ignorance as to the effects of his instructions; indeed, Grenville never acknowledged the impact of his orders, still proclaiming two years later that 'there were no cutters sent to the West Indies; no such orders to cruize on the Spanish trade ... For shame! Let it not be repeated any more.'[32] But he agreed that urgent corrective action should be taken. At his behest, the merchants themselves drew up on the spot draft instructions to officials in the West Indies intended to counter the Hovering Act.[33] Halifax dispatched these instructions to the Lords of Trade on 12 May 1764; they ran:

> It is his Majesty's intention, that Spanish vessels coming to the island of Jamaica, thro' distress, or for refreshments, as formerly, may receive the assistance they have been always allowed, provided they are not laden with, or attempt, in any manner, to bring in any foreign goods or merchandize.[34]

The orders went out to Jamaica on 6 June, and to the Floridas, Georgia and South Carolina on 15 February the following year.[35] They were received by Lyttleton in Kingston in mid-July, where the governor followed his superiors in denying actually ordering the seizure of Spanish vessels or that any ships had been seized on his orders since the Peace. Halifax's instructions encouraged some merchants to believe that the crisis was approaching resolution; one wrote from Kingston in July, 'We shall now very shortly have the trade with the Spaniards again opened ... which has given fresh spirits to the merchants here.'[36] Another wrote home from London, 'the Spanish trade you may depend is opened, as much as ye Same can be without Speaking loud.'[37] Others, however, were less sanguine. A Mr Robarts thought the new orders 'niggardly conceptions, extorted much against the grain & as it were by force'. The Manchester textile merchant Robert Hamilton stated that traders in that city did not consider the Spanish trade reopened, noting that doubts as to the orders and their efficacy continued to overshadow the trade.[38] The explicit prohibition against Spaniards bringing in foreign merchandise left Customs and Naval officers in too ambiguous a position, and the trade too vulnerable to further seizures and confiscations. The almost simultaneous issue of the Sugar Act, with its fresh anti-smuggling provisions, further complicated matters.

In July 1765 the Grenville administration fell and a new Ministry was formed under the Marquis of Rockingham. The broad commercial crisis and pressure for action to alleviate it, far from abating, redoubled in intensity. In Manchester, Hamilton began laying off workers in mid-1765, eventually firing 400 weavers. The Leeds manufacturer Robert Dawson dismissed 'near a thousand' workers by February 1766.[39] A letter published in December warned: 'If provisions should continue so dear as at present, and the poor have no work, it is to be feared that we shall soon see many terrible insurrections in this kingdom. *Hunger will break through stone walls.*'[40] The Yorkshire M.P. Sir George Savile summarised the merchants' attitude for Rockingham: 'Our trade is hurt, what the devil have you been a doing? For our part, we don't pretend to understand your politics and American matters, but our trade is hurt; pray remedy it, and a plague of you if you wont.'[41] A veritable action campaign was organised by the North America and possibly also the West India merchants, who sent circular letters to the manufacturing towns encouraging them to pressure Parliament for an enquiry and measures to end the decline in trade.[42] Petitions and protests poured in from Liverpool, Lancaster, Leicester and other towns. The greater part both of the commercial crisis and of the petitions which arose from it related specifically to trade with the North American colonies, and they led at last to repeal of the Stamp Act, and the temporary quelling of the North American crisis, in early 1766. The crisis in the Spanish trade in the Caribbean, however, remained an important aggravating factor. Ongoing correspondence from the West Indies underlined that no recovery had occurred, and that Spaniards continued to shun the British ports.[43]

Moves toward further action to restore the trade began in August 1765, when the West India merchants applied to the Treasury for a ruling as to whether bullion could, in fact, legally be imported by foreign vessels to British colonies. The administration addressed the matter in earnest in October, with the circulation by Rockingham of three anonymous papers, identified by Armytage as probably by Chancellor of the Exchequer William Dowdeswell.[44] These papers were discussed seriously and at length by members of the Cabinet. The chief points at issue were whether bullion and (less importantly) other foreign products could be legally imported in foreign vessels to British colonies under the Navigation Acts; whether and what class of goods might be exported in return; and whether such trade contravened British treaties with Spain. The close arguments and convoluted reasoning now advanced with regard to a trade clearly in Britain's interest seem surprising, but underline the extent to which Ministers were prisoners of the formidable Navigation system. One participant actually ruled that no trade by Spanish vessels could be permitted under the Navigation Acts, even for imports of bullion.[45] Others, including the Attorney-General, Charles Yorke, expressed grave misgivings about issuing overt orders protecting or fomenting the trade.[46] Nevertheless, the outcome of these Cabinet discussions was probably never in doubt. Rockingham himself pressed Yorke to place the most 'Liberal Construction' possible on his interpretation of the Acts of Trade.[47] Both the author of the three papers, and most of those commenting on them, agreed that importation of bullion at British colonies, even in foreign vessels, was clearly legal under the Acts. The export of British manufactures and produce in return was also deemed probably legal; the status of other foreign produce imported remained unclear and was thought best left to one side.

Considering that it would be impolitic to make public application to the king for the necessary remedial measures at this time, on 30 October Rockingham sent all the relevant documentation to the Attorney- and Solicitor-General for their formal opinion whether bullion might be imported into British colonies in foreign vessels.[48] The Law Officers replied on 11 November, and their opinion was adopted in an important Treasury Minute of 13 November, which ruled that by the 'true construction' of the Navigation Acts, 'Bullion may be imported into the Plantations in Foreign Bottoms.'[49] Orders were despatched forthwith to the Commissioners of the Customs,

who forwarded them to their officers in the West Indies and southern continental colonies.[50] These orders represented a second attempt (with Halifax's
instructions of May 1764) to remedy the crisis thought to have been brought
about by strict implementation of the Hovering Act. They instructed
Customs and Naval officers 'not to seize or molest foreign vessels bringing
bullion into the said plantations in like manner as has been heretofore used
& allow'd ... any late practice to the contrary notwithstanding'. They were
almost certainly intended only as a temporary measure pending full airing of
the question of the Spanish trade in Parliament, and are thought to have had
little impact in reviving the trade. Nevertheless, they won the Rockingham
administration both time and rich political rewards. Rockingham's popularity
in the mercantile and manufacturing towns soared yet higher, sealing a crucial
period of collaboration with mercantile interests over matters of commercial
policy which would have far-reaching effects the following year.[51]

When the new session of Parliament opened in January 1766, the administration was thus already committed to finding some permanent solution to
the problem of the Spanish trade. The Commons began by debating the
Stamp Act, which was repealed on 21 February, but agreed to broaden
discussions to other colonial affairs. Leading merchants were interviewed and
information on different aspects of Atlantic trade taken from a variety of
sources.[52] There is little doubt that powerful mercantile interests at this time
took advantage of the Stamp Act debates to press for broader reform of colonial trade, including reforms to set the Spanish trade on a firmer footing.
That the administration was predisposed toward some such measures was
evident during the examination of witnesses, when discussion of the North
American crisis was spliced with questions on other commercial issues and
notably on the Spanish trade. This trade was seen as significant both in its
own right and because, via the British West Indies, it provided the North
American colonies with their major, indeed virtually their only source of
specie.[53] A further striking feature of the reports amassed at this time is the
presupposition that Spaniards now undertook the bulk of the trade and that
this must necessarily remain so in future. It was at this time that the idea of
a free port in the West Indies was first canvassed openly in Parliamentary
circles. In the opening paragraph to this chapter, we saw that privately sponsored schemes for free ports proliferated after the Peace of 1763, perhaps
mainly as attempts to integrate the newly conquered territories swiftly into
the British imperial system. As it happened, among both the private schemes
for free ports and during early discussions in Parliament, most attention
focused on plans for a port in Dominica, an island of only limited relevance
to the Spanish trade.

Crucial to developments during these months was the influence of mercantile groups over the government, which now reached an absolute high;
indeed, it has been argued that at this time 'the direction of colonial policy
passed largely into the hands of the mercantile pressure groups; at no time
in the eighteenth century were Administration and Parliament more at the

command of the commercial interest than in the spring of 1766'.[54] The merchants in question by no means formed a united front, but were split into great blocs composed of merchants trading to the West Indies and those trading with North America. The story of the passage of the Free Port Act is largely one of the struggle between these two major trading blocs. The catalytic issue seems to have been the desire of the merchants trading with North America for some legal means to tap the French islands for sugar and its by-products and to sell their own produce in return, probably via a free port in the British Leewards. The West India merchants were bitterly opposed to any such scheme because it threatened their monopoly of plantation produce within the British imperial system. Probably recognising that opinion was against them, however, they reached preliminary agreement with the North American camp at a London tavern on 10 March.[55] This agreement made important concessions to the North America merchants, though not yet including a free port at Dominica, in return for safeguards on the West Indian monopoly of sugar and other plantation produce in the British market.[56] It is worth noting that on 3 April both factions also formally committed themselves to legal measures to sanction trade with the Spaniards.[57] The idea of a free port to trade with the French islands, once broached, provided an obvious solution to the conundrum of how to manage the Spanish trade, a trade in which the West India bloc was chiefly interested. The agreement of 10 March, however, appears to have been sponsored only by a minority of moderate West Indians, while the majority remained firmly opposed to the scheme. By early April the two sides were openly at issue over the question of the proposed free port in Dominica.

The Dominica scheme was supported in the House by the North America merchants and the government, notably by its leading spokesman, Edmund Burke. Opposition was led by William Beckford, the West India magnate, supported by George Grenville. Especially significant was the opposition of William Pitt, the powerful former wartime Prime Minister, who had apparently been won over by Beckford.[58] Burke made a special visit to Pitt at Hayes on 11 April in an attempt to bring him round, but found him immovable, possibly out of pique that he had not been consulted more closely. Burke remarked that when the free port was first discussed in a full Cabinet (the following day), 'the Old Stagers fritterd it down to an address to the King for the opinion of the boards on the matter &c. – so we come hopping into the house with half a measure'.[59] The debates that the affair engendered were tempestuous; one such preliminary debate was nicely sketched by Horace Walpole:

> Grenville as madly in earnest as Pitt was affectedly so, vehemently opposed that motion, and called it a *sweeping resolution*. They would next attack, he supposed, the *sacred* Act of Navigation. Burke bitterly, and Beckford and Dowdeswell, ridiculed him on the idea of any Act being sacred if it wanted correction. Lord Strange went farther; said, he would speak out; should

be for a free port in America ... Charles Townshend said ... for his part
he would call for a review of the Act of Navigation. This drew on warm
altercation between him and Grenville. [60]

For some weeks it appeared that the Bill might have to be deferred until the
next session. The Spanish ambassador thought this likely, since 'these
persons fear him [Pitt], and they do not dare to attempt anything which they
are not sure he will support'.[61] The scheme's mercantile sponsors, however,
insisted the Bill be persisted with, doubtless aware that the Rockingham
administration was collapsing and that there would be no second opportunity the next year.

In fact, opposition to the free port scheme crumbled around the end of
April and the beginning of May. Possibly decisive was a change of heart by
Pitt, who ceased actively to oppose the idea by 30 April. Pitt's harsh criticism
had been costly in political terms, 'the scheme being grateful to the City',
while he may also have become convinced of the economic benefits.[62] With
his withdrawal the moderates among the West India faction reached a new
agreement with the North Americans, drawn up in the House on 8 May. This
agreement conceded that the question of a free port in Dominica should be
discussed during the current session. In return it secured several provisions
regarding re-exports of sugar to Britain and the rum and cotton trades, which
clearly favoured West Indian interests. Most significantly, the fourth clause
specified that the Spanish trade in the Caribbean be fomented 'by a species
of Free port in Jamaica for Spanish bottoms'.[63] The establishment of free
ports oriented primarily toward the Spanish trade thus appeared almost as
an afterthought, and a trade-off for the port in Dominica long pursued by
the North America faction. This may be deceptive, a product primarily of
lacunae in the documentary record and the focus of debate on the particularly controversial Dominica question. Given the active search for a new
footing for the Spanish trade, under way since at least May 1764, it seems
likely that free ports in Jamaica remained central to Parliamentary discussions
through February to May 1766. Be all this as it may, the agreement of 8 May
was significant in clearing the final obstacle from the course of Parliamentary
approval of the free ports.

Chancellor Dowdeswell presented a Free Ports Bill to Parliament on 15
May 1766. It passed rapidly through the House, reflecting the lack of opposition it excited once agreement had been reached between the merchants. It
was referred to the Lords on 27 May and received the royal assent on 6 June;
there are no known accounts of relevant debates.[64] A colleague wrote ruefully
to Pitt, 'in a question of such importance as that now before the House,
concerning the American duties, free port, &c., only seventy members could
be found to attend their duty.'[65] Another merchant, in a passage which draws
attention to, while overstating, the almost accidental way in which the free
ports came into existence, wrote that the Bill 'passed through a very thin
house, and without much examination'.[66] It continued to cause real misgiv-

ings in some sectors, one observer commenting, 'I see they are oversetting every American idea that ever was establish'd.'[67] But in broad terms the measure won fresh mercantile accolades for Rockingham and his Ministry. The Free Port Act 'gained the administration a great weight with the mercantile part of the nation, who could not avoid being pleased at the attention that was paid to their interests'.[68] The First Lord of Trade, the Earl of Dartmouth, was granted the freedom of the city of Liverpool, while Rockingham received deputations from the West India and North America merchants expressing 'the most grateful sense of your unwearied endeavours, to establish these salutary regulations'.[69] These plaudits did not, however, save his Ministry, which collapsed on the last day of July.

The first Free Port Act opened four ports in Jamaica and two in Dominica, to function from 1 November 1766 for an initial period of seven years.[70] The Jamaican ports, both in terms of this work and in view of the subsequent development of the system, were by far the most important. The Act opened Kingston, Montego Bay, Savannah la Mar and St Lucea to foreign vessels having no more than a single deck, a size restriction apparently designed to limit the trade to small craft of local build. These vessels might import bullion and any other foreign produce, with the exception of sugar, molasses, coffee, tobacco and lesser plantation produce competing with the island's domestic agriculture. No foreign manufactures might be imported whatever. In return, all British produce and manufactures might be exported from Jamaica, excepting only a range of strategic naval supplies and iron from British North America. A further important legal export was African slaves, the trade in whom was expected to defray the expense of establishing the ports through a duty of £1 10s. on each individual exported; significantly, this was the only duty imposed upon the trade. The free ports in Dominica, by contrast (at Roseau and Prince Rupert's Bay), had a quite different constitution from those in Jamaica and were 'more in the nature of a real experiment'.[71] They were designed to secure a new legal trade in foreign plantation produce, principally with the neighbouring French islands, although in their final form this trade was diverted toward British and European continental markets rather than toward those in North America as first envisaged. For reasons which form no part of the current work, this trade failed to prosper, and the Dominica free ports themselves had a chequered existence. Though Dominica's French trade was far the more important for much of our period, the island features hereafter only with regard to its (relatively limited) trade with the Spaniards.

The British were perfectly aware that the free ports were a delicate subject, one requiring great discretion with regard to foreign powers and especially to Spain. In a passage typical of the sort of knowledgeable dissembling with which experts approached the subject ever afterward, Sir William Young acknowledged that the trade 'admits not of exposure as to its points of destination, its interior channels, and general means of success. With a view to British interests, it cannot be exhibited in detail.'[72] This secrecy served some purpose, though it failed to deceive penetrating critics like the Frenchman Dauxion Lavaysse, who called the Free Port Acts 'simply the invitations the king of England makes to the merchants of the French and Spanish colonies to undertake contraband with his subjects'.[73] It also ensured that the nature of the free ports trade and the factors which had brought it into existence remained poorly known even in Britain. Well-informed observers writing only a few years afterwards attributed establishment of the ports primarily to interest in imports of cotton, for example, or control of the slave trade with foreigners, seemingly unaware of the long debates and enquiries of the period 1764–66.[74] Nevertheless, and after the early doubts discussed in the following pages, the general advantages were rarely disputed. Young noted that to the direct commercial benefits might be added those of 'increased population, of a greater resort of shipping, of an influx and choice of British goods, or more wealthy merchants, a circulation of specie, and resource and accommodation to the landed interest'.[75] A paper written in the mid-1780s was more succinct; the free ports were established so that 'we might enjoy to the extent of the trade all the advantages of the foreign colonies without being exposed to the expense of establishing or protecting them'.[76] And historians, for their part, have underlined the remarkable, even revolutionary shift which the ports marked in British commercial policy overseas. Langford's judicious view in this sense bears repeating; the Acts were 'essentially elaborate and calculated refinements' of the Navigation system, 'yet they also evinced a new readiness to question assumptions made during the earlier history of the empire. In the last analysis they represented the first significant attempt to launch an experiment in free trade and a portentous, if small, breach in the old imperial system.'[77]

Trade at Jamaica, 1766–83: Ongoing Crisis or Recovery?

These positive assessments notwithstanding, the fundamental role the free ports were to play in the development of the Spanish trade in the ensuing decades was by no means immediately clear. Indeed, it was commonly held that the trade, at least at Jamaica, failed to recover in 1766 and remained depressed possibly for a further decade or even longer. Thus in October 1767 Jamaican trade with Cuba and Puerto Rico was still described as almost at a standstill.[78] The merchant Lowbridge Bright, complaining in the late 1760s at the scale of French smuggling, observed that 'little trade was carried on with Spaniards'.[79] In an important paper dated 1773, Governor Dalling wrote of 'the loss of the Spanish Trade having been for some years past a subject of general complaint in Jamaica', and that 'the decay of the trade has been particularly experienced since the opening of the Free Ports'.[80] Admiral Rodney asserted in October 1774 that the bullion trade all but ceased during his command in the West Indies, while a further report prepared the same year put imports of bullion from the Spaniards at around £100,000 sterling per year – still a relatively modest figure.[81] As late as 1780 the trade was said to be worth just one-third of its value earlier in the century.[82] The idea of a slump in the trade following the establishment of the free ports was endorsed by the contemporary historians Edward Long and Bryan Edwards.[83] It has continued to influence scholarly assessments of the general success of the free port system; thus Helen Allen, writing in 1928, thought that the Spanish trade sharply declined and that 'on the whole, the Free Port Act, which had been designed to encourage it, had proved to be more of a deterrent than a stimulant'. Trevor Burnard, writing in 2001, accepts contemporary accounts of a decline in trade and ascribes it in part to the free ports, 'a well-intentioned but commercially disastrous attempt to allow a measure of free trade' with the Spanish colonies.[84]

The reasons advanced by contemporaries for an ongoing crisis in the trade in the late 1760s and early 1770s were manifold. Some detected the ongoing influence of the counter-contraband decrees of 1763–64, which had permanently damaged Spanish confidence in British good faith.[85] Others blamed important innovations in the commercial legislation of European rivals in the Caribbean. In October 1765 Spain issued a decree which sanctioned direct trade between its Caribbean islands and a range of ports in the Peninsula, a first step in the process of limited commercial liberalisation known as *Comercio Libre*.[86] It has been suggested that the Free Port Act of 1766 was a reaction to this Spanish decree promulgated a year earlier, but this is unconvincing.[87] British reaction to the onset of Comercio Libre was relaxed; the British ambassador in Spain thought that the new regulations would be advantageous, 'as there will certainly be a greater call for our goods by the Spanish merchants here, now they have a free liberty of exporting them without a licence'.[88] In later years, and especially after its substantial expansion in 1778, Comercio Libre brought about rapid growth in Spanish colonial trade whose potential effect on British illicit trade in the Caribbean is discussed in the following chapter. In the period to the end of the American Revolutionary War, however, the programme's impact remained limited. The attribution of the decline in Jamaica's trade by the Spanish writer Francisco de Saavedra to 'the freedom of trade with the islands of Cuba, Santo Domingo, and Puerto Rico granted in the year 1765' was a rarity.[89] More common were complaints by Spanish monopoly merchants to the effect that Comercio Libre had actually brought about new opportunities and an expansion of illicit trade.[90] Though the question remains to some extent open, there is as yet insufficient evidence to conclude that Spanish trade liberalisation had much negative impact on British smuggling during these early years.

A further putative cause for the slump was increased competition from commercial rivals in the region, also a product of innovations in those nations' colonial legislation. In 1764, free ports were opened in the Danish islands of St Thomas and St Johns, while in 1767 the French opened ports of their own at the Mole St Nicolas in St Domingue and at St Lucia.[91] There was concern that the Spanish trade, diverted toward the French, Dutch, and Danish islands by Grenville's anti-contraband legislation, would prove difficult to recover. One observer mused that

> things having taken a new channel could not be brought back to the old, as soon as could be wished ... This has been the situation of the Spanish trade since the opening of the Free Ports in Jamaica, whereby they have not as yet answered our expectations as fully as we could have wished.[92]

There is little doubt that the Spaniards traded extensively with other nations during these years, perhaps especially with French St Domingue, now reaching the zenith of its extraordinary pre-Revolutionary prosperity. Cuban observers discussing illicit trade tended to refer to Jamaica, New Providence, and Guarico (the Spanish name for St Domingue) indiscriminately; Francisco de Arango, referring to the period before the Revolution, noted that 'our smugglers preferred then the market of Guarico, because they found there more cheaply and to their taste the principal articles of their trade ... By that rivalry and not due to our Regulation [of Comercio Libre] English smuggling had declined'.[93] The period before the onset of the Napoleonic wars in 1793 was, indeed, the last during which the French and Dutch yet presented serious commercial competition to the British in some parts of the Caribbean. In a further contribution of his 1942 article, Allan Christelow argued that less than to a loss of trade to foreign competitors, the ongoing crisis in Jamaica's Spanish trade was due at least in part to the dispersal of British trade through the greater number of colonies acquired at the Peace of Paris, notably through Florida, Dominica and Grenada. Christelow's thesis is interesting, and has been reiterated by scholars working after him, but I think that his case in this respect remains unproven.[94]

A tale told in 1773 by the Jamaican governor, John Dalling, and repeated thereafter both privately and in print, attributed the commercial crisis to an incident in which detailed records of Spaniards trading at the free ports reached the government in Madrid, which instituted harsh reprisals against implicated merchants. Although Customs practice was later revised, these events again shattered Spanish faith in the security of the trade, dealing it a further setback.[95] It now appears that this version of events must be discounted, its considerable currency among the British notwithstanding, since several years' research in Hispanic archives has revealed a complete lack of evidence to support it. The concept of a reinforcement of Spanish anti-contraband measures at this time, however, has far greater substance, and was considered by Christelow as perhaps the most likely explanation for the crisis. Though such activity should probably not be linked too closely to the establishment of the free ports, there is considerable evidence of heightened Anglo-Spanish tension during these few years. British observers including Dalling and Rodney agreed that in reaction to the Free Port Act the Spaniards reinforced their coastal vigilance, inter alia replacing local officers with fresh ones sent out from the metropolis.[96] Spanish Ministers openly declared their irritation at British smuggling in the Americas; in December

1769 the Marqués de Grimaldi expounded 'on the unbounded illicit trade we carried on in every part of the Spanish Dominions, & tho' he did not pretend to disculpate other nations, yet there was no proportion between us & them'.[97]

The hardening of Spanish attitudes during these years was evident in repeated seizures of British merchant vessels. In 1769 the British Commodore at Port Royal was moved to reflect on 'a spirit of jealousy at present in the Spaniards, which induces them to make capture of every vessel coming in their way, right or wrong'.[98] Rodney wrote in 1771 that frequent complaints reached him 'of trading ships being on the most slight and groundless pretences molested and searched by the Spanish guarda costas'.[99] Rodney also noted that British warships were now barred from entering Spanish ports even when bearing official despatches, a policy confirmed in June 1767 when the frigates *Cygnet* and *Adventure* were actually fired upon as they tried to enter Havana harbour.[100] 'Upon the first news of this affair', it was reported, Grimaldi again 'exclaimed everywhere against the violent and illicit practices of the English in America'.[101] There were also campaigns against contraband undertaken more or less energetically on local initiative in the different Spanish colonies, such as that of the Marqués de la Torre and his successor Joseph Carlos de Aguero in the province of Caracas in 1771–73.[102] It may be that British impressions of greater Spanish action against smuggling were based in part on campaigns such as these. In any case, bellicose tension in the Caribbean remained high, with an important war scare in 1771 and a flare-up of the Anglo-Spanish dispute over the island of Vieques, east of Puerto Rico, in 1771–74.[103]

To the widespread belief that the free port system had failed to restore the Spanish trade at Jamaica was added the further accusation that it had fostered large-scale smuggling, especially with the French. An advocate for the system was obliged to acknowledge that among 'the principal objections now made to the Free Port Act' was 'that it encourages smuggling'. Governor John Dalling wrote that the advantages of the Act had been 'greatly overbalanced by the importation of many commodities injurious to the manufactures and commerce both of Great Britain and this country'.[104] Perhaps of greatest concern were illicit imports of coffee; an enquiry by the island Assembly in 1773 found that 'very large quantities of foreign coffee have been imported, and large seizures made by the Customs House officers of the port of Kingston'.[105] Citing the harm arising from imports of French coffee, a group of Jamaican planters actually sought repeal of the Act as the time of its expiry in 1773 drew near.[106] Little is known of the relevant Parliamentary debates over this issue, although related papers generally reveal support for the Act, albeit often with scant enthusiasm. Dalling himself grudgingly advocated renewal, his considerable criticisms notwithstanding.[107] Another writer argued that abolition and the public debates it would engender could only increase Spanish animosity and on that account alone was to be avoided. The Spanish trade had declined some years before the passing of the Act, and only the free ports could restore it, by placing the trade on a secure basis.[108] Nevertheless, the fact that the value of the Act was seriously questioned at this time appeared confirmed by its eventual renewal in 1773 for a single year only.[109]

Be all this as it may, by the early 1770s there seems to have been growing acceptance of the utility of the free port system in purely commercial terms; that, in the words of the writer last cited, 'it must appear that whatever may have been the case at first, the Free Port Act is now rather of utility than hurt'. Indeed it is possible that we should now question the very concept of an ongoing crisis in the Spanish trade in the years after 1766, the voluminous contemporary complaints of one notwithstanding. Fragmentary evidence controverting any such crisis includes a four-fold increase in imports of foreign cotton from Jamaica to Britain by 1773, or the ongoing preference of Spanish-American merchants for Jamaica as a market for slaves (contributing to the collapse by 1772 of Spanish efforts to supply slaves direct from the coast of Africa).[110] Most strikingly, data for the entry of shipping at the Jamaican free ports suggest steady growth from the outset and a tripling in the volume of trade by 1771–72 (Table 2.1). The key to this issue appears to lie in the fact that complaints of a crisis referred principally to trade with the Spanish colonies in British vessels, which indeed seems to have declined significantly. Thus, Rodney stated in 1774 that 'since the Free Port Act ... the commerce in British bottoms has totally ceased and the persons employ'd in that commerce deserted that island'.[111] In a remarkable passage dated 1780, Francisco de Saavedra suggested that Jamaican merchants had withdrawn from the trade because of its excessive risks: 'There are today few reputable traders on this island who permit themselves to be seduced by the chimerical profits of clandestine trade, and the Jews, especially the less rich ones, are the only ones who perpetuate it.'[112] Bryan Edwards's assertion in 1793 that 'the ancient contraband system is nearly at an end' also referred to the British interloping trade.[113] But none of this implied any decline in the Spanish trade per se. A report of 1774 commented upon the decline in 'our [i.e. British] intercourse with the Spaniards', 'though the ... Spaniards from Cuba and other parts of the Spanish dominions come in here, under the Free Port Act, in their own vessels, and deal for negroes, provisions, and a variety of British manufactures, to a pretty considerable amount'.[114] A Cuban observer at this time wrote that 'contraband with foreigners does not lie with them, in reality, but with the islanders [of Cuba] themselves ... The smugglers, in essence, are the islanders.'[115] In short, the ongoing decay of trade with the Spaniards in British vessels, coming at the tail end of the general post-war slump, may have obscured modest but steady recovery in Anglo-Spanish trade as a whole following the establishment of the free ports in 1766.

Certain it is that in 1774 the Act was again renewed, and the future of the free ports secured, with the extension of the system for a further seven years. In 1773 the headquarters of the Spanish slave-trading company was transferred from Puerto Rico to Havana, and Spanish merchants were granted

Table 2.1 *Shipping entering the free ports of Jamaica, 1767–86*

	Number of vessels	Total tonnage
1767	53	1,150
1768	74	1,394
1769	86	2,062
1770	169	4,050
1771	144	3,092
1772	185	4,491
1773	117	3,180
1774	174	5,766
1775	227	5,757
1776	251	6,663
1777	279	7,595
1778	126	3,243
1779	84	3,069
1780	40	1,252
1781	35	1,433
1782	102	4,100
1783	210	10,920
1784	250	12,008
1785	311 or 259	13,269
1786	192	—

Source: Adapted from Armytage, *Free Port System*, p. 149, app. 3, table B.

permission to seek slaves in any of the neighbouring foreign colonies. Bryan Edwards argued in the same year for renewal of the Act on the grounds that the British might engross this new trade in slaves ('and on this account only'), foreseeing exports of 5,000 slaves to the Spanish colonies annually. Edwards later insisted that the slave trade had been the chief factor behind renewal of the Act, and this does not seem unlikely: to encourage this trade the Act of 1773 reduced the duty on exports of slaves from £1 10s. to just 2s. 6d. per head.[116] When the Act of 1774 expired in 1781, the system was again extended for a further six years.[117] With these Acts, the free ports remained restricted to Jamaica and Dominica until after the American Revolutionary War. Attempts in 1773–74 to secure additional free ports for Antigua and Barbados failed, as did further efforts by the same islands in 1776 and 1780 respectively.[118] Despite almost frantic petitioning by Governor Johnstone, as will be seen, no free ports were created in Florida during the twenty years of British occupation.

Evidence for Jamaica's Spanish trade during the remainder of the period covered by this chapter (to 1783) is fragmentary, though it appears to indicate further growth and reasonable prosperity. It is true that in 1774, Edward Long recorded exports to 'South America' of under £11,000 sterling, or less than 1 per cent of the island's total exports, and a balance 'gained by foreign trade, chiefly with South America' of only £35,000, but these low figures merely emphasize that Long's figures only cover part of the trade they purport to describe. His work is more useful in stressing that Jamaica exported almost none of its own produce to the Spanish colonies, but traded almost entirely in British manufactures;

> hence is obvious the vast advantage to the nation of having an island so situate and circumstanced, as to be able to extend the consumption of its manufactures, by a variety of secret and difficult channels, into those remote parts, to which no means might otherwise probably have been found of so conveniently dispersing them.[119]

There is good evidence to suggest that the expectations of 1773–74 regarding Jamaica's slave trade were broadly realised. While 235 slaves were exported from the island in 1773, some 2,321 were exported the following year. Edwards indicated that imports of slaves to Jamaica in the decade after 1773 exceeded those of the previous ten years by 22,213 slaves, and exports by a total of 5,952.[120] Such was the importance of the trade that a Cuban delegation sent to Liverpool and Manchester to study its operation caused real alarm among British slavers at the prospect that the Spanish would undertake it on their own account.[121] We have seen that a report of 1774 put imports of bullion from the Spaniards at around £100,000 sterling per year, a relatively modest figure.[122] But by 1776 an official in Cuba suggested that most of the island's illicit trade was carried on with Jamaica.[123] Francisco de Saavedra's statement to the effect that Jamaica's income from smuggling had fallen to just a third its historic value by 1780 still recorded a trade worth 1,500,000 pesos, or perhaps £340,000 per year.[124] By contrast, Bourgoing's calculation that in the period 1767–78 as a whole, 'foreigners undertook very close to half the trade of Spanish America' is based on a dubious methodology and seems clearly exaggerated.[125]

Trade at British Colonies Other than Jamaica

The Spanish trade at Dominica (besides Jamaica the only other island endowed with free ports in 1766) appeared more prosperous at the outset. Already in 1767 a group of London merchants remarked that the opening of the ports in Dominica had 'greatly encouraged the importation of foreign West Indies produce into that island, and the consumption of British manufactures'.[126] It was said that up to 595 foreign vessels visited the island in a single year, while a report dated 1773 put the fleet serving Dominica's trade at 180 vessels. In contrast to Jamaica, there seems to have been little opposition to renewal of the Dominica free ports in the latter year.[127] Not all the evidence was positive, however; Sir William Young, reviewing figures for British trade with Dominica in 1767–78, concluded that 'the speculations of advantage to British industry and trade from the establishment of this free port, seem generally to have failed'.[128] Thomas Atwood's suggestion that before the American Revolutionary War both French and Spaniards 'purchased in this island great numbers of negroes for the supply of their settlements, together with great quantities of merchandize of the manufactures of Great Britain' may be misleading, to the extent that it is clear that by far the greater part of Dominica's free port trade was with the French.[129] It appears that the only trade with the Spaniards which flourished was in slaves, of whom it was said that a better selection was usually available in Dominica than in Jamaica. The 1773 report stated that the only trade maintained with Spaniards was in slaves to Puerto Rico for the Spanish Asiento company; Kender Mason was among British merchants contracting with the Company in Cadiz for the supply of slaves to Puerto Rico via Dominica.[130]

Trade by Spanish and British merchants alike remained formally illegal in the majority of British territories yet to be granted free ports. Among the most important of these territories was West Florida, ceded to Britain at the Peace of Paris and occupied in August 1763. The Spanish trade at West Florida was to employ two quite distinct vehicles: trans-Mississippi trade with New Orleans and Spanish Louisiana, and direct Spanish maritime trade at the colony's principal ports of Mobile and Pensacola. It was the latter trade which raised the greatest hopes, and was indeed at first viewed as fundamental to the colony's success.[131] The Florida Assembly anticipated a trade worth £300,000 per year if properly regulated, and there was considerable excitement when a first Spanish trader with $40,000 put in to Pensacola in mid-1764, to be followed later the same year by a further three Spanish merchantmen with £30,000 in bullion.[132] All commentators, however, agreed that successful development of the trade was vitally dependent upon grant of free status to one or more of the colony's ports. This need was dramatically underscored when all the above-mentioned vessels were prevented from trading and actually towed out of harbour by Royal Navy vessels acting on the Hovering Act.[133] Governor Johnstone led a vigorous campaign for free ports which began with his arrival in Pensacola and was redoubled after ports were granted to Jamaica and Dominica two years later.[134] To no avail; the British government refused to grant free ports to the Floridas, which remained without any throughout their short existence as British colonies. This deficiency, combined with a less than favourable geography and powerful competition from the island entrepôts, condemned the trade, which rapidly withered away. In 1767 a further Spanish vessel was reported to have purchased $30,000 in British manufactures at Pensacola, but it was only with slight exaggeration that the commercial house of Morgan and Strothers later recalled that 'during the two or three first years a few small vessels stole into Pensacola with about $50,000, and in all the rest of the time that we were in possession there were not $20,000 more brought nor anything else except a little Campeche logwood'.[135] The British continued to make hopeful over-tures, and the authorities in Florida despatched ships to Havana in 1767 and to Veracruz in 1764, 1765 and 1770 with the intention of facilitating commer-cial relations.[136] But Montforte Browne, who left office in April 1769, was 'the last of the West Florida governors to comment with any degree of enthu-siasm on the trade or its possibilities', and later officials rarely if ever mentioned it.[137] Spanish maritime trade at British West Florida was a fleeting phenomenon, one limited to the mid-1760s and to just a handful of vessels and at most a few tens of thousands of dollars in cargo.

Much more substantial was trade across the Mississippi with Louisiana, lately ceded to Spain by the French. This trade was based partly upon the settlement of British merchants in New Orleans, partly on British treaty rights to navigation of the river, and partly on the establishment of trading posts along the left bank, including at Baton Rouge and Natchez; one such post grew so significant that the phrase 'going to Little Manchac' became synony-mous with smuggling.[138] The trade built rapidly into one of steady prosperity, checked only briefly by bursts of anti-contraband activity by the Spanish. Thus, Governor Alejandro de O'Reilly expelled most British traders in August 1769 and briefly imposed aggressive controls on British shipping on the river.[139] In April 1777, Governor Bernardo de Gálvez suddenly seized some dozen British vessels on the river and again expelled all British subjects from Louisiana.[140] But on each occasion trade swiftly resumed its former course, with the British dominating exchange on the Mississippi. One curious feature of this later period was a pair of floating British warehouses, with cabins 'fitted up with shelves and counters, as a store', which plied the river calling on the planters as they went.[141] Statistical evidence for the value of the trade is scarce and contradictory, though there is little doubt that trans-river commerce was an important factor in the economic development of the fledg-ling British colony. A Spanish report of 1776 suggested that all but a fraction of an import trade worth over $600,000 per year was enjoyed by British merchants, while elsewhere the value of the trade to the British was estimated at a (surely exaggerated) $1,000,000.[142] Charles Mowat, by contrast, suggests that British exports to Florida reached a maximum of just £67,000 in 1771, exports aimed at domestic consumption and the lucrative Indian trade as well as that with Spaniards. In any case, the advent of the American Revolutionary War brought sharp decline, and most of West Florida was conquered by Spain in 1781. During a debate over the treaty which returned them to the Spaniards in 1783, Lord Shelburne noted that the total trade of both Floridas was worth £100,000 in imports, and £120,000 in exports, but that 'this was not an object worth contending for at the hazard of war'.[143]

A further 'continental' point of exchange lay in the British settlements on the Central American coast, centred on Honduras, Black River, and the Mosquito Shore. At the Peace of Paris, Britain secured the right to maintain the logging settlements in Honduras in return for recognition of Spanish sovereignty and the demolition of British fortifications. Although never large in population terms, the settlements enjoyed some prosperity, and inevitably they served as a further entrepôt for trade with the Spaniards in Guatemala, Honduras, and Nicaragua. Reynal suggested that Jamaican merchants established trading factories in Honduras in early 1766 to supply the Mexican hinterland.[144] In 1768 economic activity on the Mosquito Shore included 'bartering with the Spaniards British commodities for silver bullion, mules, horses, black cattle etc, which they import to Jamaica', while in 1769 recorded exports included £3,500 in 'Spanish indigo and gold and silver bullion'.[145] Commercial relations between the Shore and the fort at Omoa in Nicaragua are well documented, and in 1770 the Spanish commandant was accused of being 'the boss and patron of the smugglers in that region'. A report of 1776 described British settlers near the Río Tinto, 'rich Englishmen with many slaves, these have commercial dealings with the Spaniards of the Provinces, who bring cattle, mules, indigo, raw and stamped silver'.[146] At approximately the same time, most of the plentiful sarsaparilla exported from the colony was 'purchased from the Spanyards'.[147] Besides these instances of direct trade, there was also unquestionably considerable indirect commercial exchange mediated by the Indian tribes inhabiting the regions between the British and Spanish settlements.

Such rather anecdotal evidence notwithstanding, the significance of Anglo-Spanish trade through the Honduras Bay and Mosquito Shore should not be exaggerated. The British settlements in these regions remained very much coastal enclaves, separated from the Spanish lands by vast tracts of forest and swamp. Their principal activities were logging and some small-scale cultivation, while trade with the Indians remained much more consistently significant than that with Spaniards. External trade was with Britain, Jamaica, and (increasingly) with the North American colonies, while maritime trade with other nations was mainly with the Dutch at Curaçao.[148] Relations with the Spaniards were not always peaceful, and Spain sometimes took direct action against British traders; in 1769 the schooner *Industry* was seized by the Guipúzcoa Company en route for Curaçao, while in 1776 the *Morning Star* sloop was cut out from Black River and taken to Cartagena by the guarda-costas.[149] Such incidents presented no serious obstacle to economic development in the region, but the policy of the British themselves proved more harmful. Britain refused to grant the settlements formal colonial status, perhaps because the tension they caused with Spain outweighed their relatively marginal economic value.[150] The Honduran settlers stressed that 'the trade of this place might be greatly extended ... provided we had any security that would induce merchants to risk their property here', and it was later observed that 'from 1764 to 1772 a lucrative trade might have been forced with the Spaniards, had it not been for the ridiculous restrictions of the Custom House here and the want of a civil Government there'.[151] Though good statistical data describing the trade remain elusive, it is likely that during most years sales of British goods to the neighbouring Spanish colonies through the Bay of Honduras did not exceed a few thousands of pounds' value.[152]

Trade out of the lesser British colonies seems to have remained modest before the American Revolutionary War. The Bahamas undoubtedly traded to a considerable extent, especially with Cuba, but were far from occupying the major position they would come to enjoy in the following decade. The occupation of the Turks islands in 1766 caused the Spanish ambassador in London brief concern, but the islands never became the 'considerable place of trade' and rival to Monte Christi which he feared.[153] The once major centre of Barbados, meanwhile, engaged in little Spanish trade beyond the supply of slaves to the Spanish Asiento company. Prospects at Tobago, acquired by Britain in 1763 and settled by 1771, appeared better, since the island was adjacent to Trinidad and became the British possession closest to Cumaná and eastern Venezuela. It seems, however, that no significant trade developed at Tobago, possibly due to the handicaps of slow settlement and repeated slave revolts in the early 1770s. Although Spanish launches visited the coasts, it was for wood, water, and in the hope of taking off runaway slaves rather than for purposes of trade.[154] Perhaps the most significant of the lesser centres was Grenada, which welcomed several small craft from Mexico within months of its acquisition by Britain in 1763.[155] Robert Melville, who arrived as governor of the Ceded Islands in 1765, engaged in ritual hand-wringing over the scale of contraband trade in Grenada, Dominica and St Vincent. The governor himself provoked a minor diplomatic incident in 1768 when three British vessels were captured smuggling in Venezuela with permits bearing his signature.[156] Despite various setbacks, by 1776 Grenada's exports were worth some £600,000 sterling, placing it second only to Jamaica, and its prospects were considered good.[157] Nevertheless, the island's governors, including Melville in the 1760s and Macartney in the 1770s, emphasised that the island's illicit trade was principally with the neighbouring French and Dutch islands. Grenada's role as a major entrepôt for trade with the Spaniards would wait upon the grant of free status to the port of St George's in 1787.

The View from the Spanish Colonies

Perhaps the leading Spanish-American centre for Anglo-Spanish commerce between the Peace of Paris and the American Revolutionary War was Cuba. Cuba now began a period of heady economic growth which, with its proximity to Jamaica, the Bahamas, and North America, made it a natural hot spot for the trade. The British had evacuated the island in July 1763, but the direct commercial relations established during the war persisted for several years thereafter. The Treaty of Paris granted British merchants eighteen months in which to settle their affairs, and fourteen remained in Havana after the handover. These merchants continued to despatch goods locally, to the value of perhaps 237,000 pesos in fifteen months.[158] British trade statistics record direct exports to Cuba worth some £250,000 in 1763, slumping to around £6,000 annually in 1764–65 and to £1,500 in 1766. Imports of bullion from the island were worth some £390,000 in 1763, some £21,000 in 1764, and £47,000 in 1765.[159] This tail end trade was rarely profitable to the merchants engaged in it, however, and goods worth £80,000 were eventually lost altogether – neither sold in Havana nor returned to Britain.[160] Trade with the neighbouring British colonies was similarly officially sanctioned for some years due to a chronic shortage of basic supplies in the island. The Cuban authorities licensed repeated voyages to Jamaica in 1764–65 for foodstuffs, and permitted the entry to Havana and Santiago of foreign shipping, including British, with supplies.[161] The British merchant Cornelius Coppinger was among those licensed to supply foodstuffs by the post-war Captain-General, the Conde de Ricla, with such permits authorised by royal decree in April 1767.[162] Ricla oversaw the immense programme of fortifications undertaken at Havana after the war, and was again obliged to turn to Anglo-American merchants for requisite supplies. In 1765 he signed a contract with Alexander Monroe for the supply of hundreds of thousands of bricks from North America; Monroe's vessels imported foodstuffs, alcohol, and textiles in addition to their legitimate cargoes, and at least one of them was seized and confiscated for contraband.[163]

In March 1766, a new governor, Antonio Bucarely, summarily expelled foreign shipping from Havana, including eleven British vessels loaded with bricks and flour, and ejected most foreign merchants from the city.[164] The evidence for contraband in Cuba during the following years nevertheless remains abundant. The first Intendant of the island investigated 126 cases of contraband during 1765–73, while his successor, overwhelmed by the number of cases reaching the courts, proposed a general pardon for those convicted of smuggling.[165] In two months in 1771 a Spanish squadron captured twenty British and Spanish vessels engaged in smuggling and logging along the south coast, while in 1776 fifteen small Spanish craft were taken while trading primarily with Jamaica.[166] In a valuable report dated February 1768, the treasury official Joseph de Abalos stated that 'all Havana' was complicit in contraband, with imports engrossed by ten or a dozen leading traders devoted exclusively to this activity. Profits might reach 40 per cent on contraband exports of bullion, and 75 per cent on hides, livestock and wood. Earnings on foreign imports were around 30 per cent, and the total value of illicit trade was some 700,000 pesos per year (trade at this time at least as much with French St Domingue as with Jamaica).[167] Although Cubans certainly now undertook the majority of the trade, the island also remained, like Louisiana, an important centre for British smuggling. British smugglers often combined their activities with logging of the mahogany and other precious woods for which Cuba was renowned, establishing numerous logging camps along the coast.[168] Some scholars have played down the scale of contraband in Havana in the 1770s and 1780s, and indeed it may be that the sheer number of cases recorded tends to obscure the fact that most were petty affairs, of negligible individual value compared with the rich contraband cargoes which flooded in to Havana from the mid-1790s.[169] If still relatively limited in absolute terms, however, it seems likely that contraband was now expanding rapidly in line with the Cuban economy at large, and was already endemic throughout much of the island.

Mexico seems to have been much less important as a centre for British smuggling; most observers agree that British contraband on the Mexican coasts remained limited until the late 1790s, its development hindered by the region's geography and perhaps by closer administrative control.[170] The authorities at Veracruz fended off repeated overtures for trade from the British, especially from West Florida, though British ships continued to enter the port occasionally on different pretexts.[171] Nevertheless, British smugglers were captured sporadically at lesser ports along the coast, while one estimate put the total value of contraband undertaken on the Tampico River by British, French and Catalan merchants as high as 1,000,000 pesos in the period 1765–76.[172] Meanwhile, the activity of Spanish merchants trading out of Mexico with Jamaica and the Bahamas may have been under-estimated. By whatever route, Madrid's Royal Economic Society estimated that foreigners supplied three-quarters of total Mexican imports during the period of the American Revolutionary War.[173] The principal centre for British contraband in the viceroyalty was probably the Yucatán peninsula and the Audiencia of Guatemala, where an accessible coast, sparse population, and limited legal trade fomented smuggling by British and Spaniards alike. In 1765 the governor of Mérida was imprisoned for excessive hospitality toward British visitors, while a report dated 1770 stated that thousands of Spaniards worked cutting logwood in Yucatán solely to supply British buyers. Thomas Southwell further asserted that no merchant in the province sent money to Spain willingly; all remissions went via Yucatán and Honduras to London and Amsterdam, 'to receive the returns via the same route'.[174] In 1770 Captain John Jackson, who had already made a trip from Florida to Veracruz earlier the same year, was despatched from Jamaica to the Guatemalan coast in the *Druid* after a leading Jamaican house reported receiving encouragement to trade from 'many of the most considerable merchants of Carthago'. Jackson's actions were disowned by a cautious Admiralty.[175]

A further major theatre for illicit trade was the Audiencia of Santa Fé in the viceroyalty of New Granada (broadly corresponding to modern Colombia). Studies of British trade in this region have focused on the activities of British smugglers, though it is to be stressed that local Spaniards probably already undertook the bulk of all contraband trade, and also that foreign smuggling there was still as likely to be French or (especially) Dutch as British. McFarlane suggests that contraband channels through the great port of Cartagena de Indias were 'wide open during the 1760s and 1770s', facilitated by the laxity of local officials and by permits for the slave trade.[176] A report of 1774 confirmed that 'the large quantities of gold in bars and dust which are exported from that Kingdom abroad, are shipped with those traders, by the residents of Mompós, and Cartagena'. Contraband was similarly rife in the region to the west of Cartagena and as far as Portobelo, while the Isthmus of Panama itself remained a principal focus for illegal trade in goods destined both for New Granada and the viceroyalty of Peru.[177] Perhaps more significant still were the eastern provinces of Santa Marta and Río de la Hacha, where contraband was fomented by official neglect, a propitious coast, and the perennial lawlessness of the Guajira Peninsula. At three principal landings between Cape de la Vela and the mouth of the Magdalena river, illicit trade went on uninterrupted under the passive gaze of royal guards.[178] The noted Governor of Santa Marta, Antonio Narváez y de la Torre, wrote in 1778 that the absence of legal commerce meant that trade was almost exclusively with foreigners, based on the exchange of dyewood, livestock and hides for textiles and other goods. Narváez noted that young bulls worth 5 or 6 pesos might be sold for 40 or 50 pesos in Jamaica, adding that 'in the last war they were worth up to 80, and the English took off ... around 6,000'. He further observed that 'in whatever fashion the provision of Slaves has been organised in these times, almost all their value has gone to the English in common coin'.[179] The shortcomings of the formal Spanish trading system prompted proposals for radical reform at this time: in mid-1773, Viceroy Guirior suggested that exports of surplus produce be permitted to foreign colonies, first from Santa Marta, and then from the whole of the viceroyalty.[180] In 1778 Narváez's plans for the regeneration of Santa Marta similarly centred upon the exchange of local produce for slaves from the foreign colonies. But neither proposal prospered with a Spanish government yet determined to preserve the structures of its ancient commercial monopoly.

A last great focus for contraband was the Intendancy of Venezuela, comprising Caracas and the neighbouring provinces. Again, Spaniards undertook the greater part of the trade in the region; thus, an investigation by Governor Marqués de la Torre in 1771 suggested that 'great part' of the inhabitants of Caracas were 'actively or passively' involved in smuggling. De la Torre took the unusual step of issuing a general pardon for smugglers, and by mid-October 157 individuals had accepted it, paying over 19,000 pesos in penalties.[181] The governor further remarked that foreign smugglers landed on the Venezuelan coast 'with equal security, and freedom, as if in the settlements of their own dominions', while in 1776 his counterpart in Maracaibo arrived to find 'illicit trade so open, that the goods were sold publicly in the streets'.[182] In 1773 a later governor produced data which suggested that while legal exports of hides by the Caracas Company ran at less than 8,000 units per year, illicit exports had been running at over 90,000 per year for a decade.[183] Again, in 1776, it was estimated that 95 per cent of the 500,000 pesos annual income of the lucrative cacao trade with Mexico was lost abroad.[184] Possibly the most important region in Venezuela for illicit trade with the British was the east and especially the provinces of Cumaná and Guayana. Contraband entered this region via the Orinoco and Guarapiche rivers, a trade described in picturesque terms by an observer claiming long residence in Trinidad and extensive experience of local trade:

To the banks of the Guaratipiche [*sic*] resorted formerly the different merchants of Sta. Fe and even of Peru with cargoes of money ingots of gold and other rich & valuable effects to buy up such European manufactures as were brought to them by English and French adventurers; they returned in armed troops thro' vast plains and savannahs with large caravans in spite of every impediment thrown in their way by the different Governors and Intendants.[185]

In 1773, Fray Iñigo Abbad stated that foreigners took off most of Cumaná's cacao crop (20,000 *fánegas* per year), tobacco (40,000 *arrobas*), wood, livestock, an unknown number of hides, and small quantities of coffee, cotton, indigo, drugs and medicinal oils.[186] In the same year it was reported that contraband exports of livestock from Cumaná were on such a scale as to have created a secondary rustling industry which had ruined the ranches of the province and whose effects were felt as far away as the *llanos* of Caracas.[187] By contrast, at this time British trade with the island of Trinidad a short distance to the east remained very limited. In 1776 there began the important programme of reforms which would quintuple the population of Trinidad by 1797 and greatly diversify its external trading relations. But for the moment the island's population remained very low (fewer than 3,500 inhabitants in 1777, of whom well over half were Indians) and its surplus wealth negligible. There was some low-level intercourse – in the latter year a pair of Spanish launches was captured loaded with cattle and horses for Grenada – but not as yet of any significance.[188]

The final region to be discussed is the greater Antilles, comprising the island of Puerto Rico and Santo Domingo – the Spanish part of Hispaniola. These were relatively poor territories with more modest foreign trade, and they appear to have trafficked less with the British than did other regions. Some trade there certainly was; in 1773 it was reported that British contraband in Puerto Rico was based upon the barter of merchandise for dyewoods, pepper, mules and other goods. Livestock exports appear to have been most important, Reynal commenting on the large numbers of 'good mules, though small' which were smuggled to Jamaica, St Croix and St Domingue. Known smugglers made frequent voyages between Puerto Rico and the British and Danish Virgin Islands; in 1773 fifteen vessels were captured smuggling off the south coast, and in 1774 nineteen vessels and a dozen launches were taken in a single trip. Observers both within and outside the island agreed that military subsidies (*situados*) worth hundreds of thousands of pesos per year went directly to fuel contraband with the British, Dutch, French and Danes.[189] Throughout the 1770s allegations of the participation of the island authorities in contraband were commonplace, Governor Miguel de Muesas remarking in 1770 that 'even the very lieutenants of war and urban militia officers … were the chief collaborators, opening the ports and permitting trade in all sorts of animals, produce and woods in foreign ships under hidden pacts and payments'.[190] De Muesas issued extensive regulations in the same year to island officials, among the principal aims of which was the eradication of 'illicit trade in all kinds of animals and fruits of the country'.[191]

Angel López Cantos has analysed trade between Puerto Rico and the neighbouring foreign colonies during this period, apparently under permits from the island governors. His study scarcely addresses contraband as such, but it may be suggestive of the basic characteristics of the trade. According to López Cantos's figures, the British West Indies accounted for less than 2 per cent of the total of shipping involved in the trade, and less than 1.1 per cent of its value (British North America accounted for 0.8 per cent and 1.2 per cent respectively). The Danish colonies, by contrast, accounted for 24 per cent of shipping and 20 per cent of the value of goods – emphasising that Puerto Rico traded far more extensively with the Danes and Dutch than with the British.[192] British colonies mentioned as trading partners include Antigua, Barbados, Bermuda, St Kitts, and the Turk Islands, and these were probably also the leading protagonists in contraband trade; it may be significant that neither Jamaica nor Grenada features in the list. The situation in Santo Domingo appears to have been a comparable one, of a high level of smuggling within the context of a generally poor economy, frequent petty contraband exchange with the British, especially with the Virgin Islands, but with smuggling dominated by the Danes, Dutch, and French.[193]

One branch of trade which affected the whole of the Caribbean was that in African slaves, which now reached new heights of volume and value. The British continued to dominate the supply of slaves to the Spanish colonies throughout this period. Cuba played a leading role in the trade, both as a large and growing market for slaves itself and as a centre for redistribution to other territories. In 1763, the Conde de Ricla signed a contract ostensibly with the Royal Havana Company for the importation of slaves to Cuba. Behind this contract was a group of British merchants, including the ubiquitous Cornelius Coppinger, which acquired the slaves direct from Africa and supplied them to Cuba via Jamaica and Barbados. In 1765 Ricla signed a further contract with Coppinger and David Rieuset to run for three years, covering imports of thousands more slaves and flour to feed them. Under the first contract the British supplied the Havana Company with 5,037 black men, women and children, and under the second with a further 1,987. The latter contract was disavowed by a Spanish government anxious 'to prevent British trade from taking root in these regions', concerns which contributed toward a further general shake-up in the Spanish organisation of the trade.[194] In 1765 a new Asiento for the supply of slaves was signed with a company of wealthy peninsular merchants based in Cadiz and led by Miguel de Iriarte, with the Marqués de Enrile as its president. This *Real Asiento* Company was to return the whole of the trade to Spanish hands, from Africa to the colonies, supplying 3,500 slaves per year to a base in Puerto Rico, whence they were to be distributed throughout the colonies in lesser vessels owned and manned by Spaniards. Nikolaus Böttcher has suggested that from the outset the Cadiz company represented 'not even a compromise', since it purchased slaves from British merchant houses through agents in Havana.[195] We have seen that slaves were supplied to Puerto Rico from Dominica during this period, and assuredly from other British colonies also. Certainly Spanish merchants proved unable to manage the supply of slaves from Africa, and by 1772 the Company experienced a severe crisis whose major consequences were transfer of the base of operations from Puerto Rico to Havana and the permission to source slaves from any of the neighbouring foreign colonies. From Havana the Company now 'in chartered vessels brings Negroes from the Islands of Jamaica, Barbados, or St Eustatius ... Its expeditions are frequent, and not at all expensive. It sends money from Havana, in hard pesos ... Returns are very quick.'[196]

We have seen that exports of slaves from Jamaica jumped markedly in 1773–74, and from 1773 to 1779 some 13,747 slaves were supplied to Cuba from Jamaica, other British colonies, and North America.[197] Contraband trade between Puerto Príncipe and Bayamo and Jamaica and St Domingue was such that from 1769 plans were mooted for some formal framework for the trade, perhaps based around legal exports of livestock in exchange.[198] In 1779 the Real Asiento Company's contract expired and was not renewed, leading to a further major reorganisation in the Spanish organisation of the trade (discussed in the following chapter).

One final route via which Britain traded with the Spanish colonies, a route moreover which represented something of a case apart, was through her colonies in North America. As will be seen, in later years and especially after 1796 the shipment of British manufactured goods to Spanish America via the United States in exchange for bullion occurred on a large scale. During this earlier period, by contrast, the route appears to have been of negligible significance. It is true that North American trade with the West Indies, both British and foreign, was growing throughout these years, based especially upon the exchange of agricultural produce and foodstuffs for sugar and molasses. But most American trade with the region was still limited to the British West Indies; in 1763, for example, the value of North American exports to the British colonies was some £600,000, while exports to all the foreign colonies together were worth only slightly more than 10 per cent of that sum.[199] Again, most of this (illicit) trade with other colonies went to the French sugar islands; although American trade with the Spanish colonies has been little studied for this period, it appears to have been modest.[200] Thus, American trade with Cuba (a key partner in later years) is described for the period before the Revolution as 'sporadic, often indirect, and seldom of any duration'.[201] And what trade with Spanish America did occur was based upon the export of agricultural produce, flour, fish, and wood rather than manufactured goods. Certainly, such trade generally brought returns in bullion (sugar or other plantation produce such as indigo also featured), and this bullion might then go toward payment of the North American trade deficit with Britain. There is also evidence that even at this early period, Spaniards shipped their profits back to Spain via North America so as to avoid the payment of duties.[202] Nevertheless, its limited overall scale and the nature of the exchange on which it was based appear to rule out North American trade as an important vehicle for British commerce with Spanish America before the American Revolution.

The American Revolutionary War: Short-Term Disruption, Long-Term Catalyst

The American Revolution and the war which accompanied it (1776–83) dealt a heavy blow to British power in the Americas, though in commercial terms the reverse would prove remarkably short-lived. France joined the conflict in 1778, and Spain in June 1779, partly citing ongoing British violations of Spanish territory in the Bay of Honduras.[203] Between 1778 and 1782, the French stormed the Lesser Antilles, seizing Dominica, St Vincent, Grenada, St Kitts and Tobago. The Spanish largely expelled the British from Honduras and the Mosquito Shore in 1779–80, and conquered Florida and New Providence in the Bahamas in 1780–81, so that by early 1782, in the Caribbean Britain retained only Jamaica, Antigua, and Barbados. Throughout the British West Indies the war caused severe economic hardship, principally because it substantially dislocated the crucial North American trade.[204] The war's impact on the Spanish trade, meanwhile, has been poorly researched and is harder to assess. It has been argued that a prime Spanish war aim was the extirpation of British contraband in the Gulf of Mexico and on the Mississippi.[205] From the outset, all trade with the British was banned throughout the Spanish colonies, while Cuban corsairs – the more formidable for their detailed knowledge of the Jamaican coast, acquired as smugglers during peace-time – harried the British.[206] For their part, the British contemplated seeking redress in the south for their losses in the north, one ambassador arguing:

> Let our fleets and armies evacuate North America, fall upon St Domingo, Martinico, Cuba, and force a free trade in the Gulph of Mexico, the straight road to the gold and silver mines, the sugar islands, and the revolt of the Spanish settlements ... Our Presbyterian Colonies will be more than compensated for.[207]

Spanish launches trading at Tobago were impounded at the outbreak of the war, the British Virgin Islands entered on a 'golden age' of corsairing, and the Royal Navy assaulted enemy shipping throughout the Caribbean.[208] It is true that there is evidence that the Navy limited its attacks on Spanish vessels trading with the free ports, while the Governors of Antigua and Tobago reached an accord with their counterpart in Caracas prohibiting corsair attacks on their respective coasts.[209] That some contraband trade subsisted between Jamaica and Cuba is evidenced by among the most celebrated single cases of smuggling in all Spanish-American history, one that involved the future revolutionary and *precursor* Francisco de Miranda (and which first made him a renegade from Spanish justice).[210] Nevertheless, it appears that Armytage's conclusion, that the American Revolutionary War for several years 'damaged' or even 'crippled' the free port trade, is substantially correct. The number of ships entering Jamaican free ports halved in 1778, and totalled just thirty-five in 1781, most of them Danish and Dutch vessels.[211] Dominica's trade collapsed at the outset of hostilities, and when the island was captured in 1778 its Free Port Act 'was suffered to expire' and was not renewed when the island was returned to Britain at the Peace.[212] Other British losses, especially of Florida and Grenada, momentarily closed the fresh commercial avenues which had opened in 1763. The British slave trade in the Caribbean, too, largely collapsed, provoking a chronic shortage of slaves in Cuba and elsewhere.

The commercial vacuum left by the crisis in trade with the British was filled by the merchants of nations allied or neutral to Spain, above all from the United States. The British naval blockade brought about a subsistence crisis in the Spanish colonies which could only be alleviated by recourse to neutrals, and after 1779 most of the colonies were opened to extensive neutral trade for the first time, in what was by far the most significant long-term commercial consequence of the war in Spanish America. Cuba was paradigmatic in this sense: Cuban ports were thrown open to neutral trade, first by order of the island authorities and then by formal royal decree. This trade was expressly limited to the supply of foodstuffs, especially of flour, but it inevitably gave rise to extensive contraband imports, and close commercial relations between Cuba and the United States date from this period.[213] In 1781–83 most of the other colonies were opened to trade with neutrals or with allied foreign colonies, while special permission was granted to procure slaves from the French colonies for the duration of the war.[214] Different ports in New Granada welcomed mercantile expeditions from the French, Dutch and Danish islands, while regular shipments were made from Venezuela to Martinique of livestock in return for cash.[215] Neutral and allied trade rapidly became very valuable: Francisco de Saavedra put the total value of contraband imports at Havana in the first three years of the war at over 4,000,000 pesos, and also suggested in 1781 that 70 per cent of imports of European goods to Caracas came as contraband.[216] Elsewhere it was stated that during the war the French drew 400,000 pesos from Caracas and Cumaná 'for different kinds of manufactures, they used formerly to receive from the Dutch and English'.[217] In the short term, this shift of trade toward neutrals and other foreign colonies injured British interests and contributed powerfully to the commercial crisis at the free ports. The precedent which neutral trade established in the Spanish empire during the war would not easily be forgotten, however; and in the years to come, both neutral trade and that with foreign colonies would themselves become vehicles of the first importance for British commercial intercourse with Spanish America.

Notes

1   On this controversy see Grant, 'Canada versus Guadeloupe', *passim.*

2   On the terms of the treaty, see Ward, 'The British West Indies', p. 418; Temperley, 'Peace of Paris', pp. 496, 502. Its most significant aspect in the long run, of course, was Britain's acquisition of the whole of Canada, and with it the liquidation of the French empire in North America.

3   *Philosophical and Political History*, 3:103.

4   Christelow, 'Contraband Trade', pp. 315–16, 333–4; also Armytage, *Free Port System*, pp. 36–7.

5   'Governor Johnstone's Account of West Florida', *Gentleman's Magazine*, Feb. 1765, pp. 75–7; see also Howard, *British Development of West Florida*, pp. 17–18; Born, 'British Trade in West Florida', pp. 16–17.

6   Miguel de Altarriba to Julián de Arriaga, Havana, 8 Mar. 1765, A.G.I., Santo Domingo, 2188.

7   The outstanding study of the Free Port system remains that of Frances Armytage. Though superseded in many aspects, this work is still indispensable especially for the early years.

8   4 Geo. 3 cap. 15; Beer, *British Colonial Policy*, pp. 276–84.

9   The Stamp Act crisis may be approached through Morgan and Morgan, *Stamp Act Crisis*, and the more recent Thomas, *British Politics*; for its repercussions in the West Indies see Spindel, 'Stamp Act Crisis'.

10 For a detailed account of this obsessive campaign, see Bullion, *Great and Necessary Measure*, esp. chaps. 3–4. Bullion is silent on the application of the campaign in the West Indies, however.

11 3 Geo. 3 c.22: 'An Act for the further encouragement of His Majesty's revenues and customs, and for the prevention of the clandestine running of goods …'; Beer, *British Colonial Policy*, p. 229.

12 For the text of Egremont's order see Egremont to Horatio Sharpe, Whitehall, 9 July 1763, in Sharpe, *Correspondence*, 3:102–3.

13 See the orders dated 4 Jan. and 27 Mar. 1764 in N.A., C.O. 137 / 61, ff. 233–4, 235, 243–v; and Lyttleton to Lords of Trade, Jamaica, 2 Apr. 1764, N.A., C.O. 137 / 33, ff. 131–2.

14 See also J. Robarts, 'Observations upon the Trade in General, and upon the Trade with the Spanish West Indies in particular', 2nd part, n.p., 1766?, S.R.O., D. (W.) 1778, II, no. 2113; Christelow, 'Contraband Trade', p. 320. There has been some confusion between this 'hovering clause' and the Hovering Act proper.

15 Extract of a letter to Thomas Gray, Kingston, Jamaica, 1 Feb. 1764, S.A., W.W.M., R.1 / 517c; see also Aaron Bauch Lousada to Daniel Bauch Lousada, Jamaica, 8 Mar. 1764, S.A., W.W.M., R.1 / 517a.

16 Extract, no evidence of correspondents, Jamaica, 7 Apr. 1764, S.A., W.W.M., R.1 / 517c.

17 *Gentleman's Magazine*, July 1764, p. 337; partly published in Romano, *Moneda, seudomonedas*, p. 68.

18 Extract, George Johnstone to John Pownall, Kingston, 25 Sept. 1764, S.R.O., D. (W.) 1778, II, no. 53; Johnstone to Commissioners of Customs, n.p., 15 July 1765, in 'Letters received at the Treasury, relative to Bullion …', S.A., W.W.M., R.34 / 2.

19 Extract, letter from John Rhea, Philadelphia, 11 Oct. 1765, encl. to Dennys de Berdt to Lord Dartmouth, n.p., 3 Dec. 1765, S.R.O., D. (W.) 1778, II, no. 119.

20 Testimony of William Kelly to Parliament, London, 12 Feb. 1766, B.L., Add. Mss. 33,030, ff. 130–9v.

21 Christelow, 'Contraband Trade', see esp. pp. 320, 323, 328–9.

22   Edwards, *History, Civil and Commercial*, 1:238.

23   *Gentleman's Magazine*, July 1764, p. 337; and comment by Lord Holland, 29 Oct. 1765, in Thomas, *British Politics*, p. 255.

24   'Account of Bullion imported from North America from 1748 to 1765', S.A., W.W.M., R. 34 / 5b. The respective figures are £156,390 (1763) and £116,760 (1765).

25   Bourgoing, *Tableau de l'Espagne*, 2:171; Humboldt, *Ensayo político sobre … la Nueva España*, p. 511. Rodríguez Casado's calculation of the total value of foreign contraband in Spanish America in 1765 as 12,000,000 pesos is more moderate, but his methodology is dubious; 'Comentarios al Decreto', p. 112.

26   Robarts, 'Observations upon the Trade in General', 2nd part, S.R.O., D. (W.) 1778, II, no. 2113.

27   See p. 30 above.

28   'Imports of goods have been most abundant, so that it is impossible they should be consumed here in many years'; Francisco López de Gamarra to Arriaga, Havana, 21 Apr. 1763, in Marrero, *Cuba*, 12:5–7.

29   Untitled interrogatory, n.p., marked 1763 but certainly Jan. 1766, B.L., Add. Mss. 38,373, ff. 130–1v; parallel papers in B.L., Add. Mss. 38,339, ff. 225–8.

30   Note that Christelow's article was written before the important papers now in the Sheffield Archives and Staffordshire Record Office were widely known.

31   'Here let me pause and wonder – That these profound Adepts in the knowledge of Trade and Commerce, these Grey-beards, & very *Nestors* in years & experience, did not … foresee (& the most favourable construction for them is to suppose them blind and ignorant) that they were laying the sharp axe to the root of the Spanish intercourse'; Robarts, 'Observations upon the trade in general', 2nd part, n.p., 1766 or 1767, S.R.O., D. (W.) 1778, II, no. 2113.

32   Walpole, *Memoirs of the Reign of George III*, 2:277–81, reporting a debate in the House on 3 Feb. 1766.

33   Evidence of Beeston Long, London, 17 Feb. 1766, B.L., Add. Mss. 33,030, ff. 190–5.

34   Halifax to Lords of Trade, St James, 12 May 1764, N.A., C.O. 137 / 33, f. 108.

35   Christelow, 'Contraband Trade', pp. 322–3; Armytage, *Free Port System*, p. 25; Langford, *First Rockingham Administration*, p. 113; Johnson, *British West Florida*, pp. 43–5.

36   Letter dated Kingston, 23 July 1764, in *Annual Register*, 1764, p. 107.

37   Jared Ingersoll to Godfrey Malbone, London, 7 Apr. 1765, in Ingersoll, *Selection from the Correspondence*, p. 323.

38   Evidence of Robert Hamilton, London, 13 Feb. 1766, B.L., Add. Mss. 33,030, ff. 153v–60v.

39   Evidence of Robert Dawson, London, 12 Feb. 1766, B.L., Add. Mss. 33,030, ff. 141–3v.

40   'T.M.' to Editor, West-Riding, Yorkshire, 21 Dec. 1765, in *Gentleman's Magazine*, Dec. 1765, p. 567.

41   Letter dated Rufford, 1 Nov. 1765, in Keppel, *Memoirs of the Marquis of Rockingham*, 1:252–3.

42   Sutherland, 'Edmund Burke', pp. 63–5; Armytage, *Free Port System*, pp. 29–30.

43   'We have not been able to prevail on them to return'; 'There has not a Spaniard yet ventured to come here to buy goods'; extracts, no evidence of correspondents, 30 Jan. and 10 May 1765, both in S.A., W.W.M., R.1 / 517c.

44   'Considerations on the laws made for the increase of Navigation and for Regulation of the Plantation Trade, so far as they relate to the bullion trade'; 'Memoire on the Treaties with Spain'; and 'Proposals', in B.L., Add. Mss. 35,911, ff. 109–15v, 91–8v,

79–83v respectively; there are further copies of each paper in B.L., Add. Mss. 33,030, and in S.A., W.W.M., R.34. Armytage, *Free Port System*, pp. 31–3, offers the principal secondary account of the papers; Christelow, 'Contraband Trade', pp. 324–7, also discusses them but appears to mis-attribute them to the crown Law Officers Yorke and de Grey.

45 Anon., 'Observations on the commerce of our colonies with those of Spain, so far as regards the legality of the importation of bullion in foreign bottoms', n.p., n.d., S.R.O., D. (W.) 1778, II, 136a; further copy in B.L., Add. Mss. 35,911, ff. 116–27.

46 Yorke to Rockingham, Tittenhanger, 25 Oct. 1765, S.A., W.W.M., R.1 / 515; similar sentiment in Newcastle to Rockingham, Claremont, 22 Oct. 1764, S.A., W.W.M., R.1 / 511. The three papers are also discussed in Lord Northington to Rockingham, Grainge, 23 Oct. 1765, S.A., W.W.M., R.1 / 513.

47 Rockingham to Yorke, 24 Oct. 1765, cited in Langford, *First Rockingham Administration*, p. 115.

48 Armytage, *Free Port System*, p. 33, citing Treasury Minute, 30 Oct. 1765, N.A., T. 29 / 37.

49 'Copy of the Attorney & Solicitor General's opinion', 11 Nov. 1765, B.L., Add. Mss. 35,911, ff. 88–9v; copies of the Treasury Minute of 13 Nov. 1765 in 'Copy of the Attorney ...', ff. 73–4, and N.A., T.29 / 37, f. 115.

50 The orders were despatched to the West Indies and America on 16 Nov. 1765.

51 Langford, *First Rockingham Administration*, pp. 114, 116–17; Thomas, *British Politics*, pp. 255–6.

52 Thomas, *British Politics*, pp. 257–9; Christelow, 'Contraband Trade', pp. 330–3.

53 Some, though not all, of these interviews are in B.L., Add. Mss. 33,030, ff. 130ff., dated Feb. 1766.

54 Langford, *First Rockingham Administration*, p. 200.

55 For the shift of public opinion at this time away from the West India and in favour of the North America merchants, see e.g. 'A Short Sketch of the Transactions that led to the new Regulations of Commerce ...', *Gentleman's Magazine*, May 1766, pp. 228–31.

56 'Minutes of Meeting of West Indian and North American Merchants', King's Arms Tavern, London, 10 Mar. 1766, published in Penson, *Colonial Agents of the British West Indies*, pp. 284–5.

57 Thomas, *British Politics*, p. 261.

58 See Allen, 'British Commercial Policy', p. 137.

59 Burke to Charles O'Hara, 23, 24 Apr. 1766, in *Correspondence*, 1:251–2, with the useful editor's note.

60 Walpole, *Memoirs of the Reign of George III*, 2:316–17, describing a debate 'a few days after' 22 Apr. 1766. Beckford's opposition to Grenville in this passage appears anomalous.

61 Masserano to Grimaldi, London, 15 Apr. 1766, A.H.N., Estado, 4271.

62 Walpole, *Memoirs of the Reign of George III*, 2:316–17.

63 'Agreement of the West Indian Committee', House of Commons, London, 8 May 1766, published in Sutherland, 'Edmund Burke', p. 71; important secondary commentary in Thomas, *British Politics*, pp. 269–72.

64 See e.g. *Debates and Proceedings*, 7:156–7. There is some dispute about the exact dates.

65 Thomas Nuthall to Pitt, Crosby Square, London, 8 May 1766, in Pitt, *Correspondence*, 2:417–9.

66 Quoted in Armytage, *Free Port System*, p. 41.

67 John Yorke to Hardwicke, 19 May 1766, quoted in Langford, *First Rockingham Administration*, p. 207.

68   *Annual Register*, 1766, p. 47.

69   Francis Gildart to Dartmouth, Liverpool, 6 July 1766, S.R.O., D. (W.) 1778, II, no. 2225.

70   6 Geo. 3 cap. 49. Major secondary descriptions of the Act's provisions include Armytage, *Free Port System*, pp. 42–3; Christelow, 'Contraband Trade', pp. 337–9; and Ragatz, *Fall of the Planter Class*, pp. 138–41.

71   Manning, *British Colonial Government*, pp. 275–6.

72   Young, *West-India Common-Place Book*, pp. 171–3.

73   Dauxion Lavaysse, *Voyage aux Iles de Trinidad*, 2:423.

74   'In the case of Jamaica it is conceived that cotton was the great object in view'; Sir Philip Musgrave to Earl of Dartmouth?, 'Memorandum relative to the Free Port Act of Jamaica', n.p., n.d. (late 1773?), S.R.O., D. (W.) 1778, II, no. 2160. Allen also emphasizes the importance of cotton: 'British Commercial Policy', pp. 134–5. For the slave trade, see Bryan Edwards, *History, Civil and Commercial*, 1:241–2.

75   *West-India Common-Place Book*, p. 177.

76   'Observations on the trade carried on between the British West Indies and the Spanish colonies …', possibly by Thomas Irving, 1785 or 1786, B.L., Add. Mss. 38,345, ff. 208–13v.

77   *First Rockingham Administration*, p. 207. François Crouzet takes a rather more sceptical view, of the Free Ports as 'not … a liberal measure … but rather a particularly refined form of mercantilism, adopted by a country which had secured for itself industrial supremacy'; *L'Economie britannique*, pp. 157–8.

78   Ellotson to Shelburne, Jamaica, 31 Oct. 1767, cited in Ragatz, *Fall of the Planter Class*, pp. 121–2.

79   Cited in Burnard, '"Prodigious Riches"', pp. 511–12.

80   John Dalling, tract on the Spanish trade, n.p., n.d., encl. to Dalling to Dartmouth, Jamaica, 11 Apr. 1773, N.A., C.O. 137 / 68, ff. 63–671.

81   Rodney to Stephens, London, 1 Oct. 1774, N.A., ADM. 1 / 239, n.f ; 'Queries relative to the state of His Majesty's island of Jamaica', 1774, N.A., C.O. 137 / 70, ff. 88–98v.

82   Saavedra, *Journal*, pp. 84–6.

83   Long, *History of Jamaica*, 1:500, 506–7; Edwards, *History, Civil and Commercial*, 1:239–40.

84   Allen, 'British Commercial Policy', pp. 143–4; Burnard, '"Prodigious Riches"', pp. 511–12; Penson, too, regarded the impact of the Free Port Act as 'negligible' ('The West Indies', p. 345).

85   Armytage, *Free Port System*, pp. 47–8; Williams, 'Mercados británicos', p. 97.

86   Decree of 16 Oct. 1765, published in Levene, *Documentos para la historia argentina*, 5:434–40; secondary discussion in Fisher, *Commercial Relations*, pp. 9, 13–14.

87   Ramos, *Contrabando inglés*, p. 181; Stein and Stein, *Apogee of Empire*, p. 352.

88   Rochford to Halifax, Aranjuez, 7 May 1764, N.A., S.P. 94 / 167, ff. 7–8v; Rochford to Conway, Escorial, 28 Oct. 1765, also Conway to Rochford, St James's, London, 27 Nov. 1765, latter two in N.A., S.P. 94 / 172, ff. 89–90, 126–30; and Christelow, 'Great Britain and the Trades', pp. 15–17. See also the sanguine reaction of the contemporary British historian William Robertson, in Stein and Stein, *Apogee of Empire*, p. 79.

89   Saavedra, *Journal*, pp. 83–4.

90   See e.g. the complaint of the Cadiz merchant guild, Feb. 1777, in Kuethe, 'Fin del monopolio', p. 63; also Marrero, *Cuba*, 12:16–19, 28–30.

91   Knox, *Historical Account*, pp. 87, 99; Westergaard, *Danish West Indies*, p. 250; Dubuisson and Dubucq, *Lettres critiques et politiques*, pp. 112–14.

92 'Further Considerations relative to the Free Ports', n.p., n.d. [late 1773?], S. R. O., D (W) II, no. 2161.

93 *Obras*, 1:74–6; see also especially Depons, *Travels in South America*, 2:59–60.

94 Christelow, 'Contraband Trade', pp. 340–2; also Pantaleão, *Penetracão comercial*, pp. 178–80; Ramos, *Contrabando inglés*, pp. 172–8.

95 John Dalling, tract on the Spanish trade, n.p., n.d., N.A., C.O. 137 / 68, ff. 63–71; the relevant passage is discussed in 'Considerations on the Free Port Act in Jamaica', n.d. [late 1773?], S.R.O., D (W) 1778, II, no. 2159; see Edwards, *History*, 1:239–40, which it is tempting to suppose is based on Dalling's report; Ryburn and Wilson to Maitland, Grenada, 28 Apr. 1806, N.A., C.O. 101 / 43, ff. 92–3v, and the account in Young, *West-India Common-Place Book*, pp. 171–3, may both be based on Edwards.

96 Rodney to Stephens, *Portland*, Port Royal Harbour, 12 Mar. 1774, and Rodney to Stephens, London, 1 Oct. 1774, both in N.A., ADM. 1 / 239, n.f.

97 Harris to Weymouth, Madrid, 7 Dec. 1769, N.A., S.P. 94 / 182, n.f.

98 Forrest to Philip Stephens, *Dunkirk*, Port Royal, 8 Oct. 1769, N.A., ADM. 1 / 238, n.f.

99 Cited in Brown, 'Anglo-Spanish Relations', pp. 451–60. Some half-dozen specific cases of seizures have been identified during these years; there may, of course, have been more.

100 Rodney to Stephens, London, 1 Oct. 1774, N.A., ADM. 1 / 239, n.f. On the incident at Havana see esp. the series of papers in A.H.N., Estado, 4269; Brown, 'Anglo-Spanish Relations', pp. 377–8.

101 Gray to Shelburne, San Ildefonso, 7 Aug. 1768, N.A., S.P. 94 / 180, n.f.

102 Relevant papers in A.G.I., Caracas, 81, 82.

103 Dookhan, 'Vieques or Crab Island', pp. 7–9; Torres Ramírez, 'Isla de Vieques', pp. 457–61.

104 Dalling to Earl of Dartmouth, Jamaica, 11 Apr. 1773, N.A., C.O. 137 / 68, ff. 61–2v.

105 Journals of the Assembly of Jamaica, Saturday 23 Oct. 1773, N.A., C.O. 140 / 46, f. 448.

106 Coffee planters of Jamaica to Dartmouth, n.p., n.d. [1772–73], N.A., C.O. 137 / 68, f. 83; see also Ragatz, *Fall of the Planter Class*, pp. 140–1; Armytage, *Free Port System*, pp. 46–7.

107 John Dalling, tract on the Spanish trade, n.p., n.d., N.A., C.O. 137 / 68, ff. 63–71.

108 'Considerations on the Free Port Act in Jamaica', n.d. [late 1773?], S.R.O., D (W) 1778, II, no. 2159; 'Memorandum relative to the Free Port Act', n.d. [late 1773?], S.R.O., D (W) 1778, II, no. 2160.

109 13 Geo. 3, cap. 73.

110 'Memorandum relative to the Free Port Act of Jamaica', n.d. [1773?], S.R.O., D (W) 1778, II, no. 2160; Pantaleão, *Penetraçao comercial*, pp. 169–74.

111 Rodney to Stephens, London, 1 Oct. 1774, P.R.O., ADM. 1 / 239, n.f.

112 *Journal*, pp. 84–86; for the participation of Jews see also p. 45.

113 *History, Civil and Commercial*, 1:243.

114 'Queries relative to the state of H.M.'s island of Jamaica ...', 1774, P.R.O., C.O. 137 / 70, ff. 88–98v.

115 Joseph de Abalos to Antonio María Bucarely, Havana, 17 Feb. 1768, in Marrero, *Cuba*, 12:28–30.

116 Bryan Edwards, 'Thoughts on the Spanish Assiento Contract', Jamaica, 20 Oct. 1773, S.R.O., D (W) 1778, II, no. 2135; see also *History, Civil and Commercial*, 1:242–3. The relevant Spanish decree, dated 1 May 1773, is in Levene, *Documentos*, 5:278–82. Edwards' wider proposals embraced the admission of Spanish vessels to *all* British West Indian ports, given certain precautions against smuggling.

117 14 Geo. 3, cap. 41, and 21 Geo. 3, cap. 29.
118 Poyer, *History of Barbados*, pp. 365–6; Schomburgk, *History of Barbados*, pp. 339–40; Dookhan, *History of the British Virgin Islands*, pp. 52–3; Armytage, *Free Port System*, p. 50.
119 Long, *History of Jamaica*, 1:496–503, 506.
120 Armytage, *Free Port System*, p. 50; Edwards, *History, Civil and Commercial*, 1:243.
121 William Walton to Lord Hawkesbury, Liverpool, 24 Feb. 1788, in Donnan, *Documents*, 2:575–7.
122 'Queries relative to the state of His Majesty's island of Jamaica', 1774, N.A., C.O. 137 / 70, ff. 88–98v; Burnard, '"Prodigious Riches"', pp. 511–12.
123 Ramos, *Contrabando inglés*, pp. 202–3.
124 Saavedra, *Journal*, pp. 83–6.
125 *Tableau de l'Espagne moderne*, 2:182–4.
126 London merchants to Crown, n.p., n.d. (late 1767?), N.A., C.O. 101 / 11, f. 278.
127 Christelow, 'Contraband Trade', pp. 340–2; Armytage, *Free Port System*, pp. 43–5.
128 *West-India Common-Place Book*, p. 180.
129 Atwood, *History of Dominica*, pp. 104–6; see also Jones, 'Historical Study', pp. 49–50.
130 Testimony of Kender Mason, in Committee Minutes regarding Free Ports in Dominica, Bermuda and Bahama, 14 Nov. 1786, N.A., C.O. 318 / 1, ff. 72v–4; see also 'Account of number of Slaves sold by Kender Mason and Company ... in the West Indies', n.p., n.d., in Donnan, *Documents*, 2:524.
131 'The Prosperity of Florida depends on the Success of this Intercourse'; Sir John Lindsay to Admiralty, 1765, cited in Robarts, 'Observations upon the trade', 1766 or 1767, S.R.O., D. (W.) 1778, II, no. 2113.
132 'Representation of Council and Assembly', Pensacola, 22 Nov. 1766, in Howard, *British Development*, pp. 111–16, app. 3.
133 Extract, Johnstone to Pownall, Pensacola, 31 Oct. 1764, S.R.O., D. (W.) 1778, II, no. 54; see also Born, 'British Trade in West Florida', pp. 15–16, 71–2; Johnson, *British West Florida*, pp. 13–14, 43–5.
134 On this campaign see especially Born, 'British Trade in West Florida', pp. 35–43.
135 Morgan and Strothers to Lord Hawkesbury, London, 8 Mar. 1793, B.L., Add. Mss. 38,228, ff. 355–6v.
136 Respectively: Montforte Browne to Lords of Trade, Pensacola, 29 Sept. 1767, in Howard, *British Development*, p. 128, app. 8; John Lindsay to Marqués de Cruillas, Pensacola Bay, 9 Nov. 1764, and related papers in A.G.I., Mexico, 1507a; Ramos, *Contrabando inglés*, pp. 39, 56–7, 130–1, 201; papers in N.A., C.O. 137 / 65; N.A., S.P. 94 / 185; A.G.I., Mexico, 1508.
137 Johnson, *British West Florida*, pp. 188–9.
138 Caughey, *Bernardo de Gálvez*, pp. 10–11; for an overview, Johnson, *British West Florida*, pp. 191–8.
139 Caughey, *Bernardo de Gálvez*, pp. 33–34; Born, 'British Trade in West Florida', pp. 103–5.
140 Caughey, *Bernardo de Gálvez*, pp. 70–7.
141 Martin, *History of Louisiana*, pp. 216–18.
142 Johnson, *British West Florida*, pp. 192–3; Martin, *History of Louisiana*, pp. 216–18; Born, 'British Trade', p. 114.
143 Mowat, *East Florida as a British Province*, pp. 75–6, 141.
144 Reynal, *Philosophical and Political History*, 3:492.
145 Richard Jones to Gov. Roger Elletson, Jamaica, 3 Aug. 1768, N.A., C.O. 137 / 64, ff. 9–11v; Robert Jones to William Trelawney, n.p., 4 Aug. 1770, N.A., C.O. 137 / 35, ff. 240–5.

146 Ramos, *Contrabando inglés*, pp. 85, 98, 200.
147 See the statement of Superintendent Lawrie quoted in Dawson, 'William Pitt's Settlement', p. 697.
148 Long, *History of Jamaica*, 1:318–19, 327–32.
149 For the *Industry* see esp. the papers in N.A., C.O. 137 / 64, C.O. 137 / 65, and ADM. 1 / 238; for the *Morning Star* see N.A., C.O. 137 / 71, C.O. 137 / 72, and F. O. 72 / 8.
150 Dawson, 'William Pitt's Settlement', pp. 697–8.
151 J. Maud to William Lyttleton, Honduras, 7 Oct. 1765, N.A., C.O. 137 / 34, ff. 5–6v; 'Some thoughts relative to the trade lately carried on in the Bay of Honduras', 1783, B.L., Add. Mss. 36,806, ff. 203–14.
152 Barbara Potthast-Jutkeit argues that the trade was rather more valuable, but agrees that a decline took place after the end of the war in 1763: 'Centroamérica y el contrabando', pp. 514–15.
153 Ambassador to Grimaldi, London, 10 June 1767, A.H.N., Estado, 4269.
154 Sir William Young to Board of Trade, 20 Sept. 1775, cited in Nardin, *La mise en valeur*, p. 261. Nardin rarely refers to trade with Spaniards, and neither did contemporaries; see e.g. Fowler, *Summary Account*, p. 28.
155 Jones, 'Historical Study of Anglo-Spanish American Trade', pp. 46–8; Ramos, *Contrabando inglés*, p. 212.
156 See the papers in N.A., S.P. 94 / 180, S.P. 94 / 182, C.O. 101 / 14; A.H.N., Estado, 4259. Brown, 'Anglo-Spanish Relations', pp. 379–81, publishes the passes; also Christelow, 'Contraband Trade', pp. 340–1.
157 Gov. Macartney to Lord Germain, Grenada, 30 June 1776, B.L., Add. Mss. 38,718, ff. 21–4v.
158 Conde de Ricla to Julián de Arriaga, Havana, 30 Oct. 1764, A.G.I., Santo Domingo, 2188.
159 See Böttcher, 'Trade, War and Empire', p. 162, analysing the data supplied by Sir Charles Whitworth; 'An Account of Bullion imported from Jamaica', S.A., W.W.M., R. 34 / 5c; 'Account of Bullion imported from North America', S.A., W.W.M., R. 34 / 5b.
160 Böttcher, 'Trade, War and Empire', pp. 178–9.
161 See esp. Miguel de Altarriba to Arriaga, Havana, 8 Mar. 1765, A.G.I., Santo Domingo, 2188; papers regarding voyages to Jamaica for supplies in May 1764–Nov. 1765 in A.G.I., Santo Domingo, 1206.
162 Böttcher, 'Trade, War and Empire', p. 181; Sagra, *Historia*, p. 133, citing a decree of 14 Apr. 1767.
163 Some of Monroe's mercantile papers, in English, are in A.G.I., Santo Domingo, 1159; see also Ramos, *Contrabando inglés*, p. 42. On the Conde de Ricla in Cuba see the detailed study by Jaime Delgado.
164 Pezuela, *Historia*, 3:55–6. Bucarely turned away a further three British ships in August 1766, and was also responsible for the incident in June 1767 involving the *Cygnet* and *Adventure*, described above.
165 Marrero, *Cuba*, 12:29–30.
166 Ramos, *Contrabando inglés*, pp. 71–2, 105.
167 Abalos to Bucarely, Havana, 17 Feb. 1768, in Marrero, *Cuba*, 12:28–9. Abalos estimated contraband exports of livestock at 7,000 head per year.
168 For British smugglers see e.g. Ramos, *Contrabando inglés*, pp. 46, 70, 96–7, 110, 118, 126–7, 133.
169 E.g. Lewis, 'Anglo-American Entrepreneurs', p. 120.
170 See e.g. Armytage, *Free Port System*, pp. 10–11; Ramos, *Contrabando inglés*, p. 49.
171 One such was the *John Elizabeth*, which entered Veracruz on Christmas Day 1769;

see Juan Antonio Ayanz de Ureta to Julián de Arriaga, Veracruz, 8 Jan. 1770, A.G.I., Mexico, 2844.

172 Ramos, *Contrabando inglés*, pp. 68, 305–6. Reports of British plans for strategic intervention in the region, one of which awarded Britain the port of Veracruz in exchange for support for a new Mexican Republic and a buffer-Duchy of Orizaba, all proved to be chimeras: Príncipe de Masserano to Grimaldi, London, 8 Aug. 1766, A.G.S, Estado, 6961, and related papers.

173 Stein and Stein, *Apogee of Empire*, p. 187.

174 Cited by Ramos, *Contrabando inglés*, pp. 48–9, 67–8, 108; also (for Mérida) 114–15.

175 Capt. Tonyn to Philip Stephens, *Phoenix*, Port Royal Harbour, 30 July 1770, and unsigned letter to Hillsborough, St James, London, 1 Oct. 1770, both in N.A., S.P. 94 / 185, n.f. ; also Brown, 'Anglo-Spanish Relations', pp. 381–2. Intriguingly, the house of Peter and Espret Barral & Company is described in these documents as having 'the charge & conduct of all the Bullion imported into this island'.

176 McFarlane, *Colombia before Independence*, pp. 118–19.

177 'Ynforme que acompaño al Señor Presidente de la Real Audiencia de Contratación', n.p., n.d., encl. to Consulado to Marqués del Real Tesoro, Cadiz, 12 Apr. 1774, A.G.I., Consulados, libro 86, ff. 234v–7v. On smuggling in Panama at this time see e.g. 'El Coronel Dn Pedro Jph de Urrutia … Governador que fué de Cumaná, 1781', A.G.I., Caracas, 121; Ramos, *Contrabando inglés*, pp. 60, 115–16, 118.

178 'Ynforme que acompaño al Señor Presidente …', n.p., n.d., encl. with Consulado to Marqués del Real Tesoro, Cadiz, 12 Apr. 1774, A.G.I., Consulados, libro 86, ff. 234v–7v.

179 Narváez y de la Torre, 'Relación o Ynforme de la provincia de Santa Marta, y Río Hacha …', Río Hacha, 19 May 1778, A.M.N., ms. 564, doc. 10.

180 Proposal regarding Santa Marta mentioned in Consulado to Real Tesoro, Cadiz, 27 Sept. 1773, A.G.I., Consulados, libro 86, ff. 133–v; and see McFarlane, *Colombia before Independence*, pp. 121–4.

181 De la Torre to Arriaga, Caracas, 5 Aug., 24 Aug., and 14 Oct. 1771, A.G.I., Caracas, 81.

182 Marqués de la Torre to Julián de Arriaga, Caracas, 5 Aug 1771, A.G.I., Caracas, 81; Francisco de Santa Cruz to José de Gálvez, Maracaíbo, 25 Nov. 1776, A.G.I., Caracas, 83. The Dutch were probably the greatest foreign smugglers in the region, engrossing much of the cacao trade from Curaçao.

183 Aguero to Arriaga, Caracas, 12 July 1773, A.G.I., Caracas, 82.

184 Ramos, *Contrabando inglés*, p. 171.

185 Louis Flislale, 'Observations on the Carraccas and Province of Cumana', Jamaica, 16 Nov. 1782, B.L., Add. Mss. 36,806, ff. 172–8v.

186 Abbad, *Viaje a la América*, n.f. (1 *fánega* = 1.58 bushels; 1 *arroba* = c. 11.5 kg / 25 lb).

187 Aguero to Arriaga, Caracas, 28 July 1773, A.G.I., Caracas, 82.

188 Manuel Falques to José de Gálvez, Trinidad, 29 Aug. 1777, A.G.I., Caracas, 152.

189 Ramos, *Contrabando inglés*, pp. 57, 78, 96, 113, 133, 203–4, 209–11.

190 Miguel de Muesas to crown, Puerto Rico, 21 Apr. 1770, quoted in López Cantos, 'Contrabando, corso y situado', pp. 31–2.

191 Morales Carrión, *Puerto Rico and the Non-Hispanic Caribbean*, pp. 91–2.

192 López Cantos, 'Comercio legal de Puerto Rico', esp. pp. 215–17. López Cantos has estimated that legal imports to Puerto Rico in the eighteenth century represented only 6.32 per cent of the total, but his methodology is highly dubious and he recognises that this figure is 'manifestly low'; 'Contrabando, corso', pp. 34–7.

193 See e.g. Sir Stanier Porten to Earl of Dartmouth, St James, London, 30 Dec. 1774,

and enclosures, in Stevens (ed.), *Manuscripts of the Earl of Dartmouth*, 2:529.

194 Miguel de Altarriba to Julián de Arriaga, 4 July 1765, cited in Böttcher, 'Trade, War and Empire', pp. 186–7; on the Coppinger contracts see also Marrero, *Cuba*, 9:3–7.

195 Böttcher, 'Trade, War and Empire', p. 187.

196 Joseph Antonio de Armona to Joseph de Gálvez, 'Apuntaciones de la Ciudad de la Havana', Madrid, 15 Nov. 1776, A.G.I., Santo Domingo, 2188.

197 Böttcher, 'Trade, War and Empire', p. 188; Marrero, *Cuba*, 9:7–11.

198 Armona to Gálvez, 'Apuntaciones de la Havana', Madrid, 15 Nov. 1776, A.G.I., Santo Domingo, 2188.

199 Testimony of William Kelly, 12 Feb. 1766, B.L., Add. Mss. 33,030, ff. 130–9v.

200 The best brief survey is probably Pantaleão, *Penetraçao comercial*, pp. 139–41.

201 Lewis, 'Anglo-American Entrepreneurs in Havana', p. 112.

202 'A very considerable part of the specie and bullion trade from America, is not the produce of manufacture, but Spanish property, remitted this way to Old Spain to save duties'; see the paper by Joseph Salvador, dated London, 28 Jan. 1766, B.L., Add. Mss. 38,339, ff. 225–6.

203 Headlam, 'International Relations', pp. 714–15.

204 Ward, 'The British West Indies', p. 419; Allen, 'British Commercial Policy', chap. 2.

205 Whitaker, *Spanish-American Frontier*, pp. 7–8; same author, 'Commerce of Louisiana', pp. 191, 199.

206 For the *picarones* of Trinidad in Cuba see Saavedra, *Decenios*, p. 132; same author, *Journal*, pp. 46–7.

207 Hugh Elliot to William Eden, Berlin, 28 Mar. 1778, cited in Rydjord, *Foreign Interest*, pp. 91–2.

208 Joseph Graham to Governor of Cumaná, Tobago, 17 Aug. 1779, encl. to Luis de Unzaga to José de Gálvez, Caracas, 31 Jan. 1780, A.G.I., Caracas, 85; Dookhan, *History of the British Virgin Islands*, pp. 48–52.

209 See e.g. Unzaga to [John Dalling], Caracas, 20 Jan. 1780, encl. to Unzaga to Gálvez, Caracas, 30 June 1780, A.G.I., Caracas, 85.

210 Robertson, *Life of Miranda*, 1:23–27; Saavedra, *Decenios*, pp. 187–8; Marrero, *Cuba*, 12:46–55.

211 Armytage, *Free Port System*, p. 51. For an alternative view, see Jones, 'Historical Study', p. 50.

212 Atwood, *History of Dominica*, pp. 104–6; 'Observations on the trade carried on between the British West Indies and the Spanish colonies in America ...' [1785–86], B.L., Add. Mss. 38,345, ff. 208–13v.

213 See esp. Rodríguez Vicente, 'El comercio cubano y la guerra de emancipación norteamericana'; and for contraband under this trade, Lewis, 'Anglo-American Entrepreneurs'.

214 Antúnez y Acevedo, *Memorias históricas*, p. 145; King, 'Evolution of the Free Slave Trade Principle', p. 45.

215 For New Granada: Narváez y la Torre, 'Discurso del Mariscal de Campo', p. 89; McFarlane, *Colombia before Independence*, pp. 129–30. For Venezuela: Alvarez, *Comercio y comerciantes*, pp. 35–6; for the Martinique exports, see e.g. Máximo duBouchet to Julián de Arriaga, Cumaná, 20 May 1776, A.G.I., Caracas, 121.

216 Morales Padrón, 'México y la Independencia de Hispanoamérica', p. 358.

217 Louis Flislale, 'Observations on the Carraccas and Province of Cumana', Jamaica, 16 Nov. 1782, B.L., Add. Mss. 36,806, ff. 172–8v.

CHAPTER THREE

The *Comercio de Colonias* and the Consolidation of the Free Port System, 1783–96

The Recovery of the Spanish Trade in the Immediate Post-war Years, c. 1783–87

The treaty which ended the American Revolutionary War, signed at Versailles in 1783, reversed most of the conquests lately made in the Caribbean, though not all of them. Thus, the islands of Grenada, St Vincent, St Kitts, Dominica, and New Providence were all returned to Britain, but Spain retained the Floridas, while the French kept Tobago. British rights to cut logwood in Central America were confirmed, but only in Honduras, and even in that territory all the British fortifications were to be demolished. By a supplementary convention of 1786, Britain formally agreed to evacuate the Mosquito Shore, a process which was complete by the summer of 1787.[1] The Treaty of Versailles failed to quell post-war Anglo-Spanish tension in the Americas entirely; as Allan Kuethe has noted, Spain was 'not yet a satisfied power', and continued to strike an aggressive stance in the West Indies throughout much of the 1780s.[2] This stance was a product partly of the euphoria of recent victory, and partly of perennial distrust of British intentions in the region, which the Spanish ambassador in London thought more perilous than ever since the loss of the Thirteen Colonies.[3] Throughout the Caribbean, normal relations remained perturbed for some years; British warships, for example, were routinely barred from entering Spanish ports, even when bearing despatches or on other official business.[4] The Spanish made frequent seizures of small British trading and turtling vessels, the Governor of the Bahamas writing in 1788 that 'the frequent captures made by the Spanish is really become a matter of very serious concern'.[5] Merchants in the Bahamas and Jamaica protested at seizures of large numbers of such vessels off the coasts of Cuba, Campeche and Panama, made on the grounds that they were really smugglers. Meanwhile, from Jamaica it was reported that both the Spanish and the French acted with extreme rigour against individuals engaged in contraband trade with the island.[6]

Spanish aggression in the post-war years was mirrored to some extent by anti-Spanish feeling in the British colonies, fuelled by incidents such as the imprisonment in Havana on contraband charges of the leading Jamaica merchant, Philip Allwood, in 1783.[7] In late 1786 the murder of a British sailor provoked an unusual anti-Spanish riot in Kingston, during the course of which the victim's shipmates roamed the town 'threatening to kill all the Spaniards they found'.[8] There were also naval attacks on Spanish traders to the British islands, reminiscent of those carried out under the Hovering Act of 1763 and which provoked similar mercantile protests.[9] But it is to be stressed that incidents such as these were not permitted seriously to interfere with business. As one writer observed of the Spaniards, 'notwithstanding all this they or rather their dollars are well received in all the Islands'.[10] From 1783, the governor and admiral in Jamaica were again instructed to give the Spanish trade every encouragement,[11] and in point of fact the trade appears to have made a very rapid recovery from its wartime depression. By August of the latter year, merchants in Jamaica were celebrating a 'large influx of Spanish dollars', and petitioned for a warship for remission of 'the surplus of our currency to our correspondents at home'.[12] The tonnage of foreign shipping entering Jamaica's free ports soared from little more than 4,000 tons in 1782, to reach almost 11,000 tons in 1783, over 12,000 tons in 1784, and possibly as much as 13,000 tons in 1785 (Table 2.1, p. 57). By the latter year it was estimated that Jamaica's exports to the Spanish colonies, enslaved Africans included, were worth possibly as much as £500,000.[13] Alexander von Humboldt suggested that a considerable proportion of these exports were paid for even at this early date with bills of exchange issued on commercial houses in Cadiz or Barcelona.[14] A statement of trade at the Jamaican ports each year in 1784–87 describes a diverse import trade in which livestock, dyewood, very large quantities of cotton and large quantities of indigo stand out, while registered imports of bullion feature only in the last two years and are relatively inconsequential. Registered exports do not include manufactures, but are limited to slaves and foodstuffs – especially flour, salt beef, and pork.[15]

For a few years after the war, Jamaica was the only colony which still boasted free ports, since the ports in Dominica had lapsed during the French wartime occupation and were not immediately re-established upon the island's restoration to the British in 1783. The Spanish trade at Dominica in the early 1780s appears to have been limited, though the island's intercourse with the French was much greater. The Bahamas, by contrast, may have commenced large-scale trade with the Spaniards around these years. It was reported that Spanish traders, especially from Cuba, the Floridas, and the Gulf of Mexico, now came to the Bahamas for 'British manufactures, principally linens, printed linens, striped linens, checked linens and osnaburghs; also hardware. They are beginning to take cottons. They take chiefly coarse goods and a great many fine ones.' The same source further described the goods bought and sold at the island of Grenada, now growing rapidly in prosperity and – even before the establishment of its free port in 1787 – probably already the leading British centre for the Spanish trade after Jamaica. The Spaniards took off

Slaves, flour, cotton, linen, woollens, chiefly coarse, hardware and all kinds of British manufactures, and lately a good deal of rum … They bring cotton, cocoa, coffee, horned cattle, horses, mules, asses, hides, oil, tallow, corn, fish, poultry, mahogany, nicaragua wood, fustic, logwood, brazilleto and other dye woods, lignum vita, sarsaparilla, indigo, money and bullion.[16]

Spanish traders to Grenada were generally small open launches of a mere 6–20 tons, a characteristic which persisted throughout later years. Less clear is the post-war situation of the Spanish trade at the British colonies in the Bay of Honduras and on the Mosquito Shore. A report dated 1783 described the wide range of goods imported to the Honduras settlements, including different textiles, ironware, munitions and alcohol. Of these goods, the surplus was 'generally disposed of to the Spaniard who frequently brings ready money for such commodity as he stands in need of and sometimes indigo'. The author of this report thought that with appropriate reforms to their administration and infrastructure, the Bay settlements might export 'vast quantities' of British goods to the Spanish territories.[17] Other observers were less sanguine, however; and on balance, one's overall impression is that effective exports through the Bay remained relatively modest.[18] The value of contraband on the Mosquito Shore around this time, again, was probably no more than £10,000 per year.[19] Before the Shore was evacuated in 1787, the London press had already turned against the settlers there, identifying them as a source of pointless tension with Spain; thus, one periodical asked dramatically whether the other colonies, or even Britain itself, were to be hazarded 'to enrich a few Smugglers and traders in Dyewood'.[20] Nevertheless, British withdrawal from the Mosquito Shore did not mark the end of British commercial influence there. The new Spanish governor at Black River was obliged to persuade some British merchants to remain behind after the evacuation to ensure supplies of basic goods, with imports of such goods from Britain worth over £6,500 in 1794 and 1796. Smuggling with the region out of Jamaica and Belize also remained a persistent feature.[21]

A closely analogous situation to that of the Mosquito Shore prevailed in the other major territory evacuated by the British after the war, that of East and West Florida. The Treaty of Versailles accorded the British settlers in Florida a period of eighteen months in which to settle their affairs and depart, and most abandoned the colony by late 1785 amid allegations of harsh treatment at the hands of the incoming Spaniards. The difficulties Spain experienced in attracting new settlers and particularly trade to the region, however, soon opened new opportunities to the British in the form of supply of the 'Indian trade', a key factor in the political stability of the colony. A contract for this trade was won by Panton, Leslie and Company of St Augustine, which was permitted to import goods destined for the indigenous tribes direct from Great Britain to East Florida, and to export hides and furs in return. Panton, Leslie rapidly expanded into West Florida, and for a decade the company dominated the trade of the southern tribes. Several British vessels per year plied between the Floridas and London, for example in the first two weeks of July 1786 importing 126,000 deerskins, a few beaver furs and some bullion.[22] This trade remained a matter of concern to Spanish officials, who made various attempts to return control of it to Spanish hands; interestingly, however, the essential point of purchase of the goods in Britain never seems to have come into question.[23] All such attempts proving unsuccessful, Panton, Leslie thrived, to attain an estimated capital value of $400,000 by 1794.[24]

The British supply of slaves to Spanish colonial markets recovered rapidly in the post-war years. The British possessed the most powerful slave marts in the Caribbean, a fact explained in straightforward terms by a leading merchant of the day: 'We fit out our ships for this trade more expeditiously and cheaper than the French can; our people understand the manner of carrying on the trade better, and our manufactures are better adapted to it.'[25] Spaniards once more ventured to the British colonies in great numbers in search of slaves, whether in purely contraband voyages or under dedicated licence. Recourse during wartime to licences to seek slaves in foreign colonies proved hard to suppress upon the Peace; in 1785, Antonio de Caballero y Góngora, the archbishop-viceroy of New Granada, licensed the city of Panama to import 2,000 slaves from the foreign islands, and he continued to grant such permits even after they were formally prohibited in April 1786.[26]

Unusual contracts were also signed with British merchants for the overt supply of slaves to selected Spanish colonies. A first such contract was signed in February 1784 with Edward Barry, though the business rapidly passed to the major Liverpool firm of Baker & Dawson; the latter firm then signed a second contract in 1786.[27] The first contract exploited the current Spanish efforts to develop Trinidad, and envisaged the supply of 4,000 slaves solely to that island within one year. But both contracts presented opportunities for far more extensive trade; the British minister in Madrid celebrated Barry's agreement as one 'calculated not only to produce great profit to himself ... but to bring considerable advantage to the British trade in those parts ... Mr Barry's agreement, if properly improved, may be considered as a partial renewal of the famous Asiento contract.'[28] Barry was authorised to export his returns in bullion, produce and livestock from Trinidad to Jamaica, as well as to send letters to Grenada in Spanish vessels and even to visit the mainland colonies if necessary.[29] Slaves imported to Trinidad were subsequently permitted to be re-exported to both Venezuela and Cuba, while the contract of 1786 was aimed principally at supply of the latter two markets. Some 1,800 slaves were imported to Trinidad under the Barry contract by February 1785, most of whom were re-exported due to a dearth of purchasers in the island.[30] By April 1787, a total of 2,944 slaves had been imported to the province of Caracas under both contracts, with further imports following in later years.[31] Baker & Dawson imported over 5,000 slaves to Havana between 1786 and 1789, and were said to have received 500,000 *pesos fuertes* in return, as well as hides and other produce.[32]

Total exports from Jamaican free ports numbered some 4,000 slaves in 1784, 3,400 in 1785, approximately 3,400 in 1786, and 1,700 in 1787; the establishment of free ports in Dominica and Grenada in the latter year was evident in exports of 1,655 and 257 slaves respectively from each island, making an annual total of some 3,600 slaves exported. The Jamaican trade recovered to reach a figure of some 2,500 slaves exported in 1788.[33] Young presents substantially higher figures for total exports to the foreign West Indies, of 5,182 slaves in 1787, and 11,042 slaves in 1788.[34] In 1788 Baker & Dawson began negotiations for a third contract, which failed to prosper due either to the onset of the anti-slavery movement in Britain or to strong opposition from Cuban merchants, who were eager to secure control of the trade for themselves.[35] The monopoly slave trade granted to the Spanish Royal Philippines Company during these years concerned chiefly the River Plate region, Chile and Peru, and lies beyond the scope of this work; suffice to note that here too the British dominated, even to the extreme of the Company's engaging the vessels required for the trade in London, Liverpool and Bristol.[36] The Philippines Company suspended its slave trade in 1789, paving the way for the declaration of free trade in slaves throughout the Spanish empire later the same year (as discussed below).

Bases for Further Expansion: The *Comercio de Colonias* and the Consolidation of the Free Port System

In the post-war years, almost throughout the Spanish colonies the consequences of the legalisation of trade with neutral powers and foreign colonies which had taken place during the American Revolutionary War began to manifest themselves. Most of the Spanish colonies became open to trade with foreigners to an unprecedented degree during these years, in what I would argue was the key development of the 1780s and early 1790s for British trade with the region. This trade, which has been little studied in any context, and scarcely at all with reference to commercial relations with the British, was often known as the *comercio de colonias extranjeras* (foreign colonies trade) or simply *comercio de colonias*. Most of it was undertaken by Spanish merchants under licence from the governors in the Spanish colonies, so further reinforcing the shift apparent since the 1750s in the weight of the trade toward Spanish vessels, although foreign shipping also gained far greater access to Spanish ports at this time. The onset of the *comercio de colonias* was evident immediately upon the cessation of wartime hostilities; thus, the Intendant at Havana reported in October 1783 that, whether due to the special permits granted for trade with the Americans and French during the war, or simply by entering for supplies, 'the Foreigners have become used to that tolerance … Every day many Anglo-American, French, British, and Danish vessels come to the Port … Not only the French, and Anglo-Americans do so; but also the English from Jamaica.' The change was so notable that this official suggested that more foreign ships had anchored at Havana in the few months since the war than in ten years preceding it.[37] In January 1784 his protests provoked a royal decree, effective throughout the empire, which prohibited the entry of foreign ships to Spanish ports on any pretext whatever, even if claiming imminent danger of shipwreck (*aunque aleguen que se ban a pique*).[38] The following month imports of foreign flour at Havana were again prohibited, and in 1784–85 Anglo-American traders were peremptorily expelled from the port.[39] Nevertheless, voyages in Spanish vessels to St Domingue and the United States for flour continued to be sanctioned during the years which followed.

Two further cases may serve to illustrate the widespread recourse now apparent in the Spanish colonies to trade with the foreign islands. In Venezuela, post-war trade with foreign colonies was set on a firm footing by the distinguished second Intendant of Caracas, Francisco de Saavedra (1783–88). Saavedra evoked the wartime precedents for his actions in sanctioning trade with foreign colonies, but was in fact a frank advocate for the system as the logical solution to Venezuela's economic woes, one which permitted the export of vast quantities of surplus produce in exchange for slaves, bullion, naval supplies, and a wide range of vital tools and plantation machinery.[40] Although inevitably he also devoted considerable attention to land- and sea-based anti-contraband forces, Saavedra remained convinced that only a more liberal system of trade could combat smuggling in the region effectively.[41] He issued some fifty licences for voyages to foreign colonies in two months in late 1783 alone, and during his administration quite extensive commercial relations developed between the different Venezuelan provinces and the foreign islands. This trade was based upon exports of cotton from Coro or Guayana, for example, or of mules and hides from the same provinces, from Caracas, and from Cumaná. Saavedra claimed that as early as 1784, it brought in over 300,000 pesos, 'mostly in gold', a figure which rose to 387,000 pesos at La Guaira, Puerto Cabello and Coro alone by 1787, and to 389,000 pesos by 1788, with an additional 200,000 pesos imported at Barcelona and Cumaná.[42] None of these figures, of course, acknowledges the value of the extensive contraband which might reasonably be supposed to have been undertaken under cover of the licensed voyages.

At least as striking as the Venezuelan case was that of New Granada, where already in 1783–84 most shipping entering the port of Cartagena came from foreign rather than from Spanish ports.[43] Beginning in 1784, Viceroy Caballero y Góngora developed extensive trade with foreign colonies and the United States under cover of a royal monopoly in exports of dyewood, originally intended to finance a military expedition against British incursions in the Darién.[44] Commissaries sent by Caballero to Jamaica purchased foodstuffs, tools and other supplies for the Darién scheme, in one case to the value of 100,000 pesos, while New Granadan dyewood was dispatched to the United States and thence to London and the Netherlands. There were also parallel permits for voyages to foreign colonies for emergency supplies, and a royal decree of 1786, interpreted as sanctioning such voyages, was cited repeatedly in later years to justify the practice.[45] In 1787 Spanish merchants protested at 'the many foreign vessels, which from Jamaica and other parts' frequented Cartagena, and in the fifteen months to April of the latter year alone, thirty-four Spanish ships entered from foreign ports, eighteen of them from Jamaica bringing foodstuffs on royal account.[46] The impact in Santa Marta and Río de la Hacha, centres of the dyewood industry, was particularly strong, with contraband imports estimated in 1785 at 3,000,000 pesos since the end of the war.[47] Elsewhere, it was reported that a warship entered Cartagena from Jamaica every year with dispatches, taking off 'considerable sums in bars, gold dust, silver and coin' on consignment from Spanish merchants.[48] Naval officers made rich profits from such transactions, and relations between Caballero y Góngora and the naval commander in Jamaica were said to be excellent.[49] By 1789, when Caballero's successor largely dismantled the dyewood scheme, more than 100 ships had entered Cartagena from foreign ports, and the town council of Santa Fé de Bogotá remarked that during this period, 'these provinces seemed more like English colonies than the dominions of the Catholic King'.[50] McFarlane concludes that the scale of trade with foreign colonies and contraband now began to have a serious impact on New Granada's legal trade with Spain.[51] Overt trade with foreign colonies of the kind described here extended to most of the Spanish colonies during these years;[52] the single major exception may have been Mexico, which appears to have remained without any comparable large-scale trade until after the onset of the Anglo-Spanish wars in 1796.

Closely parallel to the growth of the *comercio de colonias* in the Spanish colonies, the late 1780s and early 1790s witnessed a dramatic expansion of the free port system in the British West Indies. This process of expansion was brought about by means of further Free Port Acts passed by the British Parliament between 1787 and 1793. An Act of the former year ratified the existing four free ports in Jamaica, re-established a single port in Dominica (at Roseau), and opened new ports in Grenada (at St George's) and the Bahamas (at Nassau in New Providence).[53] An Act of 1792 opened a port in the Atlantic island of Bermuda, while a further law of 1793 added additional ports in Jamaica (at Port Antonio, on the hitherto neglected north-east coast), in Antigua (at St John's), and the Bahamas (Caicos).[54] The context to passage of the Free Port Act of 1787 has been analysed at length elsewhere, and need be sketched here only briefly.[55] The expanded system of ports was not intended to facilitate trade with the newly-independent United States of America, despite the proliferation of petitions for free ports from the British islands most concerned with that trade. Under the terms of the Act of 1787, indeed, the United States was barred from the free ports trade, via a declaration that only vessels from colonies belonging to 'a foreign European state' might take part in it.[56] More influential was the extension of the French free port system in the mid-1780s to embrace seven ports throughout the French Antilles, which it is argued provoked the British into establishing new ports in response to the perceived French commercial threat.[57] Advocates for the different colonies also advanced arguments for free ports specific to each island: the ideal situation of Dominica as a slave entrepôt, for example, or the recent rapid growth and proximity to the eastern Spanish Main of Grenada. In the broadest sense, the Acts passed between 1787 and 1793 can be regarded as final recognition of the commercial success of the system; that, in the words of the Lords of Trade, the free ports commerce 'has gradually increased to a great amount, and it is likely to increase still further, and that on this account these Free Ports are not only highly beneficial to the commerce of Great Britain, but ... contribute greatly to the prosperity of the islands in which they are established.'[58] It is not probable that the British were responding to recent developments in the Spanish colonies, although the significance of extension of the free ports almost throughout the British West Indies at precisely a time when the phenomenon of trade under official permit from the Spanish colonies was becoming increasingly generalised requires little further comment.

The new Free Port Acts passed at this time differed in significant respects from those which had preceded them. The Act of 1787 for the first time explicitly enumerated the foreign products which might be imported (the Act of 1766 had specified simply bullion and any other foreign produce, with a number of exceptions), as follows: 'wool, cotton wool, indigo, cochineal, drugs of all sorts, cocoa, logwood, fustic and all sorts of wood for dyers' use, hides, skins and tallow, beaver and all sorts of furs, tortoiseshell, hardwood or mill timber, mahogany and all other woods for cabinet ware, horses, asses, mules and cattle.' The absolute prohibition on the importation of foreign manufactures of any kind naturally remained in place. Legal exports from the free ports were to include rum, slaves, and all goods legally imported (principally manufactures of different sorts) except for naval stores, tobacco, and iron. Several further innovations were made to the free port system at this time; in 1790, in response to a mercantile petition from Jamaica, all restrictions on the tonnage of the shipping employed was lifted, though the limitation to vessels with a single deck remained.[59] In 1792 the tradition of fixed-term Free Port Acts was terminated when the Acts of 1787 and 1790 were made perpetual.[60] A further law of the same year sought to exploit the shortage of sugar in European markets provoked by the St Domingue revolt, by permitting the importation of sugar and also coffee at the Bahamas and Bermuda (islands chosen for their lack of a domestic sugar industry).[61] Trade in sugar and coffee was never very extensive at these islands, but the Act remained of value because (improbably enough) the crates in which sugar was packed provided an ideal vessel for the smuggling of bullion. Some years later a group of Bahama merchants petitioned for renewal of the Act of 1792 on the grounds that 'the chief means by which [Money] is got off is in the Sugar Boxes'. Governor Dowdeswell supported this petition, agreeing that 'the Boxes in which this article, is always packed, affords the surest means of lessening the Difficulties, attending the Smuggling of Specie from the coast of Spain'.[62]

Facilities for legal trade between the Spanish colonies and the foreign islands, as well as for access of foreign shipping at Spanish colonial ports, grew still more extensive from the late 1780s. In part this reflected the continuation of the permits for the *comercio de colonias* granted in the immediate post-war years; thus in Venezuela, Francisco de Saavedra's successor, Juan Guillelmi, maintained or even expanded the licences granted by his predecessor.[63] In New Granada, the provinces of Santa Marta and Río de la Hacha exported surplus cotton, dyewoods, and other woods to the British islands, all 'under superior permit'.[64] These years also witnessed a proliferation of permits to named individuals to export produce to foreign colonies or import specified goods in return, of which examples are known from Venezuela and especially Cuba.[65] But probably more influential than any of these permits was the advent of free trade in slaves in the Spanish colonies, by a printed decree dated 28 February 1789. This decree – which at first affected only Cuba, the province of Caracas, Puerto Rico and Santo Domingo – permitted Spanish subjects to purchase slaves freely in foreign ports, exporting specie or produce and importing only slaves in return, free of duty. Moreover, foreigners, too, were allowed to bring slaves to the Spanish colonies, albeit for a period of two years only.[66] In November 1791, fresh decrees extended the system to the viceroyalties of Santa Fé and Buenos Aires, and prolonged its term by a further six years for Spaniards and foreigners alike.[67] In the course of the next few years, numerous supplementary measures developed the system still further, for example by incorporating further regions and ports, or by granting permission for imports of agricultural tools and plantation machinery from foreign colonies if insufficient slaves were available to cover outward cargoes.[68] In my view, the free trade in slaves introduced from 1789 can be regarded in effect as extending the *comercio de colonias* which had developed out of the Spanish colonies since the American Revolutionary war, or as superseding in part the piecemeal and miscellaneous permits issued in the different colonies since the Peace. Whatever the interpretation placed upon it, it is sufficiently clear that the free trade in slaves became a prime pretext for contraband with the British and other foreign islands over the course of the next few years (as is discussed hereafter).

A final factor impinging upon the development of the Spanish trade during these years was the question of diplomatic relations between Great Britain and Spain. Peace now prevailed between the two nations for some thirteen years, until late 1796; but this remained a period of constant diplomatic tension and disputes, with differing consequences for commercial affairs. In 1789, an incident flared up over the tiny trading settlement at Nootka, on Vancouver Island in Canada, which grew into a much broader dispute about colonial rights to the North-West coast and about the navigation of the Pacific. This 'Nootka Sound controversy', which was resolved (essentially in Britain's favour) by the end of the following year, provoked a war scare in the Caribbean and the closure of Jamaican ports to foreign shipping in July 1790, with consequent brief disruption of the Spanish trade there.[69] The great slave revolt of St Domingue of 1791, for its part, which effectively destroyed the richest of the French colonies and prepared the way for the independence of Haiti, similarly led both to close vigilance of Spaniards trading at the free ports, and to a further expulsion of foreigners from Havana.[70]

More serious by far than either of these episodes was the outbreak of war with Napoleonic France in the spring of 1793, with Britain and Spain cast briefly in the unusual role of allies. The war's economic effects were mixed, since while the rich British trade with the French colonies collapsed almost entirely, the Spanish trade experienced strong and sustained growth throughout the mid-1790s. One side-effect of the war was to provide still further access for British shipping to Spanish-American ports: thus in May 1793 a 'provisional convention' was signed by London and Madrid covering mutual admittance and protection of shipping during the war, which was rapidly implemented by local authorities in the Spanish colonies.[71] Early in the war the Governor of the Bahamas openly purchased livestock in Cuba for the supply of his troops, while in 1794 the Governor of Cartagena was actually permitted to dispatch merchant vessels to Jamaica to take advantage of the British convoy system to Europe.[72] In the Spanish empire, meanwhile, the economic impact of the war was insufficient to provoke any general recourse to neutral trade as would be the case from 1797. But in Cuba, even before the onset of hostilities the local authorities opened the ports to neutrals, a policy later sanctioned by the crown, such that in practice Cuba 'enjoyed unrestricted neutral trade from 1793 on'.[73] Elsewhere, the Danish island of St Thomas now began its career as a major entrepôt for neutral trade; already in 1792 'the greatest part of the shipping that came into the harbour were American vessels, small Spanish sloops and boats, and large English merchantmen', with the Spaniards exchanging bullion for manufactured goods from Europe and provisions from the United States.[74] There is little doubt that the British benefited from this partial renewal of neutral trade, whether directly at the neutral entrepôts or through the re-export of British manufactures to Cuba and other Spanish colonies via the United States.

The Spanish Trade, c. 1787–96: General Panorama

In these conditions, then, what was the general panorama of the Spanish trade following the expansion of the free port system in the years after 1787? There is broad agreement among scholars as to the immediate commercial success of the expanded system of ports.[75] One account suggests that foreign vessels entering at all the free ports numbered 405 in 1787, but averaged 851 in the following five years. All foreign shipping entering at Kingston increased from 250 in 1784 to 169 in the first half of 1788 and 373 in the whole of 1792.[76] A different account suggests that in January to June each year from 1787–89, Spanish shipping entering at Jamaican free ports numbered 70, 98, and 84 vessels respectively. This latter account is especially valuable because it presents elusive information for the geographical distribution of Jamaica's free

Table 3.1 *Jamaica's free port trade, 1787–89*

Number of vessels entering in the half-years

Port of Origin	Jan.–June 1787	%	Jan.–June 1788	%	Jan.–June 1789	%
Cuba	25	35.7	39	39.8	44	52.4
Cartagena	9	12.9	2	2.0	3	3.6
Santa Marta	4	5.7	1	1.0	1	1.2
Río de la Hacha	2	2.9	4	4.1	2	2.4
Total, New Granada		*21.5*		*7.1*		*7.2*
Coro	2	2.9	3	3.1	2	2.4
Puerto Cabello	2	2.9	1	1.0	—	
Trinidad	—		5	5.1	1	1.2
Total, Venezuela		*5.8*		*9.2*		*3.6*
Mississippi	5	7.1	1	1.0	3	3.6
St Domingue	19	27.1	34	34.7	25	29.8
Curaçao	—		—		2	2.4
Other small ports	2	2.9	8	8.2	1	1.2
Total	70		98		84	

Source: Allen, "British Commercial Policy", chart VII, after p. 185.
Note: All percentages rounded to one decimal place.

ports trade among the different Spanish colonies at this time (Table 3.1). Cuba now accounted for over a third to a half of the trade, with New Granada and Venezuela usually taking around 7 per cent apiece and the Spanish Mississippi a smaller proportion; strikingly, Mexico does not feature in these accounts. Supplementary evidence may be found in the statistics for total British exports to Jamaica, which show strong growth and a doubling in value in the decade after 1787, from some £875,000 in 1788 to some £1,695,000 in 1796 (Table 3.2). These statistics support the suggestion that one result of the expansion of the free ports was that 'the exports of manufactured articles from the mother country to the sugar colonies were notably increased between 1787 and 1792'.[77] As a result of the Haitian revolt, Jamaica now finally overcame all French competition for the Spanish trade, one French writer commenting that 'it was after the disastrous events of St Domingo,

Table 3.2 *Total British exports to Jamaica, 1788–96*

	Value of exports and re-exports *(£ sterling at official values)*
1788	875,231
1789	905,574
1790	1,007,306
1791	1,294,134
1792	1,267,194
1793	1,429,879
1794	2,124,732
1795	1,429,446
1796	1,695,353

Source: Elaborated from P.R.O., Customs 17 / 10-18.
Note: All figures rounded to nearest pound.

that Jamaica became the general magazine of the Spaniards from the gulph of Mexico'.[78] Further fragmentary evidence supports the impression of an extremely healthy trade: the leading merchant house in Jamaica at this time made sales of £100,000–£300,000 annually, of which 'great part' was to Spaniards.[79] The Cuban writer Francisco de Arango y Parreño watched three vessels enter Kingston solely from Havana in the first three weeks of 1795, 'of which the least carried 20 merchants and 40,000 pesos'.[80] Unique statistical data from the National Archives in London, discussed below, support the notion that Jamaica survived the competition of the new British free ports to retain a strong pre-eminence in the Spanish trade as a whole.

Second only to Jamaica as a centre for the trade was the island of Grenada. Briefly the only British possession within easy reach of eastern Venezuela and Trinidad, and newly endowed with a free port, Grenada now began a period of brilliant prosperity which, however, would last less than a decade. Letters from the island in the early summer of 1787 reported that 'in the short space of 14 days, 16 Spanish launches have entered loaded with *pesos fuertes*', and that 'since St George's was declared a Free port it is filled with Spanish Ships which come over from the Continent'.[81] In its first six months, fifty-eight foreign vessels entered the free port, bringing cotton, horses, mules and oxen, 60 tons of fustic, hides, and foodstuffs.[82] A merchant resident in the island until 1791 later recalled that 'Grenada was a free port, and consequently had a great trade with Spanish South America; launches were continually coming up, bringing cargoes of mules, cattle, cotton, drugs, dye-woods, provisions, and other articles of various kinds'.[83] According to two merchants closely concerned with the trade, 192 Spanish vessels entered at St George's in 1792, 'of which no less than 133 did not exceed 25 tons'.[84]

We have unusually rich data for Grenada's trade in 1792, due to a unique report compiled at this time on the orders of Governor Edward Mathew. These data suggest that in the year to November, goods to the value of approximately £330,000 imported from Britain by sixteen major merchant houses were re-exported from Grenada to the foreign West Indies (including the French islands, with which Grenada's trade was considerable).[85] Provisions from the United States, and wines from Madeira and Tenerife, were also re-shipped for the foreign settlements. The goods exported from Grenada in July to September alone included '663 packages, 890 pieces, dry goods', and mill machinery, furniture of all sorts, hardware, earthenware, and glassware, different foodstuffs and alcohols, along with an extraordinary range of miscellaneous items including eight anchors, '40 dozen seine twine', 325 firestones and 3 bedsteads.[86] Imports from the foreign West Indies in the last six months of the year were worth a total of over £78,500 sterling, almost three-quarters of which were accounted for by cotton bales; the difference apparent between the value of imports and exports was explained in part because 'from the Spanish settlements the balance is paid in dollars'.[87] The prosperity of Grenada's Spanish trade rested on its relations with Trinidad, though the island also 'had frequent visits from the Spaniards of Porto Rico, who also brought large sums in specie'.[88] It is true that some observers argued that during this period, British mercantile success 'proceeded more from the extent of the business they were enabled to carry on, than from the largeness of their profits', which were limited by competition from other nations.[89] The war with France severely damaged trade at Grenada's free ports, which declined rapidly from 1793; nevertheless, the island would retain some portion of the Spanish trade up to the British capture of Trinidad in 1797.

The third greatest British centre for the Spanish trade was now the Bahamas, whose prosperity is best gauged by reference to the British Customs records (discussed below). The degree of local support for this trade is illustrated by an incident in which a Spanish vessel was seized by the Navy while smuggling goods into New Providence in 1791. A group of Bahama merchants 'made a purse and encouraged the Spaniards to claim, and employ'd the first law people at Nassau' to contest the seizure; the vessel was later acquitted in the island courts, 'the Chief Justice declaring that whatever Spanish vessel brought money thither should be admitted, let the rest of her cargo be what it would'.[90] At Dominica, the few years following the re-establishment of the free port at Roseau in 1787 were marked by growth in trade with foreigners and some optimism as to the commercial prospects of the island.[91] Trade with Spaniards at this time was based especially upon the slave trade, and was principally with the Orinoco, Cumaná, and (by one account) the Mississippi.[92] These hopeful prospects proved deceptive, however; already in 1791 Thomas Atwood wrote that 'the trade of Dominica is at present very much circumscribed', limited essentially to 'a few Guinea Factors, and five or six ships annually to take away the produce', a development he attributed in part to excessive enforcement of the free port regulations.[93] In any case, Dominica's free port trade was still more seriously affected than Grenada's by the French war, and from 1793 largely withered away. Also blighted by the war was the trade of Panton, Leslie and Company in Florida, which declined sharply due to French military action and to competition from the United States. The lesser British colonies in the Antilles all maintained some trade with the Spaniards, though generally at a low level. The free port at Antigua was never a major centre for the Spanish trade; neither was that at Tobago, established three years after the capture of the island from the French in April 1793.[94] An estimate by Dauxion Lavaysse to the effect that Tortola imported colonial produce worth up to 6,000,000 francs (c. 1,200,000 pesos, or £270,000) from Puerto Rico in 1788 does not seem credible in the absence of other evidence for trade on this scale.[95]

Evidence for the development of the British slave trade between the expansion of the free port system and the onset of the Anglo-Spanish wars in 1796 is sparse and rather contradictory. We have seen that figures presented by Sir William Young suggest a leap in total exports from the British colonies to the foreign West Indies from 5,182 in 1787, to 11,042 in 1788. In the latter year Dominica dominated the trade with exports of 4,653 slaves, followed by Grenada (2,543), and Jamaica (2,457), with Barbados, Antigua, St Kitts and St Vincent taking lesser shares.[96] Total exports from the British islands were estimated at some 9,500 slaves per year in 1788–92, with annual exports from Grenada of about 4,800 slaves, from Dominica of 2,800 slaves, and from Jamaica of about 2,500 slaves at this time.[97] Summary data for the period 1790–99 confirm average annual exports from Jamaica of some 2,550 slaves per year (who in the mid-1790s sold for about £45 sterling per individual).[98] A further source indicates total exports from Grenada of no fewer than 31,210 slaves in 1784–92, or average annual exports of about 3,500 slaves, though there is evidence that exports increased sharply from 1788. The Africans exported were sold for a total of £1,175,000 across these nine years, of which the three leading merchant houses of Munro, Baillie, and Tarleton between them accounted for over four-fifths.[99] Elsewhere, average exports from Grenada are given as well over 5,000 slaves annually in 1789–93, with a peak of over 7,000 in 1792, though the trade then fell away sharply with the onset of the war.[100] The slave trade at Grenada was carried on mainly in British vessels, while at the other islands, Spaniards trading at the free ports dominated it. It is to be stressed that the figures discussed here relate to exports to all the foreign West Indies, in which trade with the French sugar colonies was pre-eminent (strongly so at Dominica and Grenada). British Customs records suggest that total registered exports of slaves from the British West Indies specifically to the Spanish colonies numbered 2,283 in 1792, 3,190 in 1793, 2,867 in 1794, and 4,153 in 1795. These four years were marked by a notable concentration of the trade at the Jamaican free ports, caused principally by the collapse of the slave trade at Dominica and Grenada in the context of the French war.[101]

In the Spanish colonies, the consequences of the enhanced opportunities for overt trade with foreign colonies presented by the *comercio de colonias*, the free trade in slaves, and the expansion of the British free port system were felt to greater or lesser extent almost throughout the region. The Mexican writer Pedro Ajequiezcane later emphasised the effects of the free slave trade, especially the further encouragement it gave to smuggling by Spaniards; with this trade, the British

> ceased to trouble to come to our Coasts to supply our necessities; our ships and smugglers were admitted with open arms in all their Ports; [our merchants] took off our precious coin, and in return received, under cover of four Negroes and a few tools, their rich cloths of cotton … In all our settlements on the Continent which have enjoyed this disastrous freedom, the same lamentable effects have been experienced.[102]

Across the Gulf of Mexico in Cuba, the free trade ensured that 6,000 slaves arrived at Havana within twenty-one months, and imports averaged 5,500 slaves per year in the quinquennium 1790–94. It is noteworthy that the British firm of Baker & Dawson supplied over half the slaves imported to Cuba in 1790–91, indicating a smooth transition from the exclusive contracts held by the company in the late 1780s, to vigorous participation in the free slave trade from 1789.[103] The proportion of foreigners among all shipping entering the port of Havana first became really notable from 1791, undoubtedly reflecting the impact of the free trade in slaves. This proportion then doubled again as a result of the renewal of neutral trade in Cuba from 1793, to reach about 40 per cent in 1794–95 (Table 6.1, p. 192). More than 40 per cent of the flour imported at Havana in late 1793 came in foreign shipping, mostly from the United States, while the value of all Cuban imports from foreign ports doubled to over 2,000,000 pesos in 1794.[104] Although British penetration of neutral trade with Cuba during these years remains poorly understood, it can be noted that at least one US vessel entered Havana direct from Jamaica.[105] Cuba also remained a leading centre for British smuggling at this time, favoured by proximity to the British islands and the laxity of official controls. An anti-contraband sweep along the south-central coast in 1792 detected both British smugglers from Jamaica, and Spanish vessels trading to that island with livestock and precious woods under governmental licence. Local Spaniards collaborated closely with British smugglers and woodcutters, and the latter established extensive and well-organised camps and staithes along the coastal rivers.[106]

In New Granada, a crack-down on trade with foreign colonies by Viceroy Gil y Lemos in 1789 proved short-lived, principally as a result of the extension of the free trade in slaves to the region in 1791.[107] We are exceptionally well-informed as to the effects of this trade in New Granada due to the reports of viceroy José de Ezpeleta, who became among its most vocal opponents.[108] As the free slave trade came into operation, Ezpeleta claimed to have noticed growing public sales of illicit foreign manufactures, clearly imported under the same permit. He stated that both Spaniards and foreigners ('but principally the former') exploited the trade to engage in extensive smuggling, flooding the coastal provinces with contraband goods and contributing to a drop in the value of imports from Europe to Cartagena of over 3,000,000 pesos in the quinquennium beginning in 1789. He further suggested that most slaves imported by foreigners were re-exported for lack of a market, while imports in Spanish vessels tended to be very low in number (fuelling the suspicion that the trade was merely a cover for contraband).[109] In December 1791 Ezpeleta actually suspended the free trade in slaves throughout the viceroyalty, but in May the following year his actions were repudiated and he was instructed to implement it in full.[110] Nevertheless, a further major investigation in 1795 tended fully to endorse Ezpeleta's iden-tification of trade with foreign colonies, and specifically the free trade in slaves, as the chief vehicle for contraband trade with the viceroyalty. Informants from Cartagena, Santa Marta, Río de la Hacha, Portobelo and Panama all described how Spanish merchants exploited the legal loopholes to maintain extensive illicit trade with the foreign colonies. Imports of slaves, meanwhile, remained merely nominal – of 134 slaves to Cartagena and 92 to Santa Marta and Río Hacha in the whole of 1794, for example.[111] Certain it is that smuggling remained absolutely rife at Cartagena throughout the mid-1790s. Contraband imports to New Granada were estimated at 1,000,000 pesos per year in 1793–96, perhaps equal to half the regional market for European goods.[112]

The *comercio de colonias* may have retained a rather broader base in Venezuela than in New Granada, with perhaps a greater number of grants of special licences to particular provinces or individuals to engage in the trade. Here too, however, the free trade in slaves came to dominate, to such a degree that by 1793 the Intendant could assert that 'the trade of this Province of Caracas with the Foreign Colonies is limited to that which is permitted by ... the Negro Trade'.[113] There was concern from the outset at the potential for fraud in the system, at the small numbers of slaves imported and the large number of voyages employed to do so.[114] Nevertheless, the region's legal trade with foreign colonies grew rapidly in value: in 1793–96, total registered exports to foreign colonies from Puerto Cabello alone were worth some 480,000 pesos, of which mules and hides together accounted for over nine-tenths. Over 87 per cent of this trade was undertaken on purely Spanish account, in over 330 separate voyages. Registered imports to Puerto Cabello totalled some 615,000 pesos, of which bullion accounted for 75 per cent and slaves (to the number of 574) 18 per cent. Almost 90 per cent of this import trade was undertaken on Spanish account, in some 280 voyages; only thir-teen foreign slavers entered the port, though they brought more than half of all the slaves.[115] In 1794, total Venezuelan exports to the foreign colonies were worth some 975,000 pesos, and registered imports of slaves, tools and bullion in return some 1,175,000 pesos, figures which already represented almost a quarter of the Captaincy-General's overseas trade.[116] It should be recalled that the Dutch island of Curaçao retained a major share of Venezuela's colonies trade during these years, as it would up until its capture by the British in 1800. Naturally the figures discussed in this paragraph give no indication as to the illicit trade sustained under cover of such extensive maritime intercourse. The Intendant of Caracas anticipated a decline in Venezuelan trade in 1795, something which local merchants attributed to the strength of smuggling in the region.[117] The commander of the guarda-costas frankly acknowledged the scale of contraband trade, though ironically his proposed remedies embraced exports of hides to the British colonies and the purchase of corsair vessels there to augment his squadron.[118]

The case of Spanish Trinidad, now entering its last decade as a Venezuelan province, warrants special mention. Reference was made in Chapter 2 to Spanish efforts begun in the 1770s to promote the development of Trinidad and to increase the island's population and trade. This programme was stepped up significantly after 1783, when foreign immigration was encouraged through fiscal concessions and the distribution of land, and freedom was granted to import slaves from neighbouring foreign colonies and to export produce in return.[119] Under the effects of this legislation, Trinidad's population quintupled to almost 18,000 inhabitants by 1797, while production of cotton, sugar and coffee flourished. The growth of the island's trade with foreign colonies was especially notable: the value of Trinidad's colonies trade increased more than ten-fold between 1781–85 and 1791–95, with both imports and exports worth more than 1,100,000 pesos by the latter period. One British observer later recalled that during these years 'the trade of Trinidad was entirely in the hands of foreigners', while 'the colony had little intercourse with Spain'.[120] In the early 1780s, good part of this trade was carried on with the French West Indies, but the British then rapidly displaced the French as the principal participants. Grenada took a leading role in this process, while British commercial penetration was greatly facilitated by the Baker & Dawson contracts in force from 1784. Most cotton and (later) sugar produced in Trinidad was exported to Grenada and thence to the British market, a trade sustained by dozens of ships per year. Some estimates of the value of this trade with the British – for example, of 'a great deal more' than £1,200,000 in 1787 – appear grossly exaggerated, although it is true that the island became an entrepôt for through-trade with the continent as well as in its own productions.[121] Whatever the precise value of the trade, however, British commercial hegemony in Trinidad clearly antedated by at least a decade the formal political control which came with conquest in 1797. In late 1790 or early 1791, the government of Trinidad even attempted to raise a loan of 1,000,000 pesos (c. £225,000) in London to fuel the island's development, under a permit to this end granted earlier by Madrid.[122]

One factor affecting all Anglo-Spanish American trade during this period was *Comercio libre*, the process of limited liberalisation in Spanish colonial commerce which was discussed briefly in the preceding chapter. Following its relatively cautious origins in 1765, Comercio libre was extended in succeeding years, to culminate in the key Regulations of Free Trade of 12

October 1778. This legislation largely dismantled the ancient monopoly structure of Spanish colonial trade, permitting some thirteen Spanish ports to trade directly with most of the American colonies (Venezuela and Mexico remained excluded until 1788–89).[123] John Fisher's work has shed strong light on the revolution in Spanish Atlantic trade made possible by Comercio libre: although its effects were at first delayed by the American Revolutionary War, exports from Spain to the colonies increased no less than four-fold across the period 1778–96. Growth in imports from the Americas was more striking still, to more than ten times the level of 1778 in the years 1782–96.[124] Comercio libre did not, of course, imply any liberalisation of trade with foreigners, and the Regulations incorporated extensive provisions designed to combat smuggling in colonial trade.[125] The commercial renaissance of these years might, in fact, have been expected to depress trade with the British, as Spanish Americans gained access to a far greater range of products at cheaper prices and through legal channels. One observer thought that under the Free Trade regime, 'the foreigners and smugglers disappeared from the coasts and Ports of Spanish America [and] our provinces were supplied abundantly and at good prices'.[126] Another expert later argued that Comercio libre had 'notably diminished contraband';

> This was reduced to the very small amount that could be undertaken in small vessels which study the means to elude the vigilance of the Guardacostas … [*Comercio libre*] has torn from the hands of our bloody enemies the fat sums they took furtively from us, and with which they fed still further their insatiable avarice.[127]

Francisco de Saavedra, too, reported Jamaican merchants as stating that contraband with Cuba fell to one-quarter its former levels following the declaration of Free Trade.[128] Others, however, took an opposing view: Bourgoing suggested that total contraband exports from Spanish America increased by more than 1,000,000 pesos per year in the first six years of Free Trade with respect to the decade ending in 1778.[129] The monopoly interests which were the greatest losers by the reforms remained bitterly opposed to them, arguing repeatedly that they actually enhanced the scope for British interloping.[130] Pedro Ajequiezcane, while recognising the positive effects of the legislation, noted that it simply provoked competing nations into redoubling their efforts at penetration of the Spanish imperial system.[131] In truth, it appears that both Spaniards and the British were winners by Free Trade; that is to say, that the reforms facilitated a commercial boom from which all participants drew due advantage. The best evidence for this interpretation lies in unusual statistical data from the National Archives in London which indicate strong and sustained growth in British trade with Spanish America during precisely the years when Comercio libre was at its zenith. The following section, then, is devoted to detailed analysis of this unusual statistical series.

The Spanish Trade in the National Archives Series, 1788–95

Most studies of British overseas trade in the late eighteenth century draw principally upon the records known as the 'States of Navigation and Commerce'. These records were prepared by an officer of the Customs, the Inspector-General of Imports and Exports, in large annual volumes covering the years 1772–1808. They present historians with a number of serious problems, of which perhaps the greatest are the obsolescence of the official values accorded the various articles of trade, and the question of smuggling.[132] Additional difficulties of at least as serious a nature arise when applying them to the study of trade with the Spanish colonies. This is mainly because the States of Navigation and Commerce record only direct maritime trade with the British Isles; they do not identify commercial intercourse of any kind which went via third ports (in the case of the Spanish trade, via the Iberian Peninsula or the British West Indies). The only trade with foreign colonies in the Caribbean appearing in these official records is direct trade with a catch-all category described as 'the foreign West Indies', which included the rich French, Dutch, and other colonies as well as those belonging to Spain. Registered trade even with this category was very low throughout the late eighteenth century; in 1788, for example, total registered British exports (including re-exports) direct to the 'Foreign West Indies' were worth just £10,600 sterling, and total imports just £15,500.[133] The real volume of Britain's trade with the Spanish colonies is thus buried within the statistics for trade with Spain, the British West Indies, and other intermediary territories; for this reason, and not solely because it was a traditionally contraband trade, detailed statistical data describing British commerce with Spanish America during the colonial period are almost entirely lacking.

During the course of the current research, a highly unusual statistical series came to light in the States of Navigation and Commerce covering the years 1788–95.[134] Thomas Irving, Inspector-General of Imports and Exports since 1786, announced the change in 1788, with the introduction of a section devoted to 'such parts of our Colonial Trade as are not immediately connected to the Mother Country' (though in fact the section covers only the trade of the British empire in the Americas). Irving appears to have drawn his data from the Customs records and Naval Officer's returns for the British colonial ports concerned, although he offers no explicit evidence as to their provenance.[135] The eight volumes of the new type present accounts for maritime commerce between each British colony in the Americas and the neighbouring foreign territories, embracing shipping movements (both of British vessels, and foreign vessels trading under the Free Port Acts) and the commodities traded. In the first four volumes (covering 1788–91), full details are provided of the commodities and their quantities, but Irving offered no information as to their value, remarking only that 'difficulties have arisen as to the principle upon which these Rates of Value are to be formed that will require mature consideration'.[136] In the last four volumes, however (covering

1792–95), values were inserted for all the commodities traded, rendering the commercial accounts complete. The records for the latter four years are thus particularly valuable; indeed, the fact that the values accorded the articles of trade are up to date makes them unique among all eighteenth-century British records of their type. Taken as a whole, the series preserved in the National Archives provides what is very probably the only detailed statistical survey of a major branch of British trade with the Spanish colonies which exists for any period.[137] The series ends abruptly and without explanation in 1795; thereafter the section on colonial trade was suppressed, and the States returned to a format and content similar to that which had prevailed before 1788.

These records are deficient in a number of significant respects. An immediate problem is that the shipping and trade of each British colony is given with 'the Spanish colonies' without further differentiation. The records thus cannot be used to measure the trade of the British colonies with specific Spanish-American regions – of Jamaica with Mexico, for example, rather than with the Spanish colonies in general – with any precision. Again, they shed no light on British trade with Spanish America which went via foreign intermediary ports in the West Indies; we cannot use them, for example, to measure the substantial trade which went on via Dutch Curaçao or Danish St Thomas. Among registered imports from the Spanish colonies, as will be seen, Irving himself recognised that data for imports of bullion far understated the true value of that branch of the trade. Much the most serious defect, however, is that the commercial accounts for 1792–95, while purporting to offer full data for imports other than bullion, offer only a very limited statement of exports: the only exports recorded are slaves, rum, and a small number of sundry commodities. Irving noted that the British manufactures which made up the bulk of exports 'consist of so great a variety of articles and often in small quantities that the Officers could not take an account of them without such a degree of labour & delay as might materially injure the trade', a point which often found an echo in the officers' own statements.[138] The National Archives series is thus of use principally for the study of imports from the Spanish colonies; it offers only a limited amount of useful information on exports to those territories.

Their inherent limitations aside, the key issue regarding these records is, of course, that of their reliability: of the extent to which they may be considered accurate. Early official trade records always merit considerable circumspection, and we cannot be too sanguine about the absolute accuracy of the data discussed in the following pages. There are nevertheless grounds to suppose that the two basic problems affecting the States of Navigation and Commerce – the obsolescence of official values, and smuggling – present much less of a problem with respect to this particular series. Thus, the values accorded the articles of trade may be considered current in 1792, even if the same values were then applied throughout the three years which followed. Again, the vast majority of trade was now carried on by Spanish merchants at the British free ports and was perfectly legal in British eyes; that is to say, levels of contraband appear to have remained at a minimum during these years. Thomas Irving, the compiler of these records, was a former Inspector-General of Imports and Exports and Register-General of Shipping in North America, and claimed to be the leading British expert on 'the value of the Produce of the Western World'.[139] Irving's principal student has described his efforts to insure that the records in his charge 'were as complete and accurate as could be. He badgered and threatened any who were recalcitrant and he questioned and cross-checked everything he found sloppy or suspect.'[140] Where Irving knew his data for trade with the Spanish colonies to be defective (as with imports of bullion, or all exports) he supplied supplementary general estimates, discussed hereafter, to address the shortcoming. His own assessment of the value of the data he collected seems realistic:

> Defective ... as these American accounts may be in some instances, yet upon the whole they exhibit a view of that part of the trade of the Empire sufficiently accurate for all the general purposes required by Government and I flatter myself will be found to contain a more comprehensive and at the same time concise statement of the commercial and political importance of the British colonies than anything hitherto submitted.[141]

A final motive for optimism lies in the commercial statistics themselves, which display a substantial degree of internal consistency. This coherence is manifest in recognisable trends, which can be related quite convincingly to major external factors operating during these years – notably the onset of the French war in 1793.

The total value of imports from the Spanish colonies to the British West Indies recorded in 1792, the first year for which complete commercial data are available, was some £397,000.[142] This figure increased by some 6 per cent in 1793, fell by some 2.5 per cent in 1794, and then increased again by 21 per cent in 1795, in which year the total registered value of imports stood at just under £499,000.[143] The only important potential distortion Irving identified in his data relating to imports lay in the statistics regarding bullion. To protect the anonymity of Spaniards importing bullion, the Customs officers in the British colonies were ordered not to take strict account of imports, so that 'we may reasonably suppose that the quantity of coin and bullion stated in the official accounts bears but a small proportion to the actual importations'. After 'many conversations with well-informed men both in this country and formerly in America as to the probable quantity of coin and bullion which was annually obtained from the foreign European colonies', Irving concluded that 'upon the whole I am inclined to think that the amount of gold and silver we receive through this channel in ingots hammered money and coined dollars does not amount to less than £400,000'.[144] The vast majority of this sum, certainly more than 90 per cent, can be supposed to have come from the Spanish colonies. The registered value of bullion imported in 1792, the year in which Irving's estimate was made, was just

£70,225, suggesting an understatement of imports of bullion of perhaps around £300,000 and giving an adjusted total value of imports of around £700,000. If the rate of increase in real imports of bullion across these four years was in line with that of imports in general, then of course by 1795, too, the adjusted total value of imports would have been substantially higher than the recorded figure.

This adjustment of the total value of imports should be taken into account when comparing the value of the Spanish trade with that with the colonies of other nations in the region. This data is presented in terms of the tonnage of shipping entering at the British West Indies from all foreign colonies, and also from the United States, each year in 1788–95.[145] Shipping entering from the Spanish colonies averaged some 18,500 tons per year during this period, representing about a third of all shipping entering from foreign colonies. These mean data mask significant trends in the trade across the eight years in question. In the five years to 1792, the Spanish colonies were the origin of around a fifth to a quarter of shipping entering from foreign colonies, and more than a third only in 1791. The following three years demonstrated the effects of the war with France, which broke out early in 1793, as the substantial tonnage of shipping entering from the French colonies declined rapidly and then disappeared altogether. The overall inwards tonnage from the foreign colonies, having reached a peak in 1793, fell by more than half by 1795, though within this diminished total, shipping from the Spanish colonies became still more important, accounting for over half of all shipping entering from the foreign colonies in 1794–95. Shipping entering from the United States substantially outweighed that from all the foreign colonies combined, a feature which became much more pronounced during the war.

The tonnage of shipping is, of course, at best a crude measure of commercial activity, but similar conclusions may be drawn from data presenting the total registered value of imports from the same foreign colonies and from the United States in 1792–95.[146] In fact, the relative significance of the import trade from the Spanish colonies was substantially greater by value than in terms of tonnage of shipping: average imports were worth some £430,000 per year, or some two-thirds of the total value of imports from foreign colonies in the region. This mean figure again masks the effects of the French war, which destroyed French trade and brought the value of imports from Spanish America to a high point in 1794 of over 81 per cent of all imports from foreign colonies. Factors such as imports from the Spanish colonies which came via other foreign colonies and are hidden within the statistics for those territories, and especially the understatement in the official records of imports of bullion, may mean that the local dominance of the Spanish trade was still greater than is here supposed. Whatever the precise figures involved, however, it seems clear that the early 1790s marked the consolidation of Hispanic America as Britain's most important commercial partner in the West Indies after the United States – a position from which there would be no subsequent retreat.

The statistical series compiled by the Inspector-General of Imports and Exports clearly illustrates the degree to which the institution of the free ports and the development of the *comercio de colonias* had sealed the dominance of Spanish shipping in British West Indian trade with the Spanish colonies by the early 1790s. Of the 18,500 tons of shipping entering from those colonies in an average year, some 15,000 tons, or over four-fifths of the total, were foreign vessels trading under the Acts (of which the vast majority were Spanish).[147] Real annual figures suggest that this proportion increased to over nine-tenths in 1793–94, possibly reflecting an increased reluctance among British merchants and ship-owners to expose their property to attack in the early years of the French war. Data for the value of the goods imported in either class of shipping suggest a far greater dominance of Spanish shipping over British: in 1792–95, Spaniards brought over 95 per cent of the total value of imports from the Spanish to the British colonies.[148] This overwhelming dominance was a product principally of the concentration of imports of bullion almost exclusively in Spanish vessels (a feature discussed below). It is to be stressed that these figures describe a period of peace between Britain and Spain, when British smuggling typically declined; also that the data for trade in British vessels, as a more strictly contraband trade, may be more likely to understate its true volume than that for commerce at the free ports. The broad conclusion, however, that trade by Spaniards at the free ports now represented by far the richest branch of the trade, does not seem open to doubt.

All the British colonies in the Caribbean now took a share in the Spanish trade; the only apparent exception was Montserrat, which nevertheless recorded a modest export trade with those territories.[149] This general participation of the British islands, although predictable, has been difficult to prove, and these data provide unusual explicit confirmation that St Vincent, St Kitts, or Nevis traded with the Spaniards. Since the majority of all trade was now undertaken by Spanish vessels at the free ports, it was heavily concentrated in Jamaica, the Bahamas, Dominica, and Grenada (Antigua, the other colony with a free port, had no registered trade with Spanish shipping during these years). The free ports in Jamaica took the lion's share of shipping, accounting for some 65 per cent of the total inward tonnage from the Spanish colonies in 1788–95.[150] Jamaica's dominance in terms of the value of imports was greater still, accounting for over four-fifths of the total in 1792–95. The island appears to have benefited from the decline of trade at Dominica and Grenada, its real share of the total value of imports rising from 73 per cent in 1792, to more than 95 per cent in 1795.[151] This dominance of imports by value was a product principally of imports of bullion, which were strongly concentrated in Jamaica. Jamaica's overwhelming dominance of the Spanish trade a quarter-century after the passing of the first Free Port Act represents a further striking conclusion to be drawn from these data, one which again underlines the extent to which the widely reported slump in trade in the years after 1766, discussed at length in Chapter 2, was either illusory or of short duration.

Data for the free ports in the remaining islands suggest that trade at the Bahamas was reasonably steady and significant throughout these years, oscillating between about 5 per cent and 14 per cent of the total inward tonnage of foreign shipping. Trade at Dominica, by contrast, after hovering at around 10 per cent of the total in most years, collapsed in 1793, and accounted for less than 2 per cent of inward foreign shipping in 1795. A similar pattern prevailed at Grenada, whose free ports took from a quarter to a third of incoming Spanish shipping under the Acts until 1793, but then experienced a crisis which left the island's share at under 11 per cent by 1795. It seems clear that the trade of both islands suffered as a result of the French war, especially Dominica, unhappily situated between French Martinique and Guadeloupe. Trade by foreign vessels at the free ports aside, the leading colony for the much less significant trade in British vessels was Grenada, with an average annual share of total inward tonnage of 36 per cent, and of the total value of imports of almost 43 per cent.[152] This dominance of trade in British vessels appears anomalous, though Armytage relates British control of Grenada's slave trade with the Spanish colonies to the Baker & Dawson contracts (discussed earlier in this chapter).[153] Grenada was followed by Antigua, Jamaica, the Bahamas, and St Vincent, with the remainder of the trade distributed in portions averaging less than 5 per cent among the other colonies. Of particular interest here is the modest share of Barbados, which, well into the eighteenth century, had remained the second great centre for the trade after Jamaica.

The range of products imported by the British from the Spanish colonies is quite well-known, as the present and other secondary accounts have made clear.[154] The statistical series held in the National Archives offers fully detailed accounts of imports annually during 1792–95.[155] With the exception of specie, the most important commodities traded were livestock and hides, which accounted for more than two-fifths of the total value of imports up to 1794. Most significant among the livestock were cattle, horses, and mules; the latter featured particularly prominently, alone accounting for some 22–24 per cent of the *total value* of registered imports from the Spanish colonies until 1795! Livestock (and also most non-dye woods, foodstuffs, and slaves) were destined for use in the colonies themselves, emphasising the real significance of the Spanish trade to the local economies of the British islands, beyond its significance as a source of materials for re-export to Great Britain. The next most important commodities were dyes and dyewoods, which accounted for from 7.5 to 21 per cent of total imports until 1795, with fustic and nicaragua wood the leading products imported. There followed a range of plantation produce, accounting for from 4 to 14 per cent of total imports by value across these four years; the only commodity of any significance here was raw cotton, or 'cotton wool', for which the Spanish colonies were a source of growing importance.[156] The remaining imports consisted of lesser quantities of assorted woods (either for construction purposes, or hardwoods such as mahogany), drugs (including cortex Peru, lignum vitae, and sarsaparilla), and foodstuffs (notably bread and flour, maize, and dried fish). Miscellaneous imports not corresponding to any of these general categories included the varnish resin gum copal, tortoiseshell, and a small number of slaves.

Of particular relevance among imports was specie, in the form of Spanish dollars. From a base of the equivalent of £70,225 in 1792, registered imports of specie rose by some 75 per cent in 1793, 40.5 per cent in 1794, and 85.5 per cent in 1795, in which year they were equivalent to £320,340.[157] This rate of growth substantially exceeded the overall rate of growth of imports from the Spanish colonies, and gave specie an increasingly important share of total imports, rising from 17.7 per cent in 1792, to 64.3 per cent in 1795. The growing importance of specie came at the expense of other imports, principally of dyes and dyewoods and livestock; in fact the value of all other imports actually fell by just over 45 per cent in these four years. The likeliest explanation for this fall appears to be economic disruption caused by the French war, while the same factor may also have fuelled imports of bullion, as Spanish merchants had increasing recourse to the British for remission of bullion to Europe in the light of the French naval threat.[158] Given that the majority of imports of specie went unregistered – we have seen that by Thomas Irving's own estimate, the accounts for 1792 understated imports of bullion by at least c. £300,000 – real imports of dollars were certainly much higher than appears here. We are, of course, in the realm of speculation; if imports of unregistered specie increased at the same rate as recorded imports, for example, then real imports of bullion would have totalled some £1,687,000 in 1795, and the real total value of imports from the Spanish colonies would have been in the order of £1,866,000 in the same year.[159] The latter figure seems clearly excessive; but in my view there is little doubt that the real value of all imports from the Spanish to the British colonies, starting from a base of c. £700,000 in 1792, surpassed £1,000,000 by 1795 (and may have been substantially higher).

The contribution of the various commodities to imports as a whole varied according to whether they were brought in British shipping or in foreign shipping trading under the Free Port Acts. The relative importance of imports in each type of shipping, expressed as annual average percentages in 1792–95, sheds further useful light on the two branches of the trade.[160] It is notable that specie constituted a far more significant proportion of imports in foreign shipping than it did in British vessels. Indeed, specie was imported almost entirely by Spanish merchants in Spanish shipping, who accounted for £682,463 of the total of £686,157 in registered specie imported during these four years. Dyes and dyewoods made up a similar proportion of imports in both foreign and British shipping, of 10 per cent in each case; livestock (with specie and dyes, the basic stock of the import trade) were major imports in both foreign and British shipping, though rather more so in the former. The only other significant import in foreign shipping in percentage terms was plantation produce, especially raw cotton, emphasising that (with the major exception of livestock) Spanish merchants trafficked principally in high value goods destined for re-export to Great Britain. By contrast, imports for use in the British colonies tended to be carried in British (generally, colonial) shipping: it will be noted that foodstuffs were only imported in British vessels, and that 'other woods', including wood for construction purposes, made up a greater proportion of imports in British shipping.[161] Plantation produce constituted a higher proportion of imports in British shipping than was the case with foreign vessels (though of course, given the much lower overall value of the trade in British vessels, the value of the products imported was clearly inferior).

Comparable analysis of the make-up of the Spanish trade at each British island reveals a number of further relevant characteristics of the trade as a whole. This data is presented in terms of the average annual share of each general category of imports, whether in Spanish or British shipping, at each British colony in 1792–95.[162] It is immediately striking that the only colonies with registered imports of bullion during this period were Jamaica and the Bahamas, of which Jamaica took over 95 per cent of the total (the respective figures were £653,541, and £32,616). Other islands certainly also imported bullion during these years, with Grenada the third major port of entry; but Jamaica was clearly the leading recipient, privileged both by its general pre-eminence as a centre for the Spanish trade, and as the seat of a long-established system for monetary transfers to Europe. Specie made up an identical proportion of the value of imports in Spanish shipping at both Jamaica and the Bahamas (48 per cent); this was symbolic of a broader resemblance of the free ports trade of both colonies, which was based especially upon imports of bullion and livestock, complemented by dyes and dyewoods, other woods, and plantation produce.[163] Typical imports at the Grenadan free port, by contrast, were dominated by livestock, which together with plantation produce accounted for over 91 per cent of the total import trade. Dominica received more diverse imports based especially upon livestock, plantation produce, dyes and dyewoods, and a range of miscellaneous imports dominated by *gum copal* and *gum algobora*.[164] The import trade in British vessels, by contrast, tended to be rather more diverse than trade in foreign vessels, although Jamaica imported mainly livestock and non-dye woods in the only year in which such trade was recorded.[165] A notable conclusion suggested by the data for trade in British shipping is that the British colonies with least concern in the Spanish trade (Barbados, Nevis, and St Kitts) looked to it principally to satisfy their own immediate wants in terms of livestock, wood for construction purposes, or foodstuffs. Thus in an average year more than four-fifths of Barbados's imports consisted of wood and livestock; the same commodities constituted a similar proportion of imports at Nevis, while over half of imports at St Kitts consisted of foodstuffs and wood.

In 1788, the share of the Spanish colonies in the total free ports trade of Jamaica was still limited to about 55 per cent, with most of the remainder carried on with the French islands.[166] In the same year, about 60 per cent of Grenada's free port trade was with Spanish America, with most of the remainder again carried on with the French. Dominica, whose free ports had been first established in 1766 principally to trade with the French colonies, did about 74 per cent of its free port trade with those islands, and only about 14 per cent with the colonies of Spain. These figures remained broadly stable until 1792–93, when the imminence and outbreak of the French war provoked the collapse of trade with the French colonies and a consequent increase in the proportional importance of trade with Spanish America. By 1795, *all* of the registered shipping trading with Jamaica's free ports did so with the Spanish colonies. The corresponding figure for Grenada was over 97 per cent, and for Dominica 73.5 per cent, with all remaining shipping trading with the Danish colonies. By contrast, the free port at Nassau in the Bahamas traded almost exclusively with the Spanish colonies throughout these years. The same pattern, of the growing proportional importance of trade with the Spanish colonies in all trade at British West Indian ports from 1792 onwards, is indicated by data for the value of imports in 1792–95, although in these figures the dominance of the Spanish trade in the final years is greater still.[167]

The National Archives series furnishes not only figures for the tonnage of shipping involved in the Spanish trade in 1788–95, discussed throughout these pages, but also for the number of ships involved and for the crews who manned them. These figures make it possible to reconstruct the typical types of craft involved in the various branches of the trade.[168] Thus, Spanish vessels entering the free ports in the Bahamas or Grenada displaced fewer than 25 tons, underlining the extent to which Spanish merchants trading to these nearby islands did so in small, undecked launches. Spanish shipping trading with Jamaica and Dominica was larger, a function doubtless of the greater distance of those islands from Spanish ports; the typical vessel trading with Jamaica, for instance, displaced some 38 tons and had a crew of seven or eight men. British ships involved in the trade, by contrast, were considerably larger than these Spanish vessels; the typical British vessel trading with the Spanish colonies displaced from 60 to 70 tons and was manned by a crew of from six to seven men. British vessels trading at the Bahamas, St Vincent and Tobago – all islands in close proximity to the Spanish colonies – were typically smaller, at fewer than 50 tons and six crew, while those which entered at Dominica and Jamaica were larger, at over 85 tons and eight to nine crew in each case.

Only a fraction of exports from the British West Indies to the Spanish colonies were recorded in the accounts for British colonial trade prepared by Thomas Irving. The only exports recorded systematically in 1792–95 were slaves and rum; the majority of exports, consisting of British manufactures and especially of textiles, were not recorded by British officials in the colonies and so were not incorporated into the master volumes in London.[169] Data for the total registered value of exports to Spanish America in the four years for which they are available suggest a total value of £104,000 in 1792, rising to

£188,000 in 1795, that is to say, only around a quarter to a third of the registered value of imports during these years.[170] In his commentary on the commercial accounts for 1792, Irving noted, 'I have corresponded at different times with the principal Officers in the West Indies relative to the value of the exports to the foreign islands & from the aggregate of their information I am of opinion that the amount is not less than from 4 to £500,000.'[171] Frances Armytage thought that a value for total exports of £400,000–£500,000 may have been an underestimate,[172] and Irving's figure is very broadly comparable to my revised calculation for the total value of imports in 1792, of £700,000; though it should be noted that Irving's estimate embraces British exports to all the foreign colonies in the Caribbean, not only to Spanish America. Data in these accounts for exports of slaves to the Spanish colonies were mentioned briefly above, and have been discussed at greater length elsewhere.[173] The low total registered value of exports, combined with the very limited number of commodities accounted for, makes further analysis of most registered exports unproductive. Data for shipping movements outward from the British colonies in 1788–95, for their part, reflect closely the commercial patterns apparent in the data for inward shipping. Perhaps worthy of note is that Dominica took an annual average share of total outward tonnage of just over 11 per cent, suggesting that its share of the import trade in British shipping may have been under-estimated.

Finally, the States of Navigation and Commerce for 1788–95 also embrace the trade of the colonies in North America which remained to Britain after the American Revolutionary war. The relevant data share the characteristics and defects of those which concern the British West Indies: data are available for shipping for 1788–95, but for trade only for 1792–95; the data regarding imports purport to be complete, while those which concern exports are merely fragmentary. The total registered value of imports from the Spanish colonies to British North America and to Bermuda in the north Atlantic was trifling: the trade was worth little more than £1,000 per year until 1793, and was subject to marked decline thereafter.[174] Data on shipping suggest that, besides Bermuda, four North American colonies (Cape Breton, New Brunswick, Newfoundland, and Nova Scotia) had some share in the trade. Often a single ship a year sailed in either direction, and several of these colonies had registered trade only occasionally in the eight years in question.[175] The only fairly consistent participants were Newfoundland, and particularly Bermuda, whose free port had been established in 1793 partly with a view to waylaying Spaniards bound for the United States.[176] The National Archives series, however, does not distinguish any trade with the Spanish colonies via this free port; rather, the island's Spanish trade was carried on exclusively in British vessels. Imports from the Spanish colonies to British North America consisted entirely of coffee, white and brown sugar, molasses, and a single cargo of hides; the only recorded exports to Spanish America were of wet fish and bread and flour, worth £112, exported from Bermuda in 1793.

The Peninsular Re-export Trade, c. 1763–96: Stable Prosperity in the Twilight Years

In Chapter 1, summary account was given of what was the leading branch of British trade with the Spanish colonies, that which was based on the re-export of British manufactures via ports in the Iberian Peninsula. In conclusion to this chapter, it may be useful briefly to sketch the development of this trade between the end of the Seven Years War and the onset of the Anglo-Spanish Napoleonic wars in 1796. Tracing British activity in the re-export trade during this period is difficult given the almost entire lack of good scholarly studies, a lack which itself reflects the problematic nature of the subject as a topic for research. Virtually the only valuable study available is Allan Christelow's second major article, which considers the British re-export trades at Cadiz and Lisbon together in the period 1759–83.[177] Christelow's principal thesis is that during these years, the British became increasingly disenchanted with the re-export trade to the colonies. This was due in part to discontent at specific characteristics of the trade, especially the lengthy credit demanded and the long delays experienced in receiving returns. It was also due to late-Bourbon attacks on British commercial privileges and to protectionist measures which tended to exclude many typical British products from Spanish markets. Lastly, it reflected British consciousness of growing commercial superiority in both technological and financial terms, and hence disdain for treaties and special privileges as tools for commercial expansion. Christelow suggests that these trends fuelled greater contemporary British interest in direct penetration of Spanish-American markets through the interloping trade in the West Indies. They also contributed to a gradual withdrawal of British merchants from Spanish ports: thus, the British Factory at Cadiz boasted no more than twenty members in the two decades to 1783.[178] Forty-four Britons were registered as resident in Cadiz in 1791, and perhaps thirty-three in 1795–96, of whom only three gave their profession as merchants.[179] Christelow is careful to note, nevertheless, that this withdrawal, rather than denoting any decline in British sales by way of Spain, may simply have reflected a growing preference for outright sales at Cadiz over re-exports made through the medium of Spanish cover-men. In this sense the expert merchant Joseph Salvador noted in 1766 that although 'the British merchant trades less on his own account', yet 'there are not less British manufactures that go by way of Old Spain consumed in America in times of peace than were formerly'.[180]

Certainly, the general evidence for the scale of British trade via Spain during this period is extensive. There were periodic crack-downs on British contraband in Cadiz and other relevant ports, as well as repeated allegations of the connivance of British men-of-war in the smuggling of bullion out of the Peninsula.[181] The British packet boats provided a notorious vehicle for such smuggling, the Spanish ambassador arguing vehemently against their re-establishment in 1790 in view of 'the enormous contraband and vexations experienced with the said Packets'.[182] The scale of illicit trade could be striking: thus in eighteen months in 1775–76, the value of fraudulent imports on the coast between Cadiz and Sanlúcar de Barrameda was estimated at 1,500,000 pesos in silver bullion alone.[183] The British minister in Madrid estimated that fraud against import and export duties had cost the royal revenues some £720,000 in 1787 solely against declared trade, while 'not a tenth part of what is smuggled is seized'.[184] In July 1785 the British consul in La Coruña remarked on a late boom in trade 'in prohibited cotton manufactures of which I am told great quantities without at all being landed are clandestinely put on board the Spanish packets that sail from this port to the Havana, Carthagena, Vera Cruz and Buenos Ayres'.[185] One Thomas Lethbridge offered (in return for 'a small Reward') to describe the means by which the British smuggled up to 1,000,000 pesos per year out of La Coruña and Vigo, including up to 40,000 dollars in a single ship.[186] Statements of British imports from Cadiz, Gibraltar and other ports routinely listed large quantities of clearly American produce, and in 1792 Anglo-Spanish trade was said to rest largely upon sales of 'the wines and produce of the continent of Spain, and ... of the indigo, cacao, Tobacco, Cochineal, dyewoods etc from its colonies'.[187] Occasional confidential negotiations were held to place this exchange on a more formal footing, for example, through access to Spain for British muslins in return for admittance to British ports of Spanish-American produce in Spanish shipping.[188] These negotiations came to nothing; but the share of foreign goods in all Spanish exports to the colonies remained at around 50 per cent throughout 1778–96.[189] It was estimated that before the wars Britain supplied perhaps one-quarter of these goods, while in 1791, almost 18 per cent of shipping entering the port of Cadiz was British – a greater proportion than that of any other foreign nation.[190]

Such general evidence aside, the sources also offer some scattered indications as to the cash value of British exports to Spanish America via the Peninsula. The best such evidence relates to the 1780s and early 1790s; thus in March 1785, the British consul at Cadiz reported that British imports since the Peace had been worth at least £2,500,000, and anticipated a fall in sales that year, 'the Spanish dominions in America, & this country, being now well stocked with British commodities'.[191] In 1786 a London periodical recorded total imports of gold and silver bullion to Britain of £2,300,000 to the beginning of November, a figure likely to reach £3,000,000 by the year's end 'if, as is thought, the majority of the 6,000,000 hard dollars which have lately reached Cadiz from South America follow the same course'.[192] In December the same year the British minister in Madrid reported that imports to Spain of Spanish-American cochineal, indigo, drugs, hides and salt alone destined for British markets had been worth £700,000 in the previous eighteen months.[193] In the first six months of 1788, British woollens imported to Spain expressly for re-export to America were worth some £172,000 solely at Cadiz, and £55,000 at Seville and Sanlúcar.[194] In September 1791 it was reported that imports of American bullion to Cadiz and Lisbon were worth

£5,000,000 per year, of which £1,000,000 was re-shipped to Britain each year in exchange for manufactures; 'and so it occurs that through the superior industry of our goods and the mercantile spirit of our Merchants, the mines of Mexico, Peru and Brazil yield more solid advantages to this Kingdom than they offer the Spaniards and Portuguese themselves.'[195]

These data are few and fragmentary, and any firm conclusions must necessarily await detailed and dedicated scholarly research on this subject. Tentatively, however, the figures might indicate a trade worth from £700,000 to £1,000,000 per year in the mid-1780s and early 1790s. They appear to support current assumptions that, notwithstanding broad stagnation in the decades after 1760, re-exports via Spain remained the chief channel for British trade with the Spanish colonies (and thus, indeed, for all foreign penetration of Spanish Atlantic commerce) until the end of the eighteenth century. In view of my revised estimates for the value of trade via the Caribbean (of c. £700,000 in 1792, rising to more than £1,000,000 by 1795), they might, nevertheless, indicate that trade via the Caribbean for the first time displaced re-exports via Spanish ports as the chief vehicle for British trade with the Spanish colonies, some few years before the re-export trade collapsed altogether upon the renewal of hostilities between Britain and Spain in the winter of 1796.

Notes

1   See e.g. Becker, *España e Inglaterra*, p. 47; Dawson, 'William Pitt's Settlement', pp. 701–3. In Europe, Spain regained Minorca, seized by Britain during the War of the Spanish Succession (1702–13).
2   Kuethe, 'Havana in the Eighteenth Century', p. 24.
3   'Varias apuntaciones ... a Dn. Francisco de Mollinedo', encl. to Marqués del Campo to Floridablanca, London, 4 July 1788, A.H.N., Estado, 4236.
4   For an instance in Venezuela, see Manuel González to José de Gálvez, Caracas, 27 Apr. 1784, A.G.I., Caracas, 87; for one in Cuba, Del Campo to Floridablanca, London, 8 Sept. 1787, A.H.N., Estado, 4255.
5   Earl of Dunmore to Sydney, Nassau, 21 Apr. 1788, and other relevant papers in N.A., F.O. 185 / 5.
6   Translated extract from London press, encl. to Del Campo to Floridablanca, London, 8 Apr. 1785, A.H.N., Estado, 4232.
7   For Allwood's arrest and charges see Marrero, *Cuba*, 12:51–5. He was released in December 1784.
8   My re-translation from a translated extract from the London press, encl. to Del Campo to Floridablanca, London, 15 Feb. 1787, A.H.N., Estado, 4255.
9   Mercantile petitions dated May–June 1786, cited in Allen, 'British Commercial Policy', pp. 176–7.
10 Unsigned, undirected letter, dated Kingston, 18 Sept. 1784, A.H.N., Estado, 4232.
11 Jones, 'Historical Study of Anglo-Spanish American Trade', pp. 50–1.
12 Merchants of Kingston to Joshua Rowley, Kingston, 19 Aug. 1783, N.A., ADM. 1 / 242, ff. 278–v; see also James Gambier to Philip Stephens, *Janus*, Jamaica, 12 July 1784, N.A., ADM. 1 / 243, ff. 112–20v.
13 See esp. Manning, *British Colonial Government*, p. 279, also note 70.

14 *Ensayo político sobre el reino de la Nueva España*, p. 508.

15 Accounts in N.A., C.O. 318 / 1, ff. 129–30. Imports of bullion to Jamaica are given as $17,400 in 1786, and $53,850 in 1787.

16 Evidence of John Miller *et al.*, Minute for 1 May 1787, N.A., B.T. 5 / 4, ff. 132–3v.

17 'Some thoughts relative to the trade lately carried on in the Bay of Honduras and on the Mosquito Shore by the British merchants', 1783, B.L., Add. Mss. 36,806, ff. 203–14.

18 See e.g. the unsigned 'Account of the Spanish Main', n.d. [c. 1783], B.L., Add. Mss. 36,806, ff. 216–26.

19 Potthast-Jutkeit, 'Centroamérica y el contrabando', p. 514.

20 My re-translation from a translated extract from the London press, encl. to Del Campo to Floridablanca, London, 29 Apr. 1785, A.H.N., Estado, 4232.

21 Dawson, 'William Pitt's Settlement', pp. 705–6.

22 Del Campo to Floridablanca, London, 20 Jan. 1786, 18 July 1786, and enclosures, A.H.N., Estado, 4250; Del Campo to Floridablanca, London, 29 Mar. 1787 and enclosure, A.H.N., Estado, 4255.

23 Del Campo to Floridablanca, London, 6 Dec. 1787, 29 Dec. 1787, A.H.N., Estado, 4255.

24 Whitaker, *Spanish-American Frontier*, pp. 36–43, 177–80. Whitaker argues that the grant of the contract to a British company reflected early Spanish disquiet at US expansionism in the region.

25 Testimony of Kender Mason, Minute for 14 Nov. 1786, N.A., B.T. 5 / 4, ff. 37–8.

26 King, 'Evolution of the Free Slave Trade Principle', pp. 47–50.

27 I know of no fully satisfactory account of these contracts. The first is often known as the Barry contract, or (in Spanish sources) the Fitch contract, for Barry's correspondent in Jamaica; it is also referred to as the first Baker and Dawson contract, in opposition to the second contract signed in 1786.

28 Liston to Carmarthen, Madrid, 14 Feb. 1784, N.A., F.O. 185 / 1, no. 13; see also Liston to Fox, San Ildefonso, 11 Sept. 1783, in the same volume, no. 4.

29 'Contrata con Dn. Eduardo Barry', El Pardo, 13 Feb. 1784, A.G.I., Caracas, 466; French trans. in N.A., F.O. 185 / 1, n.f.; see Sevilla Soler, *Inmigración y cambio socio-económico*, pp. 187–8.

30 José María Chacón to José de Gálvez, Trinidad, 22 Feb. 1785, A.G.I., Caracas, 152.

31 López Cantos, *Don Francisco de Saavedra*, pp. 57–70.

32 Marrero, *Cuba*, 9:17–18; Böttcher, 'Trade, War and Empire', pp. 188–90.

33 Figures drawn from (slightly differing) accounts in N.A., C.O. 318 / 1, ff. 129–30; 'Observations on the trade', B.L., Add. Mss. 38,345, ff. 208–13v; Young, *West-India Common-Place Book*, pp. 181–4.

34 Young, *West-India Common-Place Book*, pp. 7–8.

35 See also McPherson, *Annals of Commerce*, 4:166–7.

36 Villalobos R., *Comercio y contrabando en el Río de la Plata y Chile*, pp. 62–3.

37 Juan Ignacio de Urriza to José de Gálvez, Havana, 2 Oct. 1783, 17 Oct. 1783, both in A.G.I., Santo Domingo, 2188.

38 Cédula to Intendant of Havana, El Pardo, 23 Jan. 1784, copies (with slightly different wording) in A.G.I., Santo Domingo, 2188; Caracas, 59. This decree was later partly retracted.

39 See the careful account by James Lewis: 'Anglo-American Entrepreneurs', *passim*.

40 Saavedra to Gálvez, Caracas, 25 May 1785, in Alvarez, *Comercio y comerciantes*, pp. 139–40, documentary app. 1; also Saavedra, *Decenios*, pp. 239–40. As a minister under Charles IV, Saavedra would play a decisive role in the general opening of the Spanish colonies to neutral trade in November 1797: see Ortiz de la Tabla, *Comercio*

exterior de Veracruz, esp. p.285.

41 López Cantos, *Don Francisco de Saavedra*, esp. pp. 39–41.

42 Alvarez, *Comercio y comerciantes*, p. 37; Guillelmi to Valdés, Caracas, 30 Apr. 1789, A.G.I., Caracas, 114; also Barbier, 'Venezuelan "Libranzas"', pp. 462–3.

43 McFarlane, *Colombia before Independence*, pp. 130–1.

44 McFarlane, 'El comercio exterior del Virreinato', *passim*; same author, *Colombia*, pp. 145–50.

45 Decree to Caballero y Góngora, Aranjuez, 21 June 1786, A.G.I., Santa Fé, 955.

46 Merchants' *representación*, Cadiz, 31 July 1787, and enclosures, A.G.I., Santa Fé, 955; see also Josef García de León y Pizarro to Antonio Valdés, Madrid, 20 Aug. 1787, A.G.I., Santa Fé, 955; José de Ezpeleta to Diego de Gardoqui, Santa Fé, 19 July 1796, A.G.I., Santa Fé, 645.

47 McFarlane, *Colombia*, pp. 150–1; on Santa Marta see esp. Julián, *Perla de la América*, pp. 71–4, 99, 254–6.

48 Ramos, *Contrabando inglés*, pp. 40, 205.

49 Marqués del Campo to Floridablanca, London, 17 Apr. 1787, A.H.N., Estado, 4255.

50 McFarlane, *Colombia before Independence*, pp. 155–7.

51 McFarlane, *Colombia before Independence*, pp. 160–1.

52 For example, permission was granted in 1786 to Spanish Santo Domingo to import agricultural tools and plantation machinery from foreign colonies free of duty.

53 27 Geo. 3, cap. 27; see Armytage, *Free Port System*, pp. 59–60; Allen, 'British Commercial Policy', pp. 182–3; Manning, *British Colonial Government*, pp. 277–8.

54 32 Geo. 3, cap. 43 and 33 Geo. 3, cap. 50 respectively; Manning, *British Colonial Government*, pp. 280–1.

55 See esp. Armytage, *Free Port System*, pp. 52, 56–9.

56 On petitions from British islands, see Allen, 'British Commercial Policy', pp. 129, 147–9; Wilkinson, *Bermuda*, pp. 431–3. On British policy towards trade between the United States and the West Indian colonies during the post-war decade, see Allen, 'British Commercial Policy', chaps. 3–5; Keith, 'Relaxations in the British Restrictions', pp. 2–9.

57 Allen, 'British Commercial Policy', pp. 179–82; Williams, 'Mercados británicos', p. 98; Graham, 'Origin of Free Ports', p. 27.

58 'Free Ports – Minute', 22 Feb. 1793, N.A., B.T. 5 / 8, ff. 189v–91v.

59 30 Geo. 3, cap. 29; Memorial of the merchants, minute for 7 Dec. 1789, N.A., B.T. 5 / 5, f. 219v; report on the Memorial, minute for 1 May 1790, N.A., B.T. 5 / 6, f. 99.

60 32 Geo. 3, cap. 37; Manning, *British Colonial Government*, p. 279.

61 32 Geo. 3, cap. 43; Armytage, *Free Port System*, pp. 60–3; Manning, *British Colonial Government*, pp. 279–80.

62 Merchants to Gov. Dowdeswell, Nassau, 26 May 1798, and Dowdeswell to Duke of Portland, Nassau, 28 May 1798, both in N.A., C.O. 23 / 37, ff. 147–8v.

63 See esp. Guillelmi to Antonio Valdés, Caracas, 31 July 1788, with enclosures 1–5, and Caracas, 20 Oct. 1788, both in A.G.I., Caracas, 111; Guillelmi to Valdés, Caracas, 30 Apr. 1789, A.G.I., Caracas, 114.

64 Letter by Director General de Rentas, Madrid, May 1795, A.G.I., Santa Fé, 957.

65 For the permit granted Félix de Zuasnavar in 1788 for trade with Curaçao, see the papers in A.G.I., Caracas, 111, 114–16. For permits granted Cubans including the Marqués de San Felipe and the Conde de Mompox y Jaruco between 1787 and 1796, see the papers in A.G.I., Santo Domingo, 2189–91.

66 Printed cédula, Madrid, 28 Feb. 1789; published in Levene, *Documentos*, 6:394–9.

67 Decrees dated 24 Nov. 1791, in Levene, *Documentos*, 7:3–9.

68 Excellent primary surveys of this legislation may be found in Joseph María Quirós,

'Exposición que hace a la Junta de Govierno', Veracruz, 12 Jan. 1807, copies in A.G.I., Mexico, 2515, 2997; and Real Cédula, signed by Antonio Porcel, Aranjuez, 22 Apr. 1804, A.G.N.M., Alcabalas, vol. 427, exp. 3, ff. 92–9; see also Marrero, *Cuba*, 12:42–56; King, 'Evolution', pp. 52–5; Villalobos R., *Comercio y contrabando*, pp. 66–7.

69 Manning, 'Nootka Sound Controversy', *passim*; also Allen, 'British Commercial Policy', pp. 186–7.

70 For the impact of the Haiti revolt, see the translated paper marked 'Jamaica. Montego Bay – Nov.re 18', encl. to del Campo to Floridablanca, London, 3 Feb. 1792, A.H.N., Estado, 4252.

71 See e.g. Josef Pablo Valiente to Diego de Gardoqui, Havana, 10 Jan. 1794, A.G.I., Caracas, 59.

72 Ezpeleta to Gardoqui, Santa Fé, 19 July 1793, and Cédula, Aranjuez, 29 Jan. 1794, A.G.I., Santa Fé, 957.

73 Kuethe, 'Havana', pp. 28–9; see also Marrero, *Cuba*, 10:26–7, 12:56–9; Nichols, 'Trade Relations', pp. 292–3.

74 Unreferenced quotation in Knox, *Historical Account of St. Thomas*, pp. 99–104, see also 90–1.

75 See e.g. Jones, 'Historical Study', pp. 50–2; Graham, 'Origin of Free Ports', p. 27.

76 Armytage, *Free Port System*, pp. 63–4.

77 Allen, 'British Commercial Policy', p. 188.

78 Depons, *Travels in South America*, 2:59–60.

79 Testimony of Alexander Henry, Finsbury Square, London, 21 June 1805, N.A., B.T. 1 / 25, ff. 255–7; Henry refers here to his period of residence in Jamaica in 1785–99.

80 Arango y Parreño, *Obras*, 1:74–6.

81 My re-translations of translated extracts from the London press, enclosures to Marqués del Campo to Marqués de Floridablanca, London, 13 July 1787, 21 Aug. 1787, both in A.H.N., Estado, 4255.

82 Accounts in N.A., C.O. 318 / 1, ff. 129–30; see also Allen, 'British Commercial Policy', pp. 185–7.

83 Evidence of Joseph Marryat, London, 3 June 1812, in *Parliamentary Papers*, pp. 668–83, see p. 669.

84 Guthrie and Ryburn to Charles Green, n.p., n.d., marked 'In Governor Green's of 27 April 1799', N.A., C.O. 101 / 36, n.f.; see also Young, *West-India Common-Place Book*, pp. 187–8.

85 Mathew to Earl of Liverpool, n.p., n.d. (marked 'before 19 Feb. [1793]'), and encl. 1, 'Amount of European goods imported into St. George's', in B.L., Add. Mss. 38,228, ff. 325–8v, 329.

86 Encl. 2, 'Abstract of exportations from St. Georges', B.L., Add. Mss. 38,228, f. 330. Unfortunately, no values are accorded the items recorded in this abstract. 'Firestones' were hearth stones – not flints.

87 Encl. 4, two 'Abstracts of importations', B.L., Add. Mss. 38,228, ff. 332–3; see also the cover note to these papers summarising Hawkesbury's views on them, n.p., n.d., *ibid.*, f. 324.

88 Ryburn and Wilson to Maitland, St George's, Grenada, 28 Apr. 1806, N.A., C.O. 101 / 43, ff. 92–3v.

89 Guthrie and Ryburn to Green, St George's, Grenada, 25 Feb. 1799, N.A., C.O. 101 / 36, n.f.

90 Philip Affleck to Philip Stephens, *Centurion*, off Kingston, 8 Sept. 1791, and John Lawford to Affleck, *Hound*, Port Royal Harbour, 30 July 1791, both in N.A., ADM. 1 / 244, ff. 175–7, 191–3v.

91 See e.g. Manning, *British Colonial Government*, p. 279; Allen, 'British Commercial Policy', pp. 185–7; Jones, 'Historical Study of Anglo-Spanish American Trade', p. 61.

92 Report to Committee for Trade and Plantations, encl. to Gov. Orde to Committee, Govt House, Dominica, 1 Sept. 1787, N.A., B.T. 6 / 41, ff. 212–16v.

93 Atwood, *History of Dominica*, pp. 276–81.

94 Laurence, *Tobago in Wartime*, p. 162.

95 Dauxion Lavaysse, *Viaje a las islas de Trinidad*, p. 324.

96 *West-India Common-Place Book*, pp. 7–8.

97 Armytage, *Free Port System*, pp. 66–7.

98 Minutes of Council, 23 Mar. 1800, N.A., C.O. 137 / 104, ff. 52–6.

99 'Abstract of the number and value of slaves imported and exported', B.L., Add. Mss. 38,228, f. 331.

100 'Account of the Number of Negro Slaves exported from this Port ... since the year 1788', St Georges, Grenada, 1804, N.A., C.O. 101 / 42, f. 19v.

101 Pearce, 'British Trade with the Spanish Colonies', pp. 255–7.

102 Ajequiezcane, 'British Trade with the Spanish Colonies', p. 251.

103 Marrero, *Cuba*, 9:20–2, 37.

104 Sagra, *Historia*, p. 140; Marrero, *Cuba*, 12:58.

105 Francisco de Ysla, 'Estado que manifiesta el número de barriles, y tercios de Harina, que han entrado en este Puerto desde 27 de Ag. de este año', Havana, 4 Dec. 1793, A.G.I., Santo Domingo, 2190.

106 Josef Rodríguez de Arias, 'Extracto del diario que he formado en el reconocimiento de la Costa de esta Ysla', *Magdalena*, Puerto de Cuba, 8 Apr. 1792, A.H.N., Estado, 4252.

107 On Gil y Lemos's actions, see Sánchez Pedrote, 'Gil y Lemos', pp. 186–8, 194–6; McFarlane, *Colombia before Independence*, pp. 156–7.

108 For secondary discussion of these events, see McFarlane, *Colombia before Independence*, pp. 157–9.

109 José de Ezpeleta to Pedro López de Lerena, Santa Fé, 19 Dec. 1791, A.G.I., Santa Fé, 640; three reports by Pedro Diago, dated Cartagena, 19 Nov. 1791, in A.G.N.C., Archivo Anexo: Historia, vol. 4, ff. 156–8v; Ezpeleta, *Relación de gobierno*, pp. 237–40.

110 See also Ezpeleta to Governor of Cartagena, Santa Fé, 19 Dec. 1791, and response, A.G.N.C., Archivo Anexo: Historia, vol. 4, ff. 144, 154; Ezpeleta to Gardoqui, Santa Fé, 19 Sept. 1792, A.G.I., Santa Fé, 641.

111 Ezpeleta to Gardoqui, Santa Fé, 19 May 1795, and 9 enclosures, A.G.I., Santa Fé, 645.

112 McFarlane, *Colombia before Independence*, pp. 159–61.

113 In 'Razón de los Derechos Reales y Municipales ...' [1793], A.G.I., Caracas, 485; similar statement in Juan Vicente de Arce to Miguel Cayetano Soler, Caracas, 24 May 1803, A.G.I., Caracas, 516.

114 For a specific case, see Guillelmi to López de Lerena, Caracas, 25 Oct. 1790, A.G.I., Caracas, 115.

115 Syndic General of the Real Consulado to Intendant, expediente marked no. 3, Puerto Cabello, 19 Mar. 1801, A.G.I., Caracas, 920.

116 Estevan Fernández de León, 'Resumen del Valor de los géneros y efectos introducidos por los Puertos del Distrito ...', Caracas, 31 Oct. 1795, A.G.I., Caracas, 919.

117 Fernández de León to Diego de Gardoqui, Caracas, 1 Nov. 1795, A.G.I., Caracas, 919.

118 Juan Alvarez de Verina to Gardoqui, Caracas, 24 Aug. 1794, A.G.I., Caracas, 59.

119 Printed cédula, San Lorenzo, 24 Nov. 1783, A.G.I., Caracas, 150; see esp. Newson,

Aboriginal and Spanish Colonial Trinidad, chaps. 9–10; Sevilla Soler, *Inmigración y cambio socio-económico*, p. 183.

120 Encl. to Lieut. Col. Picton to Lord Hobart, Trinidad, 22 Mar. 1802, N.A., C.O. 296 / 1, ff. 64–73.

121 See esp. Sevilla Soler, *Inmigración y cambio socio-económico*, pp. 183–9.

122 Del Campo to Floridablanca, London, 6 Jan. 1791; Floridablanca to Campo de Alange, San Lorenzo, 14 Oct. 1791; Campo de Alange to Floridablanca, San Lorenzo, 22 Oct. 1791, all in A.H.N., Estado, 4253.

123 Torres Ramírez and Ortiz de la Tabla (eds), *Reglamento y aranceles reales para el Comercio libre*; Fisher, *Commercial Relations*, pp. 13–15.

124 Fisher, *Commercial Relations*, pp. 45–9, 61–3, 87–9.

125 These are summarised usefully in a report by the Consulado de México, dated Mexico City, 23 Aug. 1809, A.G.N.M., Consulado, vol. 79, exp. 1, ff. 13–24v, see paras. 38–40.

126 Francisco Pérez Muñoz to Consulado, Veracruz, 6 Feb. 1804, A.G.N.M., Consulado, vol. 79, ff. 37–44.

127 José María Quirós, 'Memoria de instituto', Veracruz, 11 Jan. 1808, A.G.I., Mexico, 2997.

128 Morales Padrón, 'México y la Independencia de Hispanoamérica', p. 358.

129 *Tableau de l'Espagne moderne*, 2:182–4. The figures Bourgoing offers are of total contraband exports of 56,326,029 pesos in the decade to 1778, and of 83,689,799 pesos in the six years following.

130 See e.g. Bourgoing, *Tableau de l'Espagne moderne*, 2:177–82.

131 Ajequiezcane, 'British Trade with the Spanish Colonies', p. 249.

132 For lucid discussion of the problems inherent in using these records, see Clark, *Guide to English Commercial Statistics*, pp. 33–42, and T. S. Ashton's introduction to Schumpeter, *English Overseas Trade Statistics*, pp. 1–9. For attempts to resolve them, see especially Imlah, 'Real Values in British Foreign Trade'; Davis, *Industrial Revolution*; Mitchell, *British Historical Statistics*, chap. 9.

133 N.A., Customs 17 / 10.

134 N.A., Customs 17 / 10–17. I would like to express my gratitude to the staff at the National Archives for allowing me to see the originals of these records, which are normally accessible only on microfilm.

135 On the Naval Officer's returns as a historical source, see Zahedieh, 'Merchants of Port Royal', pp. 576–8; Claypole and Buisseret, 'Trade Patterns in Early English Jamaica', pp. 1–4.

136 Thomas Irving to William Pitt, n.p., n.d. [1789], N.A., Customs 17 / 10, f. 74.

137 Preliminary analysis of this series was presented in Pearce, 'British Trade with the Spanish Colonies', which may be consulted for wider discussion of its origins and characteristics.

138 Edward Mathew to Earl of Liverpool, n.p., n.d. [early 1793], B.L., Add. Mss. 38,228, ff. 325–8v; G. R. Hutchinson to Thomas Walsh, Custom House, Kingston, 14 May 1806, N.A., B.T. 1 / 29, ff. 145–v.

139 Irving's preamble to the State for 1790 (N.A., Customs 17 / 12; discussed by Clark, *Guide to English Commercial Statistics*, p. 32) is considered a significant commentary on the deficiencies of the official statistics; see also Allen, 'British Commercial Policy', p. 98.

140 McCusker, 'Colonial Civil Servant and Counter-Revolutionary', pp. 196–8 (referring to Irving's work in North America in the late 1760s and early 1770s).

141 From the preamble to the accounts for 1792, Office of the Inspector-General, London, 17 Nov. 1793, N.A., Customs 17 / 14, f. 1.

142 In the 'States of Navigation and Commerce', data is presented in three sections: West Indies, North America, and a third section covering the Bahamas and Bermuda. Irving noted that 'I was at first inclined to have attached the trade of Bermuda to North America & that of the Bahamas to the West Indies but … I found … that they could not with propriety be attached to either'. Irving's motives here do not appear convincing, and I have followed his original intention by placing the Bahamas data with that for the West Indies, and the Bermuda statistics with those for the North American colonies.

143 Statistical appendix, table A1.

144 Statement accompanying 'An Account of the Goods Wares & Merchandize Imported or Exported in Foreign Vessels …', covers 1792, N.A., Customs 17 / 14, ff. 80v–1. Irving's comments are amply supported by other testimony; see John Dalling, tract on the Spanish trade, n.p., n.d., N.A., C.O. 137 / 68, ff. 63–71; Statement of inward shipping from foreign plantations, first quarter 1799, Bahamas, N.A., C.O. 23 / 38, f. 199; Sir William Young to Earl Bathurst, Trinidad, 28 Sept. 1822, N.A., Customs 34 / 828.

145 Statistical appendix, table A2.

146 Statistical appendix, table A3.

147 Statistical appendix, table A4. Some carrying trade from the Spanish colonies was undertaken by Danish, Dutch, and other foreign merchants. But this was insignificant in terms of the number of ships involved, and even more so in terms of the value of the goods traded.

148 Statistical appendix, table A5.

149 Statistical appendix, tables A6–9.

150 Statistical appendix, table A6.

151 Statistical appendix, table A7.

152 Statistical appendix, tables A8–9.

153 Armytage, *Free Port System*, p. 68.

154 Pantaleão, *Penetração comercial de Inglaterra*, pp. 194–200; Ramos, *Contrabando inglés*, chap. 7.

155 Statistical appendix, table A10.

156 'In the year 1789, one eighth of Great Britain's total supply of cotton was, in the first instance, brought into the Free Ports of Jamaica, Dominica and Grenada by foreign vessels'; Allen, 'British Commercial Policy', pp. 134–5, 187–8; see also Armytage, *Free Port System*, pp. 73–9.

157 The term 'dollars', of course, refers to Spanish-American pesos. Registered imports of dollars in the four years for which records are available, for which only the sterling value is shown in table 10, were: 1792, $312,000; 1793, $546,200; 1794, $966,700 [*sic*, but see note to statistical appendix, table A7]; 1795, $1,423,800.

158 Note that large-scale British imports of gold bullion from Spanish America were dated to the early 1790s, and that in the fifteen years to 1810, 'the quantity brought, principally through Jamaica, has been considerable, and may be fairly computed of the annual amount of £700,000'; Koster, *Short Statement of the Trade in Gold Bullion*, pp. 16–18.

159 This calculation takes a base figure of c. £370,000 in 1792 (for which see pp. 100–1) and multiplies it by 75 per cent, 40.5 per cent, and 85.5 per cent in succeeding years, to give c. £1,687,500 in 1795; the total figure of £1,866,000 adds the registered value of non-specie imports in 1795.

160 Statistical appendix, table A11.

161 Among the 'other woods' imported, hardwood pieces or posts, pine boards, mill timber, boat timber etc, that is to say wood for local construction purposes, predom-

inated among imports in British shipping, while mahogany, ebony, and cedar, the more valuable woods with potential for re-export, dominated imports in Spanish vessels.

162 Statistical appendix, tables A12–13.

163 Statistical appendix, table A12.

164 Possibly gum arabic, or a derivative of *algarroba* (carob tree or bean); my thanks to John Fisher for this suggestion.

165 Statistical appendix, table A13.

166 Statistical appendix, table A14.

167 Thus by 1795, *all* registered imports by value throughout the British free ports in the Caribbean came from the Spanish colonies.

168 Statistical appendix, tables A15–16.

169 Miscellaneous commodities of negligible value were also recorded sporadically; these included coffee, bread and flour, brown sugar, madeira wine, salt, and some unspecified exports.

170 Statistical appendix, table A17.

171 Statement accompanying 'An Account of the Goods Wares & Merchandize Imported or Exported in Foreign Vessels ...', covers 1792, N.A., Customs 17 / 14, ff. 80v–1.

172 Armytage, *Free Port System*, p. 92.

173 P. 93; Pearce, 'British Trade with the Spanish Colonies', pp. 255–7; see statistical appendix, table A18.

174 Statistical appendix, table A19.

175 Statistical appendix, tables A20–21.

176 Allen, 'British Commercial Policy', pp. 183–4.

177 'Great Britain and the Trades', *Hispanic American Historical Review*, 27:1 (Feb. 1947), pp. 2–29. For a recent discussion of 'The Parallel Economy at Cadiz', see Stein and Stein, *Apogee of Empire*, pp. 196ff. The anonymous reader of the typescript of this book for Liverpool University Press indicated that the Spanish scholar Leandro Prados de la Escosura 'has worked on this very issue' (though principally for the nineteenth century?); unfortunately, editorial deadlines made it impossible for me to follow up this suggestion. See e.g. Prados de la Escosura, 'El comercio hispano-británico durante los siglos XVIII y XIX', and (with S. Amaral, eds.), *La independencia americana*.

178 Christelow, 'Great Britain and the Trades', pp. 16–17.

179 García Fernández, 'Negociando con el enemigo', pp. 816–18; Lario de Oñate, *La colonia mercantil británica*, pp. 105–8, 114–17.

180 Christelow, 'Great Britain and the Trades', p. 18 (the document cited is erroneously dated 1763).

181 Christelow, 'Great Britain and the Trades', pp. 7, 26–7; Brown, 'Anglo-Spanish Relations', pp. 449–51.

182 Marqués del Campo to Floridablanca, London, 28 Feb. 1790, A.H.N., Estado, 4243.

183 Gómez Gómez, 'Nota sobre el contrabando gaditano', analyses the key documents.

184 Eden to Leeds [?], Madrid, 30 Apr. 1789, N.A., F.O. 185 / 5, no. 46.

185 H. Katencamp to Carmarthen?, Corunna, 27 July 1785, N.A., F.O. 72 / 6.

186 Lethbridge to Duque de Alcudia, London, 3 July [1792], encl. to Del Campo to Conde de Aranda, London, 8 Oct. 1792, A.H.N., Estado, 4252.

187 'B: French trans., British Minister to Spanish Secretary', Madrid, 18 Feb. 1792, N.A., F.O. 185 / 10.

188 William Eden to Duke of Leeds, Madrid, 30 Apr. 1789, and encl., N.A., F.O. 185 / 5, no. 40.

189 Fisher, *Commercial Relations*, p. 46.

190 Depons, *Travels in South America*, 2:70; Walker, *Colombia*, 1:141–2, is derived from Depons; and Bourgoing, *Tableau de l'Espagne moderne*, 2:128–30.

191 James Duff to Carmarthen, Cadiz, 15 Mar. 1785, N.A., F.O. 72 / 5.

192 My re-translation from a translated extract from the London press, encl. to Del Campo to Floridablanca, London, 3 Nov. 1786, A.H.N., Estado, 4250.

193 Liston to Floridablanca, 21 Dec. 1786, one of a series of letters (in French) marked '1786', in N.A., F.O. 185 / 2.

194 Eden to Carmarthen, San Ildefonso, 16 Sept. 1788, N.A., F.O. 185 / 4.

195 My re-translation from a translated extract from the London press, encl. to Del Campo to Floridablanca, London, 13 Sept. 1791, A.H.N., Estado, 4253.

CHAPTER FOUR

Trade During Wartime (1796–1808): The Spanish Licensed Trade in the British West Indies

The war waged by Spain against revolutionary France petered out in mid-1795, and the two nations signed a peace treaty in August the following year. Already by the latter period there were signs of the coming radical re-orientation of Spanish foreign policy and of a new break with her late ally, Britain. In June 1796 the Spanish ambassador in London reported the British occupation of Demerera and Essequibo (in modern Guayana) in almost hysterical terms, as an operation 'more directed against Spain than against Holland' and 'equivalent to a declaration of war'.[1] In October the British seized Spanish vessels trading with French cargoes between Cadiz and Veracruz, a 'pre-emptive strike' comparable to the better-known seizure of Spanish treasure ships from Montevideo in late 1804. War finally came with a Spanish declaration dated 7 October 1796 and a parallel British declaration issued in mid-November. Thus began a period of conflict between the two nations which endured, with the relatively brief hiatus of the Peace of Amiens in 1802–04, until July 1808. The real reasons for this conflict were related as much to the looming threat of Napoleonic France as to inherent Spanish hostility toward the British, although publicly British military preparations in the West Indies were cited, including those designed to prevent the transfer of Spanish Santo Domingo to the French under the terms of the Treaty of Basel. Strikingly, considerable emphasis was also laid on commercial factors: on British smuggling along the Pacific coasts of South America in breach of the Nootka Convention, or the establishment of British trading companies on the banks of the Missouri.[2] Thus, in late 1796, ostensibly in part to defend its American commercial monopoly, Spain joined in a war which would destroy its commercial hegemony in the Americas forever.

The war had profound consequences for Spain's relations with its American colonies. Within a year the British had seized the island of Trinidad and shattered the Spanish fleet at Cape St Vincent, so setting the seal on British dominance of the seas.[3] In April 1797, a naval blockade was imposed on Cadiz as the key stroke in a general British embargo of Spanish Atlantic trade. Cadiz was vital because despite Comercio libre reforms which had abolished its formal monopoly of American trade, on the eve of the war the port retained about four-fifths of all colonial trade. The British blockade had an immediate, dramatic effect: in 1796, 105 ships left Cadiz for the Americas, but in 1797 the corresponding figure fell to just 12 vessels. The value of registered exports to America from all Spanish ports was over 250,000,000 reales in 1796, but collapsed to just 11,000,000 reales the following year.[4] Spanish trade with the colonies remained at very low levels throughout the period of the wars: thus during the first war (1796–1801) the average annual value of trade was less than 14 per cent what it had been during 1782–96.[5] One consequence, to be noted briefly here, was that British trade with Spanish America via the Peninsula now all but ceased. We have seen that as recently as the early 1790s, this trade may still have been worth as much as £1,000,000 per year. But with the onset of the war and imposition of the maritime blockade, foreign traders of all nations shifted their activities away from Spanish ports. The right to trade in neutral vessels from neutral ports in Europe and the United States, granted from late 1797, now offered an alternative and more attractive vehicle for trade. For this reason, in 1797–1801 and again in 1804–07, goods of native Spanish manufacture dominated exports from Cadiz, giving the illusion of a Spanish commercial renaissance in the context of a greatly impoverished trade.[6] Although we are scarcely better informed with regard to the re-export trade during these years than for the pre-war era, suffice to note that all British exports to Spain 'became negligible in 1797, and for the next two years ceased altogether'.[7] The ancient trade route linking British suppliers with Spanish-American markets via peninsular ports was thus dealt a death-blow. It experienced some recovery during the Peace of 1802–04, was carried on to some extent under the 'secret trade' after 1805,[8] and again recovered briefly after the definitive peace in 1808. But the onset of the Spanish-American Revolutionary wars in 1810, and of direct British trade with the nascent republics, ensured that it never regained more than a fraction of its former importance.

The British blockade of the Peninsula was mirrored in the West Indies by intermittent picketing of major ports (Havana, Veracruz, Cartagena, La Guaira) and by rapacious cruising by Royal Naval squadrons along the trade routes favoured by Spanish merchantmen. Privateering thrived, especially in the Virgin Islands and the Bahamas, where many of those who engaged in it were smugglers during peacetime.[9] Naval accounts for mid-1799 to February 1800, a period when relatively few Spanish ships dared venture out of port, suggest that seizures of Spanish prizes still amounted to 93 vessels for the Jamaica squadron alone.[10] The result of such seizures was that the maritime trade of most of the Spanish colonies all but collapsed in 1797. Already by July of the latter year, in Mexico, the richest of the colonies, Viceroy Branciforte lamented the effects of British naval action in the collapse of the viceroyalty's trade and the scarcity and high prices of goods still available.[11] Imports from the metropolis to Veracruz, the major Mexican port, had been worth some 6,500,000 pesos in 1796, but they fell by 92 per cent, to just 520,000 pesos in 1797. Mexican exports to Spain had been worth some

7,300,000 pesos in 1796, but fell by 97 per cent to only 240,000 pesos in 1797.[12] The Mexican case was broadly representative of what occurred in other regions: one report suggested that by August 1799, imports to the province of Caracas had fallen to one-fiftieth their previous level, while exports represented just a tenth of production.[13] Trade with New Granada fell to 'its lowest point since the previous Anglo-Spanish war' of 1779–83 and 'was reduced to a fraction of its former size'.[14] Throughout the empire, commercial activity at the ports all but ground to a halt, and an economic crisis of extreme gravity threatened. The single major exception to this dismal panorama was Cuba: by recourse to trade with neutrals, and by extensive contraband trade with the British, Cubans were able to stave off economic disaster. After 1796, exports of Cuban sugar maintained their meandering upward course, while entries of ships at Havana actually grew strongly and displayed further impressive growth in succeeding years (Table 6.1, p. 192).

From late 1797, trade by Spaniards at the free ports was granted protection from seizure under a system of licences issued by the island governors. Outright contraband by British traders appears to have undergone a general decline during the wars, but remained of some importance in certain colonies throughout the region. These long-established forms of Anglo-Spanish commerce were supplemented by a major new vehicle, that of trade in British manufactures undertaken by the merchants of neutral powers. This trade itself experienced significant change after 1804 as a result of complex operations for the transfer of Spanish-American bullion to Europe, while the year 1805 marked the onset of direct trade from Great Britain under cover of Spanish neutral trade permits (the so-called 'secret trade'). These different modes of commerce combined in the years after 1796 to sustain the totality of British trade with the Spanish colonies in the Caribbean. It is to be stressed that singling each of them out for treatment separately is to some important degree deceptive, inasmuch as there was considerable overlap between the different branches. At recurring chronological or geographical points these functioned as a seamless whole: thus, the Spanish merchants trading with the British islands were certainly also those most closely involved with British contraband trade. Merchants from neutral powers entered into commercial relations with the same relatively small group of Spanish and British traders, while much outright British contraband went on under the cover of neutral flags. It is important that this essential one-ness of a complex commercial system be born in mind over the course of the following chapters; nevertheless, a schematic separation is justified both as a descriptive tool and in view of the sharply differing characteristics of the various branches. To this end, the current chapter considers trade undertaken by Spanish merchants and vessels at the free ports in the British islands. The one which follows discusses the activities of British smugglers from the same islands on the Spanish-American coasts. Finally, Chapter 6 analyses trade in British manufactures undertaken by the merchants of neutral powers, or by British merchants trading under neutral permit, up until the Anglo-Spanish peace of 1808.

The Spanish Licensed Trade in the British West Indies: Origins and Operation

> We have thought it expedient that permission should be given to vessels belonging to the subjects of his Catholic Majesty ... to trade between the free ports established in the island of Jamaica and the Spanish colonies in America.
> —'Instructions', St James's, 20 Nov. 1797, N.A., C.O. 137 / 98, ff. 377–9.

The way in which Anglo-Spanish trade in the Caribbean had developed in the decades prior to 1796 ensured that the Spanish colonies were not the only ones which suffered by the outbreak of war late that year and by the breakdown in maritime commerce which followed. Trade at the free ports in the British colonies was immediately disrupted, when Spanish vessels caught in harbour in December 1796 were seized by the Customs.[15] In the following months, the British colonies felt the impact of the persecution of Spanish merchant shipping acutely, none more so than Jamaica, which (as we have seen) dominated trade with the Spanish colonies in general, and trade in Spanish bullion specifically. Although trade at Jamaica never ceased altogether, by mid-1797 the island was experiencing 'an uncommon scarcity of specie', attributed principally to interruption of trade with the Spanish colonies.[16] The governor, Earl Balcarres, described this scarcity as 'severely felt', and expressed concern at the possibility of 'some convulsion in consequence'.[17] To counter this crisis, Jamaicans first proposed an indirect trade with the Spanish colonies, to be carried out by renegade Spaniards and Portuguese in British ships bearing British papers.[18] But the solution ultimately adopted was far more wide-ranging, and affected all of the major British colonies, and not only Jamaica; it consisted of the licensing of trade between British and Spanish subjects in the Caribbean, the war notwithstanding.

The licensing of trade between belligerents had long-standing precedents, and support for recourse to such a mechanism had been growing since the onset of the French wars. The system began to be implemented in the Caribbean from June 1797, when within months of its capture by the British, direct trade was sanctioned between the island of Trinidad and the Spanish colonies under special licences to be granted by the governor.[19] With such an example close at hand, representatives from Jamaica, too, petitioned the Lords of Trade for a similar system to be established at that island and also in the Bahamas 'in order to remedy the present deficiency of specie'.[20] By Instructions dated 20 November 1797, this petition was granted, and a trade under licence was established between Jamaica and the Bahamas and the Spanish colonies. The system of licences in fact embraced British as well as Spanish vessels, authorising them also to trade with enemy colonies during wartime, though there is little doubt that Spaniards were the chief beneficiaries.[21] The relevant decrees were received in Jamaica and the Bahamas in late February and early March 1798 respectively, and were immediately implemented. As a result, trade by Spaniards at the free ports, interrupted in

December 1796, was resumed a little over a year later, to be maintained under licence throughout the remainder of the wars. The renewal of the free ports trade was received enthusiastically in the British islands, where officials and merchants were optimistic as to its prospects. Already by early March 1798, a letter from Jamaica suggested that some shipments had been made to Havana and Veracruz, with sales in dry goods and slaves worth more than $500,000 in just a few months.[22] It was reported from Nassau that imports from Britain for the Spanish market since the outbreak of the war amounted to £100,000, and that orders worth a further £200,000 were now gone out.[23] Both of these reports, of course, underline the fact that interruption to the Spanish trade upon the outbreak of the war was never more than partial.

Both the regulations which licensed trade with Spaniards, and the free port system itself, experienced further evolution over the ensuing months and years. In March 1798 the Instructions of November 1797 were supplanted by a new decree, one clause of which, in deference to the growing British anti-slavery movement, barred exports of slaves from the trade.[24] A further change of some significance was effected in 1798, when trade between the free ports and other British islands was made legal for the first time.[25] This permit greatly expanded the prospects for inter-island trade, though its impact was felt principally in the less significant trading colonies in the lesser Antilles. As it proved its efficacy, the licensing system was extended to further British colonies, until Grenada, Tobago, and Tortola, and also St Thomas and Curaçao (held by Britain in 1800–02 and again from 1807), also enjoyed a right to trade with the Spanish colonies during wartime. To be sure, commerce at the British free ports did not survive unaltered under cover of the licences; as will be seen, attacks by the Royal Navy on Spanish licensed vessels remained a persistent problem, one which threatened the prosperity of the trade at intervals throughout the following decade. The trade in enslaved Africans which had flourished so vigorously since 1789 declined rapidly, as British slavers were barred from Spanish ports and permission for Spaniards to seek slaves in the British islands was revoked by the Spanish authorities. Contraband trade by British merchants appears to have experienced further decline during the war, but trade by neutral powers in Spanish-American ports now began to offer serious competition to the British throughout the region. Nevertheless, trade by Spaniards at the free ports remained probably the single most important conduit for Anglo-Spanish commerce throughout the period of the wars.

Spanish Americans were made rapidly aware of the new system for trade under licence decreed in late 1797 and implemented early the following year. President Robert Hunt of the Bahamas published the Instructions of 20 November 1797 in the island Gazette, and took 'every step in my power to give it publicity in the Spanish colonies'. Hunt seems actually to have sent a copy of the Instructions to the Governor of Cuba, with a request that British vessels trading under the new regulations be admitted at Havana.[26] That the trade was widely known in the Spanish colonies is evidenced by accurate descriptions of its operation written and occasionally published there.[27] Alexander von Humboldt described commercial operations out of Veracruz and Campeche, 'whence small boats go out to seek goods at Jamaica'. Humboldt also recorded the curious local term for the commerce, of 'telegraphic routes'.[28] Smuggling by Spaniards out of Venezuela was known to be encouraged 'by the British themselves who by virtue of facilities, and Instructions from the Cabinet of St James admit our Ships freely to their Ports, and invite, and stimulate them urgently to frequent them'. The royal *Audiencia* in the same colony remarked upon 'the singular measure adopted by the British Ministry of ordering its Governors to give passports to all the Captains of Spanish Ships who wish to go to their possessions, by which means they have managed to attract many'.[29] José Ignacio de Pombo, a prominent merchant and an unusually penetrating writer on commercial matters, wrote from New Granada that in the context of the general commercial crisis provoked by the war, the licensing system 'straightaway attracted a great number of small Spanish craft to [British] ports, which, taking off some of our produce, and an immense quantity of coin, have abundantly supplied the whole Kingdom'.[30] It is noteworthy that anti-contraband proposals drawn up by Pombo are concerned almost entirely with the control of trade by Spaniards – smuggling by the British or other foreigners receiving barely a mention.[31]

The licensing system rendered trade by Spaniards at the free ports perfectly legal in the eyes of the British, despite the hostilities prevailing between the two nations. Such trade, however, remained absolutely illicit for the Spanish authorities, both because of the war and (at a deeper level) in view of the traditional mercantilist interdictions on trade with rival nations. As a result, Spanish vessels were obliged to resort to different strategies and pretexts in order to justify their journeys to the British islands. One such pretext derived from the fact that although the limited legal trade with the British established locally in recent years (the *comercio de colonias*) was naturally suspended at the outbreak of the war, commerce with neutral or friendly territories persisted and was even extended in some cases in view of the crisis affecting different Spanish-American regions. As one example, the trade with neutrals permitted by the authorities in Venezuela in May 1801 sanctioned not only the entry to port of neutral vessels, but also voyages to neutral territories in Spanish shipping and under the Spanish flag.[32] Any such legal trade might easily cover contraband with the British colonies, as the Spanish consul in Philadelphia was well aware: 'It would be useful if the Governors and Intendants refrained in their Passports from using the vague expression, *go to the friendly colonies*, with which phrase the Captains go wherever best suits them and cover better their Smuggling.'[33] The British writer William Walton suggested that the chief nominal destinations used to cover such voyages were Guadeloupe, Martinique, and St Domingue, all French colonies then allied with Spain; 'thus the clearances in the Spanish custom-houses are made nearly all for islands, to which there never existed a trade of the smallest nature'.[34] In New Granada, Viceroy Pedro de Mendinueta rejected repeated petitions for greater trade with foreign colonies in 1797–99, explicitly citing the risk of contraband. He also refused to permit trade with neutrals, decreed from November 1797, to be made a pretext for enlarged trade in Spanish vessels.[35] An alternative means by which Spanish merchants voyaged to the British colonies was under cover of perfectly legal trade between Spanish colonial ports in the region. José de Pombo noted of this trade that at first Spanish merchants acted with some caution, clearing out for another Spanish colonial port in ballast, sailing clandestinely to the British islands, and then landing their return cargoes on deserted stretches of coastline. They grew rapidly in confidence, however, and soon traded brazenly under false registers, whether from other Spanish colonies or from other ports in New Granada.[36] A last important pretext for the licensed trade, particularly in the western Caribbean during the war of 1796–1802, was that of permits for the re-purchase of prize goods in the British colonies; these permits represent something of a special case, and are discussed at length separately hereafter. In addition to these various pretexts, there is little doubt that many voyages (quite possibly the majority) were made by Spaniards simply slipping quietly away from their own coasts and sailing to Jamaica or another British colony without any legal cover whatever – a genuine Spanish smuggling trade. The remainder of this chapter, then, is devoted to the activities of these Spanish merchants trading under licence in the British colonies – first in the western Caribbean and the Gulf of Mexico, and then in the eastern Caribbean and the Lesser Antilles.

The Licensed Trade in the Western Caribbean and the Gulf of Mexico

> After a short time, scandalous thing! Our flag flew amidst our enemies in all the Ports of their Islands.
>
> —Pedro Ajequiezcane, 'British Trade with the Spanish Colonies', p. 251

The most important focus of the Spanish licensed trade was the western Caribbean, encompassing particularly Jamaica and the Bahamas on the British side, and Mexico, Cuba, New Granada and Venezuela on the Spanish. Among the evidence for the trade in this region, some of the best derives from interruptions occasioned by the Royal Navy and from the disputes with officials and merchants associated with colonial trade which resulted. The British naval command was concerned at the military implications of admitting large numbers of Spaniards at the free ports, and had long lamented the loss of British experience of the Spanish coasts which the shift toward Spanish shipping brought with it. Individual naval officers fiercely resented a trade which robbed them of large numbers of prize vessels they might otherwise have expected to take in Caribbean waters. In two letters to the Admiralty in late 1799, Admiral Sir Hyde Parker, the commander on the Jamaica station, severely criticised the way the licensed trade was administered in Jamaica and at Nassau. His chief allegations concerned 'the very loose manner in which the Governors of this island and Providence issue the licences for the Spanish trade'. Parker stated that 'the licences are granted frequently with the signature of the Governor or Secretary, but without the name of the vessel, the master, or voyage being inserted'. Such licences were purchased for $25 in Nassau, but were illicitly resold in Havana and other Spanish ports, where they fetched as much as $200 apiece. Licences were granted for periods of time deemed excessive, or even without specified duration.[37] The chief consequences were that Spaniards manipulated the protection offered by the licences to sustain trade between their own ports, or even to ship large royal or private funds from Veracruz to Havana. These allegations provoked an acrimonious dispute between Parker and the two governors implicated, particularly with Balcarres in Jamaica. The language of the dispute rapidly became very heated, and by 1800 the two men were no longer on speaking terms.[38]

Parker proved unable to sustain his particular allegations against Balcarres, but nevertheless assembled ample evidence of the skill with which Spaniards manipulated the licence system to their advantage. Governor Dowdeswell at Nassau admitted that blank licences signed by him were resold at Havana, although he argued that such a system was necessary 'because Spanish Vessells cannot come into British Ports, without Licences for that purpose, being first obtained'.[39] Once acquired, licences might be transferred from one Spanish vessel to another, which Captain Loring of the *Carnatic* thought was 'not altogether the thing'.[40] On occasion, ships were actually renamed so as to make use of a licence granted to a different vessel. Again, licences might be bought in Kingston or Nassau in the name of a purely fictitious ship or master, as a speculative venture; a buyer for the licence was afterwards procured, and the buyer and his ship assumed the names on the licence in order to make use of it. The problems occasioned by excessive time periods granted for the completion of journeys were illustrated by the capture in September 1799 of a Spanish schooner bearing a licence granted by Dowdeswell the previous December, under cover of which the Spanish master had 'been trading all round the Gulf of Mexico'.[41] The same ship was alleged to have twice carried despatches between New Orleans and Havana under cover of licensed voyages to New Providence. Further testimony supported Parker's allegation that Spanish vessels bearing British licences traded between ports on the Spanish coasts, providing economic relief and making a mockery of the British blockade.[42]

Naval seizures of enemy shipping ran at very high levels during this period; Balcarres stated in May 1800 that no fewer than 1,300 prizes had been condemned in the Jamaica Courts alone in a short period.[43] These were principally French vessels and Spanish ships taken while navigating without passes. Perhaps from early 1799, however, British cruisers began to strike an increasingly bellicose attitude toward the licensed trade itself and toward the abuses to which it was claimed to give rise. As a result, significant numbers of Spaniards began to be taken despite bearing licences from British governors. Such ships might bear licences deemed to be false, or passes showing signs of illicit interference; licences filled out at Havana from blanks procured in that port; or they might display behaviour otherwise thought suspect.[44] The total number of such seizures remains obscure, but it is clear that at intervals they were very extensive. Nor was concern at Spanish manipulation of the licence system limited to naval captains in the Caribbean. Admiral Parker's allegations prompted the Duke of Portland to issue fresh instructions to Balcarres and Dowdeswell in January 1800, imposing a tighter form on licences to be used in the trade. Licences must now bear the name of the licensee, the name and a description of the vessel concerned and of the Spanish port traded with, and must be limited to cover a single voyage, to be executed within a specified time period.[45] In the light of what follows, it is worth stressing that concern over aspects of the trade extended also to the British colonies themselves, centring principally on the issue of the spread of subversion in the region, particularly from the black revolutionaries in Haiti. Agents were thought liable to slip into British territories, 'persons of all descriptions and Countries, gaining Ingress by means of the Spanish Licenced Trade'. Balcarres determined to confiscate ships trading from Cuba or the Spanish Main with unauthorised passengers, also declaring that 'some other regulations in that trade I shall make'.[46]

These concerns notwithstanding, mercantile and official circles in the British colonies reacted with outrage to naval interference with the licensed trade. A first protest was formulated by the merchants and traders of Nassau in June 1799, listing recent seizures (including that of the *Concepción* discussed below) and suggesting that the navy's actions were placing the new trade in serious jeopardy.[47] The merchants' protest secured orders from the Admiralty to navy squadrons in the Caribbean to prevent hindrance to the trade, orders which in turn provoked Parker's letters on Spanish abuses later the same year. In November 1799 the Bahamas Agent in London insisted that due to naval interference 'great interruptions have been experienced by the merchants carrying on the trade'.[48] In 1800 the Jamaica House of Assembly suggested that the Spanish trade had sharply declined of late, in part due to the seizures by British warships, 'whose practice it has too often been, to detain and bring in the vessels employed in carrying it on, on very slight grounds'.[49] In November the following year it was stated that the trade to the Bahamas was 'rather at a stand', a situation attributed in part to captures of Spanish vessels by privateers. This new representation made a point reiterated in others of its kind, that British naval seizures had a deterrent effect upon the trade because they frightened away the Spaniards; it was said that the seizures 'greatly diminished the Confidence, which the more opulent of the Spanish Traders at First entertained of the inviolability of the Licences'.[50] In May 1801 the authorities and manufacturers of distant Dundee and Montrose lamented the decline in the Spanish-American market for their linens, caused by the trade's being lately 'much interrupted and nearly destroyed by your Majesty's ships of war'.[51] In truth, naval aggression does not seem to have had any lasting impact on the free ports trade; but it is quite clear that during particular, relatively brief periods it placed substantial obstacles in the way of its normal development.

British colonial merchants and officials frequently emphasised the contentious grounds on which British warships and privateers seized Spanish licensed vessels. Kup cites the example, eminently Royal Naval moreover, of a ship described as a brig 'brought in as being not a brig but a "hermaphrodite scow" by reason of insignificant differences in the rigging'.[52] The motive for such seizures was supposed to be venal: ships' captains seized legitimate Spanish traders in the hope of their being declared good prize by the Vice-Admiralty Courts. On occasion darker motives were hinted at, as in mid-1799 when a dispute developed between the navy and the authorities at Nassau over impressment and the desertion of naval crews for privateers, 'the result of which was they not being able to obtain what they thought justice … came to the resolution of capturing every Spanish vessel bound to New Providence, for the most frivolous pretence imaginable'.[53] Merchants and officials acknowledged that abuses of the licence system took place, but played down their significance. The Jamaica Council actually suspended the new regulations for licences issued by Portland in January 1800, arguing that they were unnecessary and that they threatened the prosperity of the trade, although Jamaican merchants proposed alternative, milder restrictions in their place. Play was made of the senselessness of interrupting a trade so wholly in the British interest:

> The Spaniards are at this moment in many parts absolutely without Clotheing to cover them – they have a great deal of produce on their hands, they come here for the express purpose of exchanging their produce and Bullion against our Manufactures – What can be more profitable to Great Britain, and to this Island than such a trade?[54]

The chief emphasis in these protests, nevertheless, was on the sheer cash value of the trade. An estimate at this time (May 1800) that more than £1,000,000's worth of British manufactures was lying on the wharves at Kingston destined for Spanish markets may have been an exaggeration.[55] But throughout these years, interested parties emphasised time and again the real importance the trade had acquired in the context of national commerce as a whole. Placing a precise figure on that value remains as problematic as ever, though the case of the schooner *Concepción* (taken en route from Veracruz and acquitted on appeal) indicates how valuable single shipments might be: this vessel carried $111,000 in bullion, the returns for a cargo of British manufactures sent out from Nassau.[56] A single merchant prominent in the trade later claimed to have exported British and prize goods worth £100,000 from the same port in 1799, in five Spanish vessels, to 'some of the most affluent Spanish merchants of the Havana and Mexico'.[57]

The Bahamas provide the best general data for the trade available for the period of the first Napoleonic war. These data indicate extraordinarily rapid growth in the period since the early 1790s, when the value of registered imports from the Spanish colonies at the Bahamas had averaged some £20,000 per year.[58] By 1799, exports of manufactured goods from Great Britain to the Bahamas were worth a total of over £500,000 sterling. Total exports from the Bahamas to the Spanish colonies in the same year were worth some £243,000, while imports from those territories (including bullion) were worth some £238,000. In the second half of the year, ninety-seven Spanish licensed vessels were employed in the export trade, and seventy-four vessels in the import trade.[59] A detailed account of imports during this period shows a trade biased heavily toward bullion and dyewood, and one from which livestock is absent (Table 4.1). As an indicator of the value of the Spanish trade as a whole, these figure are certainly substantially an underestimate. Naval action against Spanish licensed vessels was strong in 1799, and the Nassau Customs House believed trade would soon treble in value 'as it is supposed the Interruption, which it has met with, will not be continued'. Imports of bullion continued to be routinely understated in the official accounts, one Customs officer at this time noting that 'it seldom happens that so much as one half of the specie imported, is reported at the Custom House'.[60] The figures also, of course, only describe registered trade at the free ports; they do not, for instance, include any genuine British contraband trade. Although it seems unlikely that the value of the Spanish trade really trebled after 1799, it can be noted that on 17 May 1800 seven large merchantmen lay at Nassau with cargoes of typical Spanish-American

Table 4.1 *Imports to Nassau from Spanish colonies in Spanish vessels, July–Dec. 1799*

Commodity	Value ($)	% of total value
Dollars	168,800	47.6
Fustic	67,500	19.0
Logwood	28,000	7.9
Sugar, white	27,950	7.9
Sugar, brown	21,040	5.9
Indigo	20,000	5.6
Hides	15,485	4.4
Mahogany and other woods	5,000	1.4
Cotton	837	0.2
Total value	354,612	

Source: 'Bahamas. An aggregate Account of Imports into the Free Ports …', Custom House, Nassau, P.R.O., C.O. 23 / 39, f. 152.

produce and bullion worth over £82,000 ready for export to Britain. The fleet which left the port in June the same year carried 'upwards of three hundred thousand Dollars in Specie', almost all of it undoubtedly derived from trade with the Spaniards.[61]

No general data have yet come to light describing the free ports trade of Jamaica during the first war (1796–1802), though it can be expected to have been substantially richer than that of New Providence. Figures for 1803–04 (discussed immediately below) suggest that imports of bullion at Jamaica ran at more than twice the levels at the port of Nassau. Félix Berenguer de Marquina, captured en route to assume the viceregency of Mexico and detained in Jamaica for a few weeks in early 1800, was shocked to witness 'the daily entry and clearance at the port of Kingston, of vessels with the Spanish flag, the openness and liberty with which our Spaniards dealt and traded with the English on different pretexts'.[62] A French agent claimed that a hundred vessels traded solely out of Puerto Cabello in Venezuela in 1801, exporting produce, livestock and other merchandise to Jamaica and Curaçao (then under British rule). The total value of these exports was over $1,000,000, of which two-thirds consisted of cacao and cotton, while the real value of dry goods imported in return was placed at a (surely exaggerated) $1,500,000. This observer further noted that 'there have been counted in the road of Kingston, eighty Spanish vessels, all under their proper flag', and estimated the total fleet devoted to the trade throughout the region at over 400 Spanish ships.[63] Part of the profits derived from this trade may have been moderated, however, by ill-advised grants of credit by British to Spanish merchants. Jamaican traders later recalled how during these years, 'to attract the trade of the Spanish subjects to the British free ports, and to prevent them from resorting for supplies, to neutrals, credits to a considerable extent were given to the Spanish traders to this market'. Many of these credits remained outstanding at the Peace of 1802 and were still owing years later, their collection hindered by Spain's persistent regard of all such trade as illegal.[64] In November 1807, Jamaican merchants sought to have provision for recovery of such debts included in any peace settlement with Spain.[65]

Peace between Britain and its enemies was signed at Amiens in March 1802 and lasted (so far as Spain was concerned) until late 1804, a period of almost three years. With the cessation of hostilities, the licence system naturally lapsed, and trade at the free ports resumed the form it had maintained prior to the war. Some observers expected commerce to flourish once neutral traders were again excluded from Spanish ports; President Hunt wrote from Nassau that 'in case of Peace ... this island and Jamaica, as the Spanish Ports will then be shut against the Americans, and being without competitors, will probably supply them with British Manufactures to an amount hitherto unexperienced'.[66] Detailed statistical data describing the free ports trade, though still fragmentary, become more abundant from the period of the Peace of Amiens.[67] Their limitations notwithstanding, these data appear to indicate that Hunt's hopes were broadly realised. The clearest indicator, that of

Table 4.2 *Value of the licensed trade at Jamaica and the Bahamas, 1795–1807*

	Imports of bullion ($)	Total value of imports (£)	Total value of exports (£)
Jamaica			
1795	1,423,300		
1799	—	—	—
1803	1,186,500	—	—
1804	1,452,700	—	—
1805	791,000	—	—
1806	1,743,000	—	100,837 (Oct.–Dec.)
1807	1,412,000 (Jan.–June)	—	1,126,126 (see note)
Bahamas			
1795	500		
1799	168,800 (July–Dec.)	238,000	243,000
1803	486,100	—	—
1804	650,175	—	365,236
1805	753,050	—	199,037
1806	644,200	—	—
1807	177,000 (Apr.–June)	—	—

Combined totals for imports of bullion		(Sterling equivalent)
1795	1,423,800	320,676
1799	168,800 (July–Dec., Bahamas only)	38,018
1803	1,672,600	376,712
1804	2,102,875	473,620
1805	1,544,050	347,759
1806	2,387,200	537,658
1807	1,589,000 (Jan.–Jun., n.d. for Bah., Jan.–Mar.)	357,883

4.6

Note: Where appropriate, figures for total value of imports and exports have been converted from dollars to pounds sterling, at an exchange rate of £1 = $4.44 (the rate applied by the British in the early 1790s). The figure for exports from Jamaica for 1807 in fact covers the period July 1807–June 1808.

imports of bullion, shows strong growth during the Peace, while fragmentary data for exports at the Bahamas also suggest substantial growth in the trade since 1799. By 1804, exports from the Bahamas alone were worth some £365,000, while in the same year registered imports of bullion at both the Bahamas and Jamaica exceeded $2,000,000 for the first time (see Table 4.2). Commercial accounts for these years show a trade whose staples had remained essentially unaltered since its origins. Thus, imports from Spanish

America to Jamaica and the Bahamas in 1803 included over 2,000 tons of dyewood, over 7,000 head of livestock, over 11,500 hides, almost 250,000 lb of cotton wool, mahogany trunks, coconuts, and lesser imports. Imports to Jamaica alone in 1804 included some 1,350 tons of dyewood, large quantities of mahogany, some 6,700 mules, cattle and horses, over 11,000 hides, over 4,500 lb of indigo and sarsaparilla, and cotton, cacao, coconuts, and tortoiseshell. Exports from Jamaica centred on unspecified dry goods, of which over 10,000 bales and 1,400 casks, trunks and boxes were shipped in 1804. Other exports included 544 casks of ironware, 220 casks of earthenware, glassware, flour, bottled liquor and rum, and miscellaneous exports including 240 boxes of soap and candles, 180 iron pots, and 3 copper boilers.

During the Peace, the free trade in slaves with the Spanish colonies again became open to British merchants, although the aperture proved to be brief. After the war-time restrictions, slaves poured in to Spanish ports; by late October 1802, it was reported that more than 12,000 Africans had entered at Havana alone. Slaves were shipped to that port from Jamaica, the Bahamas, and other places, some of them for immediate reshipment to the United States.[68] Exports of slaves from Jamaica were reported as 2,402 in 1803, while those of the Bahamas hovered at around 2,200 per year in 1802–03.[69] In the latter year, James Moss sent 'several Cargoes of Negroes to the value of £40,000 sterling' from Nassau to Havana on consignment from merchants in Liverpool and elsewhere, although he then experienced great difficulty in securing payment from the Cubans.[70] By royal decree of 22 April 1804, the free trade in slaves was extended for a further twelve years for Spaniards and six years for foreigners, with more ample provision for parallel imports of agricultural tools and plantation machinery. The Governor at Nassau thought that this decree would 'open a new door for commercial industry'.[71] These hopes were dashed, however, when overt trade in slaves by the British again became prohibited on the renewal of war in late 1804. Two British Guineamen caught at Havana were seized in January 1805, and all British property then on hand in the city was confiscated.[72]

These years witnessed further applications from the Bahamas for a free port to be established at Crooked Island, a scheme which provoked wild optimism among its proponents.[73] At the same time, proposals from Jamaica revived earlier plans for additional free ports at St Anne's Bay, Falmouth, or Martha Brae, though Governor Nugent also thought the port at St Lucea should be closed.[74] All these applications were resolved, and the free port system itself was all but perfected, with the passing of the Consolidated Free Port Act of 1805. This Act made perpetual previous Acts issued on a temporary basis, and confirmed or extended the system to include a total of sixteen ports, in Jamaica (at Kingston, Port Antonio, St Lucea, Montego Bay, and Savannah la Mar), the Bahamas (at Crooked Island in addition to Nassau and Caicos), Bermuda, Tortola, Antigua, Dominica, Grenada, St Vincent, Tobago, and Trinidad.[75] Sir William Young could now remark that 'it may be well to consider the establishment of free ports as general, and which, in truth, it nearly is'; and certainly the free port system experienced no further significant modification after this time.[76] From April 1805, the British settlers in Honduras bay petitioned for a free port to be established at St George's Key as a remedy to a perennial shortage of supplies and the broader economic backwardness of the colony. This request was granted on limited terms a year later, and by March 1807 it was noted of Honduras that 'the Spaniards already bring a little money, and when the permission to trade becomes known throughout the neighbouring provinces, it will no doubt come in greater abundance'. Naval returns for Belize suggest that trade with the Spanish colonies dominated the licensed trade at that port later the same year.[77]

Valuable as it was, British merchants were acutely aware that the free ports trade remained vulnerable to a renewed outbreak of war with Spain. For this reason, from as early as the summer of 1803, and citing the harm done the trade by naval seizures during the late war, pressure mounted for provision to be made for an immediate renewal of the licensing system in the event of a break. Urgent petitions in this sense from Scottish manufacturers stressed the need to protect 'that confidential intercourse … on which the extensive linen and cotton trade of this quarter of the country, may be said almost wholly to depend'.[78] The issue was debated through the autumn of 1803, and late the same year instructions were sent to naval commanders and governors in the West Indies to the effect that the licensing system should be revived in the event of a new war – though no licences were issued as yet to avoid giving the impression that a break was imminent.[79] The merchants' fears seemed justified when the Los Dolores, trading from Havana to Kingston with $80,000 for the purchase of British manufactures, was captured and condemned by the Navy in December, while on Christmas day it was reported that rumours of a declaration of war had provoked the seizure of all Spanish shipping lying at the port.[80] Governor Nugent received his instructions the following month, but refused to issue licences without an explicit Order in Council authorising him to do so. Such an Order was finally issued on 5 July 1804; and thus it was that when war finally broke out in December, the licence system was immediately re-established, and trade proceeded without interruption. The relevant decrees were published in the island gazettes and easily fell into Spanish hands, drawing the attention of such acute observers as Antonio Narváez y la Torre, the colonial governor and writer on economic themes. Narváez was incensed by the fact that the British should make provision to protect a war-time contraband trade against a nation with which they were then at peace, something he regarded as 'new proof of their perfidy, and of the little store they set by Honour and the Laws of Nations, when money is at play'.[81]

The licensed trade in the western Caribbean during the second war (1804–08) displayed essentially the same characteristics as during the earlier period. Evidence for its ongoing richness includes an eye-witness report in mid-1806 of eight Spanish vessels leaving Kingston in a single month solely for the small port of Sabanilla in New Granada.[82] Viceroy Amar y Borbón prohibited all coasting trade in New Granada in February 1805, considering it particularly susceptible to abuse due to the recent British policy of 'conceding immunity and even effective protection to all those … who go to their colonies with the perverse design of employing themselves in contraband'.[83] Allegations of Spanish abuses of the licence system persisted, as did naval seizures of Spanish vessels trading under licence.[84] The cases of the *Precisa* and *Bella Americana*, taken en route for Kingston in early 1808, caused special irritation in Jamaica: the *Precisa* was a frequent trader to the island, and it was claimed that her owner had exported over $400,000 in British manufactures in the previous twelve months alone. The *Bella Americana*, from Veracruz with $34,000, had actually been insured with Lloyds of London. Though irregular prize-taking appears to have been less of a problem after 1804 than during the previous war, ongoing frustration at the licence system among naval officers was reflected in the comment of Captain Bell of the *Phipps* (captor of the *Precisa*) to the effect that 'he might as well give up cruizing as every Spanish vessel has now a licence'.[85] Abuse of the licence system ostensibly lay at the heart of an angry dispute between the governor and merchants of the Bahamas in 1807–08, which caused a brief crisis in the trade. Governor Cameron claimed that virtually every licence granted since the renewal of the war had been abused, most damagingly to transport large cargoes of bullion and produce from Mexico to Havana. The merchants insisted that Cameron's allegations were wildly exaggerated and claimed that his real motivation was pique over a reduction in the fees he was entitled to charge for the licences.[86] Partly in response to these events, in June 1808 new licences were issued for the West Indies, again revised so as to attempt to limit their abuse by Spaniards.[87]

Some commentators, both contemporary and modern, have detected a decline in the value of the licensed trade during the second war from its former levels.[88] In March 1806, orders were sent to the West Indies requiring detailed accounts for the Spanish trade in the previous two years, the first time since the 1760s that government had taken such close interest in the trade. Imports recorded in these and subsequent returns suggest some shift in the relative importance of the different commodities, with trade as a whole perhaps remaining stagnant with respect to the figures for 1803–04.[89] Thus, total imports of dyewood fell from some 2,250 tons in 1805 to some 1,500 tons in 1806, while imports of livestock rose from about 2,400 in the former year to some 4,800 in the latter (of which most were mules). Imports of hides numbered fewer than 4,000 units in both years, but those of indigo reached a remarkable 231,000 lb in 1805, and those of cacao grew to over 290,000 lb in the same year and over 670,000 lbs in 1806. Imports of cotton and of wax (a commodity new to the trade) also reached substantial levels in 1806. Jamaica took by far the greater part of all these imports, mainly at the free port at Kingston; Montego Bay and Port Antonio lay at some remove, while trade at St Lucea and Savannah la Mar was negligible. The Jamaican accounts for 1806 usefully distinguish between imports made in British vessels and those made by Spaniards, revealing that imports of dyewoods and livestock were split roughly between the two, while most foodstuffs and virtually all plantation produce were imported in Spanish vessels. Significantly, some two-thirds of all recorded imports of bullion were now made in British shipping.[90] Recorded data for exports during these years continued to be only fragmentary, the Customs officers noting that exports were all but impossible to gauge because 'the goods are generally purchased by the Spaniards themselves, from different merchants, and immediately packed up in bales without the smallest intimation being given by them to the consignees of their quality'. The data supplied suggest a decline in trade in dry goods, the principal commodity, to little more than 5,000 bales per year in 1805–06, albeit with greater diversity in exports of foodstuffs (cinnamon, black pepper and garlic in addition to flour, salt and fish) and of alcoholic drinks. Miscellaneous exports included 4,000 bricks and four iron boilers.

This evidence relating to different commodities notwithstanding, there is reason to believe that the Spanish trade in the western Caribbean experienced continued strong growth throughout these years. It is true that recorded imports of bullion at Jamaica indicate a serious slump in 1805, probably related to the renewal of trade by neutral powers at Spanish-American ports. But imports of bullion at Jamaica and the Bahamas together recovered to almost $2,400,000 in 1806, and were worth almost $1,600,000 in the first six months of 1807 alone (Table 4.2, p. 131). One well-informed source estimated that by the latter year, one-sixth of all British exports to the British West Indies were re-exported to the Spanish colonies, indicating a total value for the Spanish trade in 1805 'far superior' to £1,000,000.[91] Renny's *History of Jamaica*, published in 1807, recorded that Jamaica's currency now consisted almost entirely of Spanish and Portuguese coin.[92] In July 1808, Jamaican merchants stated that $5,000,000 (c. £1,126,000) in British manufactures had been exported by licensed vessels in the previous twelve months, and late the same year they gave a figure of at least $7,000,000 exported in the previous two years.[93] At the same time, in the context of the broader crisis in the British West Indies, the Spanish trade at Kingston was described as 'almost the only trade of consequence now left to this city, on which its existence may be said to depend'.[94] But there were renewed grounds for optimism in the American commercial embargo self-imposed in December 1807, which reduced the competition of neutrals in Spanish markets and increased the prospects for British trade.[95] The licensing system had permitted the Spanish trade to prosper through the period of the wars. When peace was finally achieved between Britain and Spain in July 1808, the system became obsolete, among with other aspects of the old commercial organisation; but Jamaica and Nassau were then well placed to exploit the opportunities of the new commercial era born with the Peace.[96]

Rescates: Pretext for the Licensed Trade with Jamaica and the Bahamas

> Those who went to the English Islands with the motive of *rescates* supplied themselves with their manufactures, introducing them by a thousand tricks suggested by greed into Spanish and American Ports.
>
> —Merchant Guild of Mexico, Mexico City, 23 August 1809 [97]

In the early seventeenth century, *rescate* (ransom) had been the standard denomination in the Spanish West Indies for all illicit trade with foreigners.[98] By the late eighteenth century, the term was used in a commercial context principally to describe the re-purchase during wartime of goods taken as prize by an enemy. This practice, it need hardly be stated, long antedated the onset of the Napoleonic wars in the 1790s. Its deep roots are apparent in British recourse to ransoms as a vehicle for illicit trade with the Spanish colonies during the years of heavy Spanish naval depredations on British shipping in the Caribbean in the 1730s.[99] Ransom operations were contemplated out of Mexico during the American Revolutionary War, although in the event none was undertaken, in part because the authorities in Jamaica opposed the scheme. By contrast, successful operations do appear to have been undertaken from Cuba during the same war.[100] Comparable permits were occasionally granted during peacetime, as in 1791, when Vicente Risel was permitted to recover goods which fell into British hands after the ship transporting them was wrecked off Tortola.[101] During the Franco-Spanish war of 1793–95, the authorities in New Granada granted permission for ransom of the cargo of a ship taken by French corsairs while en route from Cadiz.[102]

Within little more than a year of the outbreak of war in late 1796, and coinciding closely in date with the renewal of Spanish trade under licence in the British colonies, extensive *rescate* operations began to be undertaken between Spanish America and Spain and key ports in the British West Indies. Mexico and Cuba were the focal points for these operations in the colonies, while some of the most important operations were launched from Spain itself. During the current research, a single ransom also came to light out of Puerto Rico;[103] no unambiguous operations were identified from any of the other major colonies, although it would appear surprising if none was in fact undertaken. These ransom transactions were often complex, and they have been little studied, so that selected examples are described here in some detail. The ransom of prize goods itself constituted a valuable branch of British trade during these years, as the figure for prize sales at Nassau in 1799 given in the concluding paragraph to this section below suggests; but the real significance of *rescates* lay in the pretext they furnished for illicit intercourse with the British colonies. Ransom operations came to constitute a principal pretext for the licensed trade during the first Anglo-Spanish war (1796–1802) and the Peace of Amiens, providing a major vehicle for illicit trade in British merchandise during this period.

The island of Cuba became a leading base for ransom operations, a development which Cubans themselves contrived to bring about. In December 1796, the Havana merchant guild requested a general right to ransom prize vessels and cargoes taken by the British, one of a number of proposals designed to fend off the economic collapse said to threaten as a result of the war.[104] Permission to undertake ransom operations was granted by a royal decree dated 23 February 1797,[105] while a complementary order of 30 May freed ransomed vessels from import taxes and declared them fit for use in trade. In April 1798, the Cuban Captain-General, the Count of Santa Clara, wrote to President Hunt in New Providence requesting admission and protection for Spaniards seeking *rescates* in the island.[106] Ransom permits appear to have been granted routinely in Cuba from this time at least until the Peace of Amiens for merchants to sail to the British islands to re-purchase Spanish prizes. These permits were often granted without the need to specify particular vessels or their cargoes; thus, the pass granted to Juan de Arozena by Santa Clara in July 1798 read:

> I grant a passport to Don Juan Miguel de Arozena to go to the Foreign Colonies, in use of the permit granted this date by the Royal Exchequer to ransom Spanish goods and foodstuffs, captured by the British corsairs; and regarding Slaves newly brought from Africa he may bring them too, but all in a Spanish Ship.

The loose manner in which passes were issued made it particularly easy to mount operations using Cuba as a base, and merchants from other Spanish colonies frequently went to Havana for a pass prior to launching their own ransom expeditions. Arozena used his pass to purchase wine, agricultural produce, cloth and clothes in Jamaica, all purportedly from prize cargoes. The operation came under scrutiny when his ship, the *San José*, put into Campeche instead of returning to Havana, but Arozena vigorously defended its legitimacy. The resulting documentary file preserved not only his Spanish pass, but also the licence granted him by Earl Balcarres in Santiago de la Vega on 8 August the same year.[107]

Arozena stated that passes such as his were issued daily at Havana, and that imports of 'similar goods, exported by means of rescate from Enemy Colonial Ports' were 'normal and frequent'. A ship's captain, Pablo Díaz Roldán, confirmed that 'exports are daily and frequent from the foreign Colonies in Spanish Ships ... of goods ransomed by virtue of the permit and free Trade granted by the Government and Ministry in Havana, in consequence of the Royal Order they have to that effect'[108] The best statistical evidence for this trade derives from the port books for Havana, which are extant for most of the key years in question. These books show significant numbers of Spanish shipping entering Havana direct from British colonies during the first war: thirty such ships entered in 1798, 56 ships in 1799, 20 in 1800 and 6 in 1801. Most of these vessels came from the island of New Providence in the Bahamas, with only a small number arriving from Jamaica. Recorded cargoes consisted of ransomed Spanish prize goods, cloth, foodstuffs, cacao, wine, wooden boards, mill machinery and slaves, while a significant minority of ships was listed as entering in ballast.[109] In 1798, about one-third of these voyages were explicitly recorded in the port books as *rescate* expeditions, and although later arrivals are rarely recorded as such, it is probable that they too were undertaken on the pretext of ransoms. The early Cuban periodical, *Papel periódico de la Habana*, recorded the entry of precisely the same ships while suppressing all reference to *rescates*.[110] Juan de Arozena alleged that all entries of Spanish shipping from British colonies recorded in the Havana gazettes were undertaken under *rescate* permits, whether acknowledged or not – thus reinforcing the impression of a trade whose legality was known to be dubious or which was otherwise little spoken of.

Mexico was the second great centre for *rescates*; it will be observed that all of a dozen *rescate* operations for which specific documentation has come to light terminated in Mexico or Yucatán, whether by design or professed accident (Table 4.3). The importance of the ransom trade in Mexico was a

Table 4.3 *Sample* rescate *operations, 1797–1804, essential data*

Date of operation	Merchant or merchant houses involved	Ship/s ransomed	Other ship/s involved	Port of origin	British port of ransom	Port of destination
July 1798	Juan Miguel de Arozena	San Josef y las Benditas Animas		Havana	Kingston	Havana [Campeche]
Nov.–Dec. 1798	Porro & Murphy [Francisco Santa Cruz]	Bascongada, San Félix	Fidèle, Marte, Soberbio, Margarita	Veracruz / Havana	Kingston	Veracruz
Mid-1799	Santa María y Cuesta		Los Tres Amigos	Havana	Kingston	Veracruz
Mid-1799	Agustín Terrida	Mercurio; another ship		Havana	Kingston	Veracruz [Villahermosa]
Apr. 1800–1802	Torre Hermanos, other Cadiz merchants [Juan Bautista Anchorena] [Miguel de Inchausti]	Asturiana	Caribe, Dorada, María (alias Corso)	Cadiz	Kingston	Veracruz

Continued opposite

Table 4.3 *continued*

Date of operation	Merchant or merchant houses involved	Ship/s ransomed	Other ship/s involved	Port of origin	British port of ransom	Port of destination
Mid-1800	Tomás de la Cruz Muñoz		*Amable Josefa*	Havana	Kingston	Veracruz [Campeche]
Mid-1800– late 1801	José Ignacio de la Torre	*Lanzarote, Dorada*		Veracruz	Kingston	Veracruz
Mar. 1801– Nov. 1804	Bustamante Parientes Lucas Segalas	*Júpiter, Vigilante, Nueva Aguila, Caribe*		Cadiz	Kingston	Veracruz
Mar. 1801– Nov. 1804	Marco y Vergara, San Ildefonso Ruis del Río	*Vigilante, Júpiter*		Cadiz	Kingston	Veracruz
Apr.–July 1801	Juan Miguel Arozena, José Gutiérrez de Cubas	*Pelayo*	*Atrevida, Jesús María y Joseph*	Campeche	Nassau, Kingston	Campeche
Apr. 1801– Apr. 1802	Aguirre Hermanos, [Juan Manuel Rebuelta]	*Atrevida*	*Atrevido, Santa Susana*	Santander	Kingston	Veracruz
Aug. 1801 – 1803	Pío de Elizalde, Manuel de Yrasusta [Francisco de Arrillaga]	*Hipomenes, Volante*	*Paulina, Casto*	San Sebastián	Kingston	Veracruz

Notes: This table includes *all* ransom operations for which specific documentation came to light during the course of the current research; there are, of course, likely to have been many more such operations. Dates in col. 1 cover the period from the granting of the *rescate* permit in question, to the latest known date of resulting operations. Square brackets in col. 2 mark the name of the commercial agent or agents involved, as opposed to the proprietary merchants. Square brackets in the last column indicate the real, as opposed to designated, port of destination.

product of the intrinsic wealth of the Mexican market, perhaps coupled with the rather more limited access of neutral shipping there especially during the first war. *Rescates* began to be undertaken from Mexico during the administration of viceroy Miguel José de Azanza (May 1798 to April 1800), who was also responsible for overseeing the onset of trade by neutral merchants at Mexican ports. As a result, ransom operations came to be seen as of a significance comparable to neutral trade in the rapid opening of Mexican markets to foreign commerce which now took place. Humboldt, in estimating the scale of contraband in Mexico, focused on 'the years in which, either through free trade with the *neutrals*, or through the sale of *prizes*, we have witnessed a province inundated with goods from Europe and the Great Indies'.[111] Francisco Pérez Muñoz, an official of the Veracruz merchant guild, dated large-scale trade with foreign colonies and especially with Jamaica to the cover furnished by neutral trade, aggravated by permits granted in Mexico and Spain 'to go to that Island, and bring cargoes with the mistaken name of *rescate*, on exaggerated pretexts of necessity'.[112] A close identification of *rescates* with neutral trade is often to be found in the sparse discussions of ransoms in the secondary historical literature, although it is to be stressed that the two trades were in essence quite different from each other.

The *rescate* permits granted by Viceroy Azanza became a *bête noire* for Mexican monopoly merchants. Thus, the Mexican merchant guild suggested that 'never had so much silver and gold been exported by contraband as since the so-called Azanza permits'.[113] The polemicist Juan López Cancelada similarly noted that 'it is true that contraband has developed in Mexico in a scandalous manner, but because it has been authorised by the government … since the Azanza permits to *Don Tomás Murfi*'.[114] The latter reference was to the first and among the most controversial of these permits, granted to Francisco Santa Cruz, an agent of the powerful Veracruz house of Porro and Murphy. In mid-1798, with a pass obtained in Havana and under a permit from Viceroy Azanza, Santa Cruz shipped a cargo of produce from Veracruz to Jamaica in the Danish schooner *Fidèle*. In Kingston he was to ransom mercury and paper for official use and was also to procure military and other strategic information. In return he was permitted to ransom legally permitted goods and to ship them back to Veracruz. He ransomed goods principally from the cargo of the frigate *Vascongada*, and purchased the brigs *Marte*, *Soberbio*, and *Margarita* as transports. The operation was financed through sale of the outward cargo and with letters of credit on a Hamburg house with commercial ties to the house of Murphy. The *Marte* and *Soberbio* entered Veracruz in late 1798 with a rich cargo variously valued at 300,000–500,000 pesos (the *Margarita* was wrecked en route). This affair caused a scandal in Mexico and Spain, where Santa Cruz was described as 'Agent for the safest Trade the English have with New Spain'.[115] An aggravating factor was that Thomas Murphy was related to Azanza by marriage; the viceroy faced charges relating to the Santa Cruz permit during official investigations after he left office, though he was cleared on all counts.[116]

Along with Thomas Murphy, probably the leading Mexican merchant involved in *rescates* was Jose Ignacio de la Torre, a partner of the house of Torre Hermanos of Cadiz and Veracruz and Prior of the merchant guild in the latter port. In 1798, de la Torre made what may have been the first application for a *rescate* in Mexico, centred on the *Nuestra Señora del Carmen*, though the application was rejected. In mid-1800, he proposed 'to supply paper to the Tobacco Factory by Expeditions to the English Islands, especially to Jamaica', a scheme which won the support of Azanza's successor, Viceroy Félix Berenguer de Marquina. On 2 November 1800, his brig *Lanzarote* entered Veracruz from Jamaica with a cargo of over 12,000 reams of paper and some miscellaneous items, having been ransomed on a pass from Havana with the additional pretext of carrying royal despatches to Mexico. De la Torre then sought permission to ship Mexican produce to Havana and to bring a further quantity of paper and whatever mercury was available from Jamaica in return. In December he was authorised to export up to 100,000 pesos to this end, albeit with the stipulation that he export as much produce as possible in lieu of bullion, and was even accorded a monopoly of purchases of paper in the British colonies for use in the province of Campeche. In January 1801 the *Lanzarote* left Veracruz direct for Jamaica with 65,000 pesos in coin and cochineal and dyewood; and in May to December of that year, she and the *Dorada*, a second ship ransomed by de la Torre, returned to Veracruz bearing a further 25,000 reams of paper. De la Torre later claimed to have imported over 41,000 reams under this contract, supplying them to the state for 7 pesos each at a time when the going rate was some 28 pesos.[117] The operation, however, had effectively opened a sanctioned route of trade between Veracruz and Jamaica, one which it was widely suspected de la Torre exploited to maintain an extensive trade in contraband goods. It was said at this time of ransomed ships from Jamaica and New Providence that 'as soon as Ships arrive from these possessions numbers of men go on board with gold to make deals and purchase clandestine goods'.[118]

It does not appear that any blanket permission for ransoms such as that issued to Cuba ever reached the authorities in Mexico. As the foregoing examples suggest, permits for *rescates* were granted in Mexico more sparingly to commercial houses wishing to ransom specific ships or cargoes. Operations were often justified by the need to procure essential supplies, especially of mercury or paper (either for the royal tobacco factory, or the stamped paper essential for the transaction of all official business). The significance of these two products should not be exaggerated, since in my view they often provided more a pretext for the trade than its substance. In most cases, the true promoters of ransoms were merchants interested principally in the typical profitable products of Anglo-Spanish commerce (above all textiles). Nevertheless, it remains true that some *rescate* operations were launched solely with the aim of obtaining these items. In early 1799, Viceroy Azanza asked the Intendant of Havana to procure supplies of paper for the tobacco factory, an operation which was charged to the commercial house of Santa María y Cuesta. This house arranged ransom of the paper in Jamaica, and in March 1799 their schooner *Tres Amigos* entered Veracruz with some 4,750 reams and a cargo of cloth worth 20,000 pesos, all of which was permitted to be landed.[119] Azanza seems to have made arrangements with José de Gato in Nassau and José Gutiérrez Cubas in Kingston for the ongoing ransom and despatch of paper and mercury from those islands, though the details are somewhat obscure.[120]

A further justification or pretext for these voyages was the gathering of military intelligence. The captains of returning ransom ships were routinely asked to report on naval forces and preparations at British ports.[121] In some cases, as in that of Francisco Santa Cruz discussed above, this intelligence gathering was actually made a clause of the *rescate* permit. During a spell of captivity in Jamaica in early 1800, Viceroy Marquina agreed with the resident Spaniard Manuel González that the latter supply military intelligence from Kingston on a rolling basis, and licensed him to despatch ships with cargoes worth up to 10,000 pesos each time to Veracruz for this purpose. In August 1801 González despatched the Danish schooner *Suceso* with a cargo of cloth, paper, oil and cinnamon which greatly exceeded the specified value and was not accompanied by intelligence of any worth. As a result, she was allowed to land only a part of her cargo in Veracruz, although a further part was then smuggled in to the port.[122]

An important subsidiary centre for *rescates* in Mexico was the southern region from Tabasco into Campeche and Yucatán. *Rescate* operations terminating in this region often occurred in dubious circumstances; thus in 1799, Agustín Terrida ransomed the *Mercurio* in Kingston on a Cuban pass permitting him to sail to Veracruz, but instead he put in to Villahermosa in Tabasco pleading sickness among his crew.[123] In 1800 Tomás de la Cruz Muñoz put into Campeche from Jamaica with a cargo of ransomed paper, also on a permit from Havana for Veracruz. In 1798, as we have already seen, Juan de Arozena entered the same port instead of returning to Havana; and in 1801, with José de Gutiérrez and a third merchant, Arozena was responsible for probably the most significant of all the operations undertaken from Yucatán. This operation was based around the repatriation of British prisoners of war free of cost and the ransom of commercial cargoes, paper and mercury in return. Several voyages were made from Kingston and Nassau to Campeche, bringing in cloth and clothes, foodstuffs and miscellaneous items, as well as significant quantities of mercury. These operations provide further insights into dealings with the British – including the fact that most British merchants and even warehousemen were said to be fluent speakers of Spanish.[124] It is not clear how many *rescate* operations were launched from Mexico during these years, though Table 4.3 is unlikely to present a comprehensive survey. That operations thrived for several years appears to be confirmed by recorded entries at Veracruz of nineteen vessels from foreign colonies in 1800–02 alone, most of them from Jamaica.[125]

Several of the most important of all ransom operations originated in Spain itself, undertaken under permits granted for specific *rescates* similar to those issued in Mexico. A major and well-documented Spanish-based ransom was that of the *Nuestra Señora de Covadonga*, or *Asturiana*, captured off Campeche in November 1799 en route from Cadiz to Veracruz. Her cargo was the property of the house of Torre Hermanos and of a loose grouping of some sixty other merchants, which two blocs undertook formally separate ransom operations after permits to that end were procured in mid-1800. Torre Hermanos charged recovery of its share of the cargo to the ubiquitous Jose Ignacio de la Torre, while the other merchants appointed Juan Bautista Anchorena and Miguel de Inchausti as their commercial agents. The permit granted to Torre Hermanos prescribed that ransomed goods be paid for with bills of exchange or with produce exported from Veracruz. In subsequent negotiations in Mexico, however, Jose Ignacio de la Torre won important additional consent for direct exports of bullion from Veracruz to Jamaica. He despatched at least two vessels from the Mexican port under this permit, carrying almost 140,000 pesos in bullion, along with produce consisting of cochineal, dyewood, indigo, vanilla and drugs. The goods ransomed in return were transported in the brig *Caribe* (or *Amistad*), also ransomed, and in the schooner *María* (or *Corsa*), which made a number of voyages between Jamaica and Veracruz between early 1801 and mid-1802. On one such voyage the *Corsa* was intercepted by the British frigate *Apollo*, 'whose Commander, informed of my commission, let me go freely'.[126] Anchorena and de Inchausti, meanwhile, dealt with the British prize agents Willis Waterhouse, and despatched a first cargo worth about 30,000 pesos to Veracruz in April 1801, also in the *Amistad*. Anchorena then sought a right to export produce from Veracruz to pay for the balance of the ransom in the same way as had been permitted to Torre Hermanos. The crown attorney in Mexico doubted the legality of such an application, noting that 'the absolute and frank concession [*deferencia*] he aspires to, would be a safe-conduct for this traffic, against the intentions of His Majesty, which cannot have been to open by this means a direct communication with Veracruz'. Nevertheless, in July 1801 Anchorena was permitted to export the necessary produce and to bring the balance of the ransom in return in a single shipment.[127]

A second major example of a ransom operation mounted from Spain was that of the brigs *Bella María de las Mercedes* (or *Hipomenes*) and *Volante*, property respectively of the merchants Pío de Elizalde and Manuel Miguel de Yrasusta, both of the Basque port of San Sebastián. After these ships were taken prize in late 1800, the two owners obtained permits for their ransom (dated August and October 1801) and agreed to combine ransom operations. Francisco de Arrillaga, resident in Veracruz, was appointed commissary for the *rescate*, and despatched José de Monseñé to Jamaica via the United States in early March 1802 to supervise the operation. The total value of the ransom was given as some 140,000–200,000 pesos, with the cargoes consisting principally of cloth and clothes, a large quantity of paper, iron, and cinnamon.

Monseñé held letters of credit from Elizalde, but found them difficult to dispose of profitably in Jamaica; in point of fact, he railed against the British merchants as 'people who aspire to nothing more than to tyrannise as much as they can'.[128] On this pretext, he wrote to Arrillaga proposing that application be made to the viceroy for permission to send the necessary funds over from Veracruz. In April 1802, Arrillaga applied to Viceroy Marquina for permission to export up to 50,000 pesos in bullion to finance the ransom. After some hesitation, he was permitted to make a first large shipment of cash, and then 'other quantities the Interested Parties may ask for, as circumstances may require'. Under this permit, the corvette *Paulina* and brig *Casto* made several trips between Veracruz and Kingston, in late 1802 alone importing registered cargoes worth some 130,000 pesos – of which around 75 per cent were of foreign manufacture. These voyages continued well into the period of the Peace, a feature which drew explicit comment from contemporaries.[129] Nor were these the only operations which resulted in direct exports of bullion from Veracruz to Kingston; the permit granted the house of Aguirre Hermanos of Santander in April 1801 for ransom of the corvette *Atrevida* gave rise to a permit for the export of up to 40,000 pesos in bullion and produce, another operation which continued on into the peace.[130]

Rescate operations necessarily focused upon British ports with Courts of Vice-Admiralty, where naval prizes were sent for adjudication. At this time Courts existed in Kingston, in Nassau, and at Antigua (although the latter port does not appear to have been a significant centre for ransoms, presumably by reason of its location). On the whole the British were happy to encourage *rescates*, seeing them simply as another means by which Spaniards were drawn to their ports to trade. There was some concern at aspects of the business; Governor Nugent reported from Kingston that loopholes in the system governing sales of prize cargoes in that port had 'opened the door to such a system of smuggling as would astonish you'.[131] In August 1798, Governor Dowdeswell at Nassau was warned to 'keep a most attentive eye' on Spaniards coming over from Havana, amidst fears of espionage; Dowdeswell replied that to date the Spaniards had been 'perfectly submissive and orderly'.[132] None of this deterred Jamaicans from engaging vigorously in the trade, or from granting large credits to Spaniards purporting to hold ransom permits. In many cases such credit proved difficult to recover, partly because 'in many instances such licences and expeditions undertaken by them have been declared unlawful from fraud and informality'.[133]

One final and rather unlikely feature of the question of *rescates* remains to be discussed. This is the ransom by Spaniards of ships and cargoes from the United States which had been seized and condemned by the British on the grounds that they were trading to Spanish, and thus enemy, colonies. A report from the American consul in Havana in December 1801 noted:

> It is a fact, notoriously public – That the very goods taken from our Citizens and condemned at Nassau (N[ew] P[rovidence]) as Contraband, have

been instantly reshipped there under the <u>Spanish</u> Flag <u>itself</u>, and many persons, thus robbed, have come hither as passengers in the same vessel that brought what had been their own cargo.[134]

Another writer at this time confirmed that

the very Merchandize that is condemned in the port of Bahamas, which belongs to our Citizens, are sold and shipped to the port that they were intended for by the persons that own the privateers that brought them into the port of New Providence.[135]

Reports such as these could only inflame American opinion, already incensed at the growing British interference with all American shipping trading under neutral privilege in the Spanish and French colonies.[136] In a further twist, however, it was alleged that on occasion American vessels themselves gained entry to Spanish ports by claiming to have been ransomed from the British. Thus, in April 1799 merchants in Spain complained that 'on the pretext of having been ransomed, two Brigs were permitted to enter [at Veracruz], also American, from Jamaica, with goods which were sold for more than 400,000 pesos'.[137]

The phenomenon of *rescates* persisted only for the few years after 1797. Records of Spanish shipping entering Havana from British colonies are negligible for the period of the second Anglo-Spanish war (1804–08), for example, and few *rescates* have been identified as being launched from Mexico or Spain after late 1801. In November 1800 the ransom of mercury in the British islands was absolutely prohibited, and *rescates* naturally became redundant upon the suspension of hostilities in 1802.[138] In May 1805, Viceroy Iturrigaray of Mexico wrote stressing the harm which arose from the concession of ransom permits, eliciting a vague undertaking from Godoy for greater restraint in the matter in future.[139] That *rescates* did not revive during the second war may also have been a product of the fact that after 1804 neutral trade became more abundant in both Mexico and Cuba, amply supplying the requirements of both colonies for imported foreign manufactures.[140] Smuggling under the cover of trade in goods purportedly from British prizes taken by Spanish warships and privateers remained a problem, however.[141] The scale of the ransom trade during the years when it flourished was clearly considerable; thus, prize sales in New Providence alone were worth £304,000 in 1799 (sales which would have been divided between Spanish, American, and British buyers).[142] The value of British goods shipped to the Spanish colonies illicitly under cover of ransoms is harder to gauge, as befits an entirely contraband trade. Though we have no data specifically on the value of goods exported under cover of *rescates*, however, such trade is, of course, covered by the statistical evidence for the Spanish licensed trade as a whole, discussed briefly in the first part of this chapter.

The Licensed Trade in the Eastern Caribbean and the Lesser Antilles

> I know a gentleman in the Province of Cumaná who has 30,000 head of horned cattle, and is in absolute want of a coat.
> —Thomas Picton to Lieut.-Gen. Cuyler, Port of Spain, Trinidad, 25 May 1798[143]

In the eastern Caribbean, the Spanish trade was transformed by the capture of the island of Trinidad by an overwhelming British naval force under the command of Sir Ralph Abercromby in February 1797. Commercial considerations were foremost in British interest in Trinidad, something which appears clear from the rapid development of trade there in the months which followed. The first instructions issued to Governor Thomas Picton ordered him to encourage trade with the neighbouring Spanish colonies, partly with the promise of a free port in the island.[144] Picton published these instructions in an address to local Spaniards which included assurances that British views did not extend beyond trade and support for incipient independence movements.[145] Within months, Trinidad was granted a free port at San Josef (Port of Spain); still more strikingly, in June the island was granted the right to license trade with Spaniards, becoming the first British colony to enjoy such a privilege.[146] From the outset no duty was levied on the trade, while licences were supplied for a merely nominal fee and Spanish vessels were 'not required to report, enter, or clear at the Custom House'.[147] In these circumstances, and with Picton's energetic support, trade by Spaniards at the island grew rapidly. By late June 1797 Picton was reporting the daily arrival of Spanish launches bearing provisions and bullion, and his correspondence in ensuing years was littered with references to the trade as 'tolerably brisk', 'very considerable', or 'very flourishing'.[148] In April 1799, the Governor stated that Spaniards took off British manufactures worth £1,000,000 sterling per year, a claim he repeated in 1800.[149] In an authoritative article covering the first five years of British rule, Keith Radhay has calculated that the true value of the Spanish trade probably lay between around £630,000 and the figure given by Picton; an estimate by Dauxion Lavaysse, of a value of £1,600,000 in 1802, appears clearly exaggerated. Even the lowest of these figures, however, would indicate that already by 1800, Trinidad was 'second only to Jamaica among the British West Indian free ports in the volume of trade conducted with Spanish America'.[150]

Trinidad's trade was principally with the provinces of eastern Venezuela and the Orinoco, though a small part extended as far as La Guaira. The leading centre was the province of Cumaná and perhaps especially the port of Barcelona, whose merchants were said to purchase British manufactures worth $400,000 per year.[151] Though a little contraband was undertaken by the British themselves, the trade lay overwhelmingly in the hands of Spaniards trading under licence, whom Picton acknowledged to 'yield in activity and daring enterprize to no people in the world'.[152] The vessels employed were typically small launches or boats, which flocked to Port of Spain at the rate of several per day; thus, 873 Spanish launches were said to have entered in 1804 alone. The chief goods imported were specie, cotton, cacao and indigo, livestock (especially mules and cattle), and a variety of provisions. The former commodities were nearly all re-exported to Britain, while livestock and foodstuffs remained in Trinidad or were exported to neighbouring British colonies, where they played an important role in the island economies. The chief British exports, at over 80 per cent of the total, were textiles, of which the majority were cottons and linens, complemented by mill machinery, hardware, and rum; thus, 'the passion of the Spaniards for Manchester goods is so great, that all risks are run to procure them'.[153] In its early years the trade was harassed to a considerable degree by French and Spanish corsairs operating out of bases in the Gulf of Paria. Picton often discussed and, apparently, exaggerated the threat from the corsairs, and eventually oversaw military operations which drove them from the region. A threat of a different nature was the seizure of Spanish licensed vessels by British naval captains citing the same sorts of abuse of the licence system as those which prevailed at this time in the western Caribbean.[154] Privateers from the Leeward Islands and Nova Scotia also preyed on licensed vessels; in August 1800, Alexander von Humboldt took ship from Barcelona to Cumaná in a smuggling launch, and was almost carried off to Halifax by a privateer who refused to recognise the passport its captain had procured in Trinidad.[155]

Detailed data available for the period of the Peace of Amiens onwards appear to indicate some decline in the value of trade at Trinidad with respect to the earlier years. The number of launches entering at Port of Spain fell to 674 in 1805, and to 406 in the following year. The value of British exports was estimated at $850,000 in 1804, $1,000,000 in 1805, and $650,000 in the first half of 1806 (approximately £191,500, £225,250, and £146,500 sterling respectively).[156] A further source gives a figure for exports of $528,800, or c. £119,000 sterling, for the year 1808.[157] Port officials, meanwhile, estimated that imports from the Spanish colonies were worth $1,500,000 (c. £340,000) in the year to June 1804, of which $700,000 was specie.[158] Recorded imports were worth some $664,000 in 1804, $859,000 in 1805, and $528,000 in the first half of 1806 (c. £150,000, £194,000, and £119,000 sterling respectively). Data for imports may understate the true picture, however, due to routine under-registration of imports of bullion by Spaniards, while the same factor also explains the imbalance apparent between imports and exports. The Naval Officer at Port of Spain noted that Spaniards 'invariably report less [specie] than they bring', so that 'it may be fairly supposed that these statements are much under the real value'.[159] An important complementary feature of these years, and one which places the Spanish trade in proper context, was Trinidad's dependence from an early stage on trade with the United States. As early as 1800, Governor Picton was obliged to permit the importation of lumber and provisions from the United States for the supply of the island.[160] His successor, Thomas Hislop, was rebuked in 1807 for permitting imports of provisions from the United States and exports of sugar in return, but claimed that trade with Americans was twenty times greater than with any other region.[161] Whatever the case, Trinidad's trade with South America was hit hard by the onset of direct trade from Britain and of the revolutionary wars in Venezuela from 1810. The value of exports was still given as over $750,000 in 1809, but within five years it had fallen to c. $200,000, and by 1818 it had collapsed to less than $30,000.[162]

Two further territories in the eastern Caribbean newly conquered by the British during the wars also became important centres for the Spanish trade, although, unlike Trinidad, neither endured as imperial possessions. The Danish colony of St Thomas in the Virgin Islands, now at the peak of its great wealth as an entrepôt for neutral trade, was seized in 1801–02 and again in December 1807 when Denmark became allied with France.[163] At the time of its capture in 1801, steps were taken to safeguard trade with Spaniards at the island, which was guaranteed 'for provisions and indispensable supplies'.[164] The result of these measures is uncertain: one authority wrote that during the occupation of 1801–02, commerce at St Thomas was 'greatly depressed', though elsewhere it was stated that 'the trade ... experience'd no excessive diminution'.[165] After the second seizure of the island by the British, in late 1807, still more extensive measures were taken to guarantee the prosperity of the Spanish trade. Spaniards who had fled to Puerto Rico during the British blockade were invited back, and the governor anticipated their return 'with great sums of money which they had carried away with them'.[166] Although St Thomas was not granted a free port, the Customs regime established there was more liberal than in other British colonies, and trade was granted protection under licence much as at other British islands.[167] St Thomas's Spanish trade was principally with Puerto Rico, Santo Domingo, and Venezuela, and was based on the exchange of bullion and produce for British manufactures. In January 1808 it was said that British goods worth some £500,000 lay on hand in the island, and the potential value of the trade was estimated at more than £1,000,000 per year.[168] The following July imports of British merchandise, either direct or from other West Indian colonies, were estimated at £700,000 annually, and it was suggested that the potential value of the trade to the British might run as high as £1,300,000.[169] In my view these figures are excessive; total British exports to St Thomas in 1807, for example, had amounted to a (still considerable) £210,000 sterling.[170] After the Anglo-Spanish peace of July 1808, the island seems to have remained a centre for the Spanish trade of some importance, but it was returned to Denmark in 1815.

Like St Thomas, the Dutch island of Curaçao was seized by Britain in late 1800, given up during the Peace, and then retaken in 1807. Curaçao had long been the chief base for Dutch contraband trade with the Spaniards, and there is little doubt that this trade was the prime motive behind the British conquest. In 1801 the island was promptly granted both a free port (at Amsterdam) and a licensed trade with Spaniards.[171] Commerce flourished during this first period of British rule: in 21 months, 187 British and 361 Spanish ships traded at the port, and up to 60 Spanish vessels might be seen there at one time.[172] Immediately after the reconquest of the island in 1807, requests were lodged for a renewal of the earlier free port and other privileges, and these were granted by early August the same year.[173] Debate continued as to the organisation of the trade or its improvement, whether through the moderation of duties, permission to import a greater range of produce, or special facilities for trade at neighbouring Aruba and Bonaire.[174] We have little firm data on the Spanish trade at Curaçao from this time until the Anglo-Spanish peace of July 1808, although it can be noted that eighty-one licences for trade with the Spanish colonies were granted between 1 January and 28 April of the latter year.[175] Immediately upon the peace, negotiations were undertaken by the Governors of Curaçao which won significant fiscal and other privileges for trade with Venezuela.[176] This trade remained strong in 1809, but declined thereafter due to competition from American traders, and (again like St Thomas) the island was given up at the end of the wars. The cases of Curaçao and St Thomas apart, other foreign colonies conquered during these years do not appear to have become centres for the Spanish trade of any weight, whatever their broader strategic significance. French Martinique, held between 1794 and March 1802, had little direct trade with Spaniards, though it is probable that some indirect trade went on via Trinidad and other British possessions.[177] The Dutch mainland colonies of Demerera, Essequibo and Berbice, captured in 1796 and held until 1802, similarly played no significant role as entrepôts for the Spanish trade, despite considerable British investment in plantations there.[178]

Trade with Spaniards at the older-established British colonies in the Lesser Antilles declined rapidly after 1796, apparently due principally to competition from the newly conquered territories of Trinidad, St Thomas, and Curaçao. Grenada, whose trade had boomed so notably under the free port regulations since the mid-1780s, was hit particularly hard. Within a few years, it was remarked from Grenada that 'Trinidad has injured that branch of the trade of this island extremely', and that 'the loss of that commerce we had formerly with Trinidad has been severely felt'.[179] Pressure from merchants trading with Grenada led both to the concession of a licensed trade to the island in March 1798, and to the general permit for trade between the free ports and other British colonies issued the same year.[180] Trade under licence began the following December, with the arrival of three ships from the Orinoco with mules, and persisted thereafter at a low level throughout the period of the wars. As in the western Caribbean, there were allegations of abuse of the system by Spaniards, as well as naval seizures of Spaniards bearing licences.[181] As in the Bahamas, Grenada witnessed a major dispute regarding the fees levied by Customs officers on Spanish licensed vessels, a dispute which yielded much of the information we possess on the operation of the licensed trade itself.[182] One feature peculiar to this period was the proposal made in early 1805 by one William Davis Robinson, a US merchant then resident at Caracas. Robinson, who held significant commercial contracts with the Spanish authorities, sought permission to develop an extensive trade between Venezuela and Grenada in neutral merchant shipping. He was optimistic as to the benefits of this scheme, estimating the value of Venezuelan exports at almost 5,000,000 pesos per year, and the potential total value of this produce to Britain at 'not less than from 18 to 25 Millions of Dollars'. His proposal was actually approved by Governor Maitland, to run for six months from 1 August 1805; but it was unlikely to find lasting favour with the British government, and seems not to have prospered.[183]

In these circumstances, and the licence system notwithstanding, the Spanish trade at Grenada failed to recover more than a fraction of its pre-war prosperity. By February 1799, only nine licensed vessels had come to trade at St George's; in 1801 'several launches' entered, while in the last quarter of 1804 entries from the Spanish colonies rose to ten vessels.[184] In July 1805, a leading merchant house described the trade as 'at a stand' since 'no Spaniard now comes', and a small launch from Margarita with mules was said to have been the only arrival in several months.[185] In 1806 trade with Puerto Rico was said to have ceased altogether, while the Governor could still describe the trade as 'this yet unformed (or rather which is now forming) branch of commerce'.[186] We have several detailed accounts for Grenada's licensed trade during the war of 1804–08 which, though they belie these very pessimistic assessments, nevertheless describe a trade much diminished. In the two years 1804–05, total imports from Spanish America were worth just $152,680 (c. £34,000), of which assorted livestock and hides accounted for over 55 per cent and indigo almost 22 per cent. British exports in return, for which no values were recorded, consisted especially of cottons, linens, and ironware, along with a typically broad range of miscellaneous exports including shoe brushes, stationary, window glass and paint. Grenada now traded exclusively with eastern Venezuela (especially with Barcelona, Cumaná and Margarita) and the Orinoco.[187] Accounts for 1806 assign no values to the commodities traded, but show imports dominated by cacao, mules, and hides, and an export trade again based above all upon linen and cotton textiles (including large quantities of handkerchiefs).[188] Data for the first half of 1807 suggest a considerable decline in many imports, for example to only ten mules, although imports of hides rose to over 3,400; exports showed scant variation over previous years.[189] The Spanish trade at Grenada may have experienced modest recovery following the peace of 1808; thus, returns for the first eight months of the year 1813 show total imports worth a little more than $119,000, of which over $43,000 came as money (70 per cent of it in bills).[190]

Possibly the only other colony with a Spanish trade of any relevance was Tobago, which was ceded back to France in 1802 but retaken (this time definitively) in July 1803. After some vacillation, Tobago was granted a licensed trade in February 1800, and after its recapture from the French its free port was re-established under the Consolidated Free Port Act of 1805.[191] The island's trade was principally with Angostura on the Orinoco, and was based upon imports of livestock for local use, supplemented by small quantities of indigo, cotton and cacao. One report suggested that up to twenty vessels traded with Tobago per year, their crews consisting of 'Spaniards, and a race partly Spaniards and Indians, mulattoes and coloured people'.[192] Data for 1804–06, by contrast, indicate average entries from the 'Foreign West Indies' altogether of just ten ships per year, with imports worth an average of £10,000, and exports less than £4,000.[193] A different account suggests that only five Spanish vessels entered in 1804, bringing 292 mules, 5,000 hides, and small quantities of indigo, cotton and leather, while in 1805 a single ship entered with a cargo of 70 mules.[194] Further data for 1806–08 indicate a rather broader range of imports (including tobacco, drugs, rice and beef) and perhaps some growth in the trade as a whole, though overall volumes remained very modest.[195] Uniquely, most sources agree that imports to Tobago were paid for almost exclusively with specie, rather than through the export of British manufactures; thus Sir William Young remarked that 'in the three years of my Government, I have known but of two exceptions; one Spaniard taking 14 p[uncheons] of rum, another taking half a dozen chests of hats, shoes and cottons'. As at other British islands, Tobago's Spanish trade was dwarfed by its intercourse with the United States; in 1807, for example, the given value of imports from Spanish America was £7,626, while recorded imports from the United States were worth over £105,000.[196] The Spanish trade at the island surely remained modest due mainly to competition from Trinidad and elsewhere, though Young blamed repeated changes of sovereignty for impeding the natural course of its economic and commercial development.

The licensing system was rendered complete with its extension to Tortola in the Virgin Islands in 1806, in the context of British attempts to foment trade with independent St Domingue. Tortola had won its free port, at Road Harbour, in 1802, as a result of sustained pressure from island representatives, who stressed especially its capacity to compete with the Danish colony of St Thomas. In the ensuing years the island's very active agent, Patrick Colquhoun, continued to press for further privileges to encourage trade, efforts which bore modest fruit in 1806 with permission to import foreign sugar and coffee at Road Harbour free of duty.[197] Early expectations of trade at Tortola, however, were severely disappointed: in the first three months after the establishment of the licensed trade, only two licences were taken out for trade with the Spanish colonies, and a further two for St Domingue.[198] The British capture of St Thomas a short time afterwards, with its greatly superior port and commercial infrastructure, then precluded any possibility that Tortola would become an important place of trade.[199]

Tortola was the last British colony to be granted a right to trade with Spaniards under licence. The British were reluctant to extend the system to every petty colony, while the legalisation of trade between the free ports and other British islands in 1798 was seen as obviating the necessity of doing so.[200] Little evidence of any kind has come to light for trade by Spaniards at the remaining Lesser Antilles during this period. Dominica, whose petition for a licensed trade was rejected in 1797, retained some trade, but at a low level and with a tendency to decline.[201] Although five ships entered Roseau from South America in the last quarter of 1804, there is no evidence of any such trade in the first half of 1807.[202] Islands such as Barbados, St Vincent and Antigua, meanwhile, were said to supply part of the British manufactures sold to the Spaniards at Trinidad, and in return took large cargoes of the live-stock which were vital to their economies.[203] By and large, however, the strong trades yet subsisting at Trinidad or St Thomas were very much the excep-tion to the rule. The historic role played by small islands in the eastern Caribbean, as major entrepôts for trade between Britain and the Spanish-speaking continental and insular territories, was fast coming to an end.

Notes

1   Simón de las Casas to Príncipe de la Paz, London, 10 June 1796, A.H.N., Estado, 4244.
2   Printed royal cédula, San Lorenzo, 7 Oct. 1796; there is a copy of this decree in the small collection titled 'Documentos Importantes', Biblioteca de la Región Militar Sur, Seville.
3   Becker, *España e Inglaterra*, p. 58. Not all the early operations favoured the British, however, who also suffered defeats at Tenerife and Puerto Rico.
4   Fisher, 'Commerce and Imperial Decline', pp. 462–3.
5   Elaborated from Fisher, 'Commerce and Imperial Decline', pp. 471–3.
6   García-Baquero, *Comercio colonial*, pp. 48–50, 59–60; Fisher, 'Commerce and Imperial decline', p. 474.
7   Jones, 'Historical Study', p. 59.
8   See pp. 214–20 below.
9   Robert Hunt to Duke of Portland, New Providence, 5 June 1797, N.A., C.O. 23 / 36, ff. 69–71v.
10   Adm. Sir Hyde Parker to Evan Nepean, *Abergavenny*, Port Royal Harbour, Jamaica, 17 Oct. 1799, N.A., ADM. 1 / 249, no. 49; and same to same, 20 Feb. 1800, N.A., ADM. 1 / 250, no. 8.
11   Branciforte to Pedro Varela, Mexico, 3 July 1797, A.G.N.M., Correspondencia de virreyes, 186, ff. 187–9; Branciforte to Príncipe de la Paz, Mexico, 3 July 1797, A.G.N.M., Correspondencia de virreyes, 188, f. 194.
12   Ortiz, *Comercio exterior de Veracruz*, p. 263; Fisher, 'Commerce and Imperial Decline', p. 463.
13   Vicente Linares, *Acta*, 18 Aug. 1799, ff. 60–9v of 'Testimonio de los Autos creados sobre establecer en la Provincia de Venezuela y Caracas comercio con el estrangero', A.G.I., Caracas, 117.
14   McFarlane, *Colombia Before Independence*, p. 302.
15   Armytage, *Free Port System*, pp. 95–6.
16   Office of Correspondence, Spanish Town, Jamaica, 15 May 1797, N.A., C.O. 137 / 98, ff. 412–13v.
17   Earl Balcarres to Duke of Portland, Jamaica, 4 July 1797, N.A., C.O. 137 / 98, ff. 258–9.
18   Office of Correspondence to Robert Jewell, Spanish Town, 15 May 1797; Balcarres to Portland, Jamaica, 4 July 1797, both in N.A., C.O. 137 / 98, ff. 258–9, 412–13v.

19 See esp. 'Trinidada – Minute on the Draft of Instruction', 21 June 1797, N.A., Board of Trade (hereafter B.T.), 5 / 10, ff. 198v–9.

20 'Jamaica – Resolution of the Committee', Minute for 3 Nov. 1797, N.A., B.T. 5 / 11, ff. 7–8.

21 Instructions, St James, 20 Nov. 1797, and the cover letter, Portland to Balcarres, Whitehall, 22 Nov. 1797, both in N.A., C.O. 137 / 98, ff. 375–9; Portland to President Robert Hunt, Whitehall, London, 22 Nov. 1797, N.A., C.O. 23 / 36, ff. 115–16.

22 Extract of a letter, Kingston, 4 Mar. 1798, N.A., B.T. 1 / 16, f. 98.

23 Extract, Hunt to John Brickwood, New Providence, 1 Mar. 1798, N.A., B.T. 1 / 16, ff. 96–v.

24 Instructions, St James, 28 Mar. 1798, encl. to Portland to Governor Dowdeswell, Whitehall, London, 28 Mar. 1798, N.A., C.O. 23 / 37, ff. 94–v; Armytage, *Free Port System*, p. 101.

25 38 Geo. 3 cap. 39; Armytage, *Free Port System*, p. 102.

26 Hunt to Portland, Nassau, 28 Feb. 1798, and extracted translation of Count of Santa Clara to Hunt, 4 Apr. 1798, both in N.A., C.O. 23 / 37, ff. 97–8, 149–v.

27 See Ajequiezcane, 'British Trade with the Spanish Colonies', which was originally published in the *Jornal Económico Mercantil de Veracruz*, nos. 146–9, 24–27 July 1806. A noteworthy description which remained unpublished until the 1960s is that of Narváez y la Torre, 'Discurso del Mariscal de Campo ...', pp. 76ff.; Depons, *Travels in South America*, 2:55–8, was published outside the region.

28 'Sendas telegráficas'; Humboldt, *Ensayo político sobre ... la Nueva España*, p. 496.

29 *Parecer del Señor Fiscal*, Caracas, 5 Nov. 1799, and *Voto consultivo de la Real Audiencia*, Caracas, 13 Nov. 1799, both in 'Testimonio de los Autos creados sobre establecer en la Provincia de Venezuela ... comercio con el estranjero', A.G.I., Caracas, 117, ff. 96–110v, 110v–17v.

30 De Pombo, 'Informe del Real Tribunal del Consulado', pp. 14–16.

31 De Pombo, 'Informe del Real Tribunal del Consulado', pp. 23–40; also the same author's 'Memoria sobre el contrabando', pp. 71–99.

32 Officers of the Consulado to Miguel Cayetano Soler, Caracas, 29 May 1801, A.G.I., Caracas, 920.

33 Valentín de Foronda to Pedro Cevallos, Philadelphia, 23 Aug. 1804, A.H.N., Estado, 6175.

34 Walton, *Present State of the Spanish Colonies*, 2:168–9; also Depons, *Travels in South America*, 2:56–8.

35 See esp. Mendinueta to Saavedra, Santa Fé, 19 July 1798, and related material, copies in A.G.I., Santa Fé, 647; Indiferente, 2466. By February 1799, Mendinueta had himself become convinced of the need to allow Spanish trade with neighbouring neutral or foreign colonies, though his proposals fell victim to the general abolition of neutral trade in April of the same year.

36 De Pombo, 'Informe del Real Tribunal del Consulado', pp. 14–16.

37 Hyde Parker to Evan Nepean, *Abergavenny*, Port Royal Harbour, 8 Oct. 1799; Parker to Nepean, *Queen*, Port Royal Harbour, 7 Dec. 1799, both in N.A., ADM., 1 / 249, nos. 43 and 57.

38 Balcarres called Parker's allegations 'altogether unfounded in Fact, and which never had the shadow of existence'; Parker regarded this expression as 'extremely indecent and disrespectful', containing 'insolence join'd to arrogance'. The relevant correspondence may be consulted in N.A., ADM. 1 / 249, ADM. 1 / 250, and C.O. 137 / 104; see also Kup, 'Alexander Lindsay', pp. 347, 350–5. The papers from the Crawford Muniments cited by Kup, which parallel the series cited here, are now held at the National Library of Scotland.

39 Dowdeswell to Portland, Government House, Bahamas, 1 May 1800, N.A., C.O. 23

/ 39, ff. 121–2v; see also the sworn statement of Benjamin Waterhouse, dated Jamaica, 27 Jan. 1800, encl. to Parker to Nepean, *Queen*, Port Royal Harbour, 28 Jan. 1800, N.A., ADM. 1 / 250, no. 5.

40 Loring to Parker, *Carnatic*, off Cape Antonio, 30 Apr. 1799, N.A., ADM. 1 / 250, follows no. 37.

41 For these cases see Robert Plampin to Parker, *Lowestoffe*, Port Royal Harbour, 20 Oct. 1799, N.A., ADM. 1 / 249, follows no. 50.

42 R. W. Otway to Parker, *Trent*, Port Royal Harbour, 13 Nov. 1799, N.A., ADM. 1 / 249, follows no. 53.

43 Balcarres to Portland, Jamaica, 26 May 1800, N.A., C.O. 137 / 104, ff. 150–v.

44 See the examples discussed in the encl. to Parker to Nepean, *Abergavenny*, Port Royal Harbour, 17 Oct. 1799, N.A., ADM. 1 / 249, no. 49; and Parker to Nepean, *Abergavenny*, Port Royal Harbour, 20 Feb. 1800, N.A., ADM. 1 / 250, no. 8.

45 'Draft of Circular' to Balcarres and Dowdeswell, Whitehall, 6 Jan. 1800, N.A., C.O. 137 / 103, ff. 3–6v.

46 Petition of inhabitants of New Providence to President Hunt, Nassau, May 1801, N.A., C.O. 23 / 40, ff. 118–v; Balcarres to Portland, Jamaica, 29 Oct. 1799, N.A., C.O. 137 / 103, ff. 48–9v.

47 Memorial of merchants and traders of Nassau, 3 June 1799, N.A., C.O. 23 / 38, ff. 236–7.

48 'Bahamas – Memorial of Stephen Haven Esq.', Minute for 9 Nov. 1799, N.A., B.T. 5 / 11, ff. 187–v.

49 *Report from the Committee* ... (St Jago de la Vega: 1800), copy in N.A., C.O. 137 / 103, ff. 228–35v.

50 President Hunt to Lord Pelham, Govt. House, Nassau, 20 Nov. 1801, N.A., C.O. 23 / 40, ff. 58–60v.

51 The Scottish petitions are in N.A., B.T. 1 / 19, ff. 199–206v. Scottish production of cloth for Spanish-American markets grew in the last few years of the eighteenth century, replacing continental textiles whose import via North America was interrupted by the French corsairing war on American shipping; see for example the testimony of Kirkman Finlay, 20 May 1812, in *Parliamentary Papers* ..., p. 404.

52 Kup, 'Alexander Lindsay', pp. 354–5.

53 Extract of a letter, Nassau, 17 July 1799, encl. to Buchanan, Steven & Co. to Evan Nepean, Glasgow, 16 Sept. 1799, N.A., ADM. 1 / 250, follows no. 13.

54 See Minutes of Council, 10 May 1800, N.A., C.O. 137 / 104, ff. 114–23.

55 Minutes of Council, 10 May 1800, N.A., C.O. 137 / 104, ff. 114–23.

56 Memorial of the merchants and traders of Nassau, 3 June 1799, and José Gato to Dowdeswell, Veracruz, 7 June 1799, both in N.A., C.O. 23 / 38, ff. 236–7, 258–v; Parker to Nepean, *Queen*, Port Royal Harbour, 7 Dec. 1799, N.A., ADM. 1 / 249, no. 57, see also Annexe C to the same letter.

57 Petition of Robert Read of Nassau, n.p., 21 Dec. 1801, N.A., B.T. 1 / 19, ff. 421–v.

58 Statistical appendix, table A7.

59 These figures are drawn from data in *Votes of the Honorable House* ... (Nassau: 1800), in N.A., C.O. 23 / 39, see ff. 279–80; Memorial of merchants connected with the Bahamas, London, July 1800, N.A., C.O. 23 / 40, ff. 105–6; and the commercial accounts in N.A., C.O. 23 / 39, ff. 152–4.

60 See the notes to the Custom House accounts for the second half of 1799 cited in the preceding note; elsewhere it was noted that 'the Spaniards are not fond of reporting the number of dollars they import, & it is judged proper not to press them on that head'; note to account in N.A., C.O. 23 / 38, f. 199.

61 'A List of Vessells ...', Nassau, 17 May 1800, and Nathaniel Hale to John King, Nassau, 3 June 1800, both in N.A., C.O. 23 / 39, ff. 147, 353.

62 Anon., *Instrucciones que los vireyes de Nueva España dejaron a sus sucesores* ..., p. 205.

63 Depons, *Travels in South America*, 2:55–8.

64 See esp. the 'Humble Memorial' of William Robinson, n.p., n.d. [1805], N.A., B.T. 1 / 28, ff. 265–90v, specifically ff. 277–v, who goes so far as to state that 'in Jamaica, particularly, the infatuation was so great as to ruin several of the best houses in the Colony'.

65 Memorial of the merchants of Kingston, Kingston, 16 Nov. 1807, N.A., C.O. 137 / 119, ff. 203–v; discussed by Jones, 'Historical Study', pp. 149–51.

66 Hunt to Lord Pelham, Govt. House, Nassau, N.A., C.O. 23 / 40, ff. 58–60v; on the crash in US exports to Spanish America during the Peace, see Coatsworth, 'American Trade with European Colonies', p. 253.

67 For 1803–04, see esp. 'An Account of the following articles ... which have been imported in the year 1803, in the several Free Ports ...', N.A., C.O. 318 / 1, f. 82; 'General State of the Imports and Exports', N.A., C.O. 137 / 116, f. 112; and six enclosures, Bahamas, 7 June 1806, N.A., C.O. 24 / 12, ff. 92–3.

68 Vincent Gray to James Madison, Havana, 29 Oct. 1802, and Gray to Madison, Havana, 10 Nov. 1802, both in N.A.W., R.G. 59, M899, roll 1.

69 Young, *West-India Common-Place Book*, pp. 181–2, 184–5.

70 John Moss (for James Moss) to Martín de Garay, Liverpool, 13 June 1809, encl. to Juan Ruiz de Apodaca to de Garay, London, 28 June 1809, A.H.N., Estado, 5459.

71 Charles Cameron to Earl Camden, New Providence, 11 Nov. 1804, and translation of Royal Cédula, Aranjuez, 22 Apr. 1804, both in N.A., B.T. 1 / 24, ff. 320v–5v, 329–v.

72 Gray to Madison, Havana, 2 Jan., 14 Jan., and 6 Feb. 1805, all in N.A.W., R.G. 59, M899, roll 1.

73 See the papers in N.A., B.T. 1 / 21, ff. 17–18v, 23–8v, 317–18v; B.T. 5 / 13, f. 109v; and B.T. 5 / 14, ff. 81, 105, 112v–17–v. Col. Thomas Brown foresaw trade between Crooked Island and eastern Cuba to the extent of £300,000 annually; a Mr Moss thought bullion imports would be worth $1,500,000 per year.

74 'Jamaica – Letter from E. P. Lyon Esq.', Minute for 16 Apr. 1804, N.A., B.T. 5 / 14, ff. 123–v; Lieut.-Gov. Nugent to John Sullivan, Jamaica, 8 Mar. 1804, N.A., PRO. 30 / 42–9 / 13.

75 45 Geo. 3 Cap. 57; Armytage, *Free Port System*, app. 1.

76 Young, *West-India Common-Place Book*, p. 188.

77 Burdon, *Archives of British Honduras*, 2:78; 'Honduras – Information given by Mr Dyer', Minute for 21 Mar. 1807, N.A., B.T. 5 / 17, f. 91v; naval returns in N.A., B.T. 1 / 40, ff. 93–7.

78 Memorials dated Glasgow and Perth, June–July 1803, N.A., B.T. 1 / 22, ff. 299–303.

79 See the discussions in N.A., B.T. 5 / 14, ff. 51v–6v, 58–v; B.T. 1 / 22, f. 32; useful analysis in Jones, 'Historical Study', pp. 73–5.

80 William Taylor *et al.* to George Hibbert *et al.*, Kingston, 21 Dec. 1803, and annexes, N.A., B.T. 1 / 23, ff. 37–46.

81 Narváez y la Torre, 'Discurso del Mariscal de Campo', pp. 76–9, with Spanish translations of British decrees and related material, pp. 113–20.

82 Antonio Amar y Borbón to Miguel Soler, Santa Fé, 7 Dec. 1806, copies in A.G.I., Santa Fé, 653, 960.

83 See esp. Amar to Soler, Santa Fé, 20 Apr. 1807, A.G.I., Santa Fé, 654.

84 Armytage, *Free Port System*, p. 106.

85 'Minutes of a committee', July 1808, N.A., B.T. 1 / 41, ff. 115–20v; Thomas Hughan *et al.* to Board of Trade, Billiter Square, London, 25 Jan. 1809, and Record of a meeting of merchants, Kingston, July 1808, both in N.A., B.T. 1 / 44, ff. 138–v, 142–50.

86 The key, extensive documentary series on these events is in N.A., B.T. 1 / 38, begin-
    ning f. 192; there are related papers in N.A., B.T. 1 / 39 and B.T. 5 / 18.
87 Jones, 'Historical Study', p. 156.
88 Young, *West-India Common-Place Book*, pp. 181–2; Jones, 'Historical Study', pp.
    78–9.
89 'General State of the Imports and Exports ... commencing the 5th day of January
    1804, and ending the 5th day of January 1806', N.A., C.O. 137 / 116, f. 112; the
    Jamaica accounts for 1806 are in N.A., C.O. 137 / 116, ff. 312–14; C.O. 137 / 118,
    ff. 75–80.
90 But see p. 166 below. British shipping traded almost exclusively at Kingston,
    eschewing the lesser Jamaican free ports.
91 This estimate, by George Rose, is cited in Crouzet, *L'Economie britannique*, p. 159.
92 Renny, *An History of Jamaica ...*, p. 126.
93 'Minutes of a Committee', July 1808, N.A., B.T. 1 / 41, ff. 115–20v; Horsfall, 'The
    West Indian Trade', p. 177; Jones, 'Historical Study', pp. 154–5.
94 'Memorial and petition of the merchants of Kingston', n.d., N.A., B.T. 1 / 41, ff.
    116v–17.
95 'Should the present embargo in America continue for any length of time, the proba-
    bility is that the trade with the Spanish colonies will encrease'; 'Extract of the votes
    and proceedings ...', Bahamas, 22 Feb. 1808, N.A., B.T. 1 / 38, ff. 313–v. On this
    point see also Crouzet, *L'Economie britannique*, pp. 318–19.
96 Armytage, *Free Port System*, pp. 124–8, offers a brief survey covering the fifteen years
    following the Peace.
97 A.G.N.M., Consulado, vol. 79, exp. 1, ff. 13–24v, para. 6.
98 Wright, 'Rescates', p. 335.
99 Pares, *War and Trade in the West Indies*, p. 26.
100 Royal Order to Intendant of Havana, Aranjuez, 18 Apr. 1782, A.N.C., Asuntos
    Políticos, leg. 3, no. 41.
101 Vicente Risel to Conde de Lerena, Havana, 30 July 1791, A.G.I., Santo Domingo,
    2189.
102 Joseph de Ezpeleta to Diego de Gardoqui, Santa Fé, 19 Sept. 1795, A.G.I., Santa Fé,
    644; associated documentation in A.G.N.C., Colonia: Negocios Exteriores, vol. 3, ff.
    198–211, and in A.G.I., Santa Fé, 958.
103 De Castro to Soler, Puerto Rico, 15 Oct. 1799, A.G.I., Santo Domingo, 2318, and
    accompanying report.
104 Consulado to Gardoqui, Havana, 11 Dec. 1796, A.G.I., Santo Domingo, 2191.
105 The decree is discussed in Ortiz de la Tabla, *Memorias*, p. 217; José de Azanza to
    Soler, Mexico City, 28 Nov. 1799, A.G.I., Mexico, 2510; Contaduría principal de
    Mérida to Intendant, Mérida, 15 May 1801, in a report labelled 'Superior Gobierno,
    Año de 1803. Testimonio del Expediente sobre Parlamentarios despachados por el
    Gobierno de Yucatán ...', A.G.I., Mexico, 2512.
106 Extracted translation of Santa Clara to Hunt, 4 Apr. 1798, N.A., C.O. 23 / 37, ff.
    149–v.
107 Report labelled 'Superior Govierno, Año 1799. Quaderno 1º. Testimonio del
    Expediente formado sobre arribada a Campeche de la Goleta San José ...', A.G.I.,
    Mexico, 2509. The pass is on ff. 4v–5; Balcarres's licence is on ff. 141–2.
108 'Superior Govierno', ff. 78, 106v–9.
109 A.N.C., Miscelánea de libros, nos. 2787, 6737 (1798); 2787, 2518, 2021 (1799); 2787,
    2519, 2766 (1800); 1950 (1801); 1986, 2521 (1805); 6797, 1811 (1806); 6797, 2523
    (1807); 2645, 2061 (1808); 2645 (1809). 1798 is the earliest year in the sequence; the
    records are slightly defective for 1800 and 1809, and for 1802–04 are only fragmen-
    tary. I would like to thank Manuel Barcia for bringing the existence of these books to

my attention.

110 I consulted a long run of the *Papel periódico* for the year 1799 in the Biblioteca Nacional in Havana.

111 *Ensayo político*, p. 509 (the 'Great Indies', of course, referring to East India goods).

112 Letter to Junta of the Consulado, Veracruz, 6 Feb. 1804, A.G.N.M., Consulado, vol. 79, exp. 1, ff. 37–44.

113 Consulado de México, *Recopilación de noticias sobre el comercio de contrabando ...*, p. 656.

114 López Cancelada, *Ruina de la Nueva España*, pp. 38–9.

115 Report labelled 'Año de 1801. Dn Antonio de la Torre ... sobre varias representaciones ...', A.G.I., Mexico, 2509; further important papers in A.G.I., Mexico, 2510; and see Anon., *Instrucciones*, p. 205. Santa Cruz is sometimes called Clemente (rather than Francisco) in these documents.

116 Ortiz de la Tabla, *Comercio exterior de Veracruz*, pp. 206–7, 291, 327–9; Galbis Díez, 'Miguel José de Azanza', pp. 6–7, 59–60; Marichal, *La bancarrota del virreinato*, pp. 222–3; also Jiménez Codinach, *La Gran Bretaña y la independencia de México*, pp. 194–5; Souto Mantecón, *Mar abierto*, pp. 187–90.

117 Bundles marked 'No. 4. Carpeta quarta. Contiene trece documentos ...', and 'No. 6. Carpeta sexta. Contiene siete documentos ...', both in A.G.I., Mexico, 2841; further important papers in A.G.I., Mexico, 2512; ships' registers in A.G.N.M., Correspondencia de diversas autoridades, leg. 59, exp. 94, ff. 363, 368; Anon., *Instrucciones*, pp. 207–8.

118 Merchant guild to Félix Berenguer de Marquina, Veracruz, 8 June 1801, A.G.N.M., Consulado, vol. 79, exp. 1, ff. 47–50v; copy as encl. no. 11 to Guild to crown, Veracruz, 1 Mar. 1809, A.G.I., Mexico, 2997.

119 Azanza to Soler, Mexico City, 27 Oct. 1799, A.G.I., Mexico, 2510; ship's register in A.G.N.M., Correspondencia de diversas autoridades, vol. 56, exp. 82, f. 186.

120 Galbis Díez, 'Miguel José de Azanza', p. 53; Souto Mantecón, *Mar abierto*, pp. 187–8; Ortiz, *Comercio exterior de Veracruz*, p. 312.

121 See for example the copy of Alexandro Ramos to Governor, Veracruz, 21 Feb. 1801, A.G.N.M., Correspondencia de diversas autoridades, vol. 58, exp. 22, ff. 105–v.

122 Consejo de Indias en Sala de Justicia, Madrid, 27 July 1803, A.G.I., Mexico, 2511; Rodríguez del Valle, 'Félix Berenguer de Marquina', p. 139.

123 José de Iturrigaray to Soler, Mexico City, 27 Aug. 1804, A.G.I., Mexico, 2512.

124 Iturrigaray to Soler, Mexico City, 27 Dec. 1803, accompanying a report labelled 'Superior Gobierno, Año de 1803. Testimonio del Expediente sobre Parlamentarios despachados por el Gobierno de Yucatán, a los Establecimientos Yngleses', A.G.I., Mexico, 2512; for British merchants and warehousemen speaking Spanish, see the statement of Bernardo Martín, dated Campeche, 6 Aug. 1801, in this report.

125 Ortiz, *Comercio exterior de Veracruz*, p. 332.

126 Copy, José Fernández Pérez to Governor, Veracruz, 2 Oct. 1801, A.G.N.M., Correspondencia de diversas autoridades, leg. 59, exp. 56, f. 213.

127 Report labelled 'Sup.or Gov.no. Año de 1801. Testimonio del Expediente formado ... en el cargamento de la Fragata *Asturiana* sobre rescate', in A.G.I., Mexico, 2512 (for the crown attorney's view, see 'El Fiscal de Real Hacienda dice ...', Mexico, 30 June 1801, ff. 38v–40v in this report); ships' registers in A.G.N.M., Correspondencia de diversas autoridades, vol. 58, exp. 47, ff. 203–5v; exp. 56, ff. 229–30v; exp. 73, ff. 300–1; leg. 59, exp. 56, ff. 213–14v; also José Ygnacio de la Torre, Madrid, 15 July 1803, A.G.I., Mexico, 2512.

128 José de Monseñé to Francisco de Arrillaga, Jamaica, 10 Mar. 1802, ff. 5v–6v in a report labelled 'Sup.or Gov.no. Año de 1803. Testimonio del Expediente formado a

instancia de D. Francisco Arrillaga ...', A.G.I., Mexico, 2512.

129 Report labelled 'Sup.or Gov.no. Año de 1803. Testimonio del Expediente formado a instancia de D. Francisco Arrillaga...', and accompanying brief reports on two voyages by the *Paulina* and *Casto*, all in A.G.I., Mexico, 2512; ships' registers in A.G.N.M., Consulado, vol. 50, ff. 82–3; Consulado, vol. 172, exp. 21, f. 281; Marina, vol. 197, exp. 100, f. 321; also unsigned note, Mexico City, 24 Oct. 1804, A.G.N.M., Marina, vol. 170, exp. 3, ff. 102–4v.

130 References in unsigned note, Mexico City, 24 Oct. 1804, and statement of crown attorney, Mexico City, 31 May 1803, both in A.G.N.M., Marina, vol. 170, exp. 3, ff. 89–98, 102–4v; ship's register in A.G.N.M., Correspondencia de diversas autoridades, leg. 59, exp. 92, ff. 357–588.

131 George Nugent to John Sullivan, Jamaica, 8 Mar. 1804, N.A., B.T. 1 / 23, ff. 250–1.

132 Portland to Governor William Dowdeswell, London, 17 Aug. 1798, N.A., C.O. 23 / 37, ff. 157–62; Dowdeswell to Portland, Govt. House, Bahamas, 7 Jan. 1799, N.A., C.O. 23 / 38, ff. 46–v.

133 Memorial of the merchants of Kingston, Kingston, 16 Nov. 1807, N.A., C.O. 137 / 119, ff. 203–v; discussed by Jones, 'Historical Study', pp. 149–51.

134 John Morton to James Madison, Havana, 11 Dec. 1801, N.A.W., R.G. 59, M899, roll 1.

135 Copy of William Billings to Madison, New York, 21 May 1801, N.A.W., R.G. 59, M899, roll 1.

136 Madison to Monroe, Dept. of State, 12 Apr. 1805, *American State Papers*, 3:101–3; Goebel, 'British Trade to the Spanish Colonies', p. 293.

137 Consulado of Cadiz to Soler, Cadiz, 6 Apr. 1799, A.G.I., Indiferente, 2466.

138 Printed *bando*, Mexico City, 27 Oct. 1801, A.G.N.M., Bandos, vol. 22, exp. 34, f. 107; see also de Castro to Soler, Puerto Rico, 2 Oct. 1801, A.G.I., Santo Domingo, 2319.

139 Príncipe de la Paz to Soler, San Lorenzo, 30 Oct. 1805, A.G.I., Mexico, 2513.

140 References to *rescates* during the second war appear to confuse ransom operations with the new direct trade undertaken from Jamaica from 1806 as a result of the Gordon and Murphy contract; see for example Ortiz, *Comercio exterior de Veracruz*, p. 332. On Gordon and Murphy, see chap. 6 below.

141 See for example 'Sobre la suspensión de permisos para conducir ... géneros ingleses procedentes de presas', and 'Oficio del Sr Presidente de Goatemala', both in A.N.C., leg. 379, nos. 17, 28.

142 *Votes of the Honorable House ...* (Nassau: 1800), in N.A., C.O. 23 / 39, see ff. 279–80.

143 Reproduced in Fraser, *History of Trinidad*, 1:124–7.

144 These instructions are partly reproduced in Carmichael, *History of ...Trinidad and Tobago*, pp. 45–6.

145 The proclamation, dated Port of Spain, 26 June 1797, is published (with variant texts) in Walton, *Exposé on the Dissentions*, apps i–ii, doc. A; Fraser, *History of Trinidad*, 1:122–3.

146 See esp. 'Trinidada – Minute on the Draft of Instruction', 21 June 1797, N.A., B.T. 5 / 10, ff. 198v–9.

147 William Young to Earl Bathurst, Trinidad, 28 Sept. 1822, N.A., Cust. 34 / 828.

148 Picton [to Dundas], Port of Spain, 28 June 1797, N.A., C.O. 296 / 1, ff. 8–v. The key correspondence may be found in this volume and (for 1799) in B.L., Add. Mss., 36,870.

149 Picton to Dundas, Trinidad, 21 Apr. 1799, B.L., Add. Mss. 36,870, ff. 16v–18v; and 'Memorandum Trinidada', 1800, B.L., Add. Mss. 38,356, ff. 5–6.

150 Radhay, 'Contraband between Eastern Venezuela and Trinidad', pp. 33–4, 41;

Dauxion Lavaysse, *Viaje a las islas de Trinidad*, pp. 93 and lxxxi–lxxxiii, app. 1.

151 Dauxion Lavaysse, *Viaje a las islas de Trinidad*, esp. pp. 29–35.

152 Picton to Hobart, Trinidad, 18 Feb. 1802, N.A., C.O., 296 / 1, ff. 60–4.

153 Anon., 'Description of the Province of Caracas' [1797], N.A., C.O. 296 / 1, ff. 13–16.

154 Radhay, 'Contraband between Eastern Venezuela and Trinidad', *passim*; Fraser, *History*, 1:129.

155 Humboldt, *Personal Narrative of Travels to the Equinoctial Regions of America*, 3:107.

156 Data for 1804–06 in 'Estimate of the value of exports from the island of Trinidad', Trinidad, 1 July 1806, and three statements of imports, both in N.A., B.T. 1 / 30, ff. 54–v, 56–7; secondary discussion in Goebel, 'British Trade', pp. 293–4; Jones, 'Historical Study', pp. 83–4.

157 Horsfall, 'The West Indian Trade', p. 177.

158 Radhay, 'Contraband between Eastern Venezuela and Trinidad', p. 41.

159 Edwin Gardiner to Hislop, Port of Spain, 1 July 1806, N.A., B.T. 1 / 30, ff. 52–v. It was later noted that 'the specie is generally brought in small vessels, secured probably about the keel, or in such manner as to prevent the least suspicion'; Young to Bathurst, Trinidad, 28 Sept. 1822, N.A., Cust. 34 / 828.

160 Picton to Dundas, Trinidad, 9 and 20 July 1800, both in N.A., C.O. 296 / 1, ff. 45–6.

161 See the comments in N.A., B.T. 5 / 17, ff. 41v–2; Goebel, 'British Trade', pp. 294–5.

162 Armytage, *Free Port System*, pp. 120–1.

163 On both occasions, the other Danish Virgin Islands, St Croix and St John, were also seized; but their Spanish trade was in no way comparable to that of St Thomas.

164 See esp. Trygge to Dundas, and encls., *Leviathan* at sea, 12 Apr. 1801, N.A., B.T. 1 / 19, ff. 208–14; Trygge and Duckworth to Jamaica Vice-Admiralty Court, H.Q. Martinique, 24 Dec. 1801, N.A., B.T. 1 / 20, ff. 75–8v; 'Martinique. Extracts of letters', Minute for 15 Mar. 1802, N.A., B.T. 5 / 13, ff. 37–8.

165 Knox, *Historical Account of St Thomas*, pp. 91–2; also Dookhan, *History of the British Virgin Islands*, pp. 55–6.

166 Commandant Fitzroy Maclean to Castlereagh, St Thomas, 15 Jan. 1808, N.A., B.T. 1 / 40, ff. 157–8v.

167 'St Thomas – Minute on sundry memorials', 17 Aug. 1808, N.A., B.T. 5 / 18, f. 114v.

168 Petition, merchants to Governor, St Thomas, 18 Jan. 1808, N.A., B.T. 1 / 38, ff. 293–8v.

169 Memorial of merchants and manufacturers, London, July 1808, N.A., B.T. 1 / 41, ff. 40–1v.

170 Armytage, *Free Port System*, app. 3, table P, p. 158.

171 'Curaçoa – The port of Amsterdam', Minute for 15 Jan. 1801, N.A., B.T. 5 / 12, ff. 136v–7.

172 Williams, 'Mercados británicos', p. 99; Depons, *Travels in South America*, 2:55–8.

173 Memorial of merchants, Kingston, 17 Jan. 1807, and S. Cook to Castlereagh, London, 27 Apr. 1807, in N.A., B.T. 1 / 35, ff. 5–6v, 238–42v; and Minute for 16 June 1807, N.A., B.T. 5 / 17, ff. 148v–9.

174 Minutes for 7 Mar. and 12 Nov. 1807, in N.A., B.T. 5 / 17, ff. 71–v, 231–3v.

175 Crouzet, *L'Economie britannique*, pp. 318–19.

176 Jones, 'Historical Study', pp. 58–9; Lucena Salmoral, *Características del comercio exterior*, pp. 305–6.

177 See the letter marked 'Bestiaux pour les cultures', London, 11 Apr. 1798, N.A., B.T. 1 / 16, ff. 86–v; and 'Martinique – Minute on a letter', 18 Apr. 1798, N.A., B.T. 5 / 11, ff. 75v–6v.

178 Jones, 'Historical Study', pp. 71–2; Holland Rose, 'West India Commerce', pp. 35–6.

179 Frederick Maitland to William Windham, Grenada, 26 Apr. 1806, and Ryburn and

Wilson to Maitland, Grenada, 28 Apr. 1806, both in P.R.O., C.O. 101 / 43, ff. 86, 92–3v.

180 Memorial of Alexander Houston et al., Glasgow, 5 Dec. 1797, N.A., B.T. 1 / 15, ff. 241–2; Merchants to Portland, London, 8 Dec. 1797, N.A., C.O. 101 / 35, n.f. ; and Minutes for 10 Jan. and 20 Apr. 1798, both in N.A., B.T. 5 / 11, ff. 28–v, 78–v.

181 See the papers in N.A., B.T. 1 / 32, ff. 245–v, 312–20v; C.O. 101 / 46, ff. 133–5v; B.T. 5 / 17, ff. 204v–5.

182 The principal series on this dispute, which occurred in 1798–99, is in N.A., C.O. 101 / 36.

183 See the series in N.A., B.T. 1 / 28, ff. 258–90v (repeated in N.A., C.O. 101 / 42, ff. 93–113), which includes Robinson's Memorial. For his wider role in neutral trade with Venezuela, see pp. 199–200.

184 George Ferguson and Lawrence Donovan to Charles Green, Custom House, Grenada, 13 Feb. 1799, N.A., C.O. 101 / 36, n.f. ; Jones, 'Historical Study', p. 67; Armytage, Free Port System, p. 123.

185 Testimony of Messrs Wilson and Ryburn, Grenada, 23 July 1805, N.A., B.T. 1 / 28, ff. 263–v.

186 Ryburn and Wilson to Maitland, Grenada, 28 Apr. 1806, N.A., C.O. 101 / 43, ff. 92–3v; Maitland to Wyndham, Grenada, 30 Oct. 1806, N.A., B.T. 1 / 32, ff. 313–14v.

187 See the parallel accounts in N.A., C.O. 101 / 43, ff. 88–90 and 126–7; secondary discussion in Jones, 'Historical Study', pp. 82–3, and app. 7–8.

188 Accounts covering 1806 in N.A., C.O. 101 / 44, ff. 99–100 (repeated, B.T. 1 / 32, ff. 303–4); C.O. 101 / 45, ff. 48–v, 52 (repeated, B.T. 1 / 35, ff. 78, 80–1v).

189 Accounts covering Jan.–June 1807 in N.A., C.O. 101 / 46, ff. 48–9 (repeated, B.T. 1 / 37, ff. 156–9).

190 Jones, 'Historical Study', appendix, pp. 7–8.

191 Laurence, Tobago in Wartime, pp. 162–4.

192 'Tobago – Information given by Mr Robley', Minute for 25 Jan. 1805, N.A., B.T. 5 / 15, ff. 9–11.

193 See the accounts dated Inspector-General's Office, 25 Nov. 1807, N.A., B.T. 1 / 40, f. 5.

194 Customs Officials to President John Balfour, Tobago, 1 July 1806, N.A., C.O. 285 / 11, f. 28.

195 Sir William Young, 'Historical ... Account of the Island of Tobago', 1809, B.L., Stowe 922, ff. 132–3; see also Jones, 'Historical Study', pp. 81, 155–6.

196 Young, 'Historical ... Account', 1809, B.L., Stowe 922, ff. 127–8; also Goebel, 'British Trade', pp. 294–5.

197 The principal secondary account is Dookhan, History of the British Virgin Islands, pp. 52–6. Colquhoun's numerous memorials and petitions may be consulted in N.A., B.T. 1 / 20, 1 / 22, 1 / 26, and 1 / 30.

198 Extract, Lord Lavington to Castlereagh, Antigua, 19 June 1807, N.A., B.T. 1 / 37, ff. 58–60v.

199 Dookhan, History of the British Virgin Islands, p. 62; Armytage, Free Port System, p. 104, see note 1.

200 Armytage, Free Port System, p. 102.

201 'Dominica', Minute for 18 Dec. 1797, N.A., B.T. 5 / 11, f. 19; Armytage, Free Port System, pp. 102–3.

202 Jones, 'Historical Study', pp. 150–1.

203 Jones, 'Historical Study', pp. 68–9 n. 3; Dauxion Lavaysse, Viaje a las islas de Trinidad, pp. lxxxi–lxxxiii, app. 1; Radhay, 'Contraband between Eastern Venezuela and Trinidad', pp. 41–2.

CHAPTER FIVE

Trade During Wartime (1796–1808): British Contraband and the Spanish-American Perspective

LA CONTREBANDE! Dont le nom seul fait frémir le gouvernement Espagnol.
—Bourgoing, *Tableau de l'Espagne moderne*, 3:147–18

This chapter is devoted principally to what until 1796 was (with trade by Spaniards at the free ports) the other great vehicle for Anglo-Spanish commerce in the Caribbean: clandestine trade by British vessels direct upon the Spanish-American coasts. Unlike Spanish trade at the free ports, this surreptitious British intercourse was wholly illegal at point of exchange, and it remains perhaps the least known of all the means by which British goods were transferred to consumers in the Spanish colonies. The British themselves rarely referred to the interloping trade, while Spanish understanding of it was necessarily merely fragmentary, subject often to misconception and exaggeration. British contraband faced greater competition than ever during the wars, both from the thriving trade by Spaniards in the British colonies, and from the merchants of neutral powers, who for the first time trafficked in British goods on a large scale almost throughout the Spanish colonies. Some observers, indeed, thought that British contraband had now outlived its historic value and had become redundant as an appropriate vehicle for the trade:

> It is submitted that British subjects, under British flags, could not effect it; that it never can be the Interest of the British ship Owner to engage in a Trade so comparatively insignificant in a carrying view with that from the Colony to the Mother Country ... His greater object must be to quietly await the arrival of the Spanish commodities at the Free Ports without risk or danger ... being certain of a Return Cargo from Great Britain of the very Manufactures which will be wanted for the Markets of the Main.[1]

Such comments notwithstanding, and despite the limited nature of the evidence available, it appears to be the case that British contraband retained some significance in particular Spanish-American regions throughout the period of the wars. Nevertheless, it is to be stressed that the primary focus on British contraband in this chapter is to some extent simply a vehicle through which to explore *all* contraband trade with the Spanish colonies as seen from the Spanish-American perspective. This should be borne in mind particularly with regard to Spanish estimates for the total value of contraband discussed herein, which naturally refer to all clandestine trade with the British – not only that which was conducted by British smugglers.

Mexico

During the wars, Mexico emerged as an important centre for British smuggling in the Caribbean perhaps for the first time. The lighthouse which adorned the harbour at Veracruz at the turn of the century was of English manufacture, a neat symbol of the attraction the port and its hinterland held for British smugglers. Alexander von Humboldt explained this attraction in terms of the great size of the overall Mexican market and the large surplus of Mexican imports over exports.[2] Viceroy Miguel José de Azanza warned his successor Félix Berenguer de Marquina that the Mexican coasts were infested with smugglers and that contraband goods were to be found in abundance in the shops of Mexico City and the provincial capitals.[3] Marquina, who was captured on route from Spain and held in Jamaica for several weeks in early 1800, later recalled:

> I had not yet reached this kingdom ... when I received advance news of the scandalous continuous smuggling carried on in the Port and neighbouring Coasts of Veracruz ... The English Commander of the Frigate which captured the Mail Brig which brought me, and afterwards those of Jamaica ... himself confirmed to me the trade and reciprocal communication between that Island and this Kingdom.

It was alleged that British ships trading from Jamaica carried local pilots familiar with the coast, and that landings were routinely arranged with Spanish correspondents by means of 'unmistakeable signals between their ships and the coast'. Papers found on board one British ship described 'the signalling points and counter-signs for the secret communication' by which landings were to be organised.[4] Glimpses of this trade can be perceived through occasional captures of smuggling vessels or confiscations of contraband cargoes. One well-documented case was that of over 300 packages landed at Zempoala north of Veracruz by a British brig and schooner, one of whose crew claimed that the expedition had been organised by the major Jamaican merchant house of Lindo. Coastguard launches captured two British schooners, the *Sally* and *Margarita*, near Veracruz, while another small vessel loaded with contraband goods was taken off the port of Alvarado. On a separate occasion, guarda-costa brigs en route between Veracruz and Campeche captured another British schooner and a smaller vessel, also loaded with contraband goods.[5] Such occasional captures merely hint at the unquestionably much more extensive trade which went undetected.

There were allegations, current in all the Spanish colonies but particularly prevalent in Mexico, of direct participation in smuggling by warships of the

Royal Navy. Viceroy Marquina received detailed reports to the effect that 'the very British Frigates of War which Cruised ... on these Coasts, protected Contraband in return for a certain percentage on Cargoes paid their Commanders'. The merchant guild of Veracruz asserted that the two frigates blockading the port protected smuggling and transported 'for a moderate reward the funds which for this fatal trade the Spaniards wish to place in the British possessions'. Humboldt remarked that blockading warships often deposited contraband cargoes on the Isla de los Sacrificios, a small wooded islet lying in clear view of the harbour, while naval vessels were said to water on the coast nearby. In August 1801 there were unconfirmed rumours that a British frigate was grounded for seven hours off Alvarado, in full view of Spanish gunships, during which time small craft took off her contraband cargo and embarked 180,000 pesos in return.[6] Such was the degree of co-operation between the Navy and the inhabitants of Veracruz that it was 'known positively that the British Frigates cruising off the Port are aware within twenty-four hours of everything that passes in it'.[7] Allegations that the Royal Navy provided convoys for smuggling vessels or was itself involved in contraband persisted throughout the war.[8] Perhaps understandably, they find scant reflection in the British documentary record, although on the peace of July 1808 the navy in the West Indies was ordered to protect the free port trade from attacks by French privateers.[9]

It was widely acknowledged that Spaniards of all classes and professions actively participated in smuggling with the British. Papers encountered on board the schooner *Sally* provided 'the clearest proof that her Cargo came consigned to residents of [Veracruz] or its coasts'. In May 1801 a list was drawn up which gave the names and positions of a hundred individuals convicted in different contraband cases. They included an important provincial official, the *subdelegado* Pedro de Coca, and numerous merchants, military men, and members of the anti-smuggling corps, as well as simple soldiers, sailors and watchmen.[10] The case of Antonio Bonilla, a member of Berenguer de Marquina's staff detained briefly in Jamaica alongside the viceroy, caused particular scandal. When the two men proceeded to Veracruz, Bonilla took contraband goods with him worth some 60,000 pesos, apparently abusing a modest permit to this end granted him by Marquina.[11] Still more remarkable were allegations arising from perhaps the most celebrated contraband case of these years, that of part of the cargo of the schooner *Suceso* from Jamaica smuggled into Veracruz through a bastion in the city walls in August 1801. A black slave alleged that the Governor of Veracruz, García Dabila, had himself transported the goods in his gubernatorial coach and stored them in his offices. Detailed and convincing accusations notwithstanding, Marquina took no action beyond informing the crown, and García Dabila remained in his post.[12] Marquina frequently emphasised that the general participation of the residents of Veracruz made thorough-going investigation of contraband a delicate affair. The Mexican Junta Superior affirmed in 1799 that to enquire too closely 'was to risk the extreme of compromising public tranquillity', while the viceroy hinted that vigorous action on his part would expose him to malicious accusations at the statutory enquiry to follow his administration.[13]

A major secondary centre for smuggling in Mexico was Campeche and the Yucatán peninsula, whence contraband imports made their way north-west into the viceregal heartland. An investigation into smuggling in Yucatán was launched after Marquina expressed concern over large-scale clandestine trade undertaken there from Jamaica and New Providence. Enquiries were again sensitive in a region 'in which everyone is involved in such clandestine operations', but an extensive trade from Jamaica was detected under the cover of false registers, especially from Cuba, Santa Marta, and Río Hacha. The British made available to captured Spanish merchants 'ships and forged documents, so that they would be admitted in our Ports and passed by our Customs', under which cover large quantities of British manufactures were introduced at ports in the region.[14] Anti-contraband or guarda-costa forces in Mexico during this period were relatively strong on paper but largely inef-fectual in practice. There was some reinforcement of coastal vigilance in the early years of the war; the number of armed launches or gunboats rose from eight in 1796 to eighteen in 1800, and Customs surveillance was reinforced at Alvarado and Coatzacoalcos.[15] Mexican merchants, however, complained that formal naval forces in Veracruz – four frigates and four lesser ships in mid-1801 – refused to put to sea to confront the British. There even existed the suspicion of active collusion between the Navy and the enemy. In mid-1801 the Veracruz merchant guild alleged that the very warships in the harbour were 'warehouses for contraband goods', and identical allegations were made verbally to Marquina at almost the same time. They gave rise to a purportedly surprise inspection of the warships in the bay on 16 June. Merchant representatives participated in the inspection, which, however, rather to the guild's discomfiture, encountered no contraband goods.[16]

Viceroy Marquina left office in January 1803 claiming to have made impor-tant progress in suppressing contraband, and it was elsewhere asserted that during his administration smuggling was 'all but exterminated'.[17] Marquina also faced allegations of personal involvement or complicity in contraband, however, and there were more credible allegations to the effect that illicit trade continued to increase throughout these years.[18] One of Marquina's succes-sors stated that British contraband exports from Mexico were worth 500,000 pesos per month during the first Anglo-Spanish war (1796–1802), excluding exports of gold, or more than 40,000,000 pesos altogether by 'a conservative estimate'.[19] This surprising figure was endorsed by Humboldt, who thought that contraband was worth from 6,000,000–7,000,000 million pesos (c. £1,350,000–£1,575,000) in every year of the war. Humboldt further noted that the value of all Spanish exports to the viceroyalty during the war was just 2,600,000 pesos, but 'all the same, the warehouses of Mexico were filled with muslins from India and with products of English manufacture'.[20] In London, Sir Frederick Eden estimated that annual British exports to the Antilles had risen from some £2,185,000 before the war, to over £3,560,000 in 1798–1800, an increase presumably caused largely by growth in trade with the Spaniards.[21]

Humboldt's visit to Mexico coincided with the Peace of Amiens (1802–04), a period when all forms of illicit trade declined. In general terms he thought the scale of contraband had been exaggerated, calculating that throughout Spanish America smuggling accounted for less than a quarter of all imports during the peace.[22] He put unregistered exports specifically of silver bullion to Jamaica, Havana, and the Philippines at just 800,000 pesos per year, though he thought this figure was likely to rise with Anglo-American commercial penetration of the Pacific. Nevertheless, Humboldt still put the total value of contraband during the peace at 4,000,000–5,000,000 pesos per year (c. £900,000–£1,125,000). A Mexican merchant writing in February 1804 similarly estimated contraband imports to Mexico at 4,000,000 pesos per year, which he thought represented about one-third of total consumption.[23] Another writer allowed himself more generous estimates, of 20,000,000 pesos in contraband imports every year throughout the Spanish colonies, 'which sum transferred to the Foreigner enriches him every century by more than two billion (*dos mil millones*)'.[24] Some thought that contraband had actually altered the character of the Mexican market, creating a taste for luxury goods absent before the wars. Thus, contraband imports from Jamaica had 'increased, not in volume, but in their intrinsic value... Nowadays Mexico needs finer cloths and a far greater quantity of muslins, gauzes, wines and liquors than before the year 1791'.[25]

A fresh series of measures against contraband swiftly followed the renewal of hostilities with Britain in late 1804. In October 1803 important new regulations had been issued governing the guarda-costas, it has been suggested partly with the intention of countering a boom in contraband expected to follow the derogation of neutral trade legislation on the peace.[26] On 20 December 1804, Manuel Godoy issued an anti-British manifesto which vilified smugglers as 'the most abominable criminals'; this document foresaw the general closure of European ports to British trade as part of the wartime effort, and evoked a gratifying vision of the British 'perishing rabid on heaps of packages and goods repelled from all parts'.[27] Four days later, Godoy sanctioned the general renewal of neutral trade with the Spanish colonies after a brief suspension during the Peace of Amiens, and this trade itself provided a further major vehicle for British commercial relations (as discussed in Chapter 6). In January 1805, Viceroy Iturrigaray effectively closed the Mexican ports and suspended all coasting trade, a measure designed both to protect Spanish shipping from seizure and to prevent illicit trade with the British. The ban provoked an acrimonious dispute with Mexican merchants, who denied any serious link between coasting trade and contraband, despite which it remained in place for over two years.[28] In the later stages of the war guarda-costa forces at Veracruz consisted of six brigs and schooners and were considered 'the best organised in all America'.[29] The efficacy of such forces continued to be undermined, however, by the notorious corruptibility of Spanish coastguard and Customs officials. An American who took part in several neutral trade expeditions to Veracruz in 1807–08 recalled that he 'almost always found that if good faith by those engaged in smuggling is kept ... the Spanish custom house officers will never betray you.'[30]

British smugglers procured licences from the governors in the West Indies to enable them to trade with enemy colonies during wartime, but unlike Spaniards they were not restricted to use of the free ports. The bulk of the smuggling trade was based in Kingston, Nassau and other important free ports, but smugglers also sailed from the full range of lesser British West Indian ports, and indeed from any suitable cove or inlet – as befitted the nature of the trade. There is some evidence to suggest that during the wars, British vessels recovered some of the dominance within the Spanish trade which they had ceded to Spaniards in the previous half-century, but this may be misleading. Thus, the claim of one American observer in 1801 that licensed vessels trading out of New Providence 'mostly belong to British subjects' appears at best questionable.[31] British vessels accounted for some two-thirds of imports of bullion from the Spanish colonies to the free ports in 1806, and took off over 45 per cent of the total value of exports from those ports in the last quarter of the same year;[32] but these figures may be accounted for by the direct trade commenced in this year between Jamaica and Veracruz under the Gordon and Murphy contract.[33] Neither was every British expedition immediately successful; it was said in Kingston in 1800 that 'British vessels trading under Licence ... from this port in consequence of various disappointments have been employed from four to six months in one voyage, and during that time ... have anchored perhaps in twenty different places looking or waiting for Purchasers'.[34]

Assessing the value of smuggling in Mexico during the second war (1804–08) is typically problematic. Contraband goods seized by Customs officials in Veracruz were worth some 515,000 pesos in 1807, and some 885,000 pesos in the triennium 1807–09. Since seizures naturally represented only a fraction of the total trade, on the basis of these figures it was suggested that the total value of contraband in Mexico was some 2,000,000–3,000,000 pesos in 1807, or some 10,000,000–15,000,000 pesos in all the Spanish colonies, 'since the great warehouses of Jamaica, Providence, St Thomas and Curaçao have no other object nor end'.[35] Another writer thought 20,000,000 pesos in contraband imports in a five-year period was closer the mark, with clandestine exports of bullion and produce to match.[36] In 1808 Francisco de Arango y Parreño, syndic of the Havana merchant guild, noted that Mexico's legal commerce was worth no more than that of Cuba before the war, despite a population nine times greater, and 'this observation alone seems to me to prove the enormity of contraband ... in the Kingdom of New Spain'.[37] Moreover, there was universal agreement that at the peace with Britain in mid-1808, contraband was sharply on the increase. In May of the latter year, the merchant guild of Veracruz noted that 'this disorder has reached such a point, that that which is now publicly said to be carried on along the Coasts and even in the port itself is outrageous'.[38] In August Arango's counterpart in Veracruz noted that 'the progress made by contraband in this Place in recent times has been very rapid', and that two to three foreign ships now arrived daily off the port to trade. Small craft brought in hundreds of contra- band pieces by night, and took off large sums in gold, silver coin, cochineal and indigo to waiting British warships in return.[39] Under cover of legal imports, millions of pesos' worth of contraband goods circulated in the viceroyalty, and East India goods, muslins, cottons and others 'of which there are millions of *varas*' sold at less than half their former price.[40]

Cuba

Direct British smuggling almost certainly occurred on an even greater scale in Cuba than in Mexico, though the evidence to prove it is fragmentary. The Cuban coast, littered with bays and harbours and with a wild and deserted hinterland, was better suited to clandestine trade than the Mexican littoral. The British took greater liberties in Cuba: there were numerous petty assaults on isolated coastal settlements and estates; an American consul recalled that 'in some of the harbours British ships lay even during war with Spain', felling trees and stealing livestock.[41] In 1802 the British all but occupied the bay of Guantánamo in the east of the island, constructing wooden and stone jetties to facilitate exports of livestock and other contraband goods.[42] Another American observer remarked on 'the free & notorious Intercourse carried on with the Spaniards by the British themselves, both in their public & private Vessels' – the latter phrase further evidence for the participation of the Royal Navy in smuggling.[43] The National Archive in Havana preserves documents relating to many hundreds of petty contraband cases drawn from the length and breadth of the island, a largely untapped resource for micro-study of the trade. Cuba's reputation as a principal centre for contraband occasionally inconvenienced its inhabitants. A petition by Cuban merchants in 1796 for a right to import bullion free of duty from Veracruz was rejected in part because of concerns over smuggling. Similar concerns arose with regard to an application in 1798 for a right to re-export legally imported European goods from Havana to Mexico. In this context Francisco de Arango y Parreño acknowledged that contraband undertaken in Cuba was indeed scandalous, though he retorted that 'the Mexicans need neither our example, nor our help to maintain, as they now maintain, the coasts of Jamaica flooded with gold, and those of Veracruz with cloth'.[44]

Formal anti-contraband forces in Cuba were modest throughout the war, their impact on smuggling limited by low budgets and persistent apathy on the part of officialdom. At the start of the war there was a spurt of proposals for fresh measures, including the arming of corsair ships or gun-boats and the construction of watch-towers at strategic bays and harbours. It was proposed that lighthouses on the coast be furnished with skiffs 'to pursue our

Traders, and those of Providence along all its length'.[45] In May 1798 it was decided that a schooner and a launch be devoted to anti-contraband duties along the northern coast, while a single brig cruised to the south.[46] Effective maritime forces deployed against smuggling remained limited, however; at the start of 1808 just two guarda-costa ships were stationed at Havana.[47] The often powerful elements of the Spanish fleet lying at the latter port (eight ships of the line and eight frigates in May 1798), meanwhile, were rarely if ever used against smugglers. By contrast, Cuba was one of few Spanish colonies to maintain a determined and effective force of privateers. The ports of Santiago and Trinidad were important bases for both Spanish and French privateers, which harried British shipping and occasionally inflicted real damage. Rumours circulating on the Main to the effect that swarms of Cuban corsairs actually blockaded Kingston and took prizes worth millions of pesos were exaggerated, but the British themselves mentioned the 'great number of the enemies' privateers annoying the trade to Jamaica'.[48] The impact of privateering on illicit trade, however, has yet to be established, and there were frequent allegations of collusion between corsairs and smugglers.

One new modus operandi employed by British smugglers during the war attempted to exploit trade by the citizens of neutral powers at Spanish colonial ports, permitted from late 1797. Thus it was alleged that the British now used the neutral flag and false neutral papers to gain direct access to Spanish ports during wartime. The best evidence for such a trade relates to Havana and was recorded by observers from the United States. In May 1801 William Billings stated of British licensed vessels from New Providence that

> on entering the port of the Havanna, they hoist the flag of our Nation or that of the Danes, declaring either from some Southern Port of the United States or a Danish Island. In this case a clearance from either of those places secures to them an entry in the Spanish Custom House... They there make their traffick secure, and return to the Bahamas with the same security, always hoisting the Spanish Flag in the English ports.

Billings added that 'any document that is issued from our Customs' was freely available for purchase in New Providence, probably actually manufactured there. He identified the supplier of both American and Danish papers as a German called Trobe, who charged 'Sixty Dollars for what he calls the Set'.[49] In early 1805 Danish papers were again available in Havana 'in such complete sets in blank as not to be known from the originals'.[50] It is impossible to determine how many smuggling voyages were made under cover of such forged papers; suffice to note that the Havana port books recorded the entry of many hundreds of American vessels every year between 1798 and 1809, over 300 of them direct from British colonial ports.[51] A related issue was the purchase of prize ships in Cuban ports and their subsequent 'naturalisation' as American vessels. The details are somewhat obscure, but it appears that these naturalised vessels were employed in collusion with foreign smugglers, most of them British; 'those vessels being generally actually owned by Foreigners, and those Foreigners too often vicious men, pursuing [no] other than an illicit and contraband trade and often upon terms with Privateers'.[52] Such practices placed American consular and marine papers under suspicion, rendering US vessels liable to seizure by the French or Spanish, and the issue of papers to prize vessels was subject to tighter regulation in August 1801 and July 1805. Trade by Britons under false neutral papers was certainly not restricted to Havana and the other Cuban ports; an official of the Veracruz merchant guild, for example, recalled that 'the Ship which private individuals knew came from Jamaica, and its ownership foreign, for the Government and public was reputed as coming from Hamburg etc and its ownership Spanish'.[53] Viceroy Marquina recorded his suspicion that British vessels entered Mexican ports on the Pacific coast under 'forged papers of the United States'.[54]

Rare statistical evidence for the scale of contraband in Cuba outside Havana is to be found in data for exports of bullion from the capital to towns and villages in the interior. Registered exports overland amounted to some 3,275,000 pesos in 1805–11 inclusive, an average of 470,000 pesos per year (Table 5.1); including sea-borne exports, the total figure exceeded 3,700,000 pesos. The compiler of these data argued that in the absence of corresponding returns to the Cuban capital, 'there remains a rational conclusion, and it is that this surprising amount has been absorbed harmfully in clandestine trade with the neighbouring foreign possessions'. The same writer further conjectured that real exports to the provinces were likely to have been considerably larger than those recorded under register. He reinforced his argument with the observation that registered exports of goods (as opposed to bullion)

Table 5.1 *Exports of bullion from Havana to the Cuban provinces, 1805–11*
(figures in pesos)

Year	Pesos
1805	657,716
1806	487,327
1807	188,977
1808	346,306
1809	665,479
1810	544,491
1811	384,697

Source: 'Apéndice a los informes de 22 de Noviembre de 1811 sobre medios para contener la extracción de la plata y oro amonedado', in 'Expediente sobre proponer a los Sres Gefes las medidas convenientes para la eficaz persecución del contrabando en las costas de esta Ysla', Archivo Nacional de Cuba, Real Consulado y Junta de Fomento, leg. 112, no. 4715.
Note: The figure for 1811 covers Jan.–Oct. only.

from Havana overland to the provinces were worth a total of less than 142,000 pesos in the quinquennium 1806–10, or little more than 28,000 pesos per year. Even after purchases registered solely in the provinces were taken into account, this very low figure confirmed that 'the greater part of their consumption is sustained by contraband'.[55] A few years later, Arango y Parreño, a leading authority on Cuban economic affairs, observed of Santiago, Bayamo, Trinidad, Puerto Príncipe and other provincial towns that 'they have all maintained themselves and still maintain themselves by the harmful contraband with Providence and Jamaica'.[56]

There is further fragmentary evidence for the great value of Cuban contraband during these years. In November 1808, Arango y Parreño gave data which compared exports of goods of national and foreign manufacture from Spain to Cuba in two triennia of peace with Britain: 1792–94 and 1802–04. His figures suggested that exports of national goods had remained steady across the two periods, at about 43,000,000 *reales de vellón*; but exports of foreign goods had declined by more than a third, from some 58,000,000 reales to some 38,500,000 reales. Given strong Cuban economic growth in the interim, Arango wrote, 'it must be confessed that only the great increase in illicit trade can have caused this reversal and filled this gap'. On the basis of these figures, Arango estimated that goods of Spanish manufacture now accounted for just one-twelfth of Cuba's legal trade. In September 1808, the potential total value of legal trade by foreigners at Cuban ports was estimated at 1,500,000 pesos, with contraband worth a further 1,500,000.[57] In his account of November the same year, Arango y Parreño noted that 'the rock of Providence calculates its annual contraband with this island at three million pesos' (c. £675,000), and elsewhere referred to Jamaica as 'the emporium of our America'.[58] The value of all these contemporary Spanish estimates of the value of contraband, and their relationship to British estimates of the value of the same trade, is reviewed in the concluding chapter to this work.

New Granada

As in the other Spanish colonies, in the viceroyalty of New Granada the essential context to contraband trade was the collapse of commercial relations with Spain on the outbreak of the wars. Pedro de Mendinueta, viceroy of New Granada between 1797 and 1803, witnessed 'the almost complete interruption of trade between the Metropolis and the Kingdom, and its consequent substitution in part by contraband'.[59] A merchant in Cartagena de Indias later blamed smuggling on the lack of trade with Spain, the scarcity of European goods, and the absence of outlets for local produce, 'to all of which British Contraband attended with its Stores at Jamaica and New Providence'.[60] An important complementary factor in New Granada was the failure to develop any significant trade with the merchants of neutral powers by way of compensation. Although neutral trade was decreed for the viceroyalty in 1797 as for other territories, its implementation was impeded by successive viceroys, and real trade undertaken by neutrals was negligible.[61] Local observers often related the strength of contraband in New Granada to the absence of trade with neutrals; the expert merchant José Ignacio de Pombo regretted the failure to develop the trade at Cartagena, since 'with this necessary and useful measure the greater part of contraband might have been avoided'.[62] Antonio Narváez thought that the worst consequence of the formal revocation of neutral trade in April 1799 was that it 'gave greater cause for contraband' by British and Spanish merchants alike.[63] Another analyst claimed that the British

> applauded the Royal Order of 20 April 1799, which freed them from the competition of the Neutrals, offering greater scope for their clandestine Trade … Thus we saw that in the year 1800 clandestine imports experienced a visible increase, and on the arrival of the Peace America was well supplied by Contraband.[64]

These and other writers pressed repeatedly for neutral trade in New Granada, both as a good in itself and as the most efficient means to combat contraband.[65] Their arguments must be treated with caution, of course, since they were hardly disinterested. But it remains the case that, unlike in other regions, the very limited character of neutral trade, especially during the first war, restricted the development of British trade with the region much more exclusively to that which was undertaken by Spanish merchants at the free ports, and by British smugglers in the viceroyalty itself.

The general evidence for the strength of illicit trade in New Granada during the first Anglo-Spanish war is extensive. In April 1798, Viceroy Mendinueta wrote that 'it is well-known and notorious that the whole Kingdom has for some years past been supplied most abundantly with foreign goods and effects brought from the neighbouring Colonies'.[66] In February 1799, the viceroy acknowledged that illicit trade was on the increase, and came to advocate enhanced legal trade with foreign colonies as the most effective remedy.[67] In July 1801, he reviewed allegations to the effect that contraband goods had flooded the kingdom, and that national trade and Customs revenues had suffered acutely as a result. Governors along the Caribbean coast were said to protect and encourage smuggling, for example releasing ships known to have come from Jamaica, to the dismay of their captors.[68] It was reported that foreign manufactures were available in Cartagena at prices 20 per cent lower than they fetched in Spain itself, and were abundant both on the coast and in the cities of the interior.[69] The chief geographical centres for smuggling in New Granada during the wars were the provinces of Santa Marta and Río de la Hacha, the Magdalena, and the rivers Cauca, Sinu, and Atrato. The Isthmus of Panama continued to provide a major point of transit for goods en route for the Pacific coasts of New Granada and Peru, while Cartagena de Indias itself also remained a major focus. Perhaps not surprisingly, when specifically challenged Mendinueta tended to play down the significance of contraband, essentially suggesting that its scale had been over-stated for malicious or interested reasons; though elsewhere Mendinueta, too, recognised how ancient and irresoluble a problem contraband was.[70]

Smuggling in New Granada seems now to have become the preserve of Spanish traders to a still greater extent than in other regions, but some British contraband persisted throughout the wars. In July 1797 the Governor of Cartagena wrote that contraband along the coast was undertaken 'both by Spaniards and by Foreigners, who in league with their correspondents rendezvous at the places indicated and at the appropriate times, and then transfer [the goods] inland for sale, in which they find so many collaborators'. This official stated that the methodology of smuggling had changed with the years: 'Gone are the times when contraband was undertaken by brute force, and noisily, because they have learned how much more profitable it is to use small Boats, which scarcely present a target, are cheap, and also cause their owners little loss if any should go astray.'[71] A particular focus for British contraband with the region was the island of San Andrés near the Nicaraguan coast, which, although Spanish, retained a largely anglophone population from earlier British occupations. Merchants in Jamaica later recalled how 'during the late War a very extensive and lucrative trade was carried on between this island and the Spanish Main thro' San Andreas in dry goods, which by this channel reached even the most remote of the Spanish settlements in South America'.[72] Gold, of which New Granada was the chief producer among the Spanish colonies, proved especially attractive to the British: Humboldt commented that, rather than to the mints in Santa Fé and Popayán, the inhabitants took their gold directly 'to Cartagena and Portobelo, whence it leaves for the British colonies'.[73] José de Pombo wrote in June 1800 that 'the gold of the Chocó, and the silver of Mexico, run swiftly like two rivers, to meet in Jamaica, whence they flow to London, to swell the pride of the arrogant islanders'.[74] As in Mexico and elsewhere, there were persistent allegations that British warships protected or otherwise connived at smuggling in New Granada. Pedro de Mendinueta noted that a single British frigate sufficed to out-gun all the local naval forces, and intimated that the chief purpose of the British blockade of Cartagena was to ensure 'that our Guarda Costas should not pursue Contraband'.[75]

Anti-smuggling forces in New Granada at the outset of the wars consisted of four sloops, two lesser ships, and an armed launch, of which all but two sloops were based at Cartagena de Indias.[76] These vessels cost up to 150,000 pesos per year to maintain, but were widely regarded as unsuited to their task, and in the quinquennium 1796–1800 made contraband seizures to the value of less than 100,000 pesos in total.[77] In September 1796, a royal decree was issued which led to a major review of coastguard forces and strategy in New Granada during the following years.[78] After some debate, in April 1798 Mendinueta approved plans for the effective 'privatisation' of the guardacosta, which was no longer to be operated directly by the Crown. The fleet itself was to be substituted for a similar number of smaller, more lightly armed vessels, whose total cost should not exceed 60,000 pesos per year.[79] This plan was approved in September 1799, at which time Spanish naval forces were actually ordered withdrawn from Cartagena and removed to Havana 'or wherever they are most needed'.[80] Almost immediately, however, Mendinueta began to express grave reservations, emphasising both the role the guarda-costa vessels played in communications within the viceroyalty, and the risks inherent to removing the force from royal control during wartime. In October 1800 he suspended implementation of the project, and in July the following year plans to transfer the Navy away from Cartagena were similarly abandoned.[81] A constant theme in debate regarding both maritime and land-based forces in New Granada at this time was frank pessimism as to the effectiveness of any action against contraband given the geography of the region and the prevailing economic conditions. Mendinueta himself wrote that 'a most extensive and uninhabited coast, with abundant anchorages; a small number of guarda-costas, lacking many articles necessary for navigation; a decided protection of illicit trade by foreigners, and other circumstances ... have and will always render useless the most carefully-considered measures'.[82] A member of the Cartagena merchant guild agreed that all anti-contraband endeavour was 'useless and impossible not only on such extensive and open Coasts, but even in the Ports themselves where Register ships have entered with false documents'.[83]

Estimates for the value of contraband in New Granada during the first war derive from a characteristic admixture of calculation and speculation. In a report dated October 1803, the merchant guild of Cartagena noted that in the late 1780s New Granada's foreign trade had been worth some 3,000,000 pesos per year in imports and exports alike. Even assuming no growth in the years since this period, such a figure would suggest that since the end of the French war in 1795, imports and exports should have been worth around 24,000,000 pesos apiece. But real imports had been worth just 2,000,000 pesos altogether, or some 250,000 pesos per year, a phenomenon which could only reflect a 'vast and silent contraband trade, which has reduced legitimate Trade with the Metropolis to a twelfth part of what it should have been.'[84] In a report prepared for the Consulado in 1804, the Customs official Ignacio Cavero estimated that of some 11,500,000 pesos produced in New Granadan Mints during the first war, more than 8,400,000 (c. £1,900,000) were lost to smuggling, with a further 2,000,000 pesos exported as produce. The *consiliario* Santiago González, meanwhile, put the total value of British contraband exports from New Granada during the first war at 20,000,000 pesos (c. £4,500,000).[85] More modest – and in my view, more credible – figures were proffered by José de Pombo; in June 1800, Pombo calculated the value of contraband trade with Jamaica as 1,000,000 pesos per year since early 1797. Some years later, the same author estimated the total value of contraband imports to New Granada in the four years 1798–1801 at 6,000,000 pesos, or 1,500,000 pesos (c. £340,000) per year.[86]

The Peace of Amiens brought no significant recovery in New Granada's legal trade with Spain; indeed, most observers agreed that contraband actually increased during the lull in hostilities.[87] Pombo noted that peace eliminated the only factor hindering illicit trade, that of French and Cuban corsairs, so that up to thirty smuggling sloops traded at ports in Santa Marta, Río de la Hacha, Chagres and Portobelo. Pombo further emphasised the complicity of Spanish officials and the strong, even violent, opposition which any interference with trade on the part of the guarda-costas could arouse.[88] The merchant guild in Cartagena claimed that the viceroyalty was now so abundantly supplied by contraband that, in a reversal of historic patterns, the port had actually received up to a million pesos in goods from the interior provinces, while the few vessels arriving from Spain could neither dispatch their own cargoes, nor find produce to take off in return.[89] The treasury official Manuel Hernández meanwhile suggested that most trade in New Granadan cotton, cacao, indigo, dye- and other precious woods, drugs, gold, and platinum lay in foreign hands, undertaken in Spanish, British, French and Dutch vessels.[90] Hernández again emphasised the rôle of San Andrés as an entrepôt for British trade, and Jamaican merchants acknowledged that during the Peace a 'considerable trade' was carried on with San Andrés 'in dry goods, for which returns were received in cotton and specie'. In May 1804 a Spanish official described the island as 'a great warehouse stuffed with British goods for illegal shipment to the continent'.[91] Some direct trade, too, persisted during the peace; Ignacio Cavero noted that 'the British are not content with undertaking their Trade on the deserted Coasts, since the Ship *Hercules*, a Corvette and a Sloop have spent a long time in the vicinity of Cartagena and Santa Marta and have made repeated imports of goods'. José de Pombo thought that the total value of contraband rose significantly in 1802–03 to 3,000,000 pesos (c. £675,000) per year in imports of foreign goods and exports of Spanish bullion alike. These figures implied a loss to the royal revenues of 1,000,000 pesos per year solely in commercial taxes, with the total loss put at some 4,000,000 pesos in 1798–1803.[92] Cavero indignantly reported the departure from Jamaica in April 1804 of a huge commercial convoy, transporting 6,000,000 pesos in bullion and large quantities of produce to Britain.

The renewal of hostilities in late 1804 brought about the re-establishment of the British blockade and a further collapse in New Granada's legal trade. Legal imports were worth a mere 275,000 pesos in 1805, and by late September agricultural produce piling up in Cartagena included 32,000 cwt of cotton, 80,000 *arrobas* of quinoa bark, and 1,000,000 lb of cacao.[93] The commercial panorama in New Granada during the second war was complicated by limited neutral trade expeditions undertaken for the benefit of the *Caja de Consolidación de Vales Reales* in Spain, and by commercial licences granted piecemeal by Viceroy Amar y Borbón after he closed the viceroyalty's ports in early 1805. Nevertheless, illicit trade continued undiminished; thus, one neutral vessel entered Cartagena to find a market flooded by goods imported illicitly by foreigners or under private licence, 'that Port and

Kingdom being supplied abundantly for many years with all kinds of Cloth and other Articles'.[94] British interloping, too, persisted on some scale; the British sloop *Ceres* was captured at Río de la Hacha, a naval official later discussing 'the papers found on board her, and how many Spanish residents of the city of Santa Marta, Mompóx, and Río de Hacha were revealed by them to be complicit in the reprobate trade, even with our enemies the British'.[95] Commercial duties on imports, and other costs, were such that the British could 'come to our very coasts (as they do) to offer us them for 50 per cent, 80 per cent, or even 100 per cent less than what they cost us here'.[96] The flow of contraband bullion at this time through Mompóx, an inland port on the River Magdalena, was said to be so great that 'at this rate the enemy of the Nation will carry off all the gold of this Kingdom'.[97] The most striking evidence for British contraband during the second war was supplied by Domingo Negrón, a Spanish sea-captain whose vessel was taken prize by the British warship *Veteran* in 1806. After his capture, Negrón witnessed major contraband operations undertaken by Spanish vessels under British naval escort at Sabanilla, a small harbour at the mouth of the Magdalena. As part of these operations, in a single day the *Veteran* itself took off '*eight hundred thousand pesos in gold, which they carried from shore in leather-bound trunks*'; this sum was said to be the property of the admiral at Jamaica, 'the product of Goods landed on his account by Merchant Vessels at the said place'.[98] It may be no coincidence that some British maps of the early nineteenth century, even at world scale, showed Sabanilla in preference to far more important ports in the region.

In late 1806, guarda-costa forces in New Granada consisted of six sloops and a number of lesser vessels, all of which were said to be in poor repair and lacking basic supplies.[99] Anti-contraband strategy in the viceroyalty during the second war was dominated by two key issues. In early 1805, Viceroy Amar y Borbón closed the region's ports and imposed strict controls on all coasting trade. He did so citing orders from Spain designed to limit the risk to shipping during the war, but also because he claimed that coasting trade provided a key pretext for illicit intercourse with the British colonies. Amar's actions caused outrage among New Granadan merchants, who protested both at their impact on legitimate trade and at the viceroy's favouring of individual merchants with permits to export produce to other Spanish colonies.[100] Amar rejected these allegations and defended his policy, but in March 1806 he was instructed to lift the restrictions on trade (an order implemented in April the following year).[101] The other key feature was renewed strong pressure from within the viceroyalty for an opening to neutral trade, both as an economic panacea and as the only effective means to combat contraband. Some of the proposals formulated at this time, such as those prepared by Ignacio Cavero, incorporated provisions expressly designed to guard against penetration of neutral trade by the British. Others were far more radical: in the context of discussions regarding New Granada, Francisco Viana, a high-ranking colonial official in Madrid, described a proposal by the Governor of Cumaná in

Venezuela for free trade 'during peace-time, and during war-time not only with friendly Colonies, but also with enemy ones, especially since the Islands of Trinidad and Curaçao, which the British have conquered, are so close to hand'. Viana himself supported calls for neutral trade, as 'the most efficient means to contain Contraband'.[102] But these proposals proved too radical for cautious government officials in Madrid. The only anti-contraband reforms actually approved at this time were minor measures drawn up by Amar in the aftermath of the Sabanilla affair, notably the appointment of a dedicated official with responsibility for combating contraband along the river Magdalena.

Venezuela

In Caracas and the outlying provinces of Venezuela, no less than in the other Spanish colonies, legal trade suffered greatly as a consequence of the wars. Entries of Spanish shipping at La Guaira, the main Venezuelan port, ceased almost entirely in 1797 as the British blockade came into effect.[103] One source indicated that while exports of produce from the port had averaged 2,500,000 pesos each year in 1792–95, in 1797–98 they averaged less than 1,000,000 pesos, while legal imports by Spaniards averaged less than 100,000 pesos' value in each of the same two years.[104] A different source suggested that exports by Spaniards from La Guaira were worth only 425,000 pesos in seventeen months following January 1799, with imports by Spaniards worth just 212,000 pesos at the same port in the same period.[105] To the direct economic consequences of the war were added barriers to trade imposed by the local authorities: thus in 1803, Intendant of Caracas Juan Vicente de Arce placed heavy restrictions on local maritime trade and prohibited expeditions by Spaniards to foreign colonies for slaves.[106] Again, as in New Granada, in 1805 Venezuelan ports were effectively closed to shipping altogether following the renewal of hostilities, ostensibly in an attempt to protect Spanish shipping and prevent contraband trade with the British. It has been argued that the impact of the commercial crisis in Venezuela was potentially still more serious than elsewhere due to the specific character of the region's trade, which was based upon exports of produce (especially cacao and indigo) with a limited storage life.[107] By 1799, the absence of legal outlets had provoked the collapse of prices of produce, from 16–17 pesos per *fánega* of cacao to 6–7 pesos, or from 13 reales per pound of indigo to 6–7 reales.[108] Meanwhile, prices of legal imports soared, amid general reports of scarcity.

These circumstances created ideal conditions for illicit trade in Venezuela, which flourished throughout the period of the wars. Illegal trade with the region was articulated almost entirely by means of the Spanish licensed trade and through commerce undertaken by the merchants of neutral powers. In the preceding chapter we saw evidence for the strength of the licensed trade out of Venezuela, whether in the rich trade developed with Trinidad after 1797 (of which the vast majority was undertaken in Spanish vessels) or in operations based in Puerto Cabello in 1801.[109] For its part, trade with neutrals was permitted in Venezuela as early as April 1797, and was interrupted only briefly by the general suspension of neutral trade throughout the empire in April 1799. Interestingly, Venezuelan protests at this suspension emphasised that it could only increase British commercial penetration of the region, by placing illicit trade still more exclusively in British hands. One legal official thought it inevitable that 'without achieving the benefits ... of the Royal Order, these Provinces will become filled with prohibited goods and British manufactures'. The Royal *Audiencia* agreed that 'the enemies of the Crown will bring in and take off by means of clandestine trade as much, or more, than they acquired before under the cover of neutral flags'. The Governor of Cumaná protested that

> if until now our produce has been divided between the Spaniards, British, Swedes, Danes, Dutch, and North Americans, in future, except for the small amount bought by Spaniards, all the rest will go to the British; because where is the smuggler to go except to Trinidad where he can venture without any risk whatever, and they pay more for his produce and cargoes than in the other colonies, and twice what the Spaniards pay?[110]

These writers also emphasised that suspension of neutral trade during a period of acute commercial crisis would present the British with easy propaganda, increasing the threat of subversion from Trinidad and elsewhere; thus the British would 'abuse the Royal Order of 20 of April of this year, and interpreting it maliciously as is their custom, will seek to add to their subversion this proof that the Peoples of America are treated with a harshness which buries them in misery'.[111] Arguments such as these brought about a renewed opening of neutral trade in Venezuela in May 1801. Trade in British merchandise which went on under cover of this commerce is described in Chapter 6; suffice here to note that the strength of the licensed and neutral trades seems to have marginalised contraband trade by the British almost entirely. Although some such trade persisted at a low level in the eastern regions out of Trinidad, concrete evidence of trade by British smugglers in the Venezuelan heartland is scarce, and its significance within the general commercial panorama appears to have been negligible.

Venezuela's British trade was oriented principally toward Trinidad to the east, and toward Jamaica to the west, with the commercial watershed lying somewhat to the east of Caracas. Much of Caracas's trade now passed through the intermediary port of Puerto Cabello,[112] and was also directed toward Curaçao and St Thomas (whether those islands were under neutral or the British flag). Contrary to the view of the Governor of Cumaná cited in the preceding paragraph, some observers thought that British wartime action now all but drove foreign European competitors from Venezuelan markets,[113] leaving only the formidable and growing competition proffered by the United States. Investigations by a later governor of illicit trade during the first Anglo-Spanish war revealed how 'under the cover of licences and formal permits are to be discovered the falsification, bad faith, fraud, and treachery with which the enemies of the Crown ... profited from the produce of this Province'.[114] A major letter by merchants in Caracas dated May 1803 described a colony 'supplied and filled with cotton goods and also linen, deriving from the continuous and voluminous contraband undertaken with the Foreign Colonies, and especially with the island of Trinidad through the region of Cumaná, Guayana, and Barcelona'. These goods were imported via illicit trade with foreign colonies, but also under special contracts granted to foreign merchants for the export of Venezuelan produce during the war. Under cover of such licences, 'they make considerable exports of Gold and silver with the apparent aim of bringing Agricultural tools, the real object being very different, because ... the majority of the cargoes are returned in contraband goods, which are unloaded along the coasts, and even clandestinely in the Ports themselves'. Echoing similar comments by merchants in New Granada, the Caracas traders adduced as evidence for the scale of illicit trade the fact that the capital now drew its own supplies in part from the provinces, where goods sold more cheaply.[115] No contemporary Spanish estimates for the total value of contraband in Venezuela have come to light for the period of the first war and the Peace of Amiens. Alexander Walker, a Briton, thought that smuggling was worth two to three times the value of legal imports from Spain at La Guaira, which he suggested were worth some 3,115,000 pesos (£700,000) in 1796.[116] The French writer Depons, by contrast, in a passage apparently referring to the year 1801, estimated the value of contraband imports to Venezuela at less than 940,000 pesos (£210,000) per year.[117]

Anti-contraband forces in Venezuela were based at Puerto Cabello and were said by one source never to have consisted of more than two brigs, a lesser vessel, and a pair of armed launches.[118] By March 1798, both brigs had been taken prize by the British, while a third vessel was employed only on government errands, so that 'the coasts are unprotected by sea, and by land, open for the importation of as much contraband as they wish'.[119] Depons described a much larger guarda-costa squadron, comprising four schooners and half a dozen sloops, but was highly sceptical as to its efficacy:

> In the actual state of things, a contraband trader must be very unfortunate to meet one of these schooners. They only keep the sea at intervals sufficiently short and rare, and they must guard an extent of 300 leagues of coast, which everywhere furnishes suitable points for debarkation. Nor would his misfortune be without remedy, since by sacrificing one part of the cargo, it is not difficult for a Spaniard to save the other.

Nevertheless, 'a stranger would not be permitted to compound, or, if he should, the transaction would cost much more'.[120] Depons's account is distinguished by a detailed description of land-based anti-smuggling detachments in Venezuela, numbering close to 200 men with their officers but whose rigour he considered 'a commodity that only requires purchasers'. Certainly, one often has the sense that the authorities in Venezuela were more than usually uninterested in maintaining active or effective anti-contraband forces. In any case, observers agreed on the futility of anti-smuggling measures in the region. The Intendant at Caracas regarded the maritime squadron as 'entirely useless', and land-based forces as 'inadequate when the need of the importers is extreme, and the power of the protectors sufficient to silence them'.[121] Another royal official in the same city was similarly pessimistic: 'even taking all possible measures, they would never be enough to contain this disorder in the vast extent of our deserted coast.' The Governor of Cumaná thought it 'absolutely impossible to guard 150 leagues of coast, and the infinite number of navigable rivers, and streams which run through the Province'.[122]

In October 1805, Intendant Arce stated that the closure of Venezuelan ports and the consequent rise in prices had boosted contraband to scandalous levels. Arce mentioned the seizure of several valuable contraband cargoes, including one effected in the very house of the military chief at La Guaira. Seizures had been worth 127,000 pesos in two and a half years, an unprecedented sum but one which surely represented less than a tenth of all contraband imports. 'Most' contraband entered the region via the province of Cumaná, for which reason the Intendant actually banned trade between that province and Caracas.[123] The following month, Arce reiterated that 'contraband is excessive and scandalous' and insisted that 'powerful people undertake and protect it'. He stressed that the only effective defence was the promotion of trade through the legalisation of legitimate imports and exports (comments which also sought to justify the questionable commercial contracts he himself had granted in the previous two years).[124] The British were well aware of the richness of their trade with Venezuela; in February 1807, in the context of discussions regarding possible military action against the Spanish colonies, the Duke of Wellington dismissed plans for an attack on Caracas in part because 'there is reason to believe that large quantities of British produce are already conveyed into the kingdom of Terra Firma by the means of neutrals and the contraband trade'.[125]

Nevertheless, concrete statistics for the trade remain elusive for this as for the earlier period. Manual Lucena Salmoral's study of the foreign trade of Caracas in the sexennium beginning in 1807 does not address the issue of contraband and sheds relatively little light on trade with the British. Lucena's data suggest that in January 1807–September 1808, some 24–29 per cent of the registered trade of La Guaira was with foreign colonies, evidently under government licence.[126] This trade now constituted Caracas's second market after the United States, that which produced the heaviest commercial deficit and so 'really eroded the silver circulating in the province'.[127] In 1807, however, registered trade with British colonies was naturally negligible; and although the following year almost 60 per cent of registered shipments were from or to British colonial possessions (especially Curaçao and St Thomas), this period included some five months of legal trade following the Anglo-Spanish Peace.[128]

Puerto Rico and Santo Domingo

Illicit trade in Puerto Rico was undertaken with all the foreign colonies in the region, but for some time had been oriented above all toward the Danish island of St Thomas a short distance to the east. The total value of Puerto Rico's contraband trade was estimated at 500,000 pesos per year in 1792, of which four-fifths was concentrated in the capital, San Juan.[129] A good part of this trade became formally legal from late 1797, when trade with neutral merchants was permitted throughout the Spanish empire. Danish vessels from St Thomas took an important share of neutral trade with Puerto Rico, though they now also faced powerful competition from shipping from the United States. Of twenty-seven foreign vessels entering San Juan in the eighteen months following January 1800, almost 60 per cent were American and just under 30 per cent Danish, although almost half of all voyages originated in St Thomas.[130] During the Peace of Amiens, a thriving trade with foreign territories also developed in Spanish vessels under governmental licence; in the last nine months of 1803, twenty-three such vessels entered San Juan from foreign ports, while twenty-seven Spanish vessels cleared for foreign destinations. The relevance of this trade to commercial relations with the British is unclear; about 60 per cent of voyages were from or to St Thomas or the United States, though a quarter of clearances were to unspecified 'foreign islands', with cargoes consisting mainly of coffee, cotton, sugar, wood and hides.[131] Much British trade with Puerto Rico during the period of the wars is likely to have been channelled via the United States or via St Thomas, both when that island was neutral and during the two British occupations (discussed in Chapter 4).[132] It is to be supposed that trade by Spanish merchants under licence at the free ports, particularly those in the Lesser Antilles but occasionally also with Jamaica, was of comparable significance.

Harder to detect is contraband trade by British merchants in Puerto Rico during this period. The relevant volumes of governors' papers make very little mention of illicit trade of any kind, though this probably speaks more for the attitude of the authorities toward smuggling than for a lack of contraband as such.[133] Relations with the British seem to have been affected by the abortive invasion of April 1797, undertaken by the forces lately victorious in Trinidad. This event made the Puerto Ricans acutely sensitive to the presence of British shipping off the coasts or to the activities of British merchants in port.[134] Such sensitivity, with the greater facilities for trade in neutral vessels or by Spanish merchants, may effectively have limited direct British interloping to petty smuggling and perhaps logging along the coasts. It is true that several unusual cases nevertheless hint at a certain flexibility in commercial relations during these years. In 1799, a rare *rescate* was mounted from Puerto Rico of a cargo of mercury from the sloop *Elisa*, taken by a British corsair and held at St Thomas. An American merchant was contracted to ship the mercury to Veracruz in a neutral vessel, having first procured a pass from the British authorities at Tortola protecting the voyage.[135] In early 1803, two British sloops entered San Juan from Tortola with part of a cargo salvaged from the Spanish vessel *Nuestra Señora del Carmen*, which had been wrecked off Anegada en route from Malaga. Most unusually, in February 1802 the sloop *Spring Bird* entered from New Providence, despatched by John Low on the orders of the Havana merchant Juan Luis de la Cuesta. This vessel carried a cargo of assorted goods and 72,000 pesos in cash, all of which de la Cuesta offered to advance to the local treasury against future military subsidies.[136] In the event, Puerto Rico may have been the first of the Spanish colonies to open its ports to British shipping following the Anglo-Spanish Peace of mid-1808. On 1 August, the British Commandant in St Thomas informed his compatriots of this aperture, and further declared that 'every encouragement and facility be henceforth granted to all Spaniards trading to this island'.[137]

Contraband in Santo Domingo was traditionally based on cross-border intercourse with the French colony of St Domingue and on covert maritime trade with the neighbouring foreign islands. This maritime commerce was relatively poor, reflecting the general condition of the colony, and was again primarily with the Danes at St Thomas, with the British apparently relegated to a secondary role. Santo Domingo had no formal guarda-costa squadron; maritime anti-smuggling action depended principally on private corsairs, while land-based forces were thinly spread and represented little more than a token gesture at the restraint of smuggling.[138] In September 1793, Britain exploited the disorder provoked by the great slave revolt to invade French St Domingue, and for five years sought to occupy that territory before being finally expelled by the black revolutionaries in 1798. Cooperation with Santo Domingo at this time was often close, with the British purchasing large quantities of livestock from the Spaniards for the supply of their troops.[139] In 1795, Spain ceded its portion of the island to France at the treaty which ended the Franco-Spanish war begun two years earlier, a cession which was finally made effective in 1800–01. Up until this date, most trade with the British is likely to have been undertaken either by Spaniards trading under licence, or through the vehicle of neutral trade (again undertaken mainly by American and Danish merchants). Some direct British contraband certainly also persisted, part of it under the cover of false neutral papers; thus in March 1800, Spanish treasury officials noted that

> although the Flag is Danish the construction of many of the Ships ... is British, their Captains and super-cargoes are unknown here, and they do not come like others consigned to established merchants, for which reason there is more than a reasonable suspicion that they are British, sailing under the Danish Flag.[140]

Santo Domingo was restored to Spanish control in 1809 by a joint Anglo-Spanish military expedition; among the fruits of this expedition was the immediate opening of the colony's ports to British vessels, on equal terms with those of Spain.[141]

Monopoly and Taxation: Contemporary Views on the Causes of Contraband

The reasons why contraband persisted in the Spanish colonies on so vast a scale elicited broad consensus among contemporary writers, foreign as well as Spanish-American, who addressed the issue. Most placed the blame firmly at the door of the Spanish imperial trading system, which was viewed as overly complex, excessively burdensome in fiscal terms, and above all anti-quated and ill-matched to Spain's real position in the trading world. The Frenchman Dauxion Lavaysse complained that

> although Spain, with the laws, the absurd regulations and numerous taxes which weighed down and smothered its colonial trade, could neither export nor work up the products of its immense colonies, neither however would it allow them to export or work them up themselves, nor allow foreigners to export them and bring the settlers in return the goods they needed. Thus arose contraband trade.[142]

The colonial administrator Francisco Viana stated flatly that 'until the Trade of the Metropolis is such as is required to deprive smuggling of its advan-tages, contraband will be inevitable'.[143] Viceroy Mendinueta of New Granada went so far as to describe contraband as 'an evil in some ways necessary due to circumstances', one which had averted chronic shortages and possibly even civil unrest.[144] Anger and frustration at official trade policy came to be voiced with increasing frequency as the wars continued and the economic disruption which accompanied them worsened. These concerns emerged with special vigour during protests in Venezuela in 1799 over the threatened suppression of neutral trade with that colony, granted two years earlier. In this context the Governor of Cumaná asked of the settlers of his province,

> What are they to do with their estates? What measures will they take to survive, and cover their flesh, if they cannot give outlet [to their produce], and reduce it to money, and other things of absolute necessity? ... What can be the results, except poverty, misery, discontent and perhaps desperation?

The burghers of the town of Valencia called the decree suppressing trade with neutrals 'an order which will soon be the desolation and extermination of all these loyal inhabitants'. The town council of Caracas called the suspen-sion 'inhuman', and asked bitterly, 'on what are these Provinces to subsist if the provisional trade granted them with so many restrictions is suppressed? ... Can it be the mind of the Sovereign to put an end to everything, rather than fail to put an end to the provisional trade?'.[145] Such animus against offi-cial policy, so overtly expressed, belies any notion that Spanish Americans might regard contraband as morally unacceptable, much less feel inclined to heed their government's injunctions against it.

Crucial to critical analyses of the causes of smuggling was the question of excessive taxation. The merchant guild in Havana wrote to the minister in

Madrid: 'Regarding contraband, we must confess ingenuously to Your Excellency it exists, but that which exists is inevitable; its incentive lies in the heavy Duties paid by National commerce and in the exemption enjoyed in practice by clandestine trade.'[146] Alexander von Humboldt agreed that 'contraband will necessarily subsist so long as there is no diminution of the incentive through a total change in the system of the Customs'.[147] Taxation of foreign manufactures traditionally re-exported to the colonies from Spain was viewed as especially significant, since these goods naturally constituted the staples of contraband trade. The Cuban merchant Antonio del Valle Hernández put the total weight of taxes on European goods imported at Havana at 25–30 per cent.[148] Humboldt calculated that foreign goods imported in Spanish shipping to ports in Mexico bore duties of 35–40 per cent, and Miguel Lerdo de Tejada identified nine different taxes on such goods with an aggregate weight of some 36.5 per cent.[149] Francisco Pérez Muñoz demonstrated that cloth purchased in Hamburg accrued taxes of 50.5 per cent in the course of import to Spain, export to Veracruz and repatriation of the profits to the Peninsula. The same cloth imported to any British island in the West Indies carried a total duty of 5 per cent, such that British merchants could sell it there or ship it contraband to Veracruz at a price with which no legitimate Spanish trader could possibly compete.[150] José Ignacio de Pombo estimated that a piece of cloth costing 10 pesos in Europe sold for twice that sum in Cartagena de Indias due to the cumulative weight of tax, freight, commissions, and insurance. He later stated that these factors could triple the cost of European goods imported to New Granada through official channels, constituting 'the most effective stimulus that can be given to contraband'.[151]

If an outmoded monopoly and excessive taxation were the problems, then commercial reform and tax reduction were the cures. Most observers coincided in identifying such reforms – rather than enhanced guarda-costa or Customs forces – as the only practical means of combating illicit trade. José Donato de Austria, secretary of the Veracruz merchant guild, expressed the arguments of many when he emphasized the importance of 'the vital ruling principle of moderation of duties, facility of despatch, freedom of transport, and easy and uniform administration of the merchants'.[152] Del Valle Hernández argued elegantly if optimistically: 'Customs duties cannot be considered as fixed Royal income ... Their arrangement is rather a subtle rein in the hands of Government to direct and manage trade skilfully through the channels most advantageous to the Nation.' Widespread consensus on the need for fiscal and broader commercial reform, however, encountered the implacable hostility of the powerful merchant guilds, especially those of Cadiz and Mexico City, with strong vested interests in maintaining the traditional mercantile system. Serious reform of the institutional and fiscal apparatus governing Spanish imperial trade would await the onset of the emancipatory movements after 1810, and came far too late to rescue what remained of Spain's commercial hegemony in the Americas.

Notes

1   William Robinson, 'Humble Memorial', n.p., n.d. [1805], N.A., B.T. 1 / 28, ff. 265–90v, see ff. 279–v.

2   Humboldt, *Ensayo político sobre el Reino de la Nueva España*, pp. 423, 481, 496, 505.

3   Olmos Sánchez, 'Contrabando y libre comercio', p. 92.

4   Félix Berenguer de Marquina to Miguel Cayetano Soler, Mexico City, 27 July 1801, A.G.I., Mexico, 1603; Anon., *Instrucciones*, p. 205.

5   These cases are discussed by Rodríguez del Valle, 'Félix Berenguer de Marquina', pp. 130–5.

6   García Dabila to Marquina, Veracruz, 14 Aug. 1801, A.G.N.M, Correspondencia de diversas autoridades, leg. 59, exp. 36, ff. 118–21.

7   Marquina to Soler, Mexico City, 27 July 1801, A.G.I., Mexico, 1603.

8   See e.g. Depons, *Travels in South America*, 2:59–60; 'E.D.C.P.', letter dated 1 Apr. 1806, in *Jornal … de Veracruz*, nos. 50–1, 19–20 Apr. 1806.

9   Armytage, *Free Port System*, p. 115.

10   'Reos de los Contrabandos de Veracruz', Mexico City, 29 May 1801, A.G.I., Mexico, 1603.

11   Rodríguez del Valle, 'Félix Berenguer de Marquina', pp. 140–6.

12   Rodríguez del Valle, 'Félix Berenguer de Marquina', pp. 147–8; Anon., *Instrucciones*, pp. 214, 221–4. The Governor's multiple disputes with Marquina are discussed in abundant papers in A.G.I., Mexico, 2841. For the *Suceso*, see p. 142 above.

13   Marquina to Soler, Mexico City, 27 July 1801, A.G.I., Mexico, 1603.

14   See the series of papers in A.G.N.M., Alcabalas, vol. 427, exp. 3, ff. 56–82v.

15   Olmos Sánchez, 'Contrabando y libre comercio', p. 92; 'Providencias tomadas para evitar el Contrabando en las Costas de Alvarado y Goazacoalcos, 1799', A.G.N.M., Marina, vol. 141, exp. 1, ff. 1–24.

16   Merchant guild to Marquina, Veracruz, 8 June 1801, A.G.N.M., Consulado, vol. 79, exp. 1, ff. 47–50v, and the series which follows; Marquina to Juan Ygnacio Bustillo, Mexico City, 30 May 1801, A.G.N.M., Marina, vol. 143, exp. 17, ff. 488–9, and accompanying documents.

17   Anon., *Instrucciones*, p. 205; López Cancelada, *Ruina de la Nueva España*, pp. 38–9.

18   Rodríguez del Valle, 'Félix Berenguer de Marquina', pp. 70–1, 129, 142–3.

19   Real Díaz, 'José de Iturrigaray', p. 269.

20   Humboldt, *Ensayo político sobre el Reino de la Nueva España*, p. 496.

21   Cited in Williams, 'Mercados británicos en el Caribe', p. 100.

22   *Ensayo político*, pp. 423, 511; Peuchet, *Etat des Colonies*, 1:346–7, is an (unattributed) direct translation. The general methodology used by Humboldt here, which essentially compares data for coin production at Mexican Mints with registered and estimated exports, was criticised by Quirós, *Memoria de instituto*, pp. 81–2.

23   Francisco Pérez Muñoz to merchant guild, Veracruz, 6 Feb. 1804, A.G.N.M., Consulado, vol. 79, exp. 1, ff. 37–44.

24   Manuel José Elvuero to guild, Veracruz, 20 Feb. 1804, A.G.N.M., Consulado, vol. 79, exp. 1, ff. 45–6v.

25   Humboldt, *Ensayo político*, pp. 502–3; see also similar comments by Pedro Ajequiezcane, 'British Trade with the Spanish Colonies', p. 251.

26   Arregui Martínez-Moya, 'Instrucción de Guardacostas' (who also publishes the regulations in full).

27   Part of the text of the Manifesto is reproduced in Narváez y la Torre, 'Discurso del Mariscal de Campo', p. 81; its impact in Mexico may be traced in a decree issued by viceroy Iturrigaray, Mexico City, 6 May 1805, in A.G.N.M, Bandos, vol. 23, exp.

77, f. 187.

28   Real Díaz, 'José de Iturrigaray', pp. 268–72; Smith, 'Shipping in the Port of Veracruz', p. 10.

29   'Memoria sobre el establecimiento de guarda-costas', n.d. (late 1807 or early 1808?), A.M.N., ms. 149, doc. 7, f. 18.

30   Coggeshall, *Second Series of Voyages*, pp. 42–5.

31   William Billings to James Madison, New York, 21 May 1801, N.A.W., R.G. 59, M899, roll 1.

32   See the commercial accounts in N.A., C.O. 137 / 116, ff. 312–14; C.O. 137 / 118, ff. 75–80.

33   For the Gordon and Murphy contract, see pp. 208–14.

34   'A Committee appointed by the Merchants of Kingston ...', 8 May 1800, in Minutes of Council, 10 May 1800, N.A., C.O. 137 / 104, ff. 114–23.

35   Quirós, *Memoria de instituto*, p. 81; see also the reference in an earlier Memoria by José María Quirós in Ortiz, *Memorias*, pp. 208–10; and report of merchant guild, Veracruz, 28 Apr. 1810, A.G.N.M., Consulado, vol. 79, exp. 1, ff. 1–2.

36   Merchant guild to crown, Veracruz, 1 Mar. 1809, A.G.I., Mexico, 2997, f. 8.

37   *Obras*, 1:74–6.

38   Guild to Miguel Cayetano Soler, Veracruz, 28 May 1808, A.G.N.M., Consulado, vol. 79, exp. 1, ff. 26–v.

39   Francisco de Guerra y Agreda to guild, Veracruz, 12 Aug. 1808, A.G.N.M., Consulado, vol. 79, exp. 1, ff. 28–v; copy, encl. no. 14 to Guild to crown, Veracruz, 1 Mar. 1809, A.G.I., Mexico, 2997.

40   Merchants of Mexico to guild, Mexico City, 17 May 1809, A.G.N.M., Archivo Histórico de Hacienda, leg. 215, exp. 9, ff. 431–6. A *vara* was roughly equivalent to a yard.

41   Josiah Blakeley to James Madison, Santiago de Cuba, 3 Apr. 1805, N.A.W., R.G. 59, T55, roll 1; Pezuela, *Historia*, 3:283–6, 370–4.

42   Sebastián Vindelán to Marqués de Someruelos, Cuba, 18 May 1802, reproduced in Barras y Aragón, 'Noticias y documentos', pp. 546–7.

43   George Morton to James Madison, George Town, 4 June 1801, N.A.W., R.G. 59, M899, roll 1.

44   Report dated Havana, 18 July 1798, A.G.I., Santo Domingo, 2193.

45   Report on lighthouses, with Merchant guild to Diego de Gardoqui, Havana, 4 June 1796, A.G.I., Santo Domingo, 2192.

46   Merchant guild to Francisco de Saavedra, Havana, 16 May 1798, A.G.I., Santo Domingo, 2193.

47   'Memoria sobre el establecimiento de guarda-costas', A.M.N., ms. 149, doc. 7, see ff. 17–v.

48   'Noticias de la Ysla de Jamayca', A.G.N.M., Correspondencia de diversas autoridades, leg. 59, exp. 57, f. 221; W. Craigie & Co. to Gov. Charles Cameron, n.p., n.d. (early 1808), N.A., B.T. 1 / 38, ff. 222–6v.

49   William Billings to James Madison, New York, 21 May 1801, N.A.W., R.G. 59, M899, roll 1.

50   Vincent Gray to James Madison, Havana, 14 Jan. 1805, N.A.W., R.G. 59, M899, roll 1.

51   As discussed below, pp. 198–9.

52   Vincent Gray to James Madison, Havana, 29 Oct. 1802, N.A.W., R.G. 59, M899, roll 1. On this complex point see also Gray to Madison, Havana, 2 Jan. 1805; Henry Hill to Madison, Havana, 10 Nov. 1805; and 'Copy of extract from my instructions, as inclosed ... in my letter of the 16th August [1805]', all in N.A.W., R.G. 59, M899,

roll 1: Josiah Blakeley to Madison, Santiago de Cuba, 1 Nov. 1801, N.A.W., R.G. 59, T55, roll 1.

53   Letter to guild, Veracruz, 6 Feb. 1804, A.G.N.M., Consulado, vol. 79, exp. 1, ff. 37–44.

54   Anon., *Instrucciones*, p. 181.

55   'Expediente sobre proponer a los Sres Gefes las medidas convenientes para la eficaz persecución del contrabando en las costas de esta Ysla', A.N.C., Real Consulado y Junta de Fomento, leg. 112, no. 4715.

56   'Memorial interesante y documentada ... sobre comercio y la situación de la Ysla de Cuba', Madrid, 25 Aug. 1816, A.M.N., ms. 436, doc. 13; also same author, 'Informe del Síndico ...', para. 61, pp. 264–5.

57   These figures are presumably per year; see José María Quirós, 'Memoria de instituto ...', Jalapa, 23 Sept. 1811, in Ortiz, *Memorias*, pp. 203–26, p. 210.

58   *Obras*, 1:74–6; the same figure, probably drawn from Arango's estimate, is given in a report by the merchant guild of Mexico dated 23 Aug. 1809, A.G.N.M., Consulado, vol. 79, exp. 1, ff. 13–24v, para. 17.

59   Mendinueta, *Relación*, 3:102–3.

60   See the comments by Santiago González, discussed in a summary of a report by the Consulado, dated Cartagena de Indias, 24 July 1804, A.G.I., Santa Fé, 960.

61   McFarlane, *Colombia before Independence*, esp. pp. 298–302.

62   Pombo, 'Memoria sobre el contrabando', p. 103.

63   Narváez y la Torre, 'Discurso del Mariscal de Campo', p. 93.

64   See the comments by Ignacio Cavero, discussed in a summary of a report by the Consulado, dated Cartagena de Indias, 24 July 1804, A.G.I., Santa Fé, 960.

65   There are several such proposals; major examples for the period to the end of the Peace of Amiens include Pombo, 'Informe del Real Tribunal', esp. pp. 30–40, and letter by Manuel Hernández, dated Cartagena de Indias, 21 Nov. 1803, A.G.I., Santa Fé, 959.

66   Mendinueta to Marqués de las Hormazas, Santa Fé, 19 Apr. 1798, A.G.I., Santa Fé, 647.

67   Mendinueta to Miguel Cayetano Soler, Santa Fé, 19 Feb. 1799, A.G.I., Santa Fé, 648.

68   Mendinueta to Soler, Santa Fé, 19 July 1801, A.G.I., Santa Fé, 650.

69   Pombo, 'Informe del Real Tribunal', pp. 16–17.

70   Mendinueta to Soler, Santa Fé, 19 July 1801, A.G.I., Santa Fé, 650; also Mendinueta, *Relación*, 3:104–5.

71   Anastasio Zejudo to Mendinueta, Cartagena, 30 July 1797, A.G.I., Santa Fé, 647.

72   'Memorial of the subscribers', [Kingston, June 1806,] N.A., C.O. 137 / 116, ff. 174–5v.

73   Humboldt, *Ensayo político sobre ... la Nueva España*, p. 424. Humboldt anchored off the Sinu and Atrato in April 1801, and noted that the mouths of these rivers 'serve as way-side stores for the smugglers'.

74   Pombo, 'Informe del Real Tribunal', pp. 19–20.

75   Mendinueta to Miguel Cayetano Soler, Santa Fé, 19 Jan. 1800, A.G.I., Santa Fé, 649.

76   Anastasio Zejudo, 'Estado del número y calibre ...', Cartagena, 30 July 1797, A.G.I., Santa Fé, 647.

77   'Relación de los comisos o contrabandos ...', A.G.N.C., Colonia: Contrabandos, vol. 15, ff. 785–6v.

78   For the probable origins of this decree, see Ezpeleta, *Relación del gobierno*, 2:281–2.

79   See esp. Anastasio Zejudo to Mendinueta, Cartagena, 30 July 1797, A.G.I., Santa Fé, 647; Mendinueta to Marqués de la Hormazas, Santa Fé, 19 Apr. 1798, A.G.I., Santa

Fé, 647; and Zejudo, 'Ynstrucción que deben observar los Gefes ...', encl. to Mendinueta to Soler, Santa Fé, 19 Oct. 1800, A.G.I., Santa Fé, 649.

80 Mendinueta to Miguel Cayetano Soler, Santa Fé, 19 Feb. and 19 Oct. 1800, both in A.G.I., Santa Fé, 649.

81 See also Mendinueta, *Relación*, 3:181–2.

82 Mendinueta, *Relación*, 3:132.

83 Comments by Santiago González, discussed in a summary of a report by the Consulado, dated Cartagena de Indias, 24 July 1804, A.G.I., Santa Fé, 960.

84 Consulado to Viceroy, Cartagena, 20 Oct. 1803, A.G.N.C., Consulados, vol. 2, ff. 947–52.

85 Both discussed in a summary of a report by the Consulado, dated Cartagena de Indias, 24 July 1804, A.G.I., Santa Fé, 960.

86 Pombo, 'Informe del Real Tribunal', pp. 21–3; 'Memoria sobre el contrabando', pp. 60–4.

87 McFarlane, *Colombia before Independence*, pp. 302–4.

88 Pombo, 'Memoria sobre el contrabando', pp. 67–70.

89 Consulado to Viceroy, Cartagena, 20 Oct. 1803, A.G.N.C., Consulados, vol. 2, ff. 947–52.

90 Letter by Manuel Hernández, dated Cartagena de Indias, 21 Nov. 1803, A.G.I., Santa Fé, 959.

91 'Memorial of the subscribers', [Kingston, June 1806,] N.A., C.O. 137 / 116, ff. 174–5v; Parsons, *San Andrés y Providencia*, pp. 53–4.

92 Pombo, 'Memoria sobre el contrabando', pp. 60–4.

93 Barbier, 'Commercial Reform and *Comercio Neutral*', pp. 113–15; Consulado to Ministro de Hacienda, Cartagena, 20 Oct. 1805, A.G.I., Santa Fé, 960. One *arroba* = c. 11.5 kg / 25 lb.

94 Mateo Arroyo, petition on behalf of José Romero Campo, Madrid, 20 Mar. 1807, A.G.I., Santa Fé, 960.

95 Nicolás de Zubiria to Viceroy, Cartagena, 30 June 1806, A.G.N.C., Colonia: Virreyes, vol. 16, ff. 322–8.

96 Narváez y la Torre, 'Discurso del Mariscal de Campo', p. 107.

97 Silverio Lastonera to Viceroy, Mompóx, 23 Feb. and 13 May 1806, both in A.G.N.C., Colonia: Contrabandos, vol. 15, ff. 382–v, 720–v.

98 Antonio Amar y Borbón to Miguel Cayetano Soler, two letters dated Santa Fé, 7 Dec. 1806, one marked *reservada*, in A.G.I., Santa Fé, 960; further copies in A.G.I., Santa Fé, 653.

99 'Memoria sobre el establecimiento de guarda-costas', A.M.N., ms. 149, doc. 7, f. 17.

100 Consulado to Ministro de Hacienda, Cartagena, 27 July 1805, A.G.I., Santa Fé, 959; Consulado to Ministro de Hacienda, Cartagena, 20 Oct. 1805, A.G.I., Santa Fé, 960.

101 Cédula dated Aranjuez, 10 Mar. 1806, A.G.I., Santa Fé, 960; Amar y Borbón to Miguel Cayetano Soler, Santa Fé, 20 Apr. 1807, A.G.I., Santa Fé, 654.

102 The key documents here are a summary of a report by the Consulado, dated Cartagena, 24 July 1804, A.G.I., Santa Fé, 960, which discusses opinions by Santiago González, Ignacio Cavero, and Antonio Narváez; Narváez y la Torre, 'Discurso del Mariscal de Campo', which is dated 30 June 1805; and Francisco Viana to Miguel Cayetano Soler, Madrid, 16 Apr. 1807, also in A.G.I., Santa Fé, 960. Viana was *Contador General de Indias*.

103 Fisher, 'Commerce and Imperial Decline', p. 463; same author, *Trade, War*, p. 52.

104 Vicente Linares, *Acta*, Caracas, 18 Aug. 1799, in 'Testimonio de los Autos creados sobre establecer en la Provincia de Venezuela ... comercio con el estranjero', A.G.I., Caracas, 117, ff. 60–9v.

105 Manuel de Guevara Vasconcelos and Antonio López Quintana to Miguel Cayetano Soler, Caracas, 31 July 1800, A.G.I., Caracas, 117.

106 See esp. Juan Vicente de Arce to Soler, Caracas, 24 May 1803, A.G.I., Caracas, 516; Guevara Vasconcelos to Príncipe de la Paz, Caracas, 28 June 1805, A.G.I., Caracas, 61; Guevara Vasconcelos to Ministro de Hacienda, Caracas, 13 July 1805, A.G.I., Caracas, 119.

107 Fisher, 'Commerce and Imperial Decline', p. 463; also the comment in McFarlane, *Colombia*, p. 307.

108 Cabildo of Valencia, *Representación*, Valencia, 8 Oct. 1799, in 'Testimonio de los Autos creados sobre … comercio con el estranjero', A.G.I., Caracas, 117, ff. 77v–85v (1 *fánega* = 1.58 bushels).

109 Pp. 130, 146–7.

110 Vicente Emparán to Guevara Vasconcelos and López Quintana, Cumaná, 19 June 1800, A.G.I., Caracas, 117.

111 *Parecer del Señor Fiscal*, Caracas, 5 Nov. 1799, and *Voto consultivo de la Real Audiencia*, Caracas, 13 Nov. 1799, both in 'Testimonio de los Autos creados sobre establecer en la Provincia de Venezuela … comercio con el estranjero', A.G.I., Caracas, 117, ff. 96–110v, 110v–17v. Comparable arguments are advanced by different contributors throughout this lengthy report.

112 Radhay, 'Contraband', p. 33.

113 A point made by Walker, *Colombia*, 2:184–5.

114 Guevara Vasconcelos to Ministro de Hacienda, Caracas, 9 May 1805, A.G.I., Caracas, 119.

115 Representatives of Caracas merchant guild to Intendant, Caracas, 4 May 1803, A.G.I., Caracas, 921.

116 Walker, *Colombia*, 2:185.

117 *Travels in South America*, 2:62–3.

118 'Memoria sobre el establecimiento de guarda-costas', A.M.N., ms. 149, doc. 7, f. 16.

119 Prior and Consuls of Consulado to Francisco de Saavedra, Caracas, 22 Mar. 1798, A.G.I., Caracas, 919.

120 *Travels in South America*, 2:63–6.

121 Arce to Soler, Caracas, 18 Nov. 1805, A.G.I., Caracas, 486.

122 *Parecer del Señor Fiscal*, Caracas, 5 Nov. 1799, and Emparán to Intendant of Caracas, Cumaná, 21 Aug. 1799, both in 'Testimonio de los Autos creados sobre establecer … comercio con el estranjero', A.G.I., Caracas, 117, ff. 96–110v and 33v–42v respectively.

123 Arce to Soler, 31 Oct. 1805, A.G.I., Caracas, 486.

124 Arce to Soler, 18 Nov. 1805, A.G.I., Caracas, 486.

125 Memorandum dated 15 Feb. 1807, in Wellington, *Supplementary Despatches*, 6:56–61.

126 Lucena Salmoral, *Características del comercio exterior de la provincia de Caracas*, pp. 276–8, 287–8.

127 Lucena Salmoral, *Características del comercio exterior*, pp. 219, 228.

128 Lucena Salmoral, *Características del comercio exterior*, pp. 228–30, and table 4, begins p. 183.

129 Sonesson, *Puerto Rico's Commerce*, pp. 27–8.

130 'Relación certificada', accompanying Ramón de Castro to Miguel Cayetano Soler, Puerto Rico, 3 Nov. 1801, A.G.I., Santo Domingo, 2319.

131 See the commercial accounts accompanying de Castro to Soler, Puerto Rico, 14 Mar. and 25 May 1804, both in A.G.I., Santo Domingo, 2322.

132 See also Sonesson, *Puerto Rico's Commerce*, pp. 37–8.

133 This statement is based on close survey of the papers in A.G.I., Santo Domingo,

2316–24.

134 See e.g. de Castro to las Hormazas, Puerto Rico, 28 Jan. 1798, A.G.I., Santo Domingo, 2317; de Castro to Juan Manuel Alvarez, Puerto Rico, 14 Jan. 1800, A.G.I., Santo Domingo, 2319.

135 De Castro to Soler, Puerto Rico, 15 Oct. 1799, A.G.I., Santo Domingo, 2318, and accompanying report. In February 1800, de Castro was ordered not to ransom any further cargoes of mercury; see de Castro to Soler, Puerto Rico, 2 Oct. 1801, A.G.I., Santo Domingo, 2319.

136 De Castro to Soler, Puerto Rico, 1 Mar. 1802, and accompanying report, A.G.I., Santo Domingo, 2320.

137 Proclamation by Brig. Gen. Fitzroy Maclean, St Thomas, 1 Aug. 1808, N.A., B. T. 1 / 41, ff. 149–v.

138 Sevilla Soler, *Santo Domingo*, pp. 215–19.

139 See e.g. Admiral Sir Hyde Parker to Evan Nepean, *Queen*, Manchineel Bay, Hispaniola, 23 Dec. 1796, N.A., ADM. 1 / 247, no. 157.

140 Royal treasury officials to Governor, Santo Domingo, 15 Mar. 1800, A.G.I., Indiferente General, 2466.

141 Jones, 'Historical Study', pp. 161–2; Langnas, 'Relations between Great Britain', chap. 5, p. 20.

142 Dauxion Lavaysse, *Viaje a las islas de Trinidad*, pp. 326–7.

143 Francisco Viana to Miguel Cayetano Soler, Madrid, 16 Apr. 1807, A.G.I., Santa Fé, 960.

144 Mendinueta to Soler, Santa Fé, 19 July 1801, A.G.I., Santa Fé, 650.

145 Vicente de Emparán to Intendant of Caracas, Cumaná, 21 Aug. 1799; Cabildo of Valencia, *Representación*, Valencia, 8 Oct. 1799; and Vicente Linares, *Acta*, Caracas, 18 Aug. 1799, all in 'Testimonio de los Autos creados sobre establecer … comercio con el estranjero', A.G.I., Caracas, 117, ff. 33v–42v, 77v–85v, and 60–9v respectively.

146 Merchant guild to Diego de Gardoqui, Havana, 6 Jan. 1796, A.G.I., Mexico, 2507.

147 Humboldt, *Ensayo político sobre el reino de la Nueva España*, p. 496.

148 Royal Order, Zaragoza, 26 August 1802, in 'Expediente sobre cumplimiento de la Rl Orden … relativa a la situación de la agricultura y comercio', A.N.C., Real Consulado y Junta de Fomento, leg. 112, no. 4072; Antonio del Valle Hernández to Consulado, Havana, 10 May 1803, in 'Expediente sobre la introducción de contrabando y negros sospechosos', A.N.C., Real Consulado y Junta de Fomento, leg. 112, no. 4073.

149 Cited with Lerdo de Tejada in Tandrón, *Comercio de Nueva España*, p. 26.

150 Letter to merchant guild, Veracruz, 6 Feb. 1804, A.G.N.M., Consulado, vol. 79, exp. 1, ff. 37–44.

151 Pombo, 'Informe del Real Tribunal', pp. 17–18; *Informe del Real Consulado*, pp. 154–6.

152 'Memoria … para fomentar la agricultura y la industria', Veracruz, 11 Jan. 1804, in Ortiz, *Memorias*, pp. 95–122, see pp. 109–10.

CHAPTER SIX

Trade During Wartime (1796–1808): Neutral Trade, the Bullion Contracts, and the 'Secret Trade'

> In the utmost latitude given to neutral commerce in the colonies of Spain, there was an express and anxious exception of British merchandize, which was wholly without effect.
>
> —Stephen, *War in Disguise*, p. 205

The preceding two chapters have been devoted to the development during the Napoleonic wars of the two principal vehicles of Anglo-Spanish trade in the Americas in the late eighteenth century: trade undertaken by Spaniards in British colonial ports, and by the British in Spanish America. This chapter, by contrast, discusses a commerce with long-standing precedents, but which now acquired perhaps unprecedented significance in Anglo-Spanish commercial relations: trade in British goods by the merchants of neutral powers. Neutral trade with the Spanish colonies has been the subject of an extensive scholarly literature, although no general survey of the subject is available, and much remains to be learnt. It was the Spanish imperial response to the collapse of trade with the colonies in 1797 under the impact of the British commercial blockade and to the commercial and fiscal crisis which resulted (on both sides of the Atlantic). In view of Spain's manifest incapacity to supply the colonies, and fearing unilateral openings to neutral trade, such as that already proclaimed by the authorities in Cuba,[1] by decree of 18 November 1797 the crown issued a general permission for the merchants of neutral states to trade in the American colonies. This decree sanctioned commerce in permitted goods in neutral shipping from either Spanish or neutral ports, with returns to be made obligatorily to ports in Spain (though the latter provision was widely ignored).[2] It was bitterly protested by the monopoly mercantile interests in Spain and the Americas which had most to lose by it, and in fact neutral trade was abolished after only seventeen months, by a new decree dated 20 April 1799.[3] In one colony after another, however, abolition was either ignored or suspended by the local authorities;[4] and although the trade was abolished on the return to peace-time conditions in 1802, it was restored less than three years later with the renewal of hostilities, then to endure throughout the second Anglo-Spanish war (1804–08). The consequence was that, whether formally or informally, by imperial decree or local ruling, most of the Spanish colonies remained open to neutral trade from early 1798 onwards.[5]

Trade with neutrals was among the most significant of all the processes affecting Spanish America during these years. Almost throughout the colonies, it signalled the end of even formal Spanish commercial hegemony, provoking a re-orientation of economic activity toward third nations which would prove impossible to reverse. The economic impact was enormous, as neutral merchants swiftly undertook the majority of all trade with the colonies. In Mexico, the richest region, neutral traders facilitated the rapid recovery of foreign commerce after the disastrous crash of 1797. Imports from Spain at Veracruz tripled in 1798, and tripled again in 1799, to reach some 5,500,000 pesos. Exports to Spain grew ten-fold in 1798, and almost tripled again in 1799, to reach over 6,300,000 pesos (figures already representing over 85 per cent of the pre-war levels).[6] After 1804, both foreign trade at Veracruz and the share of neutrals reached still greater heights: by 1807, registered exports were worth some 22,500,000 pesos, of which neutrals accounted for over 95 per cent.[7] The Mexican case was typical of most of the other colonies; thus in Venezuela, between 1797 and 1801 neutrals accounted for c. 87 per cent of imports and 70 per cent of exports, while over 87 per cent of the external trade of La Guaira in the first half of 1807 was with the United States or neighbouring foreign colonies.[8] The degree of economic emancipation which these trade figures imply may be seen in the most extreme example, that of Cuba, where already by 1798 imports from the United States alone were worth some 8,200,000 pesos, while imports from Spain were worth just 87,000 pesos. By 1801, foreign vessels already represented almost 90 per cent of all shipping entering the port of Havana (Table 6.1); in 1806, not a single ship entered Havana from the Peninsula, while imports from neutral ports and foreign colonies were worth almost 10,000,000 pesos.[9]

The Spanish royal decree of 1797 inaugurating neutral trade was probably intended to embrace only the neutral powers of Europe; it does not appear to have contemplated the participation of the United States. The geographical proximity and burgeoning merchant marine of the United States, however, made this exclusion a dead letter. Local authorities effectively suspended the ruling throughout the colonies, and North American vessels swiftly dominated the trade. Some sense of the scale of this US commerce may be gained by reference to unquestionably the two most important centres, Cuba and Mexico. The Havana port books show many hundreds of American vessels entering the port every year throughout the period of the wars. The trade probably reached its peak in 1805–08; 600 American vessels entered at Havana in the first ten months of 1805 alone, bringing cargoes worth an estimated $6,000,000.[10] In early 1808, the American consul could note with scant exaggeration that 'when the wind continues southerly for ten or twelve days, and then favourable, our Vessels tumble in by dozens'.[11] In

Table 6.1 *Maritime trade and sugar exports at Havana, 1788–10*

	Total vessels entering port	Spanish vessels	Foreign vessels	% of foreign of ships	Sugar exports (cases)
1788	278	262	16	5.8	69,221
1789	—	—	—	—	69,127
1790	306	284	22	7.2	77,902
1791	374	290	84	22.5	71,675
1792	426	329	97	22.8	72,854
1793	417	308	109	26.1	87,470
1794	495	304	191	38.6	103,629
1795	423	253	170	40.2	70,437
1796	458	228	230	50.2	120,375
1797	630	136	494	78.4	—
1798	669	125	544	81.3	134,873
1799	837	131	706	84.3	165,602
1800	776	109	667	86.0	142,096
1801	993	104	889	89.5	159,841
1802	950	578	372	39.2	204,404
1803	785	544	241	30.7	158,073
1804	843	471	372	44.1	193,955
1805	804	77	727	90.4	174,543
1806	—	—	—	—	156,510
1807	—	—	—	—	181,272
1808	—	—	—	—	125,373
1809	1,079	437	642	59.5	230,843
1810	1,114	400	714	64.1	186,672

Source: 'Estado en que se manifesta el número de embarcaciones mercantes nacionales y extrangeras que han entrado en el Puerto de la Havana desde el año de 1788 hasta el próximo pasado de 1815 ...', annexe to Francisco de Arango y Parreño, 'Memoria interesante y documentada de ... Dn. Francisco Arango sobre comercio y la situación de la Ysla de Cuba ...', Madrid, 25 Aug. 1816, A.M.N., ms. 436, doc. 13.

Mexico, American ships began to trade with Veracruz from late 1798 'with all the activity proper to a mercantile nation, which believes the richest channel of the Globe to be open'.[12] It was reported that on 15 January 1799 alone, seven American ships lay at Veracruz with cargoes valued at 1,500,000 pesos, while a further score of shipments was expected.[13] A total of fifty-six neutral ships entered the port by the end of 1799, of which almost 80 per cent came direct from the United States.[14] Following the restoration of neutral trade after the peace of Amiens, a total of sixty-four neutrals entered Veracruz before the end of March 1807, and the latter year marked the peak of the trade, with a total of fifty-seven entries.[15] Fuelled by trade with Mexico, Cuba, and the other colonies, overall US commerce with Spanish America expanded rapidly during this period, in a boom from which there would be no lasting retreat: total exports rose from less than $1,400,000 in 1795 to more than $8,400,000 in 1801, and some $13,000,000 in 1806–07.[16] Thus the basis was laid for the outright US dominance of Hispanic markets in the Caribbean and adjacent regions which was finally achieved after mid-century, and at British expense.

The British viewed the explosive growth of American trade with the Spanish colonies with considerable disquiet. These concerns were manifest throughout the wars, but were perhaps expressed most forcefully in the influential work *War in Disguise*, attributed to James Stephen, which appeared in 1805.[17] Stephen argued that the two-legged trade which had developed between the Spanish colonies and the United States, and the United States and Europe, was permitting the colonies to flourish and making a mockery of the British blockade. This concern was principally strategic, but there was also a strong element of purely commercial rivalry: Stephen noted that 'nothing prevented the supplying of Spanish America with British manufactures, in British bottoms' during the first war except competition with neutrals.[18] Some British colonies now claimed serious damage to their Spanish trade due to American competition, with the Bahamas reported to be suffering seriously on this account in July 1800 and again in October 1806.[19] On a different tack, a House of Commons Committee reporting in 1807 on the broader commercial crisis in the British sugar colonies made repeated reference to the American role in transporting foreign colonial produce to Europe, so depriving the British West Indies of the markets on which they depended.[20]

Since the Seven Years War, the British had claimed a right to intercept neutrals trading with belligerents under conditions not permitted them during peace-time. As a result of concerns such as those expressed by Stephen, soon after the outbreak of war in 1796 this principle began to be applied to American neutral trade. The first British seizures of American shipping trading with the Spanish colonies were reported as early as October 1797, and seizures appear to have continued throughout 1798–1801.[21] Attacks on American shipping were stepped up from 1806 as Britain's commercial position in Europe threatened to deteriorate. Stephen argued that Britain should, after a period of warning, begin systematic attacks on neutral shipping trading with hostile powers.[22] The House of Commons report published in 1807 recommended that blockades be imposed on Havana, Martinique and Guadeloupe, with interception of neutral as well as belligerent shipping. Spiralling commercial warfare in Europe eventually led to the British Orders in Council of November 1807, which placed stringent and expensive controls on all neutral shipping trading with ports within the Napoleonic sphere. In response, the United States vigorously defended its rights as a neutral, and derided British hypocrisy in granting licences to its own vessels to trade with the Spanish colonies, while seeking to deny the same trade to non-belligerents.[23] British commercial aggression in the Caribbean thus fuelled the tensions which afterwards found issue in the declaration by the United States of a commercial embargo in December 1807.

These British concerns and attacks on American shipping notwithstanding, it is now clear that neutral trade itself became an important conduit for British commerce with Spanish America during these years: that neutrals, and especially Americans, with their unique degree of access to the Spanish colonies, acted as distributors of British goods there on an important scale. Little secondary work has been done on this subject, and the following pages do not aspire to present any comprehensive survey. The intention is rather to emphasise the significance of this commerce, as well as to offer summary description of some of the major ways in which it operated. The first section below presents an overview of the trade throughout the period of the wars and across the region, albeit with a focus on Mexico, Cuba, and Venezuela as the most important centres. There then follow sections on the special cases of the so-called 'Hope–Barings' and 'Gordon and Murphy' contracts, in which trade and remissions of bullion from the Spanish colonial treasuries were intertwined. Finally, the last section discusses the closely related subject of clandestine trade from Great Britain under cover of neutral trade permits – the so-called 'secret trade', which reached a peak between 1806 and the peace of 1808.

Neutral trade, 1797–1808: An Over-View

Allegations of extensive British infiltration of neutral trade began within weeks of its promulgation by the Spanish crown in November 1797. The bulk of the very first protest against the trade by the Cadiz merchant guild, the principal mercantile corporation involved in Spanish-American commerce, was devoted to the argument that the British would be the chief beneficiaries. The guild argued that the British would manipulate the trade to their advantage, intercepting neutrals carrying Spanish property while allowing those trading in British goods to pass the blockade freely.[24] Elsewhere, protests lodged by American officials at early British seizures of US shipping noted the folly of British actions when ships trading with the Spanish colonies from the United States were loaded 'principally with British manufactures'.[25] When neutral trade was revoked in April 1799, the United States Minister was assured 'that the purpose of the order was to keep out British trade' and that 'the prohibition was directed against British manufactures'.[26] A Spanish decree of July 1800 reiterating the revocation of neutral trade remarked upon the penetration of Mexican markets by foreign goods from the United States and Jamaica, and the benefit the British gained thereby.[27]

In Mexico, the richest market of all, neutral trade provoked fierce opposition among the majority of merchants excluded from its benefits. Monopoly mercantile interests soon came to date the advent of massive illicit trade in the viceroyalty to the outbreak of war in 1796 and the onset of neutral trade and *rescates* in the years immediately following. Some even went so far as to deny that contraband existed in Mexico before the war with the British:

> with just cause the trade of this place used to boast that all its business was circumscribed and limited to that which was licit and permitted by national laws … But since the year 1796 when because of the war with England … our ports were opened to neutrals … the criminal contraband became apparent.[28]

These merchants referred to contraband in the broadest sense: to the increase in direct British smuggling described in the preceding chapter, and to smuggling undertaken out of American ships alongside legitimate neutral trade. They referred to goods imported by Spaniards through the Licensed Trade, and to the contraband which went on at this time under cover of ransom permits. In a sense, their laments focused simply on the final loss of their own mercantile hegemony which the era of neutral trade brought about. This should caution us against taking their statements too literally. But it remains beyond question that neutral trade both marked and contributed to a striking increase in foreign penetration of Mexican markets during this period.

That the British were the chief beneficiaries of neutral trade with Mexico was a commonplace. The principal support for this notion was the fact that the United States had few domestic manufactures of its own, and must secure them from the British:

> The Anglo-American Colonies lacking factories, it is much to be believed that at first hand [the goods] belong to the enemy Power, their former Metropolis, with which they maintain the closest union …

> It must be supposed also that the goods, produce and effects belong wholly or in part to the British, because the Americans have no factories, but supply themselves from those of the former.[29]

The close physical and cultural similarities between British and Americans were seen as providing further proof of commercial collaboration, while making it harder to detect. The very fact that American neutral traders were almost alone in passing the British blockade was itself seen as evidence of collusion between the two nations; thus, the only neutral shipments to arrive safely were

> those prepared in the United States of North America, which are precisely those which provoke the strongest suspicion of collusion with the enemy, as is to be inferred from the intimate relationships which bind the European English and the Americans, their commercial treaties, their close and continual intercourse, their shared origins, their family connections, their identical language, clothes, usages, customs, and persons.[30]

Some commentators on neutral trade during the war of 1796–1802 sought to calculate the degree of British participation more precisely. Pedro Ajequiezcane, writing in the *Jornal Económico Mercantil de Veracruz*, estimated that during this period, 'of a hundred parts of what was imported, ninety, at least, belonged to foreigners, and much of it to enemies ... A great part of those cargoes were of British merchandise, and the rest manufactured in the North of Europe, by the allies or supporters of England'.[31] Others pointed to specific cases: 'in London an Insurance Policy to the value of £200,000 sterling has been posted on Produce to be shipped from Veracruz to North America, to be sent on to London ... This supports the belief that all, or most of the said Produce is British property'.[32] These allegations notwithstanding, the presence of unquestionably British goods in particular American cargoes has proved relatively hard to detect until after 1804.[33]

The controversy provoked by the onset of neutral trade in Mexico lost urgency for a number of years after 1800 as the revocation of neutral trade took effect and numbers of neutral vessels visiting the Mexican coasts declined. It revived with a vengeance from 1805, when Mexicans witnessed the effects of the post-war renewal of neutral trade and of the voyages made under the Hope–Barings and Gordon and Murphy contracts. As a new flood of American ships arrived at Mexican ports, and then even British warships and merchant vessels began to enter Veracruz direct from Britain and Jamaica, Mexican monopoly merchants were tempted to forget earlier woes and to postulate yet another stage in their economic marginalisation. The expert secretary of the Veracruz guild, José María Quirós, suggested that contraband 'was almost unknown until the year 1805 when the port was opened to neutral powers, and afterwards to the British ships'.[34] The Mexican guild later identified the renewal of neutral trade in 1804–05 as the middle stage in a three-part process which began with the first bout of neutral trade in 1797–99 and was capped by a decree of 1807 (discussed below) permitting re-exports of European goods from Havana.[35] Manuel Godoy, identified as responsible for the post-war renewal of neutral trade, bore the brunt of Mexican vitriol once safely out of power: 'He multiplied privileges for the direct navigation and trade of foreigners in the Ports of the Indies, and all America was filled with foreign goods preferable in quality and price to our manufactures... Eternal hate to the evil Godoy!'[36]

Mexican protests at neutral trade during the war of 1804–08 rehearsed the arguments of earlier years, perhaps now with enhanced concern for strategic considerations: 'The [British and Americans] mixing one with another, such that neither the sharpest eye nor the most extensive observation is capable of telling them apart, our enemies gain repeated opportunities of introducing themselves among the crews of American Ships in this Port, and acquiring knowledge and interesting news.'[37] Allegations of British penetration of American neutral trade found focus in one of the first vessels to arrive following the peace, the *Matchless*, dispatched to Veracruz in January 1806 by Robert Oliver of Baltimore under the auspices of the Hope–Barings contract. A 'great part' of the goods this ship brought were held to be 'notoriously British'.[38] What was more, they were mostly cottons: 'These Cotton textiles are those which produce greatest profits to England and if they are admitted among those fit for trade they will receive from our own hands an extraordinary assistance with which to sustain their unjust pretensions.'[39] Noting the serious potential consequences of permitting British cloth to enter and circulate freely, Mexican opponents of neutral trade argued that royal decrees of 1804–05 which allowed favoured American commercial houses to import 'any produce, goods and effects for trade without any exception' could not possibly have been intended to include cotton and other (principally British) textiles, which had always been strictly excluded. The Crown Attorney in Mexico City, citing a decree of September 1805 which banned 'the introduction of British effects and manufactures in the Dominions of Spain under any pretext', tended toward the conclusion that all imports of British goods should be prohibited, even when brought by merchants holding royal permits. But this argument was dismissed in Madrid with the frank acknowledgement that 'it is known that the Neutral Ships despatched under the auspices of the Royal Caja have transported great quantities of British effects and manufactures for which they were authorised by the Royal Order of 24 December [1804] and others which rule out any limitation'.[40] Allegations of American ships bringing British goods to Mexican ports persisted throughout the following years; just how well founded these claims were is best witnessed through the operations of the Hope–Barings consortium, discussed in the following section.

Much of the evidence for the penetration of neutral trade by British merchandise derives from interested critics (Spanish and Spanish-American merchant guilds, colonial officials), a fact which should urge caution with respect to the more extravagant claims made for it. Evidence of this kind is especially elusive for Cuba, where the Havana Consulado, as the representative of the most "modern"' of Spanish-American merchant communities, stood apart from most of its sister-corporations in actively supporting neutral trade.[41] Our evidence for neutral trade in Cuba often lies at one remove, for example in the protests formulated against a Cuban petition of July 1798 for a right to re-export European goods from Havana to Veracruz. This petition sought to exploit the great influx of goods to Cuba under neutral trade by securing an outlet for them in the leading Spanish-American market.[42] It prompted vigorous debate and criticism, much of which focused on British infiltration of neutral trade. The merchant guild at Cadiz protested that

the main riches will go to foreigners, and even to the very enemies of the Crown. All the goods the Havanans are able to export to New Spain, or almost all, they have because they have acquired them from Anglo-Americans, or because they proceed from prizes made from the British ... The former cannot be considered as other than purely British manufactures, since the Anglo-Americans have no other factories from which to supply themselves.[43]

The secretary of the guild of Veracruz argued that cutting supplies of gold and silver to Havana from his own port and Cartagena de Indias would deal a severe blow to the British, whose fleet in the Caribbean 'draws its subsistence from the trade they assist under the name of Americans'.[44] The Cuban petition of July 1798 fell victim to the general revocation of neutral trade in 1799, but ongoing pressure eventually secured a ruling dated 10 May 1807 which explicitly sanctioned re-exports of European goods from Havana to Veracruz.[45] To the fury of Mexican merchants, this re-export trade westwards across the Gulf of Mexico rapidly acquired significant dimensions: by 1808, European re-exports reaching Veracruz mainly from Havana were already worth almost 500,000 pesos.[46] Mexican and Spanish critics remained convinced that these goods were not the legitimate surplus of merchandise first imported from Spain, but goods imported illegally to Cuba, often under cover of neutral trade. The Consulado of Mexico wrote that the decree of May 1807 'built for clandestine trade a Royal Road, broad and safe', and that 'by these permits we see the Kingdom inundated with foreign goods of illicit trade'. Its counterpart in Veracruz insisted that 'most of the goods are brought from the foreign colonies'.[47] These statements remain simple allegations in the absence of corroborating evidence, though Ortiz de la Tabla has noted that re-exports from Havana and other ports, linked with neutral trade in the broader sense, permitted foreign goods to draw even with Spanish national products in all imports at Veracruz in the quarter-century after 1796, even before contraband is taken into account.[48]

As the preceding pages have suggested, a substantial majority of all British goods shipped to the Spanish colonies by Americans went as re-exports via the United States. There were also instances, however, of trade carried on by American merchants direct between the British and the Spanish colonies. Cuba provides the best evidence for such a trade, with the Havana port books indicating extensive commerce by US vessels entering directly from the British West Indies. Some 18 American ships entered Havana in this way in 1798; the corresponding figures for subsequent years were 42 ships in 1799, 30 in 1800, 55 in 1801, 52 in 1805, 48 in 1806, 89 in 1807, and 18 in 1808.[49] In 1805–07, American ships accounted for well over 90 per cent of all shipping entering Havana from the British colonies (the balance was made up by other neutral shipping and by occasional Spanish vessels).[50] Some US observers claimed that these ships were not American at all, but rather British ships trading under false papers. We have seen that these claims should be taken seriously;[51] but they clearly do not tell the whole story. The acting American Consul in Havana admitted in November 1798 that both 'American & Spanish Licensed vessels have been cleared out from the Custom House of Nassau, New Providence, for this port with Russia goods & oznaburghs'.[52] His successor protested at a Spanish measure whose ostensible motive was 'to prevent vessels of the United States from trading between this & English ports!'. And yet, he went on, 'not one, of the many that presented themselves from Jamaica or Providence, with or without cargoes, that wished it, but was admitted'.[53] It is impossible to identify what proportion of these ships was really American, and which were British smugglers in disguise. But it is sufficiently clear that US ships trading direct from British colonies provided an important vehicle articulating British trade with Havana during these years.

The American ships involved in this commerce operated out of a wide range of ports, from Portland in the north to Savannah in the south, although Boston, New York, Philadelphia and Charleston featured most prominently. These vessels came in to Havana from New Providence and principally from Jamaica, with Exuma in the Bahamas a distant third, and occasional entries from lesser ports. Among the consignatories for shipments in Cuba were several men with conspicuously Anglo-American surnames (Santiago Drake, Tomás Gimbal, Juan Reynolds), probably British or American merchants established in Havana. Cargoes – described only in general terms in the records – consisted of foodstuffs, sugar, rum, wooden boards, spares for plantation machinery, cloth, some miscellaneous manufactures, and slaves, while a significant proportion of ships ostensibly entered in ballast. The most curious commodity to feature in these cargoes was bullion, almost all in the form of unminted gold. Imports of gold were first apparent in 1801, and reached a peak of 141,000 pesos in 1807; the total sum imported exceeded 430,000 pesos by 1808.[54] This was essentially a Jamaican trade, with only the odd gold-bearing ship per year entering Havana from Grenada, Barbados, or elsewhere. The importation of bullion from British to Spanish colonies is an unexpected finding, and contradicts long-standing assumptions about the nature of Anglo-Spanish trade in the Caribbean. It is possible that these were imports from the United States on ships which merely passed via the British colonies en route to purchase agricultural produce in Cuba, though this seems unlikely. It may be that the gold was African, Brazilian, or even derived from the placer deposits of New Granada, imported by the British to Jamaica and exchanged from there for Spanish-American silver. But a confident explanation for what is a curious phenomenon remains elusive.

After Mexico and Cuba, Venezuela was probably the leading focus of neutral trade with the Spanish colonies. Much trade with neutrals in Venezuela was channelled via contracts granted to particular merchants, making the region something of a special case. Two of these merchants' contracts may be described briefly. In September 1799, a commercial contract was signed with the house of Robinson, Philips, and Corser of the Dutch island of Curaçao for the export of 40,000 cwt of tobacco then languishing in store. This contract was to run for three years, with four-fifths of the tobacco to be paid for in bullion or a wide range of foreign textiles, and the remainder in flour.[55] William Robinson was US consul in Curaçao, and with his partners also signed a contract to import 50,000 lb of gunpowder, payable in cacao at the leading port of La Guaira.[56] Most of the trade under-taken under these contracts used neutral shipping, and in the first half of 1802 no fewer than nine out of twenty-four foreign ships entering La Guaira came under orders from Robinson.[57] In November 1803, Robinson signed a new contract to import 1,500 slaves and flour to Venezuela, exporting tobacco and produce or mules in return.[58] Such contracts were every bit as open to abuse or to British infiltration as neutral trade in general. As the Venezuelan Captain-General observed, any contract with merchants based in Curaçao was suspect, since 'the Dutch and Danish Possessions are purely mercantile establishments peopled by all classes of people, and most of the capital is either British or maintains relations with them'.[59] The abundant imports made by Robinson and Co. in 1802 ensured that 'even the unhappiest of the common people wore nothing but muslins and cotton goods', typical British wares.[60] Of the nine vessels entering La Guaira early the same year, two came direct from Trinidad, and one from Curaçao, at that time occupied by the British. As we have already seen, in early 1805, Robinson negotiated with the British authorities for extensive trade with Grenada to be undertaken in neutral vessels, a project which was clearly designed to exploit his commer-cial privileges in Venezuela.[61]

In May 1803 a new Intendant at Caracas, Juan Vicente de Arce, prohib-ited all trade with neutrals and foreign colonies, citing the return to peace-time conditions and problems arising from the free trade in slaves decreed after 1789. Arce then proceeded to grant contracts comparable to that of Robinson to a select group of merchants, allegedly canalising trade into the hands of a small number of firms allied with him.[62] These contracts typically contemplated imports of tobacco, flour, naval supplies, plantation machinery and slaves from the United States or foreign colonies, and the export of local produce or bullion in return.[63] Such conditions were easily abused for contraband trade in British goods, and indeed several of these contracts sustained trade with the British. Perhaps most striking was the case of 'Jorge Federico Lenz', a British national who arrived in Venezuela to ransom a slave ship at the end of the first war. In July 1804, Lenz signed a contract with Arce to import several thousand slaves in foreign shipping and to export local tobacco in exchange, via Guayana. In the event, most of Lenz's early shipments were paid for in silver rather than tobacco, while he was also allowed to import flour on unusually generous terms. His contract provided the flimsiest cover for trade with the British; thus, all four Lenz vessels trading at La Guaira in 1805 came direct from Tortola, and it was rumoured that Lenz was in company with British merchants established in 'the deposit of contraband' of Trinidad.[64] Lenz's property was seized in reprisal after the return to war, but there are grounds for suspecting British involvement in several other contracts agreed at this time. Both Francisco González de Linares (contract dated February 1804) and Fernando Key Muñoz (March 1804) appear to have procured wares from the Anglo-Spanish house of

Murphy, based in St Thomas.[65] Reviewing these contracts, an exasperated Venezuelan Captain-General pondered the consequences

> if British ships, goods and effects are admitted, if precautions are not taken with Neutrals, who in these Colonies are always linked in interests and connections with the self-same British, and if by these and other means contraband, and the succour of the vassals of Great Britain is permitted.[66]

Although Americans were the greatest neutral traders in the Caribbean, it is important to stress that they were far from enjoying an empty field. On the one hand, a number of neutral European colonies continued to serve as major centres for trade between both neutrals and belligerents alike. Some sense of the magnitude of this trade may be gained by reference to probably the most significant example, that of St Thomas in the Danish Virgin Islands. We have already seen that St Thomas was seized by the British on two occasions during the wars, largely on account of its rich trade.[67] But even between these occupations, the island acted as a leading entrepôt for commerce between the British and Spanish. During the war of 1796–1802, St Thomas became a focus of the British slave trade with the Spanish colonies.[68] Still more strikingly, during that of 1804–08, one account stated that 'several million dollars worth of British manufactures' and from 50,000 to 60,000 barrels of provisions were exported via the island every year. A hundred Danish vessels were said to serve the Spanish trade, with from ten to twenty Spanish launches arriving daily and twenty large merchant vessels serving trade with Britain. In addition, 'near one million dollars in specie have been given in payment for British government Bills, sold here in one year, the greater part of which specie was introduced in the aforesaid small Spanish vessels'.[69]

On the eve of its capture by the British in late 1807, anxious merchants emphasised the 'immense amount' of British property then on hand in St Thomas, with annual exports 'principally calculated for the Spaniards' amounting 'to a sum almost incredible'.[70] The great fires which devastated the island in 1804 and again in 1806 destroyed an estimated 11,000,000 and 5,000,000 pesos' worth of merchandise respectively, of which 'the majority' was said to be British.[71] These accounts are impressionistic and possibly inflated, but we have already seen that registered British exports to St Thomas in 1807 totalled over £210,000 (of which some 87 per cent by value were cotton and linen textiles or manufactures).[72] By the latter year, 83 per cent of trade with foreign colonies at La Guaira in Venezuela was with St Thomas (77 of 93 consignments).[73] Nor was St Thomas the only neutral port of trade between British and Spaniards; Dutch Curaçao played an important role in neutral trade in British goods with Venezuela,[74] and St Bartholomew and St Eustatius also played comparable, though lesser, roles.

Americans also faced competition from the merchants of neutral states in Europe, principally from the northern countries and especially from Germany. These merchants traded in the Caribbean either via entrepôts, such as St Thomas or Curaçao or directly with the Spanish colonies, operating either under licence from the Spanish government or without permit. Commerce in British goods by European neutrals lies in even deeper shadow than that undertaken by Americans, although there is no reason to doubt that the trade was other than considerable. As early as December 1796 a former Spanish ambassador to London expressed concern at the flow of British merchandise through Hamburg to ports in Spain and Spanish America, and news of the onset of neutral trade was received with jubilation in the latter city and in Amsterdam.[75] In September 1797, another observer suggested that more than forty vessels were fitting out from Hamburg for St Thomas and thence for the Spanish colonies, while three or four ships headed directly for Havana to take advantage of the opening of that port by the local authorities. The discussion in Madrid which resulted from this report overtly addressed the risk of British penetration of this trade.[76] In mid-May 1799, four named vessels were stated to have left Hamburg for Veracruz and Havana, and the Spanish consul reiterated his suspicion that many of the cargoes consisted of British manufactures.[77] A London merchant, John Braddick, who undertook extensive trade with the Spanish colonies through European neutrals during these years, remarked in 1803 that

> on the arrival of a Neutral Vessel at the Spanish Colonies in South America … application was made to the Spanish Governor or Commandant of the Port at which the said ship arrived … who instantly winked at the Trade, on receiving a Bribe, though he well knew the nature of the Trade that was carried on, and that the Goods were British Manufacture, and always permitted a Return Cargo.

Braddick further claimed that return voyages were often made direct to London, rather than to the neutral port of origin.[78] Certainly, throughout the later stages of the Napoleonic wars, the British continued to regard neutral trade at Hamburg and the access of British goods there as objects of the first importance, their blockade of the Weser and Elbe rivers notwithstanding.

Finance and Neutral Trade: The Hope–Barings Contract

As noted in the opening paragraph to this chapter, neutral trade operated in most of the Spanish colonies throughout the period 1797–1808, with only a brief interruption during the Peace of Amiens (1802–04). Although this statement is accurate in general terms, in its particulars neutral trade operated in a rather different fashion after its re-establishment in 1804 than it had before 1802. During the first war, the trade operated under a general permission to any neutral merchant wishing to engage in it. From December 1804, by contrast, commerce was concentrated in the hands of a relatively small number of merchants expressly licensed by the crown; the Spanish decree re-establishing neutral trade mentioned eleven houses in Europe and the United States, though further firms were added subsequently.[79] This change made little difference to British trade with the colonies, since the neutral houses involved traded in the same range of goods as before, including many British manufactures. It may, however, have represented a significant shift in Spanish attitudes towards imperial trade. Jacques Barbier has explored this shift in a series of complex and perceptive articles; Barbier argues that during the first war the purpose of neutral trade had been 'above all economic', designed to maintain some level of Spanish Atlantic trade despite the British blockade. But from 1804, it ceased to bear any relation to the economic interests of the colonies, instead becoming 'narrowly financial' and designed 'solely to secure enough revenues to stave off bankruptcy'.[80] And this new purpose was articulated through a close link now established between neutral trade and massive transfers of bullion from the colonial treasuries to the mother country.

By far the most important neutral trade operations undertaken during the second war, and something of a case apart in the commercial history of these years, were those which became known as the 'Hope–Barings' and 'Gordon and Murphy' contracts. The Hope–Barings contract sustained probably the greater part both of neutral trade with Mexico as a whole, and of British penetration of it, and also provides a uniquely well-documented illustration of the way in which this trade operated. The Gordon and Murphy contract also prompted extensive commercial intercourse with Mexico, part of it direct from Jamaica, though its sphere of influence also extended as far as Havana and New Granada. Both contracts demonstrate most clearly the link between bullion remissions and commercial transactions posited for this period by Barbier; indeed, the driving motive behind both was the remission of bullion. The current and following sections of this chapter, then, present summary discussion of both contracts; it should be appreciated that both were too complex for full justice to be done them here.[81]

The origins of both the Hope–Barings and Gordon and Murphy contracts lay in agreements designed to secure the transfer to Spain of funds from the colonial treasuries, despite the British blockade of the Atlantic. These funds were destined principally to pay huge sums of money owing to France under the 'Treaty of Subsidies' of October 1803.[82] The architect of the first such agreement in 1804 was the French banker Gabriel Ouvrard, but by mid-1805 the business had passed to Hope & Co., the leading bank of the Netherlands and among the largest banks in the world.[83] By the same period, the basic features of what became the Hope–Barings scheme were already established, based on two key elements: first, Hope & Co. was to cash Spanish royal bills of exchange against the Mexican treasury and provide for transportation of the resulting funds to Europe. Secondly, and partly to facilitate these financial operations, it was to organise extensive trade with Mexico, to be undertaken in neutral shipping on its own account or by firms allied with it. To sustain both operations, Hope received bills on the Mexican treasury worth several million pesos, as well as large numbers of blank licences permitting voyages to the Spanish colonies in neutral vessels.[84] Hope & Co. was to charge relatively low commissions on both the bullion shipments and trade, but the real profits of the operation lay in the exchange rate applied to Spanish-American pesos delivered in Europe.[85] Strikingly, the bulk of the funds transferred from Mexico were to be the product not of regular royal income, but of the forced sale of clerical property in the viceroyalty – among the most controversial and divisive of all colonial policies of the period.[86] Also unusually, for reasons both of practicality and security, the whole of this business was to be realised not directly with Mexico, but routed via the United States of America.

The transactions proposed by Hope & Co. appeared highly objectionable in a British point of view, since the substantive profits from both the commercial and financial operations were ultimately to be paid to France to fulfil Spanish treaty obligations. Yet the risk of seizure of the neutral shipping to be employed made some degree of British collaboration indispensable. For negotiations with the British, Hope & Co. turned to Baring Brothers, the powerful London bank, to which it was linked by marriage.[87] Barings soon became the second major partner in these transactions, playing a vital role particularly in the receipt of incoming funds from the Americas. In negotiations with the government held throughout 1805, its principal goal was to secure licences protecting neutral vessels employed by Hope from seizure by British warships. In this it appears to have been unsuccessful; but in the broader sense, and some initial reservations on the part of Prime Minister William Pitt notwithstanding, the British consented to the scheme. Indeed, British collaboration with Hope–Barings ultimately went so far as to embrace the dispatch of a warship to collect funds directly from Veracruz, and even the purchase of Mexican bullion by the Bank of England, paid for with bills of exchange on Hope & Co.[88] British motives for actively colluding with Hope–Barings in this way are by no means immediately apparent;[89] imports of millions of pesos of Mexican bullion do not appear to offer a sufficient explanation, since the majority of the funds were destined for the French.[90] The most convincing explanation lies in the commercial dimension – in the prospect of 'a great vent' for British merchandise in the Spanish colonies, to be achieved on the back of the financial transactions. Certainly it was this prospect which Hope & Co. urged upon Barings, and through them on the government.[91]

With Hope & Co. in possession of both bills of exchange on the Mexican treasury and licences for neutral trade with the Spanish colonies, and with British consent to the scheme secured, all was in place for realisation of the contract. Hope appointed David Parish, a young merchant based in Hamburg, to supervise its operations in the United States. Parish was to organise extensive trade with Mexico in neutral vessels, partly in return for organising bullion remittances and partly to facilitate those operations. This trade was to be based upon the export of cargoes of manufactured goods and the import from Mexico of bullion and produce. Parish arrived in New York in January 1806, later establishing his headquarters in Philadelphia.[92] He employed two sub-agents to assist him: Vincent Nolte in New Orleans on the

Gulf of Mexico, and Armand de Lestapis, who settled in Veracruz under the assumed identity of Gabriel de Villanueva.[93] Parish organised some trade with Mexico out of New Orleans under the supervision of Vincent Nolte, but he lacked both the capital and the local expertise required to operate independently on the scale required. He thus came to rely mainly upon agreements with local firms, which were of two types: either Parish sold his neutral licences outright to interested merchants, or he surrendered the licences in return for a commission on cargoes and a share of net profits on sales.[94] All of the shipments despatched by merchants working with Parish were consigned to Villanueva in Veracruz, who thus took receipt of incoming cargoes, arranged for the sale of merchandise locally, and oversaw the dispatch of vessels on the return voyage to the United States.[95] As will be seen, Villanueva and his assistants handled the reception of some seventy vessels on behalf of Parish and Hope–Barings over the course of the following three years.

Parish initially found it difficult to agree with local merchants over the disposal of his neutral trade licences. There were a number of reasons for this, including uncertainty as to the character or validity of the documents, but the main cause was probably mercantile competition in trade with Veracruz. When Parish attempted to launch trade with Veracruz on behalf of Hope–Barings in early 1806, he found that other merchant houses had already initiated the same trade under the decree of December 1804 or later permits.[96] Prominent among these was John Craig of Philadelphia, who in partnership with Robert Oliver of Baltimore had already sent six shipments to Mexico by March 1806.[97] Parish's first instinct when faced with this problem was to appeal to the Spanish minister in the United States to quash his rivals' trade, but when this tactic failed he adopted the alternative strategy of joining forces with them. Thus, Parish signed a contract with Robert Oliver in early March under which he surrendered the bulk of his commercial licences in return for a commission of 2½ per cent on outward cargoes and a third of net profits from sales in Mexico.[98] As a result, Robert Oliver came to undertake the majority of all trade with Mexico launched from the United States on behalf of Hope–Barings. It controlled a large slice of the total overseas trade of Veracruz: the Olivers dispatched at least thirty-eight shipments to Mexico during the period 1806–08, with a total sales value running as high as $3,000,000 during the first two of these years alone.[99] Oliver accounted for no less than 40 per cent of all trade between the United States and Veracruz in the same biennium.[100] Finally, chiefly due to the activities of the Olivers, during this brief period, Baltimore became the leading centre for American trade with Mexico, dispatching and receiving more merchant vessels than any other port in the United States.[101]

The trade undertaken by the Olivers in Veracruz cannot be distinguished from that of other neutral merchants, whose value and broad characteristics are discussed briefly below. It is worthwhile exploring the presence of British merchandise among the cargoes shipped by the Olivers, however. In July

1806, the Olivers received a list of recommended merchandise forwarded by Villanueva which consisted largely of British goods: 'Echeverría had recommended assortments of such "English Goods" as fancy chintz, callicoes, corded dimity, cambrick dimity, and black velvets.'[102] Had these recommendations been followed, much of Robert Oliver's exports to Veracruz might have consisted of British goods. In the event, the Olivers found it difficult to obtain supplies of these goods in the quantities required. One problem was that British goods imported for consumption in the United States were different from those required for the Mexican market, making it difficult to source the Mexican cargoes locally. Another was that the Olivers were reluctant to import extensively from Britain themselves, lest unforeseen events put an end to their Mexican trade, leaving them with large stocks of goods on hand. Eventually, other merchants in Baltimore imported the goods required from Britain, under a guarantee from the Olivers to purchase them. By 5 March 1807, Robert Oliver had bought dry goods from these houses to the value of $100,000; in February 1808, the firm had stock on hand, apparently from the same source, worth some $293,000.[103] It appears that ultimately, the bulk of all cargoes was made up of British and German textiles, supplemented by goods from the East Indies and other regions.[104] The share of British manufactures in the whole thus cannot be known with any precision, although Robert Oliver claimed that his firm had exported 'upwards of Two Millions of Dollars [c. £450,000] worth of British Manufactures' to Mexico in the twelve months to September 1807 alone.[105] The returns both from these commercial operations and from the cashing of treasury bills in Veracruz were remitted from the United States to Europe not as bullion, but converted into staple articles of North American trade (sugar, coffee, cotton, tobacco, or rice). Rather than purchase these commodities himself, Parish advanced large sums of money to other US merchants who used them to buy cargoes of the appropriate goods, later repaying the loans to Hope & Co. or Baring Brothers out of proceeds of sales.[106]

The second aspect to Parish's responsibilities in the United States – indeed, almost certainly the first in his employers' priorities – was the cashing of Spanish bills in Mexico and remission of the resulting funds to Europe. It will be recalled that these funds were principally the product of the expropriation of Mexican Church wealth under a controversial decree of December 1804. Shipment of the funds was particularly problematic, since they remained the property of the Spanish crown and were vulnerable to seizure by the Royal Navy. Hope–Barings thus employed three main methods for transferring the funds to the United States and Europe: first, Robert Oliver shipped some 1,450,000 pesos of royal bullion alongside its commercial shipments, ostensibly as its own property and thus immune from seizure.[107] Second, Parish dispatched vessels to Veracruz in ballast exclusively to collect the funds remitted by Villanueva. These vessels were fast schooners, built to Parish's own specification so as to outrun British warships,[108] and altogether shipped perhaps as much as a further 5,000,000 pesos in royal bullion from Veracruz to the United States.[109] Lastly, at Sir Francis Baring's request, in May 1807 the British frigate *Diana* was despatched directly to Veracruz to collect bullion on behalf of the consortium. The ship arrived in June with Sir Charles Baring, a junior member of the banking dynasty, aboard as supercargo.[110] Within a fortnight, it took on board some 3,679,835 pesos, or £828,792 sterling – a sum which made the *Diana* the largest single risk covered by Lloyds of London during the Napoleonic wars.[111] The exportation of such a huge sum from a hostile colony in a British warship represents perhaps the most extraordinary feature of the Hope–Barings contract as a whole, the more so since the final destination of the bulk of the funds was France. But then, as will be seen shortly, the *Diana* was not the first British warship to take off royal funds from Veracruz during the war, nor would it be the last.[112]

Hope–Barings' operations in the Americas were run down in early 1808, and ceased altogether by the middle of the same year. Trading conditions had become increasingly difficult since late 1807, in part due simply to ever more cut-throat commercial competition in Veracruz, but partly also to the increasingly aggressive stance taken by the Royal Navy.[113] The death-blow to the contract came with the political revolution in Spain of May 1808, which resulted in the refusal of the authorities in the colonies to cash any further treasury bills issued by the former administration.[114] Assessing the precise scale of the commercial operations undertaken by Hope–Barings between 1806 and 1808 is problematic, largely because the value of shipments cannot be distinguished from the value of all neutral trade in Mexico during the same period. All that can be noted is that the consortium dispatched some seventy vessels to Veracruz in all, with cargoes shipped by the Olivers in 1806–07 alone worth some $3,000,000.[115] Assessing the value of the treasury drafts cashed by Hope–Barings is also challenging, given both the complexity of the operations and contradictions in the sources. The aggregate of the sums cited in the preceding paragraph indicates a total of some 10,130,000 pesos, or approximately £2,280,000 sterling, although other studies have put the figure as high as 12,500,000 pesos *exclusive* of the treasure taken on board the *Diana*.[116] An oft-cited figure of total bullion exports from Veracruz under Parish's supervision of 33,000,000 pesos seems certain to be an over-estimate, even supposing that it embraces both royal bullion and commercial profits.[117] Hope–Barings's profits on these operations were estimated at $3,828,390, or £862,250 sterling, although this figure appears to cover only part of the contract and in my view is likely to be an under-estimate.[118] Parish's personal share of these profits amounted to around $1,000,000; the most reliable estimate of the profits made by Robert Oliver (which were distinct from the earnings of the consortium) is $775,000 on all trade with Veracruz in 1805–08.[119]

What was the total value of the trade in British goods by Americans and other neutrals? Over the period 1805–08, imports by neutrals at Veracruz were worth 19,202,918 pesos (c. £4,325,000), while exports by neutrals were worth 31,627,890 pesos (c. £7,123,000), of which bullion accounted for over 88 per cent. In 1807 alone, imports by neutrals were worth 10,134,000 pesos (c. £2,282,000), while exports were worth some 21,400,000 pesos (c. £4,820,000).[120] The British share in these figures cannot be known with any accuracy, but in the latter year the cotton manufactures in which Britain excelled accounted for almost 63 per cent of total imports (over 6,350,000 pesos). In evidence given at a British Parliamentary enquiry in 1812, the banker and High Bailiff of Birmingham, Thomas Atwood, suggested that before the imposition of the American commercial embargo in December 1807, perhaps one-fifth of all British manufactures exported to the United States were re-exported from thence, in many cases to the Spanish colonies.[121] Total British exports to the United States in 1807 were worth some £7,500,000 at official values, making Atwood's estimate worth some £1,500,000;[122] and indeed, Kirkman Finlay, another witness and an eminent Glasgow merchant with establishments in New Orleans and the Bahamas, estimated the total value of British manufactured re-exports from the United States to Spanish America during the same period at 'a great deal more' than £1,000,000 sterling per annum.[123] Unsatisfactorily vague testimony, perhaps, but it lends credence to the still more nebulous allegations of Mexican and Spanish critics of neutral trade as it operated in Spanish-American ports. And it is worth noting that after the commercial disruption and conflicts of the period 1808–12, Americans resumed this intermediary role on an even greater scale. A decade after Atwood and Finlay's testimony, British consular officials in Spanish America complained that British manu-factures re-exported from the United States actually undersold direct exports from the home country. By the mid-1820s, 'the Atlantic and gulf ports of the United States supplied … a considerable proportion of the British manufac-tures consumed in Mexico and Colombia'.[124]

The Gordon and Murphy Contract

Standing somewhere between the Hope–Barings affair and the 'secret trade' (discussed in the following section), and running during virtually the same period, was the contract held by the house of Gordon and Murphy. The agreements signed by Gordon and Murphy with the British and Spanish governments in 1806 have been called 'perhaps … the most important of the era granted to private individuals, and without question the most remarkable for New Spain'.[125] The Murphys were an Irish Catholic family which settled in Andalusia in the eighteenth century and entered the wine trade to Britain. Thomas (or Tomás) Murphy moved to Mexico around 1790, where he was joined by his brother Matthew Lawrence (or Mateo Lorenzo). Thomas became one of the leading merchants in Veracruz, even serving for several years as consul in the merchant guild founded there in 1795.[126] He cultivated friendships with dignitaries including Viceroy Revillagigedo (1789–94) and Manuel Godoy, and was related by marriage to Viceroy Azanza

(1798–1800).[127] We have seen that he was widely suspected of having exploited the latter relationship to gain access to the *rescate* trade from 1798 onwards,[128] and he was also among the principal merchants involved in neutral trade with Mexico during the first Anglo-Spanish war. The house of Gordon and Murphy was founded in London around 1802 by John Murphy, another brother, and William Gordon, a British MP and nephew to James Duff, the long-serving British consul in Cadiz.[129] Its commercial network eventually spread not only to Cadiz and Veracruz, but also to Havana and St Thomas, New York, Boston and New Orleans, Lisbon, Malaga, Hamburg and Copenhagen. By exploiting this network, and partly as a result of the operations described in these pages, the firm rapidly became among the largest in London, employing some 360 clerks and with profits estimated in 1811 at £237,000 sterling, on earnings of £7,000,000.[130]

Gordon and Murphy later claimed that the initiative behind their American contract originated with the Spanish government through an approach to John Murphy in 1805.[131] Later the same year, a Spaniard named Saratea arrived in London to negotiate via Gordon and Murphy for licences for exports to Spanish America, against the promise of Spanish permits for imports of Spanish-American bullion to Britain.[132] In December 1805, the merchants signed a draft contract with the Treasury which gave a clear indication as to the nature of their plans. This contract bound Gordon and Murphy to procure $10,000,000 in Spanish-American bullion and to deliver this sum either to the Bank of England or the Governor of Jamaica within fifteen months, at a stipulated rate. To facilitate this operation, the Lords of the Treasury undertook to supply them with licences protecting any vessels employed from seizure. They were also permitted to use Spanish vessels to trade between Jamaica and the Spanish colonies on business relating to the contract.[133] This draft agreement was signed jointly with the house of Reid, Irving & Co., who became junior partners in the scheme.[134] A formal contract between the partners and the Treasury was then signed on 27 March 1806. The precise circumstances remain obscure, but this contract was agreed soon after the extension of the 'secret trade' to the Caribbean (as discussed below) and it seems likely that pressure from Gordon and Murphy proved crucial in the development of that trade.[135] The formal contract closely mirrored its draft predecessor, committing the firm to 'bringing to this Country 10,000,000 of Dollars from Spanish America'.[136] These events were profoundly alarming to Hope–Barings, engaged in its own discussions with government regarding large-scale imports of Spanish-American bullion; and indeed, the following years were marked by strong competition, but also considerable co-operation, between the two concerns.[137]

Their contract with the British in hand, Gordon and Murphy next signed dual accords with the Spanish government, dated 8 and 18 May 1806. The terms of these contracts were set out by Minister of Finance Miguel Cayetano Soler in an order to the Viceroy of Mexico the next day.[138] Gordon and Murphy were to organise extensive voyages to Veracruz in neutral vessels from Europe and North America, for which they must procure licences from the British government. One-third of the outward cargoes for these expeditions was to be reserved for goods shipped on royal Spanish account, including mercury for the silver mines and paper for the royal tobacco factory. One-quarter of return cargoes was similarly reserved for royal property: 'Soconusco cacao, cochineal, indigo and any other produce'. All of this property was to be 'neutralised', that is to say, made to appear the property of neutral merchant houses, although it belonged to the crown of Spain. The remainder of outward cargoes might be made up of 'every kind of goods, produce and effects, without any exception whatever', for the benefit of Gordon and Murphy and Reid, Irving, with returns to consist of the 'money, produce and products' of Mexico. In addition to these commercial operations, Gordon and Murphy were to organise a monthly mail service in Spanish shipping between Jamaica and Veracruz, Cartagena de Indias, and Havana, and a similar service in neutral vessels between Lisbon and Veracruz and Havana. This service was to carry royal Spanish correspondence as well as the merchants' own, with the mail forwarded to London and thence to Spain, and must also be protected by British licence. The mail ships might carry any goods whatsoever for sale in Veracruz, giving them a powerful commercial potential. Finally, 'in compensation for these services', Gordon and Murphy might export from Veracruz and Cartagena up to 10,000,000 pesos fuertes free of all duties, to be paid out of royal revenues. These revenues were to draw principally upon funds belonging to the *Real Caja de Consolidación*, the Spanish state corporation which received and distributed income resulting from the forced sale of clerical property and which had also funded the bulk of the bullion shipped by Hope–Barings.

On 5 June, Gordon and Murphy duly applied to the Lords of Trade for ten licences for neutral vessels to be loaded in any Spanish port and for any Spanish colony, carrying both British and Spanish manufactures, and with outward and return voyages to be made either directly or indirectly. These licences were granted on 6 June, 'without mention of whether the cargoes should be British, Neutral, or otherwise', although with the restriction that cargoes must be the property of Gordon and Murphy or of other British or neutral merchants, and that return voyages must be made to British or British colonial ports.[139] Lord Auckland, President of the Board of Trade, had to convince Gordon and Murphy that the shipping must be neutral rather than Spanish, and that British manufactures must make up a proportion of cargoes;[140] and indeed, the subsequent history of the contract became a tug of war between the merchants and the government, in which the former sought ever more favourable conditions. In October 1806, Gordon and Murphy stated that a further ten licences were required to bring the full $10,000,000 in bullion from Spanish America, and five such permits were granted by 8 December. On 22 January 1807, they contrived to have ten of the licences explicitly endorsed for the carriage 'in the whole or in part [of] Spanish property' – a quite exceptional concession. This and other conditions caused the King's Advocate considerable hand-wringing over the ensuing weeks, since (as he remarked) as they now stood the licences did 'not require much less ensure the Conveyance of a single Bale of British Manufacture'.[141] In the summer of 1807, Gordon and Murphy applied for a further five licences on the grounds that a similar number of their vessels had been seized by British cruisers, their permits notwithstanding, or lost at sea; these were granted by 29 October.[142] Finally, although the principal focus in these pages is upon Gordon and Murphy's trade with the Caribbean, they also sent expeditions to the River Plate in 1806–07; it is unclear whether these were an offshoot of their contract, or constituted distinct commercial ventures.[143]

The British and Spanish each had their own motives for consenting to these highly unorthodox transactions. In the case of the British, this motive is fairly clear: it was to obtain a large supply of silver coin for the purposes of government, in the darkening days of early 1806. Bullion appears to have weighed more heavily than trade in British agreement to the Gordon and Murphy contract, even if ultimately it also brought significant commercial benefits.[144] The Spanish case is rather more complex: Minister Soler's letter to the Mexican viceroy in May 1806 emphasised Gordon and Murphy's role in transporting mercury, tobacco paper and other royal property to Mexico, and bringing colonial produce in return. This emphasis should perhaps be taken at face value, given the fundamental role played by mercury as a factor in silver production at Mexican mines, or by the tobacco monopoly as a source of royal income, with the interruption of supplies of both during the war.[145] Soler also dwelt on the role of the Gordon and Murphy contract in securing regular communications with the colonies, through the mail services to be established between Jamaica and Lisbon and Veracruz, Havana, and Cartagena de Indias. The importance of such communications needs hardly be stressed, although it renders British consent to this aspect the more surprising. Lastly, with regard to the exportation from Mexico of $10,000,000 in bullion, Soler's letter is cast in peculiar terms, as though this was merely a subsidiary aspect of the contract. This surely cannot have been the case: these funds, even after a heavy discount in favour of Gordon and Murphy, were to be paid directly to the *Consolidación* fund in Spain. In contrast to the Hope–Barings scheme, then, the Spanish government itself, rather than the French, was to be the beneficiary of this sum of money – no minor incentive to consent to the affair as a whole.[146]

The first Gordon and Murphy vessels reached Mexico in December 1806, and included the American frigate *Eliza and Ana* and a mail boat from Jamaica. Most neutral vessels employed subsequently were chartered in the United States, Portugal, or Hamburg, while all cargoes were consigned to Thomas Murphy or to fellow agents in Veracruz.[147] Also reaching Mexico in December 1806 was the British frigate *Resistance*, which took off a first large shipment of bullion, the product of bills of exchange presented earlier by Murphy.[148] Over the duration of the contract, all such bullion was promptly sold by Gordon and Murphy to the British authorities at pre-agreed rates, either in Jamaica or London, and then paid for with bills of exchange to the Spanish *Consolidación* fund.[149] The British came to doubt the value of these transactions; as early as June 1806, Lord Grenville hoped to reduce imports by Gordon and Murphy from $10,000,000 to $2,000,000, having received 'an offer of dollars on much better terms' (almost certainly from Hope–Barings).[150] It was later said of Thomas Murphy that 'there is little confidence in his House and his character is not at all reputable, many complained of being deceived by him during the war'.[151] The Spaniards found a great deal more to complain at; the contract was later categorised as 'a very serious, thorny, and complicated business', with Gordon and Murphy accused of failing to devote sufficient cargo space to merchandise on royal account, and importing only half the stipulated quantities of mercury and paper. By the conclusion of the contract, Gordon and Murphy themselves admitted to owing the Spanish Treasury 14,000,000 *reales* in taxes.[152] After the Peace of July 1808, two of their ships were rejected at Veracruz by the colonial authorities. But they then secured further commercial privileges by way of compensation, and in 1810 the British government contracted with the Murphys for a further supply of Mexican bullion. The brothers' involvement in Mexico endured throughout the Independence period and beyond.[153]

Two features of Gordon and Murphy's American affairs stand out above all others. The first was the intercourse undertaken between Jamaica and Veracruz in mail boats. Carlos Marichal suggests that a mail boat left Kingston for Mexico almost every month from mid-1806 until early 1808, and registers for many of these voyages are preserved in Mexican archives.[154] Carriage of mail apart, these vessels were employed to develop an extensive trade direct between the British and Spanish colonial ports. This trade, in Spanish vessels and under licence, to all intents and purposes formed simply another aspect of the Licensed Trade at large, albeit an economically important one. The difference was that the mail boats enjoyed the full sanction of the Spanish crown, and indeed worked partly on its behalf, making this wartime trade between British and Spanish colonies all the more remarkable. Arguably more extraordinary still was the large-scale exportation of bullion from Veracruz in British warships. We have already seen that in June 1807 the frigate *Diana* took off some 3,679,835 pesos from Veracruz on behalf of the Hope–Barings consortium. But the first such voyage had been undertaken on behalf of Gordon and Murphy in the dying days of 1806, when the *Resistance* took off 3,100,000 pesos (c. £698,000). By the peace of July 1808, five warships had exported a total of 7,651,641 pesos on behalf of the firm, equivalent to some £1,723,343 sterling (see Table 6.2).[155] The Mexicans could scarcely be unaware of either of these exceptional phenomena, and viewed both with understandable outrage. The Secretary of the merchant guild of Veracruz later recalled how its members 'watched the arrival … with notable frequency of ships with the name of mail boats from Jamaica bringing

Table 6.2 *Exports of bullion from Veracruz in British warships,*
Dec. 1806–Mar. 1808

Date of sailing	Name of vessel	Sum exported (pesos)	Contract
29 Dec. 1806	*Resistance*	3,100,000	Gordon and Murphy
20 June 1807	*Diana*	3,679,835	Hope-Barings
20 Aug. 1807	*Thames*	2,000,000	Gordon and Murphy
29 Oct. 1807	*Veteran*	551,641	Gordon and Murphy
3 Feb. 1808	*Adamant / Diamond*	1,000,000	Gordon and Murphy
21 Mar. 1808	*Topaz*	1,000,000	Gordon and Murphy
Total		11,331,476 (c. £2,552,134)	

Source: Joseph María Quirós, 'Nota de las partidas embarcadas por las Casas de Comercio de Dn. José Gabriel de Villanueva, y Dn. Tomás Murphy, en plata y frutos ...', Veracruz, 7 May 1808, A.G.N.M., Consulado, vol. 113, exp. 7, f. 220–v; Marichal, *La bancarrota del virreinato*, p. 240, table VI.2.

Note: This table covers all shipments in British warships occurring before the peace of July 1808. The total sum exported was much greater than appears here (it exceeded £4,000,000), due to exports by Hope-Barings which were routed via the United States.

every class of goods, and how ships of the royal British navy came to our coasts to take on millions in silver coin'.[156] This official further lamented 'the exports of silver and valuable produce made in all these ships for countries then enemies, and by those of the royal British navy'.[157] The guild itself went further, calling the Gordon and Murphy contracts 'abominable, treacherous, and criminal permits, granted in the moments of madness'.[158]

Jiménez Codinach suggests that Gordon and Murphy dispatched a total of 38 vessels to Veracruz in 1806–08. Twenty of these sailed from Europe or North America (13 from Spain and 7 from neutral ports in Portugal, Germany, and the United States), while a further 18 traded directly from Jamaica.[159] Mail boat shipments from Veracruz to Jamaica in 1806–08 may have numbered as many as 25, although this figure possibly includes voyages for Europe which merely touched at Jamaica.[160] Whatever the precise number, the trade sustained by means of these shipments was clearly rich. The total value of the 38 shipments indicated by Jiménez was some 9,260,923 pesos, or almost £2,100,000. The value of exports from Veracruz to Jamaica in mail boats recorded by Marichal was 4,340,877 pesos, or almost £1,000,000 (of which 45 per cent was in bullion and the remainder in produce). Impressively, the register of a single mail boat which entered Veracruz from Jamaica on 5 October 1807 indicates a cargo worth almost 4,200,000 pesos, or some £950,000 sterling.[161] The profits accruing from these shipments are not known, although a furious Veracruz merchant guild estimated Gordon and Murphy's profits at 'two or three million pesos' on sales it calculated (apparently conservatively) at 6,000,000 pesos.[162] The bullion transactions, too, yielded large profits for the firm: it purchased silver from the Spanish government at 885 pesos to the thousand, a discount of 11.5 per cent. It then sold on to the British at a considerable premium, according to one report selling as high as 51 pence per peso.[163]

Beyond the immediate profits, assessing the implications of these transactions for British trade with Spanish America is problematic. Gordon and Murphy's contract explicitly reserved one-third of cargo space in outward voyages for Spanish royal property, especially mercury and stamped paper. It has been suggested that, in contrast to rivals such as Hope–Barings, the cargoes dispatched by Gordon and Murphy included a 'high proportion' of Spanish wares, including Galician hats, Catalan textiles, Valencian silks, and alcohol.[164] Certainly, Gordon and Murphy's British licences quite exceptionally permitted them to carry Spanish property. Nevertheless, the few scholars who have discussed this issue tend to agree that in the event, the remaining two-thirds of cargo space was loaded entirely or principally with British manufactures.[165] Indeed, a Spanish report later accused Gordon and Murphy of failing even to reserve a third of outward cargoes for Spanish goods as stipulated, among other misdemeanours.[166] Meanwhile, in the mail boats dispatched directly from Jamaica 'the predominance of British textiles was notorious'.[167] The rich cargo of the mail boat which entered Veracruz in October 1807, for example, consisted of two-thirds 'cotton textiles, foreign contraband' – almost certainly British goods. It was also alleged that the firm substituted full-size merchant vessels for mail boats, converting neutral or Spanish commerce into outright British trade. We again find ourselves in the realm of speculation, but given a tentative total valuation of trade by mail boats with Jamaica of around £1,000,000, and of all exports in Gordon and Murphy expeditions of close to £2,100,000, it seems perfectly possible that the contract generated sales of British manufactures in the Mexican market alone in excess of £1,000,000 sterling. This sum is not, of course, to be taken in isolation, but rather went to swell the value of the Spanish licensed trade at Jamaica, of trade in British goods by neutrals, and of the 'secret trade'.

The 'Secret Trade': British Trade under Neutral Permit, 1805–08

The current and the past two chapters have explored the different ways in which British trade with the Spanish colonies was sustained after 1796, even in the context of a long war with Spain. Whether by means of trade by Spaniards under licence at the free ports, British smuggling in the Spanish colonies, or the sale of British goods by merchants belonging to neutral states, British trade with the region flourished throughout these years. Despite this rapid growth, however, there were some merchants – particularly those without experience or contacts in West Indian commerce, or who traded mainly via Cadiz and other Spanish ports before the war – to whom none of these routes was satisfactory. As a result, from shortly after the outbreak of the wars, British firms applied to the government for permission to trade with Spanish America on their own account in neutral shipping, either directly from Britain, or via Spain or third countries. These merchants thus sought to exploit the opening offered by neutral trade directly, organising their own commercial expeditions rather than selling cargoes outright in the United States or Europe for onward shipment. To do so, they had first to acquire neutral trade licences from the Spanish crown, which they did either by purchasing licences already granted to Spanish merchants or royal favourites, or through payment of a bribe. A good example of such a scheme is that proposed in 1798 by the house of Thelusson Brothers on the basis of an agreement with Francisco de Bustamante and Co. of Cadiz. Thelusson Brothers sought permission to send a neutral vessel from Cadiz to Veracruz with a cargo consisting 'chiefly of German and other linens'. This and a second neutral ship would then bring back from Mexico a cargo consisting of up to 2,000 bags of cochineal and a small amount of logwood and cotton, all to be shipped direct to a British port.[168] The house of Bird, Savage and Bird similarly sought a licence to trade in neutral vessels with the Spanish colonies at this time, apparently in part to recover debts owing from the region.[169] The total number of such applications during these years is unknown, though they may have been quite numerous.[170]

Throughout the war of 1796–1802 and until 1805, the British government remained resolutely opposed to the mode of trade proposed by these merchants, and their applications were uniformly rejected. This reticence sprang partly from concerns as to the legality of permitting direct trade with the Spanish colonies; thus, the Earl of Liverpool commented that 'nothing less than an Act of Parliament can further open this trade, or give it a greater extension'. It was also felt that there were 'no sufficient means of ensuring the due execution of the conditions under which such a licence might be granted', such that the trade might easily be abused. Interestingly, forty years after the establishment of the free ports, the government's attitude also reflected a firm conviction of the benefits of the free port system and its sufficiency to sustain British trade with the Spanish colonies. Liverpool rejected Bird, Savage and Bird's application partly on the grounds that they could perfectly well undertake the trade they desired via the Spanish Licensed Trade.[171] Another merchant was informed that 'with respect to the trade with South America there could be no doubt but that where it could be carried on thro' the Free Ports, it would be undoubtedly better that it should be so carried on'.[172] Even Sir Frances Baring, on the very eve of his negotiations with the government in support of Hope & Co.'s operations via the United States, observed 'that the Free Port Trade in the West Indies should be encouraged by every possible means, as upon the whole the most advantageous'.[173]

These reservations notwithstanding, under the impact of ongoing mercantile pressure, on 17 June 1805 the attitude of the government shifted, and the first licences for British merchants to trade with the Spanish colonies under neutral permit were granted. At this stage, the protection of the free ports was yet to be abandoned, and the new trade was limited to the River Plate, Chile, and Peru (regions not in direct competition with them): 'Licences should be granted to neutral vessels to trade to Rio de la Plata and the parts adjacent, and to the ports of the western coast of South America ... such licences to be granted to British subjects, and to protect neutral, as well as British property.'[174] Several of these licences were granted to British businesses with interests in Cadiz which needed a vent for stocks accumulated there before the renewal of hostilities. Such was the case with among the best documented of these ventures, the one mounted to Lima in the *Hermosa Mexicana* by Anthony Gibbs. Gibbs's licence was among the earliest of those granted (December 1805), and was unusual in permitting him to employ a Spanish rather than a neutral or disguised British vessel. He loaded property worth at least £15,000 in this ship, which finally sailed a year after the granting of the licence. The voyage was a successful one in commercial terms, though Gibbs saw relatively few of the profits due to prior indebtedness and apparent sharp practice by the Spaniard who fronted for him.[175]

Trading expeditions such as this were of questionable legality, and indeed the commerce launched from June 1805 under government licence and generally under neutral permit was sometimes referred to informally as the 'secret trade'. It was anathema to the naval officers charged with enforcing the Spanish blockade, who were forced to look on passively as merchant vessels entered or left enemy ports. Nelson himself, on the Cadiz blockade, wished that 'ministers at home would only stop the abuse of granting licenses for British vessels to enter the blockaded ports'.[176] The Navy particularly objected to the licensing of Spanish vessels for use by British merchants, as in the case of Gibbs; Vice-Admiral Lord Collingwood wrote in late 1806,

> A ship sailed yesterday from Cadiz for Lima with British goods, having a passport from the King. The Captain came to me to shew his pass, and request a convoy to see him clear of the French privateers, which he understood were looking out for him. What an odd war this is! A Spanish ship coming to the English fleet to seek protection from the depredations of their great ally![177]

Naval complaints at the trade persisted throughout its duration.[178] Nevertheless, in early 1806, the government agreed to grant licences on a still wider scale. On 21 February, the Privy Council reviewed a petition from the merchant John Turnbull 'that the directions contained in their Lordships' Minute of the 17th June last, may be extended to the port of La Vera Cruz'. Both Gordon and Murphy and John Taylor (of whom more below) made similar requests at the same session. The Council ruled that these licences be granted, and a week later confirmed those of Turnbull and Gordon and Murphy.[179] The extension of the 'secret trade' to the Caribbean – to Veracruz, Caracas and Havana as well as the River Plate, Chile, and Peru – thus dates from February 1806. It reflected the new thinking of a new ministry, that of 'All the Talents' formed after the death of Pitt in January. It was the product of still greater pressure from merchants, as well as of growing conviction as to the advantages to be gained. Lord Auckland now remarked that 'an exchange of British manufactures for dying woods, cochineal, and dollars, is so peculiarly expedient in our actual circumstances',[180] while Lord Grenville added that 'in a commercial point of view, this question does not admit of doubt'. The shift also reflected the waning of the concerns which had first delayed it; Auckland, the president of the Board of Trade, reasoned that 'the trade of our free ports with the Spanish settlements is entirely a contraband trade and, under such conditions, cannot be seriously affected by the open transport of British manufactured goods in neutral shipping'.[181] Auckland was surely mistaken here on principle, though perhaps right in practice. Extension of the 'secret trade' to the Caribbean did present competition to the free ports, but the bulk continued to be with the River Plate and Pacific coast, while the Spanish Licensed Trade was too large and too well established rapidly to succumb to any rival. For the time being, both trades could thrive; only later would Jamaica have cause to lament the advent of direct British trade with Spanish America.

François Crouzet, whose work on the 'secret trade' all later scholars have followed, distinguishes four classes of licence granted under the February 1806 ruling. The first and most straightforward authorised voyages from Britain to the Spanish colonies and back in a neutral vessel. Cargoes were to consist of British manufactures, but some ships might call at a neutral port (often Lisbon or Hamburg) to round out with foreign goods, such as wine, mercury, or paper. A second class of licence permitted exports from a neutral port ('almost always Lisbon'), with returns necessarily to Britain, and cargoes to consist of two-thirds British and one-third foreign merchandise. The third type of licence allowed exports from a Spanish port with returns to Britain; Crouzet includes within this category both the Gordon and Murphy contract, and exports by British merchants based in Spain of stocks held there since before the war. The fourth and final class of licence permitted imports to Britain of cargoes from the Spanish colonies, these voyages to represent the returns from earlier exports.[182] This system of licences remained under review, and was subject to adjustment in 1807, when it was decreed that all voyages must depart from Great Britain.[183] Within a few weeks of the original ruling, Auckland urged that 'it is surely desirable to encourage and multiply our licences as much as possible for the export of British produce and manufactures to the Spanish settlements',[184] and indeed the records of the Privy Council record the concession of a great many of the different species of licence over the ensuing three years. Thus, throughout 1806, 16 vessels were licensed to trade from Britain to the Spanish colonies, and another 50 for trade in mostly British merchandise from the Channel Islands, Gibraltar, Malta, Portugal and Spain, while 81 ships were authorised to import cargoes from Spanish America to Britain. In 1807, 24 licences were granted for voyages from Britain to the Spanish colonies, and 28 for imports from that region. Lastly, in the first six months of 1808, before the peace, 12 vessels were authorised to export cargoes from Britain to Spanish America, and 21 to import from there. A further 45 licences were granted for exports from Britain by the end of the same year.[185]

The most unusual of these licences were surely those which authorised imports of bullion from Spanish-American colonial treasuries. The greatest of the resulting contracts, that of Gordon and Murphy, was discussed at some length in the previous section, but it may not have been the only example. John Taylor, whose petition for a licence was reviewed alongside that of Gordon and Murphy at the Privy Council meeting of 21 February 1806, promptly expanded his request to include the purchase of treasury bills at Madrid to be cashed in the colonies, with returns to be made in bullion to Britain.[186] Taylor worked with the firm of Fermín de Tastet and Co., which in June was granted a licence to purchase bills to the value of $1,000,000 to be cashed in Mexico or another colony, with the bullion to be transported to Jamaica or another British colony. Fermín de Tastet further received a licence to purchase bills on Buenos Aires worth £45,000 ($200,000), with the bullion also to be shipped to Jamaica.[187] This is the only known example of a 'secret trade' licence to purchase Spanish treasury bills other than the Gordon and Murphy affair, though there were echoes of the latter in the request of Gorman Brothers in May 1807 for a frigate to be dispatched to Lima to bring $3,000,000 in bullion, the returns for an outward cargo of British manufactures, mercury and stamped paper worth £500,000.[188] A British official later remarked of Gorman Brothers' licence that 'it was some private agreement with the Treasury, and adds that in Ld Auckland's time there was a good deal of that sort of thing going on'.[189]

It should be noted that it is unclear whether Fermín de Tastet ever put their licence into effect, while Gorman brothers never called on the services of a British warship.[190] The influence of bullion imports in the extension of the 'secret trade' to the Caribbean – that is to say, whether it was the prospect of a flow of treasure which proved decisive in the Council's decision of February 1806 – remains obscure. But certainly bullion contracts were upmost in Auckland's mind during the weeks in question,[191] while the coincidence of Gordon and Murphy and John Taylor at the crucial Council meeting seems suggestive.

Assessing the value of the 'secret trade' at its peak between 1806 and 1808 is no less problematic than for other branches, not least because there is no guarantee that all the licences were actually made use of. Crouzet suggests that 'total exports under licence to the Spanish colonies from Great Britain reached a real value in 1806 of at least £500,000',[192] but this may be an underestimate. In September of the same year, Auckland wrote (apparently with some consternation) that the government had 'granted licenses within the last four months to ten principal houses engaged in the secret trade to South America; to the extent certainly of one million sterling, and perhaps more than double that amount'.[193] The Customs records show a sudden leap in British exports to "South America and the Foreign West Indies" from £185,000 in 1805, to £1,473,000 in 1806 at official values (though figures for the latter year were distorted by a boom in trade with the River Plate, occupied by a British expeditionary force in June; thus, the official value of exports to Veracruz in 1806 was still less than £19,000).[194] In 1807, Crouzet estimates that the value of the trade was 'certainly superior to £500,000', while the official value of British exports to the Spanish colonies was some £407,000 – both figures again likely to be under-estimates. Over four-fifths of official trade in 1807 was with the River Plate and Peru, though some 17 per cent, worth £68,000, was now with Veracruz.[195] In March, indeed, Baring Brothers warned Robert Oliver with regard to its Mexican trade that 'several expeditions have sailed from England on secret services and the public entertain an opinion that some of them are intended for South America'; in September the Olivers responded that a 'great many' British licences had been granted to vessels 'trading from Spain and carrying Spanish property'.[196] Lastly, in 1808, British exports to the Spanish colonies (defined only as Buenos Aires, Montevideo, Lima, Caracas, Pensacola, and Cuba) were worth some £644,000, although 'their real value was certainly much higher'.[197] That these figures represent only a part of the real trade appears to be confirmed by the departure of eleven vessels for Chile and Peru in the winter of 1807–08 with cargoes worth a total of £933,000. Most of these were intended as smuggling voyages, although at least some 'embarked under his Majesty's licence & prompted by the suggestions of the Right Hon.ble Lords of Trade and Plantations'. Six of the vessels were later rumoured or confirmed captured by the Spaniards.[198]

Given the absence of fully reliable figures, the use of official rather than real values in Customs records, and difficulties with geographical categories, these statistics at best provide an approximate guide. The question of geography is particularly thorny in the context of the current study, since not only was the 'secret trade' distorted in 1806–07 by the boom at Buenos Aires, but in general it was far more active with the River Plate, Chile, and Peru than with ports in the Caribbean (the outstanding exception, of course, arising from the Gordon and Murphy contract). Again, the records do not generally permit a distinction between the precise character of trade with Veracruz or Caracas and that with Buenos Aires, Montevideo, or Lima. Within all British exports to the 'foreign West Indies' and (where data are available) the Spanish colonies, cotton goods (whether printed, plain, or manufactures) were dominant throughout 1806–08, taking 46 per cent, 49 per cent, and 62 per cent of total exports in those years respectively. Woollen goods were also significant, while the main non-textile export was wrought iron. Imports were more diverse: in 1806, the leading commodities were tallow, sugar, and raw cotton, while in 1807, Peruvian bark, cochineal, and unwrought copper made up over 85 per cent of the total. In 1808, Peruvian bark and hides accounted for 24 per cent and 20 per cent of total imports respectively, though the full range of imports ran to fifty-nine headings and included such products as jalap, 'ostrich feathers' and 'elephants' teeth', goose quills and flower roots.[199] Scrutiny of two voyages made to the River Plate and Lima in April and August 1806 by Boulton, Walker, and Collins of Birmingham illustrate some of the problems which affected the trade, including low real profits and extreme slowness of returns. The latter problem was key – Boulton and Co. only received final settlement for the April 1806 venture in 1815 – and ensured that 'only Houses with large capitals could engage in this trade'.[200]

It is its geographical distribution which arguably lends the 'secret trade' its lasting significance in the history of Anglo-Spanish American commercial relations. This significance should not be over-stated. If these events indeed 'inaugurated a new phase in the British penetration of Spanish America',[201] this was the case above all in Chile and Peru and in the River Plate, which the British invasions of 1806–07 anyway made something of a special case. The 'secret trade', it is true, has a claim to represent the onset of direct commercial relations with Spanish America from Great Britain. Even this claim is at best relative, however, since we have seen that though the merchants and merchandise were mainly British, much trade continued to be routed via third ports, and almost all was undertaken in neutral rather than British shipping. In short, it would be a further fifteen years before direct and overt trade between ports in Britain and Spanish America became the norm. Nevertheless, the fact that most direct trade from Britain in its earliest stage was concentrated in the River Plate provided a significant foretaste of commercial patterns to come. British trade with Hispanic America from the close of the present study until around 1860 is poorly understood, but despite many setbacks and much disruption, this period may have marked the high point of British commercial hegemony across the region.[202] By 1860, British commercial and financial interests had already become heavily concentrated in Brazil, Chile, Uruguay, and above all Argentina, a pattern which prevailed throughout the remainder of the nineteenth century and well into the twentieth.[203] Thus, until 1808, the Caribbean remained overwhelmingly the most important market for British traders with Spanish America, as it had since the days of Hawkins. The half-century which followed was one of transition, but after 1860 British attention became ever more focused on the regions pioneered by the small number of 'secret traders' in 1805–08. By the later nineteenth century, the Caribbean had become a relative backwater in terms of British interests; and the brilliant Spanish trade of the British islands in the half-century following the Peace of Paris in 1763 was merely a memory.

Notes

1   Garcia-Baquero, *Comercio colonial*, p. 138; Fisher, *Trade, War*, p. 54.
2   Decree, San Lorenzo, 18 Nov. 1797, in Levene, *Documentos para la historia argentina*, 7:134–5.
3   Royal decree, Aranjuez, 20 Apr. 1799; published in Levene, *Documentos para la*

historia argentina, 7:157–9, and in Quirós, 'Reflexiones sobre el comercio libre', pp. 202–4; discussed by García-Baquero, *Comercio colonial*, pp. 146–8; Ortiz, *Comercio exterior de Veracruz*, pp. 305–9.

4   For Cuba, see Marrero, *Cuba*, 10:27–9, 12:70–2; for Mexico, Ortiz de la Tabla, *Comercio exterior de Veracruz*, pp. 309–12; for Venezuela, Manuel de Guevara Vasconcelos to Miguel Cayetano Soler, Caracas, 7 Dec. 1799, A.G.I., Caracas, 117.

5   The major exception was New Granada, which, through unusual viceregal policy, remained largely closed to neutrals throughout most of the wars; see McFarlane, *Colombia before Independence*, pp. 298–302.

6   Fisher, 'Commerce and Imperial Decline', p. 465; Ortiz, *Comercio exterior de Veracruz*, pp. 263–4.

7   Ortiz, *Comercio exterior*, pp. 230–1, 325, and tables on pp. 241, 247, 250; also Real Díaz, 'Iturrigaray', pp. 276–7.

8   Radhay, 'Contraband', pp. 27–8; Lucena Salmoral, *Características del comercio exterior*, pp. 267–8.

9   Fisher, 'Commerce and Imperial Decline', pp. 465–6, 476; García-Baquero, *Comercio colonial*, p. 182; see also the useful statistics in Sagra, *Historia*, p. 155.

10 Henry Hill to James Madison, 1 Nov. 1805, N.A.W., R.G. 59, M899, roll 1.

11 James Anderson to James Madison, Havana, 9 Feb. 1808, and Anderson to Madison, Havana, 11 Jan. 1808, both in N.A.W., R.G. 59, M899, roll 2.

12 Joseph Donato de Austria, 'Noticias y reflexiones acerca del Comercio de 1798', Veracruz, 7 Feb. 1799, A.G.I., Mexico, 2508.

13 Consulado of Cadiz to Miguel Cayetano Soler, Cadiz, 6 Apr. 1799, A.G.I., Indiferente, 2466.

14 Ortiz, *Comercio exterior*, p. 327; see also the table in Arcila Farías, *Reformas económicas*, 1:155–8.

15 Ygnacio José de la Peoza y Casas, 'Noticia del comercio que han hecho los buques neutrales en el puerto de Veracruz', n.p., n.d., A.M.N., ms. 317, f. 22.

16 The principal studies of US trade with Spanish America during this period are the articles by Nichols, Coatsworth, Cuenca Esteban, and García-Baquero, listed in the bibliography; see also Barbier and Kuethe, *The North American Role*.

17 [James Stephen?], *War in Disguise; or, the Frauds of the Neutral Flags* (London: C. Whittingham, 1805).

18 Stephen thus seems to have been unaware that most Anglo-Spanish trade in the Caribbean was now undertaken by Spanish merchants in the British islands; Stephen, *War in Disguise*, p. 201.

19 Memorial of Bahamas merchants, London, 'July 1800', N.A., C.O., 23 / 40, ff. 105–6; Petition of James Moss, London, 28 Oct. 1806, N.A., B.T., 1 / 30, ff. 180–1v.

20 House of Commons Committee, *Report from the Committee on the Commercial State of the West India Colonies* ([London: House of Commons], 1807).

21 Extract, G.L. Morton to Secretary, Havana, 18 Nov. 1798, N.A.W., R.G. 59, M899, roll 1; William Savage to Timothy Pickering, Kingston, 5 June [1800], N.A.W., R.G. 59, T31, roll. 1; and series dated Aug.–Nov. 1801, in N.A., C.O., 137 / 106, ff. 428–33.

22 Stephen, *War in Disguise*, pp. 137, 203.

23 *General Advertiser* (Philadelphia), 25 Jan. 1806, copy in A.H.N., Estado, 6175, and Madison to Monroe, Dept. of State, 12 Apr. 1805, *American State Papers*, 3:101–3 (both on the case of the US brig *Aurora*).

24 Consulado to crown, Cadiz, 3 Dec. 1797, A.G.I., Indiferente, 2466.

25 John Junno to Rufus King, London, 30 Oct. 1797, N.A., B.T., 1 / 15, ff. 204–5.

26 Nichols, 'Trade Relations', pp. 301–2.

27 Cédula, 18 July 1800, published in Levene, *Documentos para la historia argentina*,

7:181–3; also in Quirós, 'Reflexiones sobre el comercio libre', pp. 221–2.

28   Consulado de Veracruz to Viceroy Iturrigaray, Veracruz, 13 Aug. 1808, encl. no. 15 to Consulado to Crown, Veracruz, 1 Mar. 1809, A.G.I., Mexico, 2997; similar sentiment in Merchants to Consulado, Mexico City, 17 May 1809, A.G.N.M., Archivo Histórico de Hacienda, leg. 215, exp. 9, ff. 431–6.

29   Consulado de Veracruz to Miguel Cayetano Soler, Veracruz, 28 Feb. 1799, and the third enclosure with the same letter (Consulado to Viceroy Azanza, Veracruz, 12 Feb. 1799), in A.G.I., Mexico, 2996.

30   Consulado to Soler, Veracruz, 15 Nov. 1805, A.G.I., Mexico, 2997.

31   Ajequiezcane, 'British Trade with the Spanish Colonies', p. 252.

32   Consulado de Cadiz to Miguel Cayetano Soler, Cadiz, 6 Apr. 1799, A.G.I., Indiferente, 2466.

33   One case in point is that of the *Citizen*, which arrived at Veracruz in March 1799; see the summary of a letter by Viceroy Félix Berenguer de Marquina dated Mexico City, 27 Aug. 1802, and accompanying papers, in A.G.I., Mexico, 2515.

34   Quirós, *Memoria de Instituto*, p. 81.

35   Representation of Consulado de México, Mexico City, 28 June 1811, A.G.I., Mexico, 2514.

36   Consulado de México to Viceroy, Mexico City, 1 June 1811, A.G.N.M., Archivo Histórico de Hacienda, leg. 215, exp. 9, ff. 506–21v.

37   Consulado de Veracruz to Miguel Cayetano Soler, Veracruz, 15 Nov. 1805, A.G.I., Mexico, 2512; see also Consulado de Veracruz to Crown, Veracruz, 24 Feb. 1806, A.G.I., Mexico, 2513.

38   Consulado de Veracruz to Crown, Veracruz, 24 Feb. 1806, A.G.I., Mexico, 2513.

39   Copy, Consulado de Veracruz to Viceroy Iturrigaray, Veracruz, 13 Feb. 1806, A.G.I., Mexico, 2997.

40   See the documentary series in A.G.I., Mexico, 2514, which culminated in the private ruling to Viceroy Iturrigaray dated 20 Aug. 1807.

41   Manuel Moreno Fraginals provided a brilliantly perceptive analysis of the Cuban mercantile community and of the role of the Consulado and its spokesmen during this period: *El ingenio, passim*.

42   Report of Francisco de Arango, Havana, 18 July 1798, A.G.I., Santo Domingo, 2193; major secondary commentary in Ortiz, *Comercio exterior de Veracruz*, pp. 178–210; Marrero, *Cuba*, 12:64–9; Stein, 'Caribbean Counterpoint', pp. 32–40. The smuggling of re-exports from Cuba to New Spain had deep roots: see Stein and Stein, *Apogee of Empire*, p. 149.

43   Consulado de Cadiz, *Representación*, Cadiz, 5 Mar. 1799, A.G.I., Indiferente, 2466.

44   Joseph Donato de Austria, 'Noticias y reflexiones acerca del Comercio de 1798', Veracruz, 7 Feb. 1799, A.G.I., Mexico, 2508.

45   Royal Decree, Aranjuez, 10 May 1807, copies in A.G.I., Mexico, 2513; A.G.N.M., Archivo Histórico de Hacienda, leg. 215, exp. 9, f. 430.

46   José María Quirós, 'Memoria de Instituto', Jalapa, 23 Sept. 1811, published in Ortiz, *Memorias*, pp. 203–26, see p. 209.

47   Consulado de Mexico, *Representación*, Mexico City, 28 June 1811, A.G.I., Mexico, 2514; Report of Consulado de Mexico, Mexico City, 23 Aug. 1809, A.G.N.M., Consulado, vol. 79, exp. 1, ff. 13–24v; Consulado de Veracruz to Marqués de las Hormazas, Veracruz, 6 June 1810 A.G.I., Mexico, 2514; see also Consulado de Cadiz, *Representación*, Cadiz, 24 Sept. 1811, A.G.N.M., Archivo Histórico de Hacienda, leg. 215, exp. 9, ff. 615–22v.

48   Ortiz, *Comercio exterior de Veracruz*, p. 239.

49   A.N.C., Miscelánea de libros, nos. 2787, 6737 (1798); 2787, 2518, 2021 (1799); 2787,

2519, 2766 (1800); 1950 (1801); 1986, 2521 (1805); 6797, 1811 (1806); 6797, 2523 (1807); 2645, 2061 (1808); 2645 (1809).

50   In 1798, about a dozen more American ships last at British colonies were brought in to Havana as French prizes. My calculations in this paragraph exclude these ships, and also British and other warships entering under flag of truce. All figures include a margin of error probably not greater than one to three ships, the product of ambiguous entries in the port books.

51   See pp. 168–9.

52   Extract, G. L. Morton to Secretary, Havana, 18 Nov. 1798, N.A.W., R.G. 59, M899, roll 1.

53   John Morton to James Madison, Havana, 11 Dec. 1801, N.A.W., R.G. 59, M899, roll 1.

54   Most imports were recorded only as so many 'onzas de oro'. The figures in this paragraph represent a calculation based on a rate of 1 ounce gold = c. 17 pesos (I draw this rate from internal evidence in the sources consulted).

55   Manuel de Guevara Vasconcelos, 'Provincia de Venezuela. Sobre extracción e introducción de tabaco ...', Caracas, 28 June 1805, A.G.I., Caracas, 61; Barbier, 'Venezuelan "Libranzas"', p. 473.

56   Guevara and Antonio López Quintana to Soler, Caracas, 23 Dec. 1800, A.G.I., Caracas, 117.

57   José Vásquez y Telles, 'Lista de los Buques Extrangeros que han entrado en este Puerto ...', La Guayra, 26 June 1805, encl. to Captain-General to Sr. Generalísimo, Caracas, 28 June 1805, A.G.I., Caracas, 61.

58   Guevara Vasconcelos to Ministro de Hacienda, Caracas, 27 Sept. 1805, and third encl., William Robinson to José Rafael Gómez, Cumaná, 19 July 1805, A.G.I., Caracas, 119.

59   Guevara Vasconcelos to Ministro de Hacienda, Caracas, 25 June 1805, A.G.I., Caracas, 119.

60   'Apoderados del comercio de Caracas' to Intendant, Caracas, 4 May 1803, A.G.I., Caracas, 921.

61   See pp. 149–50.

62   Guevara Vasconcelos to Príncipe de la Paz, Caracas, 28 June 1805, A.G.I., Caracas, 61; Guevara Vasconcelos to Ministro de Hacienda, Caracas, 13 July 1805, A.G.I., Caracas, 119; the Intendant's account of his actions is in Arce to Soler, Caracas, 24 May 1803, A.G.I., Caracas, 516.

63   All the contracts discussed in this paragraph are described in Guevara Vasconcelos, 'Provincia de Venezuela. Sobre extracción e introducción de tabaco ...', Caracas, 28 June 1805, A.G.I., Caracas, 61.

64   José Vásquez y Telles, 'Lista de los Buques Extrangeros que han entrado en este Puerto ...', La Guayra, 26 June 1805, encl. to Captain-General to Sr. Generalísimo, Caracas, 28 June 1805; Guevara Vasconcelos to Príncipe de la Paz, Caracas, 28 June 1805, both in A.G.I., Caracas, 61.

65   See also Guevara Vasconcelos to Ministro de Hacienda, Caracas, 9 May 1805, A.G.I., Caracas, 119; El Capitán-General al Sr Generalísimo, Caracas, 28 June 1805, A.G.I., Caracas, 61.

66   Guevara Vasconcelos to Príncipe de la Paz, Caracas, 28 June 1805, A.G.I., Caracas, 61.

67   The Spanish trade of St Thomas during the British occupations is discussed on p. 148.

68   Extract, Brigadier-General Fuller to Lord Hobart, St Croix, 12 Jan. 1802, N.A., B.T. 1 / 20, ff. 81–v.

69   Petition of resident merchants to Brig. Gen. Maclean, St Thomas, 18 Jan. 1808, N.A., B.T. 1 / 38, ff. 293–8v; discussed in Williams, 'Mercados británicos', p. 101.

70   Petition of merchants trading to St Thomas, Lancaster, 3 Oct. 1807, and Memorial of merchants trading to St Thomas, London, 5 Oct. 1807, both in N.A., B.T. 1 / 37, ff. 160–1v, 164–5v.

71   Knox, *Historical Account*, p. 92; Torivio Montes to Príncipe de la Paz, Puerto Rico, 6 Nov. 1806, A.G.I., Santo Domingo, 2323a.

72   Armytage, *Free Port System*, app. 3, table P, p.158; see also p. 87.

73   Lucena Salmoral, *Características del comercio exterior*, table 4, pp. 183ff.

74   For Curaçao, see also Memorial of the merchants of Kingston, Kingston, 17 Jan. 1807, copies in N.A., B.T. 1 / 35, ff. 5–6v, and C.O. 137 / 118, ff. 56–7.

75   Marqués del Campo to Príncipe de la Paz, Paris, 20 Dec. 1796, A.H.N., Estado, 4244; Ortiz de la Tabla, *Comercio exterior de Veracruz*, p. 271.

76   Nicolás Blasco de Orosco to Príncipe de la Paz, Hamburg, 12 Sept. 1797, and correspondence between the Marqués de las Hormazas and the Príncipe de la Paz, dated San Lorenzo, 9 Oct.–15 Nov. 1797, in A.G.I., Indiferente, 2466.

77   Ortiz de la Tabla, *Comercio exterior de Veracruz*, pp. 319–22.

78   Statement of John Braddick, 7 June 1803, in Memorial of William Davis Robinson, n.p., n.d., N.A., B.T. 1 / 28, ff. 265–90v, see ff. 286v–8v.

79   Cédula reservada, San Lorenzo, 24 Dec. 1804; see also Cédula, Miguel Cayetano Soler to Marqués de Casa Yrujo, 1 Mar. 1805, both with Consulado de Veracruz to Crown, 1 Mar. 1809, A.G.I., Mexico, 2997.

80   Barbier, 'Peninsular Finance and Colonial trade', pp. 31, 34, 36–7; 'Venezuelan "Libranzas", 1788–1807'; 'Anglo-American Investors and Payments on Spanish Imperial Treasuries'; and 'Commercial Reform and *Comercio Neutral* in Cartagena de Indias'. Barbier notes that the change in fact dated to 1801, but that its effects were masked by the peace of the following three years, and thus were seen only from 1804.

81   An article titled 'The Hope–Barings Contract: Finance and Trade between Europe and the Americas, 1805–1808' has been completed and will be published separately.

82   On the Treaty of Subsidies see Marichal, *La bancarrota del Virreinato*, pp. 174–5, 185–6; Redlich, 'Payments between Nations', p. 699; Buist, *At Spes Non Fracta*, p. 284.

83   This is a highly simplified account of events. On Ouvrard, see the biographies by Lévy, Wolf, and Payard cited in the bibliography. On his contract of 1804, see Marichal, *La bancarrota del virreinato*, pp. 187–9; Bruchey, *Robert Oliver*, pp. 271–2. The standard work on Hope & Co. from its origins in the 1770s through to the end of the Napoleonic wars is Buist, *At Spes Non Fracta*.

84   Marichal, *La bancarrota del virreinato*, pp. 189–90; Buist, *At Spes Non Fracta*, pp. 292–3.

85   Thus, the rate of exchange of the peso against the franc in Mexico was 1 to 5; the rate applied to pesos delivered in Europe was 1 to 3.75. See Buist, *At Spes Non Fracta*, p. 325; Wolf, *Ouvrard*, p. 104.

86   On the sale of clerical property in Mexico see Hamnett, 'The Appropriation of Mexican Church Wealth'; Lavrín, 'The Execution of the Law of *Consolidación* in New Spain'. The relevant decree, dated 26 Dec. 1804, is published in Sugawara, *La deuda pública de España*, doc. 1, pp. 13–26.

87   On Baring Brothers, see the studies by Hidy, Orbell, and Ziegler cited in the bibliography.

88   On these negotiations, see Memorandum of Sir Francis Baring, marked 'R[eceived] 11 Dec. [1805] Secret', B.L., Add. Mss. 38,737, ff. 107–10v; also Jiménez Codinach, *La Gran Bretaña*, p. 211; for the role of the Bank of England, Crouzet, *L'Economie*

Britannique, pp. 120–1.

89 As was noted by François Crouzet almost half a century ago: *L'Economie Britannique*, pp. 120–1.

90 Buist, *At Spes Non Fracta*, p. 324, suggests that 'four-fifths or five-sixths' of the Mexican bullion imported to Britain was destined for re-export to Spain and France.

91 See Pierre Labouchère to Sir Francis Baring, Amsterdam, 10 May 1805, quoted in Bruchey, *Robert Oliver*, pp. 273–4.

92 Walters and Walters, 'The American Career of David Parish', pp. 150–1; see also Herbert Lasky, 'David Parish: A European in American Finance, 1806–1816' (unpub. PhD diss., Ann Arbor, Michigan, n.d.).

93 Nolte wrote a lengthy account of his activities on Parish's behalf: see Vincent Nolte, *Fifty Years in Both Hemispheres*, esp. pp. 56–170. William Hervey Allen made Nolte's activities in New Orleans those of the hero of his vast novel *Anthony Adverse* (New York: Farrar & Rinehart, 1933).

94 See esp. Bruchey, *Robert Oliver*, pp. 278–82.

95 Marichal, *La bancarrota del virreinato*, pp. 198–206, is fundamental for Villanueva's activities in Veracruz.

96 For neutral vessels trading at Veracruz in 1805, see Joseph María Quirós, 'Balanza de comercio de Veracruz correspondiente al año de 1805 ...', Veracruz, 24 Feb. 1806, A.G.I., Mexico, 2513; published in Lerdo de Tejada, *Comercio exterior de México*, app. 18.

97 Bruchey, *Robert Oliver*, pp. 267–70.

98 Bruchey, *Robert Oliver*, pp. 280–2, 299–303.

99 Marichal, *La bancarrota del virreinato*, pp. 202–3; Jiménez Codinach, *La Gran Bretaña y la independencia de México*, p. 215. The figure given by Jiménez Codinach for the value of sales in 1806–07 is $2,918,652.

100 Bruchey, *Robert Oliver*, pp. 262–3.

101 In 1805–08, 56 out of 119 ships (47 per cent) entering Veracruz from US ports did so from Baltimore. New Orleans accounted for 43 shipments (36 per cent) during the same period; see Smith, 'Shipping in the Port of Veracruz', p. 13, table v.

102 Bruchey, *Robert Oliver*, p. 304.

103 On these questions, see Bruchey, *Robert Oliver*, pp. 304–7.

104 Textiles aside, other exports included Spanish paper, silks and brandy, and Italian steel; Bruchey, *Robert Oliver*, p. 305. Note that in 1806 re-exports (as opposed to domestic exports) accounted for no less than 78 per cent of all US exports to Spanish America; Coatsworth, 'American Trade with European Colonies', p. 257 n. 38.

105 Bruchey, *Robert Oliver*, p. 324.

106 Buist refers to this system as 'prepayment or partial financing'. This is a heavily simplified account of these transactions, which in reality were rather more complex: see Buist, *At Spes Non Fracta*, pp. 318–19; also e.g. Bruchey, *Robert Oliver*, pp. 273, 295–6. Walters and Walters, 'The American Career of David Parish', p. 153, suggest that Parish sent $1,250,000 direct to the Hopes in late 1806, but this appears to be an error.

107 Bruchey, *Robert Oliver*, pp. 286–9, 291–5.

108 Barbier, 'Peninsular Finance and Colonial Trade', pp. 34–5.

109 Buist, *At Spes Non Fracta*, pp. 317–18.

110 On the voyage of the *Diana*, see e.g. Buist, *At Spes Non Fracta*, p. 329; Marichal, *La bancarrota del virreinato*, p. 199.

111 Joseph María Quirós, 'Nota de las partidas embarcadas por las Casas de Comercio de Dn. José Gabriel de Villanueva, y Dn. Tomás Murphy, en plata y frutos ...', Veracruz, 7 May 1808, A.G.N.M., Consulado, vol. 113, exp. 7, f. 220–v. For the

Lloyds point, see Hidy, *The House of Baring*, pp. 35–7.

112 Hope–Barings also acquired bills worth 700,000 pesos on each of the royal treasuries in Havana and Caracas; for their attempts to cash these sums, see Buist, *At Spes Non Fracta*, pp. 327–31.

113 Oliver had three ships seized, in Nov. 1806 and Aug.–Sept. 1807; Bruchey, *Robert Oliver*, pp. 319–23.

114 Buist, *At Spes Non Fracta*, pp. 353–6.

115 Marichal, *La bancarrota del virreinato*, pp. 202–3; Jiménez Codinach, *La Gran Bretaña*, p. 215.

116 Marichal, *La bancarrota del virreinato*, p. 210, analysing John Alexander Jackson, 'The Mexican Silver Schemes: Finance and Profiteering in the Napoleonic Era, 1796–811' (unpub. PhD diss., University of Carolina, 1978).

117 Nolte, *Fifty Years in Both Hemispheres*, discussed by Bruchey, *Robert Oliver*, p. 333. The total value of bills issued against the Mexican treasury in 1804–08 was just under 30,000,000 pesos; Barbier, 'Peninsular Finance and Colonial Trade', pp. 35–6.

118 Bruchey, *Robert Oliver*, p. 333.

119 There are conflicting estimates of the Olivers' profits; see Buist, *At Spes Non Fracta*, p. 315; Jiménez Codinach, *La Gran Bretaña*, p. 215; the figure of $775,000 is in Bruchey, *Robert Oliver*, pp. 326–7.

120 José María Quirós, 'Estado o Balanza general del comercio ...', Veracruz, 18 Apr. 1821, A.G.I., Mexico, 2994; published in Lerdo de Tejada, *Comercio exterior de México*, app. 14.

121 Evidence of Thomas Atwood, 29 Apr. 1812, *Parliamentary Papers* ..., pp. 1–19, see p. 15.

122 'A Comparative View of the State of the Trade of Great Britain ...', N.A., Cust. 17 / 29, ff. 113v–15.

123 Evidence of Kirkman Finlay, 20 May 1812, *Parliamentary Papers* ..., pp. 396–423, see pp. 401–2, 411.

124 Humphreys, 'Anglo-American Rivalries', pp. 144–6.

125 Ortiz de la Tabla, *Comercio exterior de Veracruz*, pp. 332–3.

126 See also Stein, 'Caribbean Counterpoint', pp. 31–2.

127 Ortiz de la Tabla, *Comercio exterior de Veracruz*, pp. 206–7.

128 P. 140.

129 Jiménez Codinach, 'An Atlantic Silver Entrepôt', p. 155; Marichal, *La bancarrota del virreinato*, pp. 221–2.

130 The best work to date on Gordon and Murphy is Jiménez Codinach, *La Gran Bretaña*, chap. 6; this is usefully reprised in English in the same author's 'An Atlantic Silver Entrepôt', esp. pp. 154–63.

131 Jiménez Codinach, 'An Atlantic Silver Entrepôt', p. 156.

132 Buist, *At Spes Non Fracta*, pp. 324, 327.

133 'Draft contract between the Lords Commissioners of his Majesty's Treasury and Messrs Reid, Irving & Co. and Gordon and Murphy', [Dec. 1805], B.L., Add. Mss. 38,766, ff. 1–11v.

134 The role of Reid, Irving remains poorly understood. One document shedding some light on the relationship is Dick, McCall & Co. to Thomas Walsh, Kingston, 6 July 1807, N.A., C.O. 137 / 119, ff. 96–v.

135 See e.g. Lord Auckland to Lord Grenville, Palace Yard, 16 Feb. 1806, in Historical Manuscripts Commission, *Report on the Manuscripts of J. B. Fortescue*, 8:59.

136 The contract is described briefly in Minute for 7 Aug. 1807, N.A., P.C. 4 / 15, ff. 285–99, see f. 285. To my knowledge, the original document has yet to come to light.

137 See esp. Bruchey, *Robert Oliver*, pp. 315–17; Jiménez Codinach, *La Gran Bretaña*,

pp. 214–15.

138 This paragraph draws on Miguel Cayetano Soler to viceroy, Aranjuez, 19 May 1806, A.G.N.M., Inquisición, vol. 1543, ff. 413–17; see also Jiménez Codinach, *La Gran Bretaña*, pp. 229–30; Jiménez Codinach, 'An Atlantic Silver Entrepôt', p. 157; Marichal, *La bancarrota del virreinato*, pp. 227–9.

139 Minute for 7 Aug. 1807, N.A., P.C. 4 / 15, ff. 285–99, see ff. 285–6.

140 Auckland to Grenville, Palace Yard, 5 June 1806, in Historical Manuscripts Commission, *Report on the Manuscripts of J.B. Fortescue*, 8:178.

141 All this information draws on Minute for 7 Aug. 1807, N.A., P.C. 4 / 15, ff. 285–99.

142 See also Minute for 29 October 1807, N.A., P.C. 4 / 15, ff. 557–9.

143 Minutes for 19 and 28 June 1806, N.A., P.C. 2 / 170, ff. 418, 504; Minute for 20 Aug. 1807, N.A., P.C. 4 / 15, ff. 342–3.

144 See e.g. Crouzet, *L'Economie Britannique*, p. 181.

145 This case is made strongly by Marichal, *La bancarrota del virreinato*, pp. 211–6, 231–2. Gordon and Murphy not only sourced mercury for Mexico from Saxony, but even designed the flasks for its transportation: Jiménez Codinach, *La Gran Bretaña*, p. 230.

146 A point made briefly by Jiménez Codinach, *La Gran Bretaña*, pp. 223–4; Jiménez Codinach, 'An Atlantic Silver Entrepôt', pp. 154–5.

147 Jiménez Codinach, 'An Atlantic Silver Entrepôt', p. 157; on the Murphys' agents, see Marichal, *La bancarrota del virreinato*, p. 224 n. 44.

148 Viceroy Iturrigaray to Soler, Mexico City, 29 Dec. 1806, A.G.I., Mexico, 2513.

149 'The Spanish Government was then contented to permit the sale of dollars at La Vera Cruz at a very depreciated price and to allow them to be exported on the security of Bills given by individual merchants in London'; Spencer Percival to George Canning, London, 6 Mar. 1809, N.A., F.O. 72 / 90, ff. 97–100v.

150 Grenville to Auckland, Downing Street, 5 June 1806, in Historical Manuscripts Commission, *Report on the Manuscripts of J. B. Fortescue*, 8:178–9; see also the series in N.A., C.O. 137 / 119, ff. 94–6v.

151 'Irene's [?] proposal to Capt. Fleming', n.p., n.d. [1810], N.A., F.O. 185 / 23, n.f.

152 Jiménez Codinach, 'An Atlantic Silver Entrepôt', p. 158; same author, *La Gran Bretaña*, p. 232.

153 For the Murphys' activities after 1808, see Jiménez Codinach, *La Gran Bretaña*, pp. 231–60.

154 Marichal, *La bancarrota del virreinato*, p. 235; ships' registers in A.G.N.M., Consulado, vol. 46, ff. 22–3, 70–1, 273, 305; vol. 148, exp. 12, f. 244, exp. 29, ff. 439–40; vol. 153, exp. 7, f. 43, exp. 25, f. 185, exp. 26, f. 187, exp. 30, ff. 197–200; vol. 167, ff. 49, 51–2, 340–1. This list is unlikely to be exhaustive.

155 This figure was confirmed by Gordon and Murphy's partners: 'we have lately been concerned in bringing eight millions of dollars for the use of the British government.' See Reid, Irving & Co. to Wm. Huskisson, Broad Street Buildings, London, 6 July 1809, N.A., F.O. 72 / 90, ff. 230–1.

156 José María Quirós, 'Memoria sobre la alteración que experimentó el comercio de Indias en el anterior reinado', Veracruz, 24 Dec. 1810, in Ortiz, *Memorias políticas y económicas*, pp. 195–202, see p. 199.

157 Quirós, 'Memoria de Instituto en que se trata del comercio ... general, libre y directo por los extranjeros', Jalapa, 23 Sept. 1811, in Ortiz, *Memorias políticas y económicas*, pp. 203–26, see p. 212.

158 Consulado to Viceroy Francisco Xavier Venegas, [Veracruz], 14 Sept. 1811, A.G.N.M., Archivo Histórico de Hacienda, leg. 215, exp. 9, ff. 586–90.

159 Jiménez Codinach, 'An Atlantic Silver Entrepôt', p. 157.

160 Marichal, *La bancarrota del virreinato*, p. 236, table VI.1.

161 Register of entrance for the sloop *Correo*, Veracruz, 26 Mar. 1808, A.G.N.M., Consulado, vol. 148, exp. 29, ff. 439–40. It is unclear why this register is dated some six months after the voyage it describes.

162 Consulado to Venegas, [Veracruz], 14 Sept. 1811, A.G.N.M., Archivo Histórico de Hacienda, leg. 215, exp. 9, ff. 586–90.

163 Jiménez Codinach, 'An Atlantic Silver Entrepôt', pp. 157–8; same author, *La Gran Bretaña*, pp. 230–1.

164 Marichal, *La bancarrota del virreinato*, p. 233.

165 Jiménez Codinach, *La Gran Bretaña*, p. 229; also Marichal, *La bancarrota del virreinato*, p. 237 n. 76.

166 Jiménez Codinach, *La Gran Bretaña*, p. 232.

167 Marichal, *La bancarrota del virreinato*, p. 233.

168 Two unsigned and undated papers, both in N.A., B.T. 1 / 16, ff. 192–4v, ff. 204–5; Minute for 2 Aug. 1798, N.A., B.T. 5 / 11, ff. 91v–2v.

169 'The Earl of Liverpool relative to the applications for leave to trade with the Spanish colonies', n.p., Nov. 1799, B.L., Add. Mss. 38,355, ff. 111–12v.

170 Armytage, *Free Port System*, pp. 109–10; Lynch, 'British Policy and Spanish America', p. 24; Jones, 'Historical Study of Anglo-Spanish American Trade', p. 60 n. 1.

171 All the latter references from 'The Earl of Liverpool relative to the applications for leave to trade with the Spanish colonies', n.p., Nov. 1799, B.L., Add. Mss. 38,355, ff. 111–12v.

172 'Linens: Minute on the attendance of Messrs Turnbull ...', 13 May 1805, N.A., B.T. 5 / 15, ff. 82–3.

173 Minute for 15 May 1805, N.A., P.C. 4 / 13, ff. 125–31.

174 Part of Minute for 17 June 1805, N.A., P.C. 4 / 13, ff. 157–9, also N.A., B.T. 5 / 17, f. 161v; Lynch, 'British Policy and Spanish America', pp. 25.

175 This description draws on Gibbs, *The History of Anthony and Dorothea Gibbs*, chap. 8.

176 Cited in Gibbs, *The History of Anthony and Dorothea Gibbs*, p. 166 n. 2 (no date given).

177 Vice-Admiral Collingwood to Lady Collingwood, off Cadiz, 20 Dec. 1806, in Collingwood, *A Selection from the Public and Private Correspondence*, p. 225. A minor discrepancy in dates notwithstanding, the ship referred to here was almost certainly the *Hermosa Mexicana*; see Gibbs, *The History of Anthony and Dorothea Gibbs*, p. 171.

178 See e.g. Thomas Grenville to Auckland, Admiralty, 26 Feb. 1807, B.L., Add. Mss. 34,457, ff. 231–2v.

179 Minutes for 21 Feb. 1806, 28 Feb. 1806, both in N.A., P.C. 4 / 14, ff. 51–2, 53–7.

180 Auckland to Grenville, Palace Yard, 18 Feb. 1806, in Historical Manuscripts Commission, *Report on the Manuscripts of J.B. Fortescue*, 8:36.

181 Crouzet, *L'Economie Britannique*, pp. 179–80.

182 Crouzet, *L'Economie Britannique*, p. 182.

183 Crouzet, *L'Economie Britannique*, pp. 234–5; Gibbs, *The History of Anthony and Dorothea Gibbs*, p. 177; for one of the relevant rulings, see Minutes for 23 Jan. 1807, 27 Jan. 1807, N.A., P.C. 4 / 15, ff. 5–77; related debate in Minutes for 23 June 1807, 10 Aug. 1807, N.A., P.C. 4 / 15, ff. 130–4, 307–9.

184 Auckland to Grenville, Eden Farm, 9 Apr. 1806, in Historical Manuscripts Commission, *Report on the Manuscripts of J. B. Fortescue*, 8:87–8.

185 Crouzet, *L'Economie Britannique*, pp. 182–3, 235, 318, 362.

186 John Taylor to Board of Trade, New Broad Street, 19 Mar. 1806, B.L., Add. Mss. 34,456, f. 434.

187 'Bills of Exchange. Messrs Fermin de Tastet & Co. allowed a license to obtain some

from Spain', Minute for 3 June 1806, N.A., P.C. 2 / 170, ff. 310–12.

188 Memorial of Messrs Gorman Brothers, New Broad Street, 19 May 1807, N.A., B.T. 1 / 35, ff. 68–9v; 'Spanish Main – Minute on a memorial of Messrs Gorman Brothers …', 20 May 1807, N.A., B.T. 5 / 17, ff. 125v–6; also Minute for 11 Aug. 1807, N.A., P.C. 4 / 15, ff. 321–2. Crouzet, *L'Economie Britannique*, p. 235 n. 79, and Armytage, *Free Port System*, pp. 110–11, mistakenly give Veracruz for Lima.

189 Unsigned note, 20 Nov. [1809], N.A., F.O. 72 / 90, f. 299.

190 Gorman Brothers to Earl Bathurst, New Broad Street, 14 Nov. 1809, N.A., F.O. 72 / 90, ff. 290–1v.

191 Auckland to Grenville, Palace Yard, 16 and 21 Feb. 1806, both in Historical Manuscripts Commission, *Report on the Manuscripts of J. B. Fortescue*, 8:59, 63.

192 Crouzet, *L'Economie Britannique*, p. 183.

193 Auckland to Grenville, Eden Farm, 14 Sept. 1806, in Historical Manuscripts Commission, *Report on the Manuscripts of J. B. Fortescue*, 8:331–2.

194 Elaborated from commercial accounts in N.A., Cust. 17 / 28 (which is unfoliated).

195 Crouzet, *L'Economie Britannique*, p. 235; commercial accounts in N.A., Cust. 17 / 29, ff. 84v–8, 113v–155; see also Lynch, 'British Policy and Spanish America', p. 28.

196 Bruchey, *Robert Oliver*, pp. 322, 324.

197 Crouzet, *L'Economie Britannique*, p. 362 (the figure for exports given by Crouzet, of £621,000, excludes trade with Cuba); commercial accounts in N.A., Cust. 17 / 30, ff. 109v–14.

198 See esp. 'Memorial from the merchants trading to the coasts of Peru and Chili', London, 3 Apr. 1809, and 'Memorial of merchants trading to the coasts of Peru and Chile', London, 28 July 1809, N.A., F.O. 72 / 90, ff. 111–14v, ff. 242–4v, with related papers; also Humphreys, *British Consular Reports*, p. 127 n. 2.

199 All these figures elaborated from the appropriate tables in N.A., Cust 17 / 28–30.

200 Crouzet, *L'Economie Britannique*, p. 183 n. 57; see also Langnas, 'Relations between Great Britain and the Spanish Colonies', chap. 3, p. 27.

201 Lynch, 'British Policy and Spanish America', p. 28, following Crouzet, *L'Economie Britannique*, p. 184.

202 See Miller, *Britain and Latin America*, pp. 71–3. The fullest account of British trade with Spanish America between the close of the present study and 1860 is Platt, *Latin America and British Trade*, part 1.

203 Platt, *Latin America and British Trade*, provides the fundamental study.

CHAPTER SEVEN

Conclusions

In the opening chapter to this book, I presented an overview of British trade with the Spanish colonies from its origins in the sixteenth century until the end of the Seven Years War. The core of the book, embracing Chapters 2–6, then described (in considerable detail) the development of the trade in the forty-five years between 1763 and the Anglo-Spanish peace of July 1808. In these concluding comments, I wish to begin by summarising in a few pages what I regard as the key features of that development. I then devote a separate section specifically to reviewing the question of what British trade with Spanish America was worth during this period, and how it stood within the generality of British overseas trade at this time. Finally, and partly in the light of what has gone before, I suggest the broader significance of this work within the British imperial and Spanish-American historiographies.

Key Trends: Growth, Legalisation, Diversification

The key characteristic of British trade with Spanish America between 1763 and 1808 was surely its rapid growth. The specific evidence is recapped below, but if my figures are accepted as reasonably reliable, then growth of the order of 300–400 per cent occurred across these four and a half decades. What stood behind this growth, of course, was British industrial development (the 'Industrial Revolution') and its fruits in terms of ever-cheaper products, manufactured to ever-higher standards and in ever-greater quantities. British industrial and commercial development – and the financial and other apparatus which sustained it, from banking to ship-building – enabled British manufactures to out-compete foreign rivals and rendered them immensely attractive to Spanish-American consumers. This broader context has been studied in great detail by British economic and industrial historians, and is necessarily taken for granted here. My own focus has been on explaining how the great surplus of goods produced in British factories and workshops was transmitted to ready markets in Mexico, Cuba, Venezuela, and the other colonies.

In my view, the key factor facilitating the growth of British trade during this period consisted of its legalisation in practical terms. In a strict sense, all British trade with Spanish America was illegal, albeit one great branch – via Andalusia in southern Spain – operated through the legal framework of Spanish Atlantic trade. Commercial relations in the Caribbean (the other great branch) were contraband almost from their origins, under the colonial laws and commercial monopoly of both Spain and Britain. Chapter 2 of this work demonstrates how the British broke with this tradition by opening the first free ports in their colonies in the West Indies in 1766. The establishment of the free ports occurred due to specific commercial and political circumstances, in which contingency played a not insignificant role. But perhaps the key factor was a shift in the carriage of the trade toward Spanish vessels some fifteen years earlier, and British recognition – provoked by a minor crisis in the trade, itself caused partly by new anti-contraband legislation – that banning Spaniards from trade with their islands was not in their interest.

The advent of the free ports rendered trade by Spaniards in the British West Indies legal for the first time in its history. Spaniards might now import bullion (of most interest to the British) and most agricultural produce, but no manufactures of any kind. They could export almost the full range of British manufactured goods, as well as enslaved Africans; and they could do all this quite openly, in their own vessels. This was no more than a unilateral legalisation; while the trade became fully sanctioned by the British, it remained illegal in the eyes of the Spanish, and Spaniards trading with the free ports were subject to seizure by their own authorities. Whether it remained contraband in international law also is an interesting and possibly delicate question. But let there be no mistake, this nonetheless represented a major shift in the basis of Anglo-Spanish commercial relations in the Americas. For the first time, a fully legal platform was provided for commercial exchange between the two nations, which for the most part would no longer be undertaken furtively on deserted stretches of coast, or under threat of sudden seizure by Customs or Naval officials. Small wonder that the free ports proved as commercially successful as they did, or that the great majority of Anglo-Spanish trade rapidly became concentrated in them. The free ports, because they provided a legal venue for trade, became crucial to the rapid growth of British commerce in the decades which followed.

After a somewhat shaky start (there were doubts for a decade as to the success of the free ports in Jamaica, by far the most important centre), the free port system was consolidated and expanded in later years. By 1805, it embraced some sixteen ports in a dozen islands throughout the Caribbean, a network which in effect covered the whole of the region. Free ports became a key demand for British colonies, and failure to secure them could bring serious consequences (as with the short-lived British colony of West Florida). Grenada experienced an extraordinary commercial boom after a free port was granted to St George's in 1787, only to see this trade shift away to Trinidad when that island was captured from Spain and granted its own free port a decade later. The rapid grant of free ports to Trinidad and to St

Thomas and Curaçao (captured from the Danes and Dutch in 1800) demonstrated British awareness of the crucial commercial significance of the institution by that date. One consequence of the expansion of the British empire in the West Indies (with the incorporation of Dominica, Grenada, St Vincent, Tobago, Trinidad, and other islands) and of the concession of free ports to all these islands, indeed, was a significant geographical diversification of the trade. Although Jamaica retained its primacy, other colonies – above all the Bahamas and Trinidad, though also briefly St Thomas and Curaçao – also became substantial bases for trade. And a further consequence of the free port system was to reinforce still further the predominance of Spaniards as carriers of the trade, to the prejudice of British smuggling, which seems to have declined in the late eighteenth century.

If Chapter 2 explored the establishment of the free ports by the British in the mid-1760s, Chapter 3 discusses what may be regarded as a parallel process of legalisation undertaken by Spaniards in the 1780s and 1790s. During the American Revolutionary War, the Spanish colonies were thrown open to trade with neutral colonies and the United States as an enforced reaction to wartime economic dislocation. Over the following two decades, this opening was extended to embrace ever-greater legal commercial relations with foreign colonies in the region, including the British colonies. This trade was known to Spaniards as the *comercio de colonias*, or 'colonies trade', and it acquired real economic significance in several regions. It was generally undertaken under licences granted by the governors of poorer and more isolated regions – eastern New Granada, for example, or the eastern provinces of Venezuela – and was justified by the absence of commercial alternatives or the simple need for supplies (often foodstuffs). In many cases, such licences were granted without reference to, and possibly without the knowledge of, the Spanish crown. But in 1789, Madrid itself contributed to the process, with a decree of free trade in slaves throughout the colonies. This trade permitted both voyages to foreign colonies in search of slaves, and the entry to Spanish ports of foreign vessels bringing enslaved Africans. In my view, the free trade in slaves operated as equivalent to an extension of the *comercio de colonias*, and certainly it brought about a marked increase in legally sanctioned trade between the Spanish and British.

Two points should be emphasised with regard to the *comercio de colonias*. First, it had a lengthy history before the 1780s; thus, there were precedents for wartime openings to neutral trade in the Spanish colonies, and many for the licensing of trade with foreign colonies. This was not a new phenomenon, as were the free ports; although it became more generalised than ever from the American Revolutionary War onwards. Secondly, this represented only a partial legalisation of trade by Spanish subjects. Such regions as Santa Marta, Río de la Hacha, Cumaná and Guayana certainly benefited to a considerable extent, and even major colonies such as Cuba, New Granada, and Venezuela now engaged in overt trade with the British on a large scale. Nevertheless, the richest colony of all (Mexico) seems to have remained excluded, and elsewhere the *comercio de colonias* was vulnerable to changes of governor or sudden dictates from the imperial centre. It is true that the free trade in slaves opened Spanish ports throughout the region to British trade, but the resulting scope for legal intercourse in no way compared with that which was offered by the free ports in the British islands. Nevertheless, the *comercio de colonias*, too, played its part in the growth of British trade with the region. Wherever it operated, it provided the vital counterpart to the free ports by rendering trade by Spanish merchants fully legal in the eyes of their own authorities. Spaniards could sail openly and direct to the British colonies, secure in the knowledge that their licences would protect them from harassment en route to the free ports.

The year 1796 marked the onset of the Anglo-Spanish Napoleonic wars, which (with the brief exception of the Peace of Amiens in 1802–04) endured until 1808. These wars constituted a period of great turbulence, which brought about the most substantial realignment of Anglo-Spanish American commercial relations in more than two centuries. Despite some short-term disruption, the same key trends, of growth, legalisation, and diversification, were nevertheless apparent throughout these years. In one major sense, this was a time of loss for Anglo-Spanish trade, since British re-exports via Spain itself ceased altogether as a result of the British naval blockade, and never recovered more than a fraction of their former value. The loss of the re-export trade might have represented a serious blow, since this branch had been the richest since its very origins in the early sixteenth century. In the event, however, an extraordinarily rapid expansion of trade via the Caribbean, and the emergence of entirely new branches, more than compensated for the loss of re-exports via Spain. The trend of rapid growth in British exports was thus not only maintained during the wars, but growth actually increased in pace with respect to earlier decades.

The transformations to which British trade was subject during the wars were described in Chapters 4–6. Chapter 4 discusses trade by Spaniards at the free ports, and particularly the efforts made on both sides to safeguard the legal status of this trade, the hostilities notwithstanding. The outbreak of the wars caused a brief crisis, when Spanish vessels found lying at the free ports were seized as enemy. This crisis prompted loud protests from merchants and authorities in the West Indies, and within less than a year, the British implemented a system of licences protecting Spanish vessels trading at the free ports. These licences were granted to Spanish merchants by the governors in each colony, and guaranteed against seizure by the Royal Navy. Having begun in Trinidad in June 1797, the system was extended first to Jamaica and the Bahamas in November the same year, and afterwards to Grenada, Tobago, Tortola, St Thomas and Curaçao. Although naturally suspended during the Peace of Amiens, provision was made for its restoration even before the return to hostilities in 1804, so that trade by Spaniards at the free ports remained fully legal throughout the period of the wars. In practice, this legal status did not provide the complete protection it offered in principle, and Spanish vessels continued to be seized by naval captains irate at the loss of opportunities for prize cargoes. But despite occasional interruptions, trade by Spaniards at the free ports grew richer than ever, and probably became the principal path by which goods were transferred from British producers to consumers in the Spanish colonies. There were late eighteenth-century European precedents for the protection of trade with enemies during wartime along these lines. But this systematic defence of the legal status of trade with Spaniards in the West Indies throughout the French Revolutionary wars remains deeply impressive.

Spanish defence of legal trade with the British was much weaker during the wars, as was hardly surprising. As perceived in official circles in Madrid, Spain had little to gain and much to lose by trade with the British, and the limited avenues for legal commerce established before the war were eliminated upon its outbreak. No *comercio de colonias* permits could operate openly after 1796, and the free trade in slaves was naturally also suspended so far as the British colonies were concerned. For the most part, voyages by Spaniards to the free ports during the wars thus again became contraband, undertaken under pretext of voyages to neutral colonies or other Spanish ports, and subject to interception by Spanish anti-smuggling forces if detected. The principal exception to this rule during the war of 1796–1802 was trade under cover of permits for the ransom (*rescate*) of prize ships and cargoes held in the British islands. Such was the scale of British predation on Spanish Atlantic trade, and such the necessity in the Spanish colonies both for vital supplies and for standard goods of trade, that ransom permits were granted on a large scale in Cuba and Mexico. Some ransom expeditions were even organised from Spain itself, under direct permit from the crown. Spanish vessels engaging in ransom expeditions thus held a licence from their own government protecting them from Spanish anti-contraband vessels, and a licence from the British protecting them from seizure by the British navy. Under this legal protection, a rich trade was sustained between Mexico and Cuba, and Jamaica and the Bahamas, at the very height of the war. During the war of 1804–08, meanwhile, the legal protection granted by Spain to commercial relations with the British in the Americas was still greater, albeit in the very different form of the Hope–Barings and comparable commercial contracts.

If trade by Spaniards at the free ports flourished more than ever during the wars, trade by British smugglers on the Spanish-American coasts appears to have declined. This decline is described in Chapter 5, and seems to have marked the continuation of a process evident since at least the 1750s. I say 'seems' because British contraband is much harder to trace than Spanish trade at the free ports. The British rarely mentioned their own smuggling, while Spanish accounts are often vague, opaque, or probably exaggerated (reflecting the difficulty of knowing a secretive trade launched from elsewhere, rather than any lack of percipience among Spanish observers). In Spanish reports of contraband, particular caution is required over whether the vessels and individuals referred to are British or Spanish. My conclusion that British smuggling declined after 1796, and indeed since several decades earlier, is necessarily a tentative one. But we may reasonably ask of British contraband in the Spanish colonies, 'Why would it *not* decline?' From 1766, trade by Spaniards at the free ports was legal and safe, while trade by the British in Spanish America remained illegal and dangerous. A great many Spaniards were eager to trade with the British, but there was always the risk of deception or entrapment, and Spanish anti-contraband forces or zealous officials posed a constant threat. As was pointed out by at least one contemporary, it thus made little sense for the British to hazard expeditions to the Spanish coasts, when they could trade all they wished with the Spaniards without straying from their own colonies. This shift in trade away from British smuggling and towards trade at the free ports, of course, only bolstered the practical legalisation of Anglo-Spanish commercial relations during these decades. Nevertheless, British contraband by no means disappeared altogether. It continued at some level in particular colonies, and retained considerable significance in regions where local circumstances were favourable. Probably the key example of such a region was Cuba, which combined an exceptionally propitious coast with particularly poor official oversight. There is also evidence of trade by the British on the coasts of Mexico and New Granada (including at that perennial smuggling centre, the Isthmus of Panama).

Perhaps the most surprising wartime developments in trade were those which derived from the opening of the Spanish colonies to the merchants of neutral powers. Spain was again obliged to throw its colonies open to neutral merchants in November 1797, as the only means to maintain some level of Atlantic trade in the face of the British blockade. Although this permit was formally revoked in April 1799, in practice the majority of the Spanish colonies remained open to neutrals virtually throughout the period of the wars. This may be regarded in effect as a new trade, the precedents for wartime recourse to neutrals notwithstanding, since that which developed after 1797 was immeasurably greater in scale and had far more significant consequences. By far the greatest beneficiary was the United States of America, which was supremely well placed to exploit neutral trade, both geographically and in terms of mercantile potential. North American vessels flooded into Spanish colonial ports, particularly into Havana and Veracruz, but also La Guaira in Venezuela and elsewhere (the sole major exception was New Granada, which remained largely closed to neutrals). The result was a great boom in US trade with Spanish America, the origins of a lasting commercial hegemony.

The potential for the British to penetrate neutral trade with the Spanish colonies was significant. This potential is discussed in Chapter 6; on the one hand, neutral merchants enjoyed fully legal access to Spanish-American ports, and provided an ideal vehicle for the carriage of British goods. On the other, the United States – the dominant neutral power – still had a relatively limited industrial base, and was obliged to import many of its trade goods from Europe, perhaps especially from the British. The result was that after 1797 great quantities of British goods were exported to the Spanish colonies in neutral shipping, above all via the United States. During the war of 1796–1802, neutral trade operated under a general permit for all neutral merchants (rather than under the more controlled regime which prevailed after 1804). British goods were exported to the United States (and also neutral northern Europe), sold outright there, and re-exported to Spanish America by their new owners. Trade in British goods by neutrals was illegal, though in reality few practical obstacles stood in the way of exports. Because it was illegal, trade in British merchandise during the first war is difficult to follow in detail, but the general significance of the commerce remains clear. Neutral trade very rapidly came to constitute a major new branch of British trade with the Spanish colonies. It can be regarded as substituting and compensating for the loss of re-exports of British merchandise via Spain itself during these same years. Its development after 1796 marked a further significant diversification of British trade, subsequent to expansion via the new British colonies in the West Indies in the decades after the Peace of Paris.

Neutral trade adopted a rather different form after 1804 than it had before the Peace. It now operated under individual permits to named merchant houses, both in the United States and Europe, rather than as a general permission. The greatest of the resulting commercial operations were those undertaken by the Hope–Barings consortium, based in Holland and Britain. The origins of the Hope–Barings contract lay in Spain's need to find means to transport bullion from the colonial treasuries across the Atlantic, despite the British blockade. The resulting operations were managed via the United States by an agent of Hope–Barings, David Parish, with bases in New York and Philadelphia. They were mounted from the major ports of the Atlantic seaboard and from New Orleans on the Gulf of Mexico, but came to be handled above all by the house of Robert Oliver based in Baltimore. They resulted in very extensive commercial operations, involving exports of millions of dollars' worth of British and other manufactures to Veracruz. They also involved exports of many millions of pesos in Mexican royal bullion from the same port, some of which was routed via the United States, while some was despatched direct to Britain aboard a British warship. In this context, it will be noted that during the war of 1796–1802, trade by neutral merchants in British goods had been formally illegal, even if informally smiled upon. From 1804, by contrast, the right of Hope–Barings and other neutral houses operating on behalf of the Spanish crown to export British merchandise was openly acknowledged.[1] Hope–Barings and the other houses granted rights for neutral trade after 1804 held impeccable credentials from the Spanish government, and their trade was fully legal.

Comparable to the Hope–Barings contract, and rivalling it in scale, was the affair mounted by the Anglo-Spanish house of Gordon and Murphy during precisely the same years (1805–08). This second contract similarly originated in Spain's need to import bullion from the colonies, and Gordon and Murphy competed directly with Hope–Barings in both commercial exports to Mexico and imports of royal Spanish bullion from Veracruz. Gordon and Murphy organised several dozen expeditions in neutral shipping to Mexico, from Spain, neutral Europe, and the United States. It also operated a monthly mail boat service between Jamaica and Veracruz from mid-1806 to early 1808, which carried large commercial cargoes in addition to the royal Spanish mail. To collect royal bullion from the Spanish colonies Gordon and Murphy used British warships in the same way as Hope–Barings, having five frigates dispatched to Mexico between December 1806 and March 1808. Like Hope–Barings, Gordon and Murphy received the full backing of both the British and Spanish governments, with which the house held separate agreements. Indeed, the protection afforded Gordon and Murphy was if anything still greater than that enjoyed by the former house. The mail boats between Jamaica and Veracruz were Spanish, and were granted licences by the British to trade with the free port at Kingston; but uniquely, these voyages were also fully sanctioned by Spain, in the same way as *rescate* expeditions had been during the war of 1796–1802. This was once more fully legal trade, in contravention of Spain's monopoly of colonial commerce and between nations at war.

Chapter 6 closes with discussion of the 'secret trade' which developed between Britain and the Spanish colonies also between 1805 and 1808. The Gordon and Murphy contract arguably formed part of this trade, although its circumstances were exceptional. Secret trade voyages were mounted by British firms to the Spanish colonies in neutral shipping, often passing via Spain or neutral ports in Europe and the United States. Cargoes consisted primarily of British manufactures, typically rounded out with foreign merchandise taken on board in Spanish or neutral ports. The secret trade developed out of the dissatisfaction of British merchants with the other commercial options available, together with the obvious opportunities offered by neutral trade with Spanish America. It operated under licences granted by the government to individual merchant houses, and with neutral trade permits acquired legally or illegally from the Spanish. From June 1805, secret trade licences began to be granted for voyages to the River Plate, Chile, and Peru, and coincided with the ill-fated British occupation of Buenos Aires and Montevideo in 1806–07. From February 1806, they were also granted for voyages to the Caribbean, especially to Veracruz, Havana and Caracas. Many dozens of such licences were issued between the latter date and 1808, covering both outward and inward voyages. Some scholars have regarded the secret trade as inaugurating 'a new phase in the British penetration of Spanish America', though I have argued that this is only relatively true.[2] It nevertheless remains the case that these expeditions provided an indication of the future course of British trade, both in those voyages that were undertaken direct from Britain (eschewing entrepôts and third ports) and above all in the geographical concentration of trade upon the 'southern cone' and especially the River Plate.

The Value of British Trade with the Spanish Colonies

Assessing the value of British trade with Spanish America poses serious challenges. Throughout its history, detailed statistical data exist solely for the years 1792–95, and even these are problematic. For other periods, we are obliged to rely upon more or less well-informed estimates or guesswork formulated by contemporaries, whether government officials, expert merchants or mercantile bodies, or interested writers and travellers. This procedure is of course deeply unsatisfactory, since the external controls with which to verify the isolated and often fragmentary estimates available are modest. A small number of reports and opinions from different observers scattered across several decades provides a singularly unpromising basis upon which to judge the worth of the commerce with confidence. Nor is the only problem the reliability of available estimates; as we will see, there are also serious difficulties in distinguishing and comparing between figures given for different branches of the trade. I fully expect the estimates given in this book to be subject to strong scrutiny and criticism; nevertheless, the information on which they are based, verified to the degree possible by other evidence, is all we have. While unsatisfactory, it is these figures or nothing, and I hope that readers and reviewers will bear this basic point in mind. The alternative, of abdicating the responsibility of indicating what I regard as the most reliable estimates for the trade, in the context of a study of this length, would be absurd.

In point of fact, the scenario is not quite so bleak as we might expect, such that there are grounds to suppose that the figures given in this work are not entirely arbitrary. One basic point to emphasise is that the estimates offered by the British may be generally more reliable than those encountered among the Hispanic sources. This is not because Spaniards were less competent or perceptive observers than their British counterparts, but simply reflects the reality of the trade. Throughout its existence as a contraband commerce, the British could enquire relatively freely among their own people as to the value of exports and imports, albeit with no guarantee that the answers they received were reliable. The Spaniards, by contrast, for the most part could only attempt to guess at the scale of the secretive intercourse carried on along their shores, of which those involved had excellent reason to remain silent. After the establishment of the free ports in 1766, the balance of credibility shifted far more firmly toward the British, who could now enquire quite openly after a trade which was fully legal in their islands (even if they still took few formal records of it). During the free ports era, British colonial governors could ask respectable merchant houses in Kingston, Nassau, or Port of Spain quite openly about the value of goods bought and sold, and the merchants had little real reason to dissemble (other than perennial mercantile bravado or deliberate under-reporting). The same holds true for other legal or semi-legal branches of trade, including that of Hope–Barings and Gordon and Murphy in 1805–08. Hard statistical data are still lacking, but the occasional estimates available appear to draw upon a more solid base than in earlier periods.

Additionally to these points, we are not entirely in the dark as to the course of the trade. There do not appear to be grounds to doubt that British trade with Spanish America grew, and grew strongly, during the period embraced by this study. On this point all observers, both British and Spanish, agreed, and it also rings logically true given the rapid contemporary progress of British industry and commerce. The challenge is to measure the rate and value of this growth, rather than establish the fact of it; and it transpires that the scattered estimates available from British sources do mark a clear upward trend. This trend is not only positive in a general sense, but in detail shows a measured and credible, albeit rapid, progression, and one moreover which can be related to well-known external factors. Thus, to take the case of re-exports via the Caribbean, we witness a trade which experienced a post-war depression in the 1760s, exacerbated by broader political and commercial factors in the British colonies. This trade was seen to be well on the way to recovery by the 1770s, notably through the agency of the free ports, and by the mid-1780s had already reached more than double its recent historic levels. It then experienced particularly rapid growth in the early 1790s in the context of the St Domingue revolt and the Franco-Spanish war, before commencing a new and still more rapid expansionary phase after the onset of the Anglo-Spanish wars in 1796. The British estimates, then, though few in number and diverse in origin, trace a clear and credible progression, and one which marked a late-eighteenth-century departure in terms of British commercial hegemony. This progression also enables us to identify occasional figures given for the trade which clearly lie outside the realms of the credible, for example when they multiply other known figures ten times over. It establishes a benchmark against which the generally less consistent figures given by Spanish observers can be measured. In short, the figures presented here can certainly never be regarded as more than guidelines, but the factors indicated provide grounds for at least cautious optimism.

Until 1796, two main sets of figures must be combined to achieve a figure for the total value of British trade: those for re-exports via Spain, and for trade via the British entrepôts in the Caribbean. A third figure, for re-exports via Portugal and Brazil, should also be included, although data for this branch are exceptionally scarce. Although the English traded with the Spanish colonies from within only a few years of Columbus's voyage, the trade seems to have become substantial only from the early seventeenth century, and reasonably good data are available only from the 1670s. By 1670, English exports to Andalusia (of which the great majority were destined for re-export to the Americas) were already worth some £368,000, a figure which rose to £400,000 by 1700.[3] In the Caribbean, the only significant entrepôts during this period were Barbados and particularly Jamaica, which already dominated the trade. Jamaica's Spanish commerce was worth less than £20,000 as late as 1679, but then grew rapidly to reach a figure of perhaps £100,000 in 1690.

By the eve of the War of the Spanish Succession in 1700–02, several reports put the value of Jamaican exports as high as £150,000 to £200,000.[4] There must also have been some unquantifiable trade via the Colonia do Sacramento in Brazil, founded in 1680. Taken together, then, the English may have exported goods to the Spanish colonies worth at least £350,000 in the 1670s, a figure which it seems safe to assume rose to well above £500,000 by the turn of the century.

Anglo-Spanish relations at the beginning of the eighteenth century were marked by the War of the Spanish Succession (1702–13), during which British merchants were expelled from Spain and their trade via Andalusia was naturally suspended. Commerce via Jamaica appears to have been worth between £100,000 and £200,000 per year during the war, reaching a peak of £275,000 in exports in 1707 despite stiff competition from the French.[5] Taken as a whole, then, the War of Succession dealt a serious blow to British trade, with a decline in total exports probably exceeding 50 per cent. It was followed by the era of the British-held *Asiento de Negros* (1713–39), when British slave-traders established factories in major Spanish colonial ports, and the South Sea Company sent large merchant vessels to the great trade fairs at Portobelo and Veracruz. Conditions such as these provoked envy among the Spanish and hubris among the British, and estimates for the value of the trade during the Asiento era embrace a particularly wide range. One Spanish observer suggested a figure of almost £2,000,000 per year, while an estimate based on British sources suggests £600,000 per year in the 1730s. My own (perhaps conservative) view is that Britain's Spanish trade in the Caribbean was worth at least £300,000 per year during 1713–39, representing a signif-icant if not extraordinary increase with regard to earlier periods.[6] These years witnessed fierce competition between supporters of the Asiento and merchants involved in the long-established re-export trade via Spain, which was renewed after the Peace in 1713. Figures cited by Sir Charles Whitworth suggest that British exports to Spain grew steadily, from some £600,000 in 1722, to £820,000 a decade later.[7] The proportion of these exports which was re-exported via Andalusia is unknown, though it was certainly high. It may be, then, that the value of British exports surpassed £1,000,000 per year for the first time in the 1730s, buoyed up both by sales via the Asiento and Spanish re-exports.

The period from the late 1730s to the early 1760s witnessed two major bouts of warfare, the wars of Jenkins' Ear and the Austrian Succession (1739–48) and the Seven Years War (1756–63, joined by Spain only in 1761). Although good statistical data are lacking, it appears that re-exports via the West Indies flourished during the war of 1739–48, suspension of the Asiento notwithstanding. There followed a post-war depression around 1750, a period which also marked the transition towards mainly Spanish carriage of Anglo-Spanish trade in the Caribbean. Some accounts suggest that trade remained depressed until the late 1750s, though it picked up again by the early 1760s after Spanish entry into the war. Taken as a whole, British re-exports principally via Jamaica may have been worth around £200,000 per year on average during 1739–63, a significant regression from the quarter-century to 1739.[8] The first estimate for the value of British re-exports via Spain to surpass £1,000,000, meanwhile, dates from 1741 (presumably referring to the immediate pre-war period). By 1761, the British share in re-exports via Cadiz was estimated at just under £1,100,000.[9] And the sole available statistic for the value of British re-exports via Portuguese Brazil dates from the same period, of £200,000 annually in 1762.[10] The isolated nature of the latter estimate, together with what seems a surprisingly high figure (perhaps equivalent to all re-exports via the West Indies), make it difficult to interpret. But, given the above figures, we may tentatively conclude that all British trade with Spanish America was worth at least £1,300,000 per year by the early 1760s. This figure matches an oft-cited Spanish estimate of 6,000,000 pesos (c. £1,350,000) for 1761, though this estimate was apparently intended to refer only to re-exports via the Caribbean. The figure of c. £1,300,000 does not include the exceptional exports of £250,000 made to Cuba during the British occupation of Havana in 1762–63, many of which went direct from Britain rather than from Jamaica.

In the mid-1760s, trade with Spaniards in the West Indies experienced a further crisis, related to post-war glutting of the markets exacerbated by ill-considered British anti-contraband measures. This crisis – which fuelled the debate which led to the creation of free ports in the British islands in 1766 – is difficult to measure accurately. One estimate suggests a value of exports from Jamaica of less than £70,000, the lowest figure of the eighteenth century, though this appears to refer to the late 1750s.[11] As late as 1774, imports of bullion at Jamaica were estimated at only £100,000, well below the average figure for recent decades.[12] By this date some unquantifiable trade was also carried on through the new British colonies in the region, above all Grenada and the Floridas. But whatever the precise extent of the post-war crisis, it seems to have been over by the late 1770s, when the late-eighteenth-century take-off of British trade with the region began. Before 1780, there commenced a boom which would carry Anglo-Spanish trade far beyond its previous levels. In the latter year, an (admittedly dubious) Spanish estimate already indicated trade worth c. £340,000 at Jamaica, while in 1785 a British source put the figure at £500,000 (no British source had recorded so high a figure for any previous era).[13] Unusually good statistical data suggest that by 1792, the total value of imports from the Spanish colonies throughout the British West Indies was around £700,000.[14] And, although data from the same series become more difficult to interpret over the following years, in my view there are solid grounds to suppose that the figure rose above £1,000,000 by 1795 (and possibly considerably higher).[15] Although Jamaica still took more than four-fifths of total imports, other colonies now also played significant roles (principally the Bahamas, Dominica, and Grenada). This startling boom in British trade from around 1780 is to be attributed to general British industrial and commercial progress, in the context of the buoyant Spanish

Atlantic economy brought about by *Comercio libre* reforms. It was boosted in the early 1790s particularly by the elimination of French commercial competition, the strongest in the West Indies, with the St Domingue revolt of 1791 and the Franco-Spanish war of 1793–95.

Data for British re-exports via Spain are particularly unsatisfactory for the late eighteenth century, but such evidence as is available suggests broad stability between the 1760s and 1790s, at the level perhaps of between £700,000 and £1,000,000 per year.[16] This stability over the course of four decades in fact represented stagnation with respect to the relatively rapid growth of the early eighteenth century. It also signified a loss of ground relative to competitors, explaining the generally pessimistic assessments of British observers during this period. Lastly, it meant that the value of re-exports via the West Indies surpassed that of trade undertaken via Spain for the first time, perhaps in the early 1790s. It is probable that some ongoing trade was also undertaken via Brazil at this time, even after the elimination of Colonia do Sacramento as a smuggling base by the Spaniards in 1777. In sum, I would tentatively suggest a total value for British exports to the Spanish colonies of at most £2,000,000 per year in the mid-1790s, on the eve of the outbreak of the Anglo-Spanish wars.

Calculating the value of British exports during the wars presents more formidable challenges than ever. In part this is because available data, although quite abundant, are still more difficult to interpret. In part also, it becomes more difficult to distinguish between different branches of the trade as it became ever more diverse. The Spanish Licensed Trade experienced further rapid growth after 1796, as formal Spanish commerce all but disappeared and Spaniards were driven to British ports for trade. Major new centres now developed in the British islands; good data for the Bahamas (relatively insignificant until as recently as the mid-1790s) suggest the remarkable figures of around £240,000 in 1799, and £365,000 in exports in 1804.[17] Trade at Trinidad (captured only in early 1797) may have been worth between £630,000 and £1,000,000 per year by 1800, though my instinct places it close to the lower figure. Trinidad's trade declined by 1804, when the value of imports was variously recorded as £150,000 or £340,000 (and exports as a little over £190,000).[18] The first British suggestion that trade out of Jamaica surpassed the £1,000,000 mark, meanwhile, dates from 1800. The latter evidence is of little value in itself, but the figure is not an unlikely one given the recent trajectory of the trade at its most important centre.[19] By 1804, *recorded* imports of bullion (certainly only a fraction of the true figure) at Jamaica and the Bahamas were worth some £474,000, passing the $2,000,000 mark for the first time.[20] And there were further important centres, notably St Thomas and Curaçao (held by Britain in 1800–02); though the data to prove it are lacking, it is perfectly possible that trade worth several hundred thousand pounds took place at these islands.[21] Although a degree of speculation is inevitable, given figures of this order, it seems certain that trade by Spaniards at the free ports was worth at least £1,500,000 by 1800 (and conceivably as much as £2,000,000). Whatever the precise sum, the wartime years marked the peak of the free ports' influence, when they briefly constituted the single most valuable conduit for Anglo-Spanish American trade.

Given my comments as to the probable greater reliability of British statistics over those to be found in Spanish sources, it may be instructive to review what Spaniards said about contraband in their colonies during the war of 1796–1802. New Granada serves as a useful 'control' in this sense, since – unlike the other major Spanish colonies – it remained largely closed to neutral shipping, and its foreign trade was limited to trade under licence at the free ports and to British smuggling. A wide range of estimates is available for the value of contraband with New Granada during the war. These include some 10,400,000 pesos (c. £2,340,000) in bullion and produce, or rather less than £470,000 per year for all foreign contraband; up to 22,000,000 pesos (c. £5,000,000) from mid-1795 to late 1803, or about £625,000 per year; and even 20,000,000 pesos during the war (c. £4,500,000) for contraband solely with the British (about £900,000 per year). The most modest (and, in the light of the data presented in the preceding paragraph, in my view the most credible) statistics suggested some 1,500,000 pesos (c. £340,000) per year in 1798–1801 for all foreign contraband, with Jamaica taking perhaps 1,000,000 pesos (c. £225,000) per year. The same cautious source suggested that the value of smuggling in New Granada rose significantly during the peace of 1802–04, to 3,000,000 pesos (c. £675,000) per year in 1802–03 for all foreign trade.[22] Elsewhere, estimates for contraband in Venezuela range from little more than £200,000 in 1801 (embracing trade by both Spaniards and neutrals), to between £1,400,000 and £2,100,000 in 1796 (!); while in Mexico, no less careful an observer than Alexander von Humboldt put the value of contraband at from 6,000,000 to 7,000,000 pesos (c. £1,350,000–£1,575,000) in each year of the war.[23] My object in this paragraph, then, is simply to underscore the point that observers in the Spanish colonies necessarily had a much less clear idea of the true value of contraband than the British. Their estimates tend to vary widely, and often inflate the likely true figures (sometimes to an extraordinary degree). They tend to be of use principally where it is possible to check them against the more credible, or at least more consistent, statistics offered by the British.

Trade at the free ports underwent a certain transformation during the war of 1804–08, though the overall level of exports remained broadly stable and may even have increased. At Trinidad, commerce declined with respect to the years immediately after 1797. Registered exports were worth c. £225,000 in 1805, and perhaps £290,000 in 1806 to judge by data available for the first half of the year only. By 1808, this figure may have fallen to less than £120,000 (probably due to competition from Curaçao, recaptured in late 1807).[24] On the other hand, an increase occurred in trade via other islands and particularly via St Thomas (also recaptured in late 1807). Separate estimates dated 1808 indicate trade worth more than £500,000 at St Thomas, while the *minimum* credible figure appears to be in excess of £200,000.

Exports from Curaçao may well have been of comparable magnitude to those at St Thomas.[25] No statistics regarding the Bahamas have come to light for this period, though we have seen that exports from these islands were worth £365,000 in 1804. Meanwhile, expert testimony dated 1805 suggests that exports from Jamaica were now 'far superior' to £1,000,000. In 1808, it was stated that $5,000,000 (c. £1,125,000) in British merchandise had been exported within twelve months, though an alternative estimate suggested $7,000,000 (c. £1,576,000) in the biennium 1807–08.[26] Registered imports of bullion at Jamaica and the Bahamas (again, only a fraction of true imports) were worth close to £540,000 in 1806, and more than £350,000 in the first half of 1807 alone.[27] Trade at Jamaica was boosted after 1805 by the intercourse with Mexico undertaken in Spanish, British, and neutral vessels under the Gordon and Murphy contract. Data for this trade square in general terms with the figures summarised in this paragraph; thus, the value of trade with Veracruz in Gordon and Murphy mail boats alone has been estimated at almost £1,000,000 for imports and exports alike between mid-1806 and early 1808. British warships also brought to Jamaica some portion of the Mexican bullion exported by Gordon and Murphy in the same period (and may have distorted the figures for trade in British shipping at the free ports).[28] In any case, the levels recorded at Jamaica, St Thomas, Trinidad, and probably Curaçao and the Bahamas would suggest an annual figure of at least £2,000,000 for the total value of trade via the Caribbean by 1807.

Expansion via the British West Indies during the wars helped compensate for the absolute loss of re-exports via Spain, which may still have been worth up to £1,000,000 in some years until 1796. Further compensation for this loss came in the form of the very rapid development of exports of British goods by neutral merchants during the same period. Measuring these exports is more difficult than for any other branch, because they were secretive and were divided between several different routes: principally via the United States, Europe (including Spain), and neutral entrepôts in the West Indies. No useful estimates at all have come to light for the value of British exports by neutrals during the war of 1796–1802. After 1804, the data become more extensive, though they are still difficult to interpret confidently. Much neutral trade via the United States was handled by the Hope–Barings consortium, which despatched some seventy vessels to Mexico from US ports between 1806 and 1808. The value of commercial cargoes shipped in these vessels was some $3,000,000 in 1806–07 alone, while the principal merchant house working with Hope–Barings claimed to have exported more than $2,000,000 (c. £450,000) in British merchandise to Veracruz in the year to 1807. Nor did Hope–Barings ever secure a monopoly on trade via North America, since other US firms also traded with Spanish America, often in British merchandise. By 1807 it was estimated that one-fifth of all British exports to the United States were re-exported to third countries; and, if not all these re-exports were destined for the Spanish colonies, the total value of those that were was credibly stated to be 'a great deal more' than £1,000,000 during the same period.[29]

Trade in British goods via neutral ports in Europe is still more difficult to follow. The single most important firm concerned was Gordon and Murphy, which is known to have dispatched 38 vessels solely to Veracruz in 1806–08 (the firm also traded with other ports including La Guaira). Many of these vessels sailed from Europe: thirteen from Spain and others from Portugal and Germany, with the remainder sailing from the United States and Jamaica. The total value of all thirty-eight shipments was 9,260,923 pesos, or almost £2,100,000; no separate data are available for the value of shipments sent via Europe. Part of the merchandise exported by Gordon and Murphy was Spanish or neutral property, but it is probable that at least two-thirds consisted of British manufactures.[30] In 1807 (the peak year) the total value of goods imported to Veracruz by all neutral merchants (via the United States, Europe, and elsewhere) was over £2,280,000, while exports by these merchants (consisting overwhelmingly of bullion) were worth over £4,800,000. There is no way of knowing the British share in this trade, though British firms surely stood behind the majority of shipments, and the cotton manufactures in which Britain now specialised accounted for almost 63 per cent of total imports.[31] Nor was Veracruz the only port involved; neutrals also traded on a large scale with Cuba, Venezuela, and other Spanish colonies. Lastly, not all trade with neutrals was located in Spanish America; the third major route was via neutral entrepôts in the West Indies, where Spaniards themselves went to trade with neutral and British merchants alike. The most important such entrepôt, outside its two periods of occupation by the British, was Danish St Thomas. By one account, 'several million dollars worth' of British manufactures were exported via St Thomas every year during the war of 1804–08, and certainly registered British exports to the island totalled over £210,000 in 1807.[32] St Thomas may have been the richest of the neutral entrepôts, but it was far from the only one; other leading centres included Curaçao, and St Bartholomew and St Eustatius in the Lesser Antilles.

I have left out of this discussion the exports of royal Spanish bullion from Mexico handled by Hope–Barings and Gordon and Murphy between 1806 and 1808. We have seen that Hope–Barings exported at least 10,130,000 pesos in bullion from Veracruz, or approximately £2,280,000, either directly in a British warship or indirectly via the United States. Gordon and Murphy arranged for the export of 7,651,641 pesos of treasure, equivalent to over £1,720,000, exclusively in British warships. The total sum embarked by both houses was thus in excess of £4,000,000; but these were not commercial shipments, and the bulk of the money was not destined for British use. At least four-fifths was ultimately delivered to France, in payment of Spanish wartime subsidies. This is not, of course, to say that either firm failed to profit individually from the enormous financial and commercial operations with which they became involved. Hope–Barings's profits amounted to at least £862,250 over the course of their contract, and Gordon and Murphy's may not have been greatly inferior.

One last piece of the puzzle remains to be considered, in the form of the 'secret trade' undertaken from Britain under neutral licence in 1805–08. We have seen that over 100 licences were granted by the Privy Council for voyages under this trade up to July 1808, while 130 licences were granted for return voyages. Judging the value of this trade is complicated by the fact that by no means all the licences were made use of, while much trade was concentrated in the River Plate and other regions outside the Caribbean. François Crouzet estimated the value of the 'secret trade' as at least £500,000 in 1806, and a greater sum in 1807, while registered exports to the Spanish colonies were worth some £644,000 in 1808. In my view, Crouzet's figures for 1806–07 seem excessively conservative; a leading minister, for example, estimated the value of licences granted in four months in 1806 alone at from £1,000,000 to £2,000,000.[33] The picture is further complicated by the emergence of new trades at this period, symptoms of the collapse of Spanish imperial dominance which was shortly to follow. In June 1806, the British occupied Buenos Aires and the River Plate, sparking a commercial boom which prompted registered exports of over £1,000,000 by the end of the year.[34] Not all this trade was undertaken under neutral permit, though some of it was; twenty-five of the 'secret trade' licences granted in 1806 were for voyages to the occupied River Plate.[35] The British were expelled from Buenos Aires the following year, but continued to trade there from this time onwards, either directly via the collaboration of local officials, or via Brazil; the latter route was particularly rich, with exports estimated at £120,000 in the second quarter of 1808 alone.[36] And in the winter of 1807–08, eleven British vessels sailed for the west coast of South America (Chile and Peru) with cargoes worth some £933,000.[37]

What, then, are we to make of the data for British exports during the wars of 1796–1808? Re-exports via Spain were lost altogether after 1796, and there must have been some brief loss of ground over the course of the next few years while trade readjusted. By 1800, however, the commerce of Spaniards at the free ports was already worth at least £1,500,000, and possibly considerably more. No data have come to light for the value of trade by neutrals during the war of 1796–1802, making it impossible to offer any general figure for this period. After 1804, trade at the free ports grew still more prosperous, to reach a figure of at least £2,000,000 by 1807. Trade in British goods by neutral merchants via the United States may well have been worth a further £1,000,000 by this time. Neutral trade via Europe is more difficult to judge; Gordon and Murphy alone exported goods worth c. £2,100,000 in 1806–08, but not all of these were British, and perhaps half the shipments went from Jamaica or North America and should be included in those branches of trade. No data are available for shipments of British goods made from European ports by other neutral houses. Trade worth at least £200,000 was carried on through neutral entrepôts in the West Indies, notably St Thomas, but also Curaçao; though again, this trade shifted 'sector' after both islands were captured by the British in late 1807 and granted free ports, and should not be counted twice. Finally, voyages made under neutral permit from Britain (the 'secret trade') were concentrated in South America outside the West Indies, though those which operated in the Caribbean were indistinguishable from, and certainly went to swell the volume of, other neutral arrivals. Taken together, in my view these figures indicate total trade worth between £3,000,000 and £4,000,000 in 1807 (a figure which may have declined somewhat in 1808 as a result of the American embargo and consequent drop in US trade). Such a figure finds some support in registered imports by neutrals at Veracruz in Mexico alone worth over £2,280,000 in 1807, a statistic which includes non-British as well as British goods but does not include imports by Spaniards from the free ports. The figure of from £3,000,000 to £4,000,000 represents 'normal' trade at this time; it does not include the exceptional trade undertaken with the River Plate in 1806–07, nor the expeditions to the Pacific in 1807–08, of uncertain commercial outcome.

The standard figures for the value of British trade with Latin America (including both the Spanish colonies and Brazil) date from over a quarter of a century ago. Ralph Davis's *The Industrial Revolution and British Overseas Trade* offers data for British exports to all parts of the world in the triennia '04–'06 for every decade between the 1780s and 1850s. Exports and re-exports to Latin America combined are accorded a figure of £1,209,000 in 1804–06, in the context of global British exports of £51,069,000 (about 2.4 per cent). The corresponding figures for imports are £1,270,000 and £55,558,000 respectively (2.3 per cent).[38] However, Davis's study was constrained by the limitations of the commercial records on which it was based, which is to say, those of the Inspector-General of Imports and Exports. As we saw in Chapter 3, a major problem with these records is that (except for an exceptional series covering 1788–95, analysed in this book for the first time) they record only direct trade with Britain, and none which went via third ports. Davis's figures thus necessarily exclude not only trade with the Spanish colonies routed via the United States or Europe, but even that which was routed via the free ports in the British West Indies. Furthermore, Davis's figures were affected by his selection of the years '04–'06, which in the case of the triennium 1804–06 meant they included the quite exceptional exports of the latter year to Buenos Aires. For earlier decades, his figures are extremely low; total British exports to Latin America in 1794–96, for example, appear as £89,000 (0.3 per cent of the total), when data from the same sources (discussed in Chapter 3) suggest a probable figure of over £1,000,000 by 1795 in Spanish imports to the British West Indies alone. Given the absence from Davis's figures of trade routed via the West Indies, North America, or Europe, it is hardly surprising that the new estimates presented here should be so much higher than those which resulted from the earlier study.

What are the implications of an estimate of c. £3,000,000–£4,000,000 for British trade with Spanish America in 1807? Such a figure is some three times higher than that offered by Davis for all trade with Latin America in 1804–06. With British exports worth a little over £50,000,000 per year in these three years,[39] the Spanish colonies may have taken *at least* 6.0 per cent of the total, as opposed to the 2.4 per cent suggested by Davis (for trade which also included Brazil). This revised estimate for Spanish America does not require any correction of Davis's total figure for British exports, since this is not 'new' trade, previously unrecorded by the Customs. Trade with Spanish America, rather, has been buried until now in the commercial records for trade with the West Indies, the United States, and Europe. British exports to those territories were 'real' enough, but in most cases the ultimate market was not Jamaica, New York, Lisbon, or Cadiz (the recorded destinations), but Mexico City, Havana, Bogotá, or Caracas. It has long been apparent that exports to the West Indies exceeded the demand capacity of the British islands, such that there must have been a surplus for re-export. It now appears that estimates for domestic demand in other regions, including the United States, should be revised in the light of the volume of goods re-exported to the Spanish colonies. None of this detracts from Davis's general series for the growth of British global exports, whose value rose from c. £20,400,000 in the mid-1780s to £34,300,000 in the 1790s, and above £50,000,000 in 1804–06.[40] But the contribution to this growth of Spanish-speaking America seems to have been significantly under-estimated. Lastly, this contribution was never more significant than from late 1806, when the Continental Blockade seriously threatened British exports to Europe. John Lynch has argued that the blockade might have proved crucial had Britain not possessed expanding outlets elsewhere.[41] These outlets were concentrated in the New World, above all in the West Indies and the United States; and it is now clear that behind both lay the markets of Spanish America, to a hitherto unsuspected degree.

The implications of this adjustment of Davis's figures go beyond the first decade of the nineteenth century. Davis, we recall, estimated British exports to Latin America as a whole at £1,209,000 in 1804–06, equivalent to about 2.4 per cent of total British exports. The suggestion here is that real exports to Spanish America, at from £3,000,000–£4,000,000, made up at least 6.0 per cent of total British exports in 1807. Davis then goes on to indicate exports and re-exports combined to Latin America of £2,587,000 in 1814–16, constituting 3.9 per cent of the total. The corresponding figures for later decades are £5,281,000 in 1824–26 (10.7 per cent), £5,352,000 in 1834–36 (9.5 per cent), £6,084,000 in 1844–46 (8.8 per cent), and £9,332,000 in 1854–56 (7.6 per cent). Two general points may be made about these figures. Firstly, Latin America's role as a significant market for British exports clearly began earlier than we have been accustomed to think. Indeed, this role dated not only to the decade to 1810; my estimate for exports in the mid-1790s, of c. £2,000,000, though necessarily tentative, would suggest a similar share of around 6 per cent (in the context of total British exports of a little over £32,000,000). Secondly, Davis indicates some retreat in the 1810s with regard to my figure for 1807 (to a little over £2,500,000 in 1814–16). This decline could easily be explained by the turbulence of the decade, of insurrection, warfare, and commercial blockade. But it is possible that the same issue which affects Davis's figures for 1804–06 – the absence of indirect as opposed to direct trade with Spanish America – also affects those for 1814–16. We know that trade via the West Indies remained strong in the 1810s, and only fell away later; in 1817, for example, Jamaica may have exported manufactured goods to the value of $9,000,000 (c. £2,000,000).[42] In short, it seems likely that Davis's figure for 1814–16 underestimates the true value of trade with Spanish America, because it excludes exports via the West Indies (and indeed via North America). If this is the case, then British trade may have remained buoyant continuously from the turn of the century onwards.

Concluding Comments

What are the broader conclusions to arise from this work? To consider the Spanish-American dimension first, the implications are both economic and political. In economic terms, this book demonstrates the extent to which the Spanish commercial monopoly was undermined in the closing decades of the colonial era by foreign competition, and particularly by the British. This competition grew rapidly even during the period of apparent commercial renaissance brought about by 'Free Trade' reforms in the Spanish empire after 1765; indeed, the rapid growth of British trade coincided closely with those reforms. By the mid-1790s, British penetration was already substantial, and posed a significant threat to Spanish commercial hegemony; but from 1796 and the outbreak of the Anglo-Spanish wars, the rate of growth redoubled, and the trade acquired wholly unprecedented dimensions. During a dozen years of warfare, the commercial barriers surrounding the Spanish colonies collapsed, until by 1807 the British alone did business there to the extent of at least 13,000,000 pesos. This represented a first moment of something approaching free trade with foreign nations, managed and promoted moreover in no small part by Spanish Americans themselves. It is the latter issue which holds the key to the political dimension to the work; for scholars have long been concerned with the relationship between independence in Spanish America and foreign trade. Points of contention have included the degree to which control of trade was a key grievance of Spanish-American patriots, and the extent to which free trade was a key goal of the independence movements. The degree of effective economic emancipation indicated by the scale of British trade in the early 1800s – together (perhaps) with the vigorous participation of Spanish-American merchants in this trade – hints at both the vigour with which these debates were staged, and the progress made in terms of effective commercial independence, even before outbreak of the revolutionary movements in 1809–10.

Lastly, in its British aspect, my work ties in with long-standing debates about the relationship between economic growth and overseas trade during the era of the 'Industrial Revolution'. These debates embrace the extent to which foreign trade stimulated or sustained industrialisation at home, or the development and diversification of British overseas markets. Spanish America provided a far richer field for British goods during this period than we have been accustomed to think, one which seems to have taken at least 6 per cent of all British exports before 1810. This market absorbed significant quantities of manufactures and particularly of textiles, and it also supplied large amounts of the raw materials on which British trade and industry depended. These raw materials included cotton, dyewoods, and drugs, and above all the abundant supply of bullion on which British global commerce, particularly with Asia, relied. Trade with the Spanish colonies also fuelled economic growth indirectly, by supplying the plantations in the West Indies with mules, horses, cattle and other livestock essential to their operations. The Spanish-American market proved significant from at least the 1790s, but it may never have been more influential than in 1806–08, when it helped compensate for the wartime crisis in British trade with Europe. As a British Latin Americanist, nevertheless, I find still more interesting the question of the development of British relations with Spanish America. My work has traced the development of those relations in the half-century before Independence, particularly in the economic sphere. A great deal remains to be learnt, and many of my conclusions necessarily remain provisional pending further detailed research. But I think their tendency, at least, is to push the rise of British commercial hegemony in the region back by perhaps two decades; to show to just what extent, and by what means, the foundations of Britain's intense nineteenth-century relationship with Latin America were laid before the onset of political Independence.

Notes

1   See pp. 202–8.
2   Pp. 214–20.
3   P. 6.
4   P. 17.
5   P. 17.
6   P. 25.
7   P. 9.
8   P. 32.
9   P. 10.
10   P. 11.
11   Pp. 30, 45.
12   P. 52.
13   Pp. 58, 81.
14   Pp. 100–1
15   P. 104.
16   P. 110.
17   Pp. 129, 131.
18   Pp. 146–7.
19   P. 128.

20 Table 4.2, p. 131.
21 Pp. 148–9; compare trade in British goods at St Thomas and Curaçao while still neutral, p. 210.
22 Pp. 173–4.
23 Pp. 178, 164.
24 P. 147.
25 Pp. 148–9.
26 P. 135.
27 Table 4.2, p. 131.
28 P. 213.
29 P. 208.
30 Pp. 213–14.
31 P. 208.
32 P. 201.
33 P. 218–19.
34 Combined figure for exports and re-exports to Buenos Aires and Montevideo, from 'A Comparative View of the State of the Trade of Great Britain with all Parts of the World ...', in N.A., Cust. 17 / 28, n.f.
35 Crouzet, *L'Economie britannique*, pp. 179–84.
36 Goebel, 'British Trade to the Spanish Colonies', pp. 309–10; Lynch, 'British Policy and Spanish America', p. 29.
37 P. 219.
38 Davis, *Industrial Revolution*, table 43, p. 96 (exports); table 51, p. 104 (re-exports); table 59, pp. 114–15 (imports).
39 Davis, *Industrial Revolution*, table 37, p. 86.
40 Davis, *Industrial Revolution*, table 37, p. 86 (computed values of British overseas trade excluding Ireland).
41 Lynch, 'British Policy and Spanish America', pp. 25–6; also Platt, *Latin America and British Trade*, pp. 28–9.
42 Armytage, *Free Port System*, pp. 92–3.

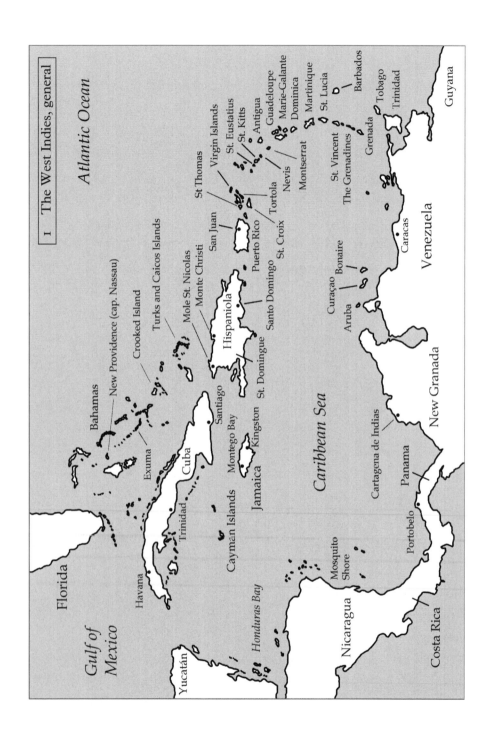

1   The West Indies, general

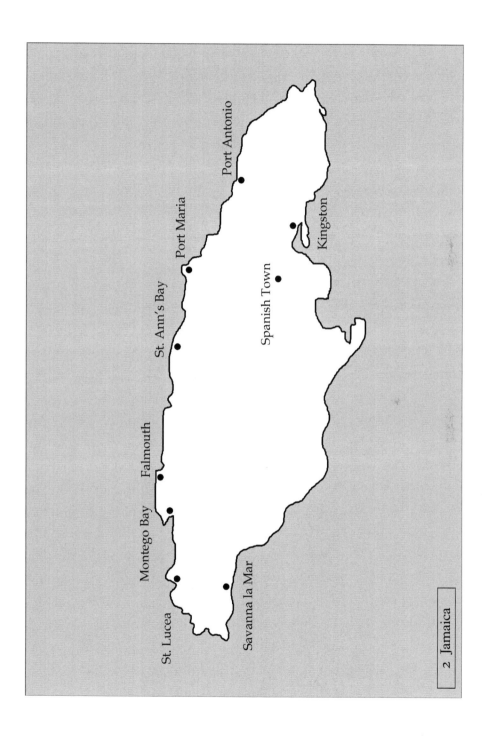

2 Jamaica

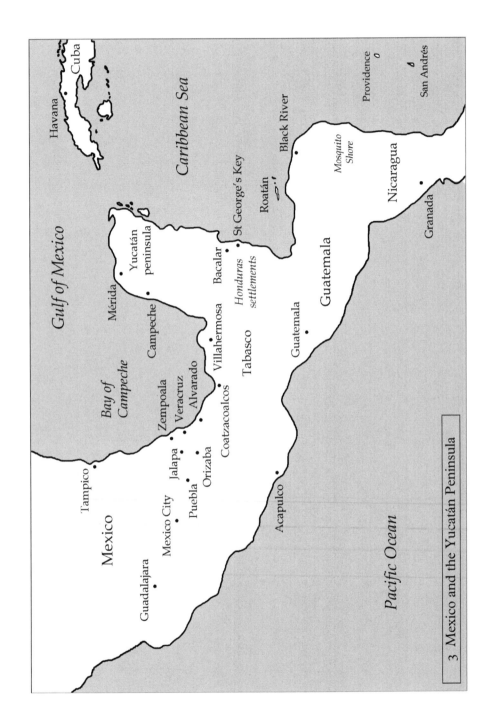

3 Mexico and the Yucatán Peninsula

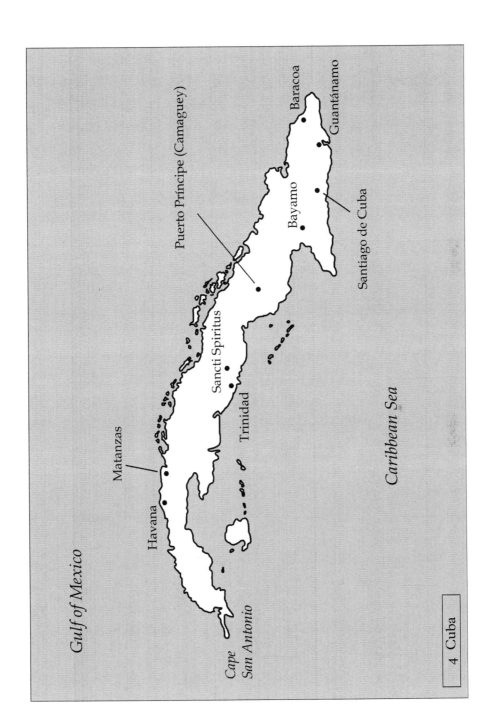

Gulf of Mexico

Matanzas

Havana

Cape
San Antonio

Puerto Príncipe (Camaguey)

Sancti Spiritus

Trinidad

Baracoa

Guantánamo

Bayamo

Santiago de Cuba

Caribbean Sea

4 Cuba

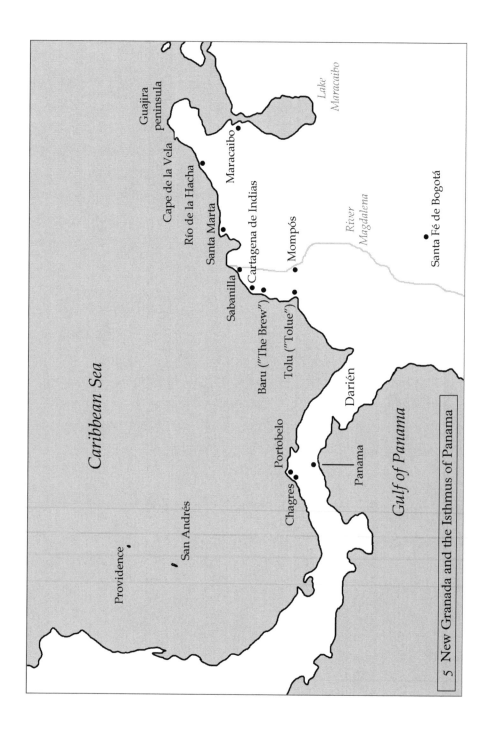

5 New Granada and the Isthmus of Panama

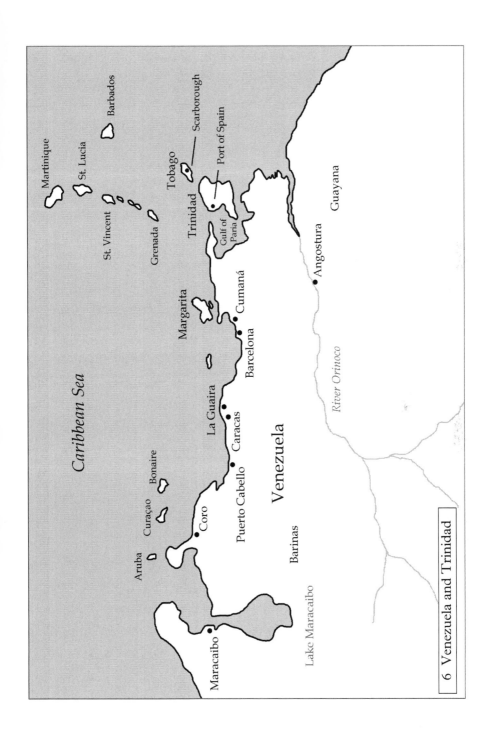

6 Venezuela and Trinidad

Caribbean Sea

Portobelo

Caracas / La Guaira

Trinidad

Atlantic Ocean

Cartagena de Indias

Panama

Santa Fé de Bogotá

Popayán

Quito

Guayaquil

Paita

Trujillo

Lower Peru

Salvador da Bahía

Lima / Callao

Cuzco

Arequipa

Chuquisaca
(Sucre)

Brazil

Arica

Potosí

Upper Peru

Río de Janeiro

Paraguay

Asunción

Pacific Ocean

Colonia do
Sacramento

Montevideo

Valparaíso

Buenos
Aires

River Plate

Santiago

Concepción

Valdivia

Falkland Islands

7 South America

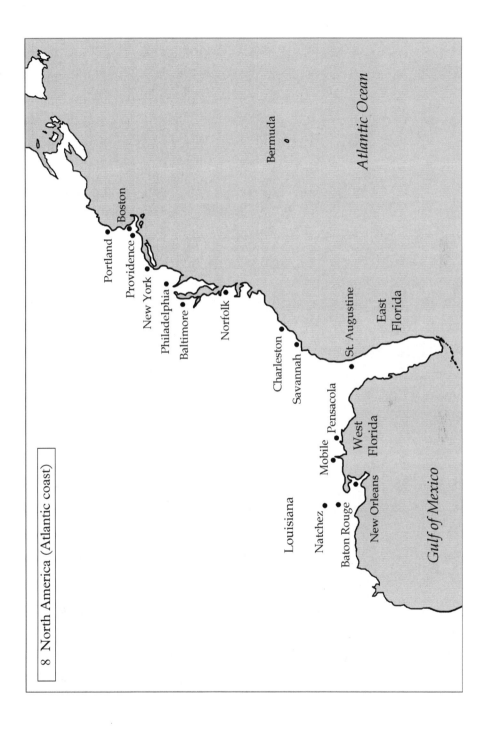

8 North America (Atlantic coast)

Portland
Boston
Providence
New York
Philadelphia
Baltimore
Norfolk
Charleston
Savannah
St. Augustine
Pensacola
Mobile
West Florida
East Florida
Louisiana
Natchez
Baton Rouge
New Orleans
Bermuda
Atlantic Ocean
Gulf of Mexico

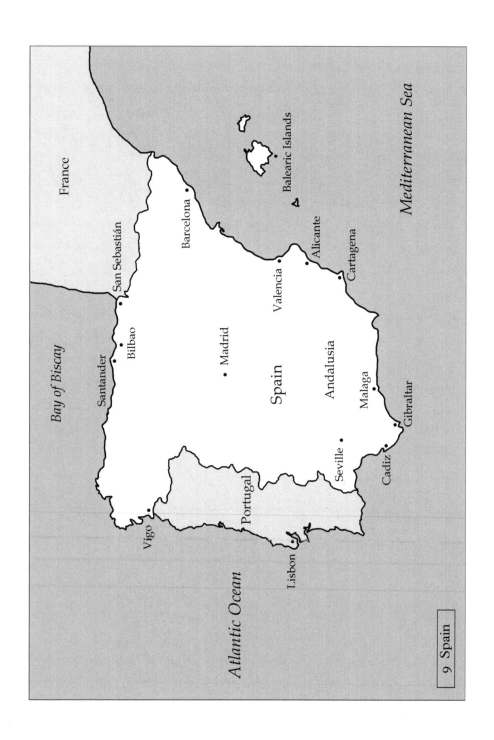

9 Spain

British Trade with the Spanish Colonies, 1788–95

Table A1 Total registered value of imports from the Spanish colonies to the British West Indies, 1792–95

1792	396,693-3-5
1793	420,577-0-7
1794	410,281-6-9
1795	498,562-1-6

Source: N.A., Customs 17 / 14–17.
General note to tables: All figures for value in pounds sterling-shillings-pence. All percentages are rounded to first decimal place; as a result in some cases the figures may not total 100.0. Unless otherwise stated, data covers the period 5 Jan.–5 Jan. of each year.

Table A2 Tonnage of shipping entering at the British West Indies from foreign colonies and the United States, 1788–95

Colonies	Tons	%	Tons	%	Tons	%
	1788		**1789**		**1790**	
Spanish	12,525	23.1	13,494	25.1	12,605	21.4
Danish	3,153	5.8	1,906	3.6	2,613	4.4
Dutch	16,916	31.2	17,817	33.2	24,585	41.7
French	19,084	35.2	18,114	33.7	16,199	27.5
Swedish	2,528	4.7	2,348	4.4	2,939	5.0
Total	54,206		53,679		58,941	
United States	68,447		97,500		91,504	
	1791		**1792**		**1793**	
Spanish	21,885	34.8	17,451	26.3	29,139	38.4
Danish	3,432	5.5	5,469	8.2	3,275	4.3
Dutch	17,703	28.1	15,535	23.4	26,185	34.5
French	17,688	28.1	24,495	36.9	10,065	13.3
Swedish	2,261	3.6	3,424	5.2	7,192	9.5
Total	62,969		66,374		75,856	
United States	87,244		108,746		91,712	
	1794		**1795**			
Spanish	21,697	54.2	19,008	50.4		
Danish	1,821	4.6	1,465	3.9		
Dutch	14,227	35.6	16,310	43.2		
French	—		—			
Swedish	2,266	5.7	944	2.5		
Total	40,011		37,727			
United States	91,839		132,435			

Source: N.A., Customs 17 / 10–17.

Note: Table covers trade both in British vessels and in foreign vessels under the Free Port Acts. In 1788, the principal foreign colonies were: Danish: St Thomas, St Croix, St John; Dutch: Curaçao, St Eustatius; French: Martinique, Guadeloupe, Marie-Galante, St Lucia, Tobago; Swedish: St Bartholomew. Tobago was captured by Britain in April 1793, and Martinique and St Lucia in 1794.

Table A3: Total registered value of imports from foreign colonies and the
United States to the British West Indies, 1792–95

Colonies	Value	%	Value	%
	1792		**1793**	
Spanish	396,693-3-5	64.6	420,577-0-7	53.2
Danish	11,190-11-9	1.8	15,021-3-10	1.9
Dutch	112,198-8-9	18.3	209,028-18-10	26.5
French	85,721-14-7	14.0	99,266-12-9	12.6
Swedish	8,043-4-0	1.3	46,065-18-2	5.8
Total	613,847-2-6		789,959-14-2	
United States	n/a		612,607-7-10	
	1794		**1795**	
Spanish	410,281-6-9	81.6	498,562-1-6	66.0
Danish	3,690-17-6	0.7	4,126-17-0	0.5
Dutch	77,819-9-3	15.5	250,484-3-7	33.2
French	—		—	
Swedish	10,893-8-3	2.2	2,015-13-0	0.3
Total	502,685-1-9		755,188-15-1	
United States	644,315-6-4		991,258-2-0	

Source: N.A., Customs 17 / 14–17.
Note: Table covers both trade in British vessels and in foreign vessels under the Free Port
Acts. No data available for United States in 1792. Figure for United States in 1794 includes
£378,749-7-10 for foreign vessels entering by Governors' Proclamation – which were
overwhelmingly American.

Table A4 Share of British and foreign vessels of shipping entering from the Spanish colonies at the British West Indies, 1788–95 (figures for total tonnage)

Colonies	Tons	%	Tons	%	Tons	%
	1788		**1789**		**1790**	
British vessels	2,720	21.7	3,316	24.6	2,836	22.5
Foreign vessels under the Free Port Acts	9,805	78.3	10,178	75.4	9,769	77.5
Total	12,525		13,494		12,605	
	1791		**1792**		**1793**	
British vessels	4,387	20.0	3,185	18.3	2,716	9.3
Foreign vessels under the Free Port Acts	17,498	80.0	14,266	81.7	26,423	90.7
Total	21,885		17,451		29,139	
	1794		**1795**			
British vessels	1,884	8.7	3,743	19.7		
Foreign vessels under Free Port Acts	19,813	91.3	15,265	80.3		
Total	21,697		19,008			

Source: N.A., Customs 17 / 10–17.

Table A5: Share of British and foreign vessels of registered value of imports from the Spanish colonies to the British West Indies, 1792–95

	Value	%	Value	%
	1792		**1793**	
Imports in British vessels	21,806-1-5	5.5	24,835-4-6	5.9
Imports in foreign vessels under the Free Port Acts	374,887-2-0	94.5	395,741-16-1	94.1
Total	396,693-3-5		420,577-0-7	
	1794		**1795**	
Imports in British vessels	11,597-1-9	2.8	18,410-17-3	3.7
Imports in foreign vessels under the Free Port Acts	398,684-5-0	97.2	480,151-4-3	96.3
Total	410,281-6-9		498,562-1-6	

Source: N.A., Customs 17 / 14–17.

Table A6 Share of each British colony of the registered tonnage of foreign shipping entering from the Spanish colonies, 1788–95 (figures for total tonnage)

Colony	Tons	%	Tons	%	Tons	%
	1788		**1789**		**1790**	
Antigua	n/a		n/a		n/a	
Bahamas	484	4.9	918	9.0	1,183	12.1
Dominica	1,075	11.0	944	9.3	977	10.0
Grenada	2,886	29.4	3,365	33.1	3,040	31.1
Jamaica	5,360	54.7	4,951	48.6	4,569	46.8
Total	9,805		10,178		9,769	
	1791		**1792**		**1793**	
Antigua	n/a		n/a		—	
Bahamas	1,055	6.0	708	5.0	1,949	7.4
Dominica	827	4.7	1,364	9.6	685	2.6
Grenada	4,290	24.5	5,019	35.2	4,912	18.6
Jamaica	11,326	64.7	7,175	50.3	18,877	71.4
Total	17,498		14,266		26,423	
	1794		**1795**			
Antigua	—		—			
Bahamas	n/a		2,120	13.9		
Dominica	542	2.7	255	1.7		
Grenada	3,499	17.7	1,614	10.6		
Jamaica	15,772	79.6	11,276	73.9		
Total	19,813		15,265			

Source: N.A., Customs 17 / 10–17.
Note: The Free Port in Antigua opened only in 1793. Data for Bahamas for 1794 lacking.

Table A7 Share of each British colony of the registered value of imports in foreign shipping entering from the Spanish colonies, 1792–95

Colony	Year	%	Year	%
	1792		1793	
Antigua	n/a		—	
Bahamas	19,270-11-3	5.1	22,068-14-4	5.6
Dominica	24,189-5-3	6.5	13,793-10-6	3.5
Grenada	57,905-15-6	15.4	63,884-17-9	16.1
Jamaica	273,521-10-0	73.0	295,994-13-6	74.8
Total	374,887-02-0		395,741-16-1	
	1794		1795	
Antigua	—		—	
Bahamas	18,938-0-6	4.8	—	
Dominica	4,663-7-0	1.2	5,991-10-6	1.2
Grenada	41,060-0-9	10.3	16,792-6-9	3.5
Jamaica	334,022-16-9	83.8	457,367-7-0	95.3
Total	398,684-5-0		480,151-4-3	

Source: N.A., Customs 17 / 10–17.

Note: In the Inspector-General's account for imports to the Bahamas in 1794 (Customs 17 / 16, f. 90v) the value of specie imported is given as £99-16-0 and its equivalent in dollars as '$199,600'. The true sterling equivalent of $199,600, at the current exchange rate of c. $4.44 to the pound, is £44,914-10-0 – an increase which would materially affect the total value of imports to the Bahamas. I have here assumed, however, that the sterling figure of £99-16-0, though certainly an understatement of real imports of bullion, is the figure supposed correct by the Inspector General.

Table A8: Share of each British colony of the registered tonnage of British shipping entering from the Spanish colonies, 1788–95 (figures for total tonnage)

Colony	Tons	%	Tons	%	Tons	%
	1788		**1789**		**1790**	
Antigua	62	2.3	775	23.4	960	33.9
Bahamas	25	0.9	71	2.1	105	3.7
Barbados	275	10.1	163	4.9	140	4.9
Dominica	634	23.3	53	1.6	198	7.0
Grenada	440	16.2	919	27.7	1,160	40.9
Jamaica	46	1.7	332	10.0	150	5.3
Martinique	n/a		n/a		n/a	
Montserrat	—		—		—	
Nevis	191	7.0	334	10.1	—	
St Kitts	394	14.5	457	13.8	63	2.2
St Vincents	592	21.8	212	6.4	60	2.1
Tobago	n/a		n/a		n/a	
Tortola	61	2.2	—		—	
Total	2,720		3,316		2,836	
	1791		**1792**		**1793**	
Antigua	804	18.3	508	15.9	161	5.9
Bahamas	669	15.2	462	14.5	356	13.1
Barbados	130	3.0	342	10.7	—	
Dominica	—		53	1.7	86	3.2
Grenada	1,219	27.8	1,453	45.6	379	14.0
Jamaica	1,088	24.8	184	5.8	1,286	47.3
Martinique	n/a		n/a		n/a	
Montserrat	—		—		—	
Nevis	—		31	1.0	192	7.1
St Kitts	35	0.8	106	3.3	79	2.9
St Vincents	442	10.1	46	1.4	112	4.1
Tobago	n/a		n/a		65	2.4
Tortola	—		—		—	
Total	4,387		3,185		2,716	

	1794		**1795**	
Antigua	222	11.8	278	7.4
Bahamas	n/a		279	7.5
Barbados	104	5.5	—	
Dominica	—		—	
Grenada	1,330	70.6	2,012	53.8
Jamaica	109	5.8	53	1.4
Martinique	n/a		264	7.1
Montserrat	—		—	
Nevis	—		—	
St. Kitts	32	1.7	—	
St. Vincents	87	4.6	273	7.3
Tobago	—		584	15.6
Tortola	—		—	
Total	1,884		3,743	

Source: N.A., Customs 17 / 10–17.
Note: Data for Bahamas for 1794 lacking.

Table A9: Share of each British colony of the registered value of imports in British shipping entering from the Spanish colonies, 1792–95

Colony	Value	%	Value	%
	1792		**1793**	
Antigua	2,804-18-9	12.9	24-5-0	0.1
Bahamas	3,974-10-8	18.2	3,204-3-0	12.9
Barbados	3,755-0-0	17.2	—	
Dominica	917-0-0	4.2	390-12-6	1.6
Grenada	10,216-12-0	46.9	7,672-17-6	30.9
Jamaica	—		11,558-6-6	46.5
Martinique	n/a		n/a	
Montserrat	—		—	
Nevis	138-0-0	0.6	1,268-0-0	5.1
St Kitts	—		92-0-0	0.4
St Vincent	—		625-0-0	2.5
Tobago	n/a		—	
Tortola	—		—	
Total	21,806-1-5		24,835-4-6	
	1794		**1795**	
Antigua	683-17-3	5.9	366-5-0	2.0
Bahamas	1,387-17-0	12.0	995-17-0	5.4
Barbados	60-5-0	0.5	—	
Dominica	—		—	
Grenada	8,801-17-6	75.9	6,093-3-9	33.1
Jamaica	—		—	
Martinique	n/a		3,359-7-6	18.2
Montserrat	—		—	
Nevis	—		—	
St Kitts	317-17-6	2.7	—	
St Vincent	345-7-6	3.0	2,809-0-0	15.3
Tobago	—		4,787-4-0	26.0
Tortola	—		—	
Total	11,597-1-9		18,410-17-3	

Source: N.A., Customs 17 / 14–17.

Table A10: Registered imports from the Spanish colonies to the British West Indies, 1792–95

Year	General category	Commodity	Value	% of total value
1792	Specie	Dollars	70,225-0-0	17.7
	Dyes and dyewoods	Brazil wood	2,400-0-0	20.8
		Cochineal	863-4-0	
		Fustic	70,146-5-9	
		Indigo	2,432-15-0	
		Logwood	116-0-0	
		Nicaragua wood	6,446-0-0	
	Other woods	Cedar boards	6-1-4	1.0
		Ebony	8-0-0	
		Hardwood pieces	318-10-0	
		Mahogany	1,095-8-4	
		Mill timber	2,607-0-0	
	Drugs	Cortex Peru	2,406-19-0	0.6
		Lignum vitae	85-5-0	
	Livestock and hides	Cows and oxen	28,039-0-0	40.5
		Hides	16,276-13-0	
		Horses	18,972-0-0	
		Mules and asses	96,608-0-0	
		Poultry	54-1-0	
		Sheep and hogs	901-0-0	
	Foodstuffs	Indian corn	540-0-0	0.1
	Plantation produce	Cocoa	152-12-6	13.9
		Cotton wool	54,924-2-6	
	Miscellaneous	Gum copal	13,544-6-0	5.3
		Tortoiseshell	280-0-0	
		Negroes	7,245-0-0	
	Total		396,693-3-5	

1793	Specie	Dollars	122,894-10-0	29.2
	Dyes and dyewoods	Brazil wood	44-0-0	9.8
		Cochineal	5,600-0-0	
		Fustic	21,758-1-0	
		Indigo	800-7-6	
		Logwood	241-8-6	
		Nicaragua wood	12,654-12-0	
	Other woods	Boat timber	6-5-0	1.9
		Cedar timber	12-0-0	
		Ebony	10-10-0	
		Hardwood	752-6-6	
		Mahogany	6,524-1-8	
		Mill timber	158-0-0	
		Pine boards	50-0-0	
		Shingles and staves	399-19-0	
	Drugs	Balsam	710-0-0	0.6
		Lignum vitae	300-0-0	
		Sarsaparilla	1,312-10-0	
	Livestock, hides, and tallow	Cows and oxen	54,213-0-0	45.8
		Hides	18,163-0-8	
		Horses	23,400-0-0	
		Mules and asses	95,500-0-0	
		Poultry	6-18-0	
		Sheep and hogs	721-0-0	
		Tallow	468-9-0	
	Foodstuffs	Bread and flour	825-5-0	0.3
		Indian corn	91-7-6	
		Rice	165-12-0	
	Plantation produce	Cocoa	430-13-0	11.2
		Cotton wool	43,526-16-3	
		Sugar	3,206-0-0	
	Miscellaneous	Gum algobora	4,500-0-0	1.3
		Gum copal	665-0-0	
		Negroes	135-0-0	
		Pitch and tar	30-0-0	
		Tortoiseshell	300-8-0	
	Total		420,577-0-7	

1794	Specie	Dollars	172,697-6-0	42.1
	Dyes and dyewoods	Brazil wood	466-10-0	7.5
		Fustic	10,957-9-9	
		Indigo	8,275-10-0	
		Logwood	327-0-0	
		Nicaragua wood	10,744-10-0	
	Other woods	Cedar timber	134-10-0	1.2
		Hardwood posts	52-13-0	
		Hoops and staves	226-0-0	
		Mahogany	4,289-7-6	
		Mill timber	24-0-0	
		Pine boards	7-0-0	
	Drugs	Balsam capavia	0-15-0	0.2
		Guaiacum	247-10-0	
		Lignum vitae	307-10-0	
		Sarsaparilla	75-18-9	
	Livestock, hides and tallow	Cows and oxen	60,228-0-0	44.5
		Hides	10,242-12-6	
		Horses	21,582-0-0	
		Mules	88,580-0-0	
		Poultry	18-8-0	
		Sheep and hogs	1,853-5-0	
		Tallow	59-6-0	
	Foodstuffs	Coconuts	78-0-0	0.2
		Beef and pork	372-12-0	
		Indian corn	331-12-6	
	Plantation produce	Cocoa	48-8-9	4.2
		Coffee	835-5-0	
		Cotton wool	15,362-15-0	
		Pimento	28-0-0	
		Sugar	973-0-0	
	Miscellaneous	Gum copal	210-0-0	0.2
		Salt	30-0-0	
		Negroes	405-0-0	
		Tortoiseshell	209-12-0	
	Total		410,281-6-9	

1795	Specie	Dollars	320,340-0-0	64.3
	Dyes and dyewoods	Brazil wood	155-0-0	2.2
		Fustic	1,618-6-4	
		Indigo	581-17-6	
		Logwood	22-6-0	
		Nicaragua wood	8,689-16-0	
	Other woods	Cedar posts	3-0-0	0.2
		Hardwood posts	57-15-0	
		Mahogany	542-14-2	
		Pine boards	255-0-0	
		Staves	54-0-0	
	Drugs	Cascarilla	37-10-0	0.0
		Lignum vitae	12-14-3	
	Livestock and hides	Cows and oxen	32,229-0-0	20.9
		Hides	5,316-0-6	
		Horses	20,196-0-0	
		Mules	45,900-0-0	
		Poultry	28-2-0	
		Sheep and hogs	628-10-0	
	Foodstuffs	Bread and flour	764-1-0	0.4
		Coconuts	140-0-0	
		Dry fish	521-18-0	
		Indian corn	430-0-6	
		Pease	25-13-0	
		Rice	282-18-0	
	Plantation produce	Brown sugar	183-18-0	11.9
		Cocoa	142-10-0	
		Coffee	630-10-0	
		Cotton wool	57,984-6-3	
		Tobacco	181-5-0	
	Miscellaneous	Deerskins	90-0-0	0.1
		Gum copal	52-10-0	
		Negroes	315-0-0	
		Pitch and tar	150-0-0	
	Total		498,562-1-6	

Source: N.A., Customs 17 / 14–17.
Note: Percentages of less than 0.05% are entered as 0.0%. Includes both imports in British vessels and in foreign vessels under the Free Port Acts.

Table A11 Make-up of imports from the Spanish colonies to the British West Indies, 1792–95, in British and foreign shipping

General category of imports	Percentage of total value of imports in British shipping (annual average, 1792–95)	Percentage of total value of imports in foreign shipping (annual average, 1792–95)
Specie	4.8	41.4
Dyes and dyewoods	9.8	9.6
Other woods	7.8	0.7
Drugs	1.9	0.2
Livestock and hides	26.4	37.6
Foodstuffs	5.2	—
Plantation produce	26.3	9.3
Other	17.8	1.2
Total	100.0	100.0

Source: N.A., Customs 17 / 14–17.

Table A12 Make-up of imports from the Spanish colonies at each British colony, 1792–95; imports in foreign shipping (percentages)

British colony	Specie	Dyes and dyewoods	Other woods	Drugs
Bahamas	48.0	6.5	4.5	—
Dominica	—	13.2	0.2	3.6
Grenada	—	3.7	0.6	0.9
Jamaica	48.0	10.3	0.6	0.1

British colony	Livestock and hides	Foodstuffs	Plantation produce	Other
Bahamas	35.4	—	5.7	—
Dominica	37.2	0.3	19.2	26.3
Grenada	57.7	0.1	33.6	3.4
Jamaica	35.0	—	5.9	0.1

Source: N.A., Customs 17 / 14–17.

Note: Figures for the Bahamas represent an average percentage share for the three years (1792–94) in which imports at that island's Free Ports were registered.

Table A13 Make-up of imports from the Spanish colonies at each British
colony, 1792–95; imports in British shipping (percentages)

British colony	Specie	Dyes and dyewoods	Other woods	Drugs
Antigua	—	27.0	8.9	—
Bahamas	38.6	7.7	—	0.1
Barbados	—	1.0	68.6	—
Dominica	—	—	—	—
Grenada	—	15.0	2.5	0.4
Jamaica	—	5.3	17.3	11.4
Martinique	—	—	—	—
Nevis	—	9.8	5.5	—
St Kitts	—	—	22.4	—
St Vincents	—	—	1.6	—
Tobago	—	—	—	—

British colony	Livestock and hides	Foodstuffs	Plantation produce	Other
Antigua	53.3	—	10.8	—
Bahamas	33.7	12.5	0.8	6.4
Barbados	14.9	—	15.4	—
Dominica	—	—	100.0	—
Grenada	6.7	8.1	27.9	39.4
Jamaica	54.2	—	11.8	—
Martinique	—	—	100.0	—
Nevis	75.1	—	—	9.6
St Kitts	—	33.9	43.6	—
St Vincents	1.0	—	97.5	—
Tobago	100.0	—	—	—

Source: N.A., Customs 17 / 14–17.
Note: Only Antigua, the Bahamas, and Grenada had registered imports in all four years;
figures for the other colonies represent the average percentage share in years for which
imports were registered.

Table A14 Trade of the British Free Ports with neighbouring foreign colonies:
average percentage shares, import and export trades combined

| | Percentage shares of total tonnage | | | | |
	Spanish colonies	Danish colonies	Dutch colonies	French colonies	Swedish colonies
1788					
Dominica	14.2	3.0	8.6	73.8	0.5
Grenada	60.1	7.0	4.0	28.4	0.7
Jamaica	54.6	3.3	4.4	37.7	—
Bahamas	100.0	—	—	—	—
1789					
Dominica	15.6	—	4.4	80.0	0.2
Grenada	55.2	1.4	15.1	28.0	0.5
Jamaica	49.9	—	4.9	45.3	—
Bahamas	100.0	—	—	—	—
1790					
Dominica	14.3	3.2	3.2	79.0	0.5
Grenada	57.8	2.9	8.4	31.1	—
Jamaica	51.4	0.5	5.2	41.6	1.4
Bahamas	100.0	—	—	—	—
1791					
Dominica	14.1	2.7	7.3	75.9	0.1
Grenada	54.0	5.5	4.5	36.0	—
Jamaica	78.2	0.5	6.9	14.3	0.3
Bahamas	97.5	—	—	2.5	—
1792					
Dominica	37.1	2.0	10.2	50.7	—
Grenada	47.4	3.7	3.7	45.4	—
Jamaica	50.8	—	5.5	43.8	—
Bahamas	98.9	—	—	1.1	—

1793

Dominica	46.0	16.5	12.4	21.6	3.6
Grenada	68.8	5.0	5.6	18.6	2.2
Jamaica	88.7	0.9	1.4	8.9	0.2
Bahamas	100.0	—	—	—	—

1794

Dominica	62.0	34.2	2.6	—	1.2
Grenada	93.9	5.9	0.3	—	—
Jamaica	96.6	0.9	2.6	—	—
Bahamas (No data in this volume)					

1795

Dominica	73.5	26.5	—	—	—
Grenada	97.2	2.9	—	—	—
Jamaica	100.0	—	—	—	—
Bahamas	100.0	—	—	—	—

Source: N.A., Customs 17 / 14–17.

Table A15 Trade of the British West Indies with Spanish America in foreign
shipping under the Free Port Acts, 1788–1795: total numbers of ships,
tonnage and crew

			Import trade		
British colony	*Ships*	*Tonnage*	*Crew*	*(Average tonnage)*	*(Average crew)*
Bahamas	345	8,417	1,540	24.4	4.5
Dominica	188	6,669	1,764	35.5	9.4
Grenada	1,274	28,625	8,658	22.5	6.8
Jamaica	2,077	79,306	15,785	38.2	7.6

Source: N.A., Customs 17 / 10–17.

Note: Averages rounded to one decimal place. 'Ships' represents the number of voyages made, not necessarily the real number of ships employed in the trade.

Table A16 Trade of the British West Indies with Spanish America in British
shipping, 1788–95: total numbers of ships, tonnage and crew

			Import trade		
British colony	*Ships*	*Tonnage*	*Crew*	*(Average tonnage)*	*(Average crew)*
Antigua	57	3,770	427	66.1	7.5
Bahamas	46	1,967	243	42.8	5.3
Barbados	17	1,154	88	67.9	5.2
Dominica	12	1,024	92	85.3	7.7
Grenada	140	8,912	888	63.7	6.3
Jamaica	37	3,248	371	87.8	10.0
Martinique	4	264	24	66.0	6.0
Montserrat	—	—	—		
Nevis	11	748	69	68.0	6.3
St Kitts	18	1,166	105	64.8	5.8
St Vincent	35	1,824	199	52.1	5.7
Tobago	13	649	100	49.9	7.7
Tortola	1	61	8	61.0	8.0
Total		24,787			

Source: N.A., Customs 17 / 10–17.

Note: Averages rounded to one decimal place. 'Ships' represents the number of voyages made, not necessarily the real number of ships employed in the trade.

Table A17 Total registered value of exports from the British West Indies to
the Spanish colonies, 1792–95

1792	103,600-15-0
1793	150,044-0-0
1794	136,686-10-0
1795	188,449-2-0

Source: N.A., Customs 17 / 14–17.

Table A18 Exports of slaves from the British West Indies to the Spanish
colonies, 1792–95

Colony	Number of slaves exported	%	Number of slaves exported	%
	1792		**1793**	
In British vessels				
Antigua	8	1.0	10	1.2
Bahamas	8	1.0	—	
Barbados	—		—	
Dominica	579	70.4	—	
Grenada	170	20.7	524	61.0
Jamaica	27	3.3	265	30.8
St Kitts	30	3.6	—	
St Vincent	—		60	7.0
Total	822	36.0	859	26.9
In foreign vessels under the Free Port Acts				
Bahamas	—		—	
Dominica	251	17.2	6	0.3
Grenada	1,102	75.4	625	26.8
Jamaica	108	7.4	1,700	72.9
Total	1,461	64.0	2,331	73.1
Grand total	2,283		3,190	

	1794		1795	
In British vessels				
Antigua	—		—	
Bahamas	48	7.3	—	
Barbados	60	9.1	29	11.1
Dominica	—		—	
Grenada	248	37.7	228	87.0
Jamaica	132	20.1	5	1.9
St Kitts	140	21.3	—	
St Vincent	30	4.6	—	
Total	658	23.0	262	6.3
In foreign vessels under the Free Port Acts				
Bahamas	8	0.4	—	
Dominica	—		—	
Grenada	207	9.4	73	1.9
Jamaica	1,994	90.3	3,818	98.1
Total	2,209	77.0	3,891	93.7
Grand total	2,867		4,153	

Source: N.A., Customs 17 / 14–17

Table A19 Total registered value of imports from the Spanish colonies to British North America and Bermuda, 1792–95

1792	1,097-14-4
1793	1,079-16-6
1794	639-10-0
1795	475-5-9

Source: N.A., Customs 17 / 14–17.

Table A20: British North America: share of each British colony of the registered tonnage of British shipping entering from the Spanish colonies, 1788-95

	1788		1789		1790	
Bermuda	69	(100.0%)	—		—	
Cape Breton	—		—		—	
New Brunswick	—		62	(6.5%)	—	
Newfoundland	—		543	(56.5%)	66	(100.0%)
Nova Scotia	—		356	(37.0%)	—	
Total	69		961		66	
	1791		1792		1793	
Bermuda	61	(100.0%)	102	(28.6%)	64	(30.3%)
Cape Breton	—		—		—	
New Brunswick	—		—		—	
Newfoundland	—		102	(28.6%)	147	(69.7%)
Nova Scotia	—		153	(42.9%)	—	
Total	61		357		211	
	1794		1795			
Bermuda	—		32	(16.0%)		
Cape Breton	—		—			
New Brunswick	—		—			
Newfoundland	—		—			
Nova Scotia	—		168	(84.0%)		
Total	None		200			

Source: N.A., Customs 17 / 10-17.
Note: From 1793 onwards, the Inspector-General's records for the continental colonies cover the *twelve months following 10 Oct.* of the year concerned.

Table A21: British North America: share of each British colony of the registered tonnage of British shipping clearing outwards for the Spanish colonies,
1788–95

	1788		1789		1790	
Bermuda	242	(72.2%)	69	(100.0%)	39	(100.0%)
Cape Breton	20	(6.0%)	—		—	
New Brunswick	73	(21.8%)	—		—	
Newfoundland	—		—		—	
Nova Scotia	—		—		—	
Total	335		69		39	

	1791		1792		1793	
Bermuda	125	(100.0%)	—		38	(100.0%)
Cape Breton	—		—		—	
New Brunswick	—		—		—	
Newfoundland	—		—		—	
Nova Scotia	—		—		—	
Total	125		None		38	

	1794		1795	
Bermuda	—		67	(34.9%)
Cape Breton	—		—	
New Brunswick	—		—	
Newfoundland	—		—	
Nova Scotia	—		125	(65.1%)
Total	None		192	

Source: N.A., Customs 17 / 10–17.
Note: From 1793 onwards, the Inspector-General's records for the continental colonies
cover the *twelve months following 10 Oct.* of the year concerned.

Note on Archival Sources

Research for this work was undertaken in the following archives and archival sections:

United Kingdom

National Archives	Admiralty, Board of Trade, Colonial Office, Papers of H.M. Customs, Foreign Office, Privy Council, State Papers Foreign, Treasury
British Library	Additional Mss., Egerton Mss., Stowe Mss.
Staffordshire Record Office	Dartmouth Papers
Sheffield Archives	Wentworth Woodhouse Muniments, Rockingham Papers

Spain

Archivo General de Indias	Gobierno (sub-sections Caracas, Mexico, Santa Fé, Santo Domingo), Indiferente General, Consulados
Archivo Histórico Nacional	Estado
Archivo General de Simancas	Estado
Archivo del Museo Naval	General manuscript series

Mexico

Archivo General de la Nación	Alcabalas, Archivo Histórico de Hacienda, Bandos, Consulado, Correspondencia de Diversas Autoridades, Correspondencia de Virreyes, Inquisición, Marina

Cuba

Archivo Nacional	Asuntos Políticos, Correspondencia de los

de Cuba	Capitanes Generales, Miscelánea de Libros, Real Consulado y Junta de Fomento

Colombia

Archivo General de la Nación	Archivo Anexo: Historia, Colonia: Consulados, Colonia: Contrabandos, Colonia: Historia Civil, Colonia: Negocios Exteriores, Colonia: Virreyes

United States

National Archives	Record Group 59 (Despatches from United States Consuls)

Bibliography for the Study of British Trade with the Spanish Colonies

This bibliography, besides furnishing referential support for the text, aims to present a research-level guide to published sources for the study of British trade with the Spanish colonies, especially in the Caribbean in the half-century following the Seven Years War. The intention has been to include most major work published in English, Spanish, French and Portuguese, particularly since c. 1950, although many older works are included where appropriate. Although listings are as comprehensive as possible, the field covered is now a very large one, and a degree of selectivity has been required. Thus, for example, general works of economic or national history with potential relevance to the topic have usually been excluded.

The works listed were consulted in the auxiliary libraries of the archives listed in the Note on Archival Sources and in the following institutions: the British Library; Senate House Library, University of London; the library of the Escuela de Estudios Hispano-Americanos, Seville; Biblioteca Nacional, Madrid; the Library of Congress, Washington; Biblioteca Nacional, Mexico; library of the Colegio de México, Mexico City; Biblioteca Nacional José Martí, Havana; and the Biblioteca Nacional, Bogotá. Supplementary collections included the Sydney Jones Library, University of Liverpool; Library of the West India Committee, Institute of Commonwealth Studies, London; John Rylands University Library of Manchester; library of the Universidad Hispalense, Seville; Biblioteca de la Región Militar Sur, Seville; library of the Instituto Mora, Mexico City; and the Biblioteca Luis Angel Arango, Bogotá.

Printed Primary Sources and Early Histories to 1860

Abbad, Iñigo, Fray, *Viaje a la América* (1772–73: facsimile edn by Carlos I. Arcaya, Caracas: Banco Nacional de Ahorro y Préstamo, 1974).

Ajequiezcane, Pedro, 'British Trade with the Spanish Colonies: Pedro Ajequiezcane's Letter on Commercial Matters (1806)', ed. Adrian J. Pearce, *The Americas*, 61:2 (Oct. 2004), pp. 245–56.

American State Papers. Documents Legislative and Executive of the Congress of the United States … Class 1. Foreign Relations (Washington, 1832; Buffalo, NY:

William S. Hein & Co., 1998).

The Annual Register ..., 80 vols. (London: J. Dodsley, [1762?]–1838).

Anon. (ed.), *Instrucciones que los vireyes de Nueva España dejaron a sus sucesores* ... (Mexico City: Imprenta Imperial, 1867).

Antúnez y Acevedo, Rafael, *Memorias históricas sobre la legislación, y gobierno del comercio de los Españoles con sus colonias en las Indias occidentales* (Madrid: 1797); facsimile edn by Antonio García-Baquero González (Madrid, 1981).

Arango y Parreño, Francisco de, 'Informe del Síndico en el expediente instruído por el Consulado de la Habana sobre los medios que conviene proponer para sacar la agricultura y comercio de la isla del apuro en que se hallan' (Havana, 29 Nov. 1808), in José Carlos Chiaramonte (ed.), *Pensamiento de la Ilustración: Economía y sociedad iberoamericanas en el siglo XVIII* (Caracas: Biblioteca Ayacucho, 1979), pp. 249–76.

Arango y Parreño, Francisco de, *Obras*, 2 vols. (Havana: Howson y Heinen, 1888).

Atkins, John, *A Voyage to Guinea, Brazil, and the West Indies, in His Majesty's Ships the Swallow and Weymouth* (London: Caesar Ward & Richard Chandler, 1735).

Atwood, Thomas, *The History of Dominica* ... (London: J. Johnson, 1791).

Bourgoing, Jean François de, Baron, *Tableau de l'Espagne moderne*, 2nd edn, 3 vols. (Paris, 1797).

Burdon, John Alder, Sir, *Archives of British Honduras*, 3 vols. (London: Sifton Praed & Co. for the West India Committee, 1931).

Burke, Edmund, *A Short Account of a Late Short Administration* (London: J. Wilkie, 1766).

Burke, Edmund, *The Correspondence of Edmund Burke*, ed. Thomas W. Copeland, 10 vols. (Cambridge: Cambridge University Press, 1958–78).

Coggeshall, George, *Second Series of Voyages to Various Parts of the World, made between the Years 1802 and 1841* (New York: D. Appleton & Co., 1852).

Collingwood, Vice-Admiral Lord, *A Selection from the Public and Private Correspondence of Vice-Admiral Lord Collingwood, Interspersed with Memoirs of his Life*, ed. G.L. Newnham Collingwood (London: James Ridgway, 1828).

Colmenares, Germán (ed.), *Relaciones e informes de los gobernantes de la Nueva Granada*, 3 vols. (Bogotá: Banco Popular, Fondo de Promoción de la Cultura, 1989).

Consulado de México, *Recopilación de noticias sobre el comercio de contrabando con las posesiones de España en América* (16 Sept. 1818), *Boletín del Archivo General de la Nación* (Mexico), 29.4 (1958), pp. 611–704.

Dauxion Lavaysse, Jean Joseph, *Voyage aux Iles de Trinidad, de Tabago, de la Marguerite, et dans diverses parties de Vénézuela, dans l'Amérique Méridionale*, 2 vols. (Paris: F. Schoëll, 1813).

Debates and Proceedings of the British House of Commons ...

Defoe, Daniel, *A General History of the Pyrates*, ed. Manuel Schonhorn (1724: London: J.M. Dent & Sons, 1972).

Defoe, Daniel, *A Plan of the English Commerce, being a Compleat Prospect of the*

Trade of this Nation, as well the Home Trade as the Foreign (London: Charles Rivington, 1728).

Defoe, Daniel, *Mercator: or, Commerce Retrieved, Being Considerations on the State of the British Trade; particularly as it respects Holland, Flanders, and the Dutch Barrier; the Trade to and from France, the Trade to Portugal, Spain, and the West Indies* ..., nos. 169–74 (19 June–3 July 1714).

Defoe, Daniel (but Anon.), *The Interests of the Several Princes and States of Europe Consider'd, with respect to the Succession of the Crown of Spain and the Titles of the several Pretenders thereto, Examin'd* (London, 1698).

Depons, François Joseph, *Travels in South America, during the years 1801, 1802, 1803, and 1804* ..., 2 vols. (London, 1807; facsimile edn: New York: AMS Press, 1970).

Donnan, Elizabeth (ed.), *Documents Illustrative of the History of the Slave Trade to America*, 4 vols. (1930; New York: Octagon Books, 1965).

[Dubuisson, Paul Ulric, and 'Dubucq'], *Lettres critiques et politiques sur les colonies et le commerce des villes maritimes de France* ... (Geneva: n.p., 1785).

Eden, Frederick Morton, Sir, *Eight Letters on the Peace and on the Commerce and Manufactures of Great Britain* (London: J. Wright, 1802).

Edwards, Bryan, *The History, Civil and Commercial, of the British Colonies in the West Indies*, 3 vols. (London: John Stockdale, 1793–1801).

Ezpeleta y Galdeano, Joseph de, *Relación del gobierno del Exmo. Sor. Dn. Josef de Ezpeleta, etc., en este Nuevo Reino de Granada* ... (3 Dec. 1796), in Germán Colmenares (ed.), *Relaciones e informes de los gobernantes de la Nueva Granada*, 3 vols. (Bogotá: Banco Popular, Fondo de Promoción de la Cultura, 1989), 2:153–311.

Flanagan, Mrs (attributed to), *Antigua and the Antiguans* ..., 2 vols. (London: Saunders & Otley, 1844).

Florescano, Enrique, and Fernando Castillo (eds.), *Controversia sobre la libertad de comercio en Nueva España (1776–1818)*, 2 vols. (Mexico: Instituto Mexicano de Comercio Exterior, 1975).

Fowler, John, *A Summary Account of the Present Flourishing State of the Respectable Colony of Tobago* ... (London: A. Grant, 1774).

The Gentleman's Magazine, 103 vols. (London: various publishers, 1731–1833).

[Hall, F. Ayrer], *The Importance of the British Plantations in America to this Kingdom* ... (London: J. Peele, 1731).

Headlam, Cecil (ed.), *Calendar of State Papers, Colonial Series. America and West Indies, 1704–1705* (London: H.M.S.O., 1916).

Headlam, Cecil, *Calendar of State Papers, Colonial Series. America and West Indies, January 1719 to February 1720* (London: H.M.S.O., 1933).

Headlam, Cecil, *Calendar of State Papers, Colonial Series. America and West Indies, 1724–1725* (London: H.M.S.O., 1936).

Historical Manuscripts Commission, *Report on the Manuscripts of J.B. Fortescue Esq. preserved at Dropmore*, 10 vols. (London, 1892–1927).

House of Commons Committee on the Commercial State of the West India Colonies, *Report from the Committee on the Commercial State of the West India*

Colonies ([London: House of Commons], 1807).

Humboldt, Alexander von, *Ensayo político sobre el reino de la Nueva España* (Mexico: Editorial Porrúa S.A., 1966).

Humboldt, Alexander von, *Ensayo político sobre la isla de Cuba* (Madrid, Valladolid: Junta de Castilla y León, 1998).

Humboldt, Alexander von, *Personal Narrative of Travels to the Equinoctial Regions of America, during the years 1799–1804*, 3 vols. (London: Henry G. Bohn, 1852–53).

Humphreys, Robin Arthur (ed.), *British Consular Reports on the Trade and Politics of Latin America, 1824–1826* (London: Royal Historical Society, 1940).

Ingersoll, Jared, 'A Selection from the Correspondence and Miscellaneous Papers of Jared Ingersoll', ed. Franklin B. Dexter, *Papers of the New Haven Colony Historical Society*, 9 (1918), pp. 201–472.

Jornal Económico Mercantil de Veracruz (Veracruz periodical; commenced publication 1 Mar. 1806).

Juan, Jorge, and Antonio de Ulloa, *Noticias secretas de América*, ed. Luis J. Ramos Gomez (Madrid: Historia 16, 1992).

Julián, Antonio, *La Perla de la América. Provincia de Santa Marta reconocida, observada y expuesta en discursos históricos* (Madrid: Antonio de Sancha, 1787).

Keppel, George Thomas, Earl of Albemarle, *Memoirs of the Marquis of Rockingham and his Contemporaries*, 2 vols. (London: Richard Bentley, 1852).

Knox, John P., *A Historical Account of St. Thomas, W. I. ... and incidental notices of St. Croix and St. Johns* (New York: Charles Scribner, 1852).

Koster, John Theodore, *Short Statement of the Trade in Gold Bullion*, 2nd edn (Liverpool, 1811).

Lerdo de Tejada, Miguel, *Comercio exterior de México desde la Conquista hasta hoy* (Mexico: Rafael Rafael, 1853).

Levene, Ricardo (ed.), *Documentos para la historia argentina*, 20 vols. (Buenos Aires: Facultad de Filosofia y Letras, Instituto de Investigaciones Históricas, 1913–29).

Long, Edward, *History of Jamaica*, 3 vols. (1774; facsimile edn by George Metcalf, London: Frank Cass & Co., 1970).

López Cancelada, Juan, *Ruina de la Nueva España si se declara el comercio libre con los extranjeros ...* (Cadiz, 1811), in *Controversia que suscitó el comercio de Nueva España con los países extranjeros (1811–1821)*, ed. Luis Chaves Orozco (Mexico: Banco Nacional de Comercio Exterior, 1959), pp. 3–63.

Manning, William R. (ed.), *Diplomatic Correspondence of the United States Concerning the Independence of the Latin-American Nations*, 3 vols. (New York: Oxford University Press, 1925).

Martin, François-Xavier, *The History of Louisiana from the Earliest Period* (1827–29; New Orleans: James A. Gresham, 1882).

McPherson, David, *Annals of Commerce, Manufactures, Fisheries and Navigation ...*, 4 vols. (London and Edinburgh: Nichols & Son *et al.*, 1805).

Mendinueta y Músquiz, Pedro, *Relación del estado del Nuevo Reino de Granada ...* (Dec. 1803), in Germán Colmenares (ed.), *Relaciones e informes de los gober-*

nantes de la Nueva Granada, 3 vols. (Bogotá: Banco Popular, Fondo de Promoción de la Cultura, 1989), 3:5–191.

Narváez y la Torre, Antonio, 'Discurso del Mariscal de Campo ... D. Antonio Narváez y la Torre, sobre la utilidad de permitir el comercio libre de neutrales en este Reyno ...', (30 June 1805) in Sergio Elías Ortiz (ed.) *Escritos de dos economistas coloniales: Don Antonio de Narváez y la Torre y Don José Ignacio de Pombo* (Bogotá: Banco de la República, 1965), pp. 67–120; also edited by Carlos Restrepo Canal in *Revista de Indias*, 91–92 (Jan.–June 1963), pp. 280–316.

Nolte, Vincent, *Fifty Years in Both Hemispheres; or, Reminiscences of a Merchant's Life* (London: Trubner & Co., 1854).

Ortiz de la Tabla Ducasse, Javier (ed.), *Memorias políticas y económicas del Consulado de Veracruz, 1796–1822* (Seville: Escuela de Estudios Hispano-Americanos, 1985).

Ouvrard, Gabriel Julien, *Mémoires de G.J. Ouvrard sur sa vie et ses diverses opérations financières*, 3 vols. (Paris, 1826–27).

Papel periódico de la Habana (Havana periodical: commenced publication 1790).

Parliamentary Papers: 1812, Minutes of Evidence taken before the Committee of the Whole House ... Relating to the Orders in Council, vol. 3 ([London: House of Commons], 1812).

Peuchet, Jacques, *Etat des Colonies et du Commerce des Européens dans les deux Indes, depuis 1785 jusqu'en 1821 ...*, 2 vols. (Paris: Amable Costes et Cie., 1821).

Pitt, William, Earl of Chatham, *Correspondence of William Pitt, Earl of Chatham*, ed. W.S. Taylor and J.H. Pringle, 4 vols. (London: John Murray, 1838–40).

Pombo, José Ignacio de, 'Informe de Don José Ignacio de Pombo ... sobre asuntos económicos y fiscales, (18 Apr. 1807), in Sergio Elías Ortiz (ed.) *Escritos de dos economistas coloniales: Don Antonio de Narváez y la Torre y Don José Ignacio de Pombo* (Bogotá: Banco de la República, 1965), pp. 121–34.

Pombo, José Ignacio de, *Informe del Real Consulado de Cartagena de Indias a la Suprema Junta Provincial ...* (Cartagena, 1810) in Sergio Elías Ortiz (ed.) *Escritos de dos economistas coloniales: Don Antonio de Narváez y la Torre y Don José Ignacio de Pombo* (Bogotá: Banco de la República, 1965), pp. 135–271.

Pombo, José Ignacio de, 'Informe del Real Tribunal del Consulado de Cartagena de Indias ... sobre el origen y las causas del contrabando, sus perjuicios, los medios de evitarlo y de descubrir los fraudes' (June 1800), in Jorge Orlando Melo (ed.), *Comercio y contrabando en Cartagena de Indias* (Bogotá: Ed. Linotipia Bolívar Ltda., 1986), pp. 11–47.

Pombo, José Ignacio de, 'Memoria sobre el contrabando en el Virreynato de Santa Fé ...', (Mar. 1804), in Jorge Orlando Melo (ed.), *Comercio y contrabando en Cartagena de Indias* (Bogotá: Ed. Linotipia Bolívar Ltda., 1986), pp. 49–122.

Postlethwayt, Malachy, *The Universal Dictionary of Trade and Commerce, translated from the French of ... Monsieur Savary ... with large Additions and Improvements ...*, 2 vols. (London: John & Paul Knapton, 1751–55).

Poyer, John, *The History of Barbados, from the First Discovery of the Island, in the Year 1605, till the Accession of Lord Seaforth, 1801* (London: J. Mawman, 1808).

Quirós, José María, *Memoria de instituto en que se manifiesta que el comercio marítimo ha llamado siempre la atención de todas las naciones* ... (Havana, 1814), in *Controversia que suscitó el comercio de Nueva España con los países extranjeros (1811–1821)*, ed. Luis Chaves Orozco (Mexico: Banco Nacional de Comercio Exterior, 1959), pp. 65–94.

Quirós, José María, 'Reflexiones sobre el comercio libre de las Américas ...' (1817), ed. Manuel Carrera Stampa, *Boletín del Archivo General de la Nación* (Mexico), 19:2 (Apr.–May 1948), pp. 169–215.

Renny, Robert, *An History of Jamaica with Observations on the Climate, Scenery, Trade, Productions, Negroes, Slave Trade, Diseases of Europeans, Customs, Manners, and Dispositions of the Inhabitants* (London: J. Cawthorn, 1807).

Reynal, l'Abbé, *A Philosophical and Political History of the Settlements and Trade of the Europeans in the East and West Indies*, trans. J. Justamond, 4 vols. (London: T. Cadell, 1776).

Saavedra de Sangronis, Francisco de, *Journal of Don Francisco de Saavedra de Sangronis during the commission which he had in his charge from 25 June 1780 until the 20th of the same month of 1783*, ed. Francisco Morales Padrón (Gainesville: University of Florida Press, 1989).

Saavedra de Sangronis, Francisco de, *Los Decenios (autobiografía de un sevillano de la Ilustración)*, ed. Francisco Morales Padrón (Seville: Excmo. Ayuntamiento de Sevilla, 1995).

Saco, José Antonio, *Colección de papeles científicos, históricos, políticos y de otros ramos sobre la isla de Cuba, ya publicados, ya inéditos* ..., 3 vols. (Paris: Imprenta de D'Aubusson y Kugelmann, 1858–59).

Sagra, Ramón de la, *Historia económico-política y estadística de la isla de Cuba* (Havana: Imprenta de las Viudas de Arazoza y Soler, 1831).

Sánchez Pedrote, Enrique (ed.), 'Gil y Lemos y su memoria sobre el Nuevo Reino de Granada', *Anuario de Estudios Americanos*, 8 (1951), pp. 169–212.

Savary de Bruslons, Jacques, *Dictionnaire universel de commerce* ..., 3 vols. (Paris: Jacques Estienne, 1723–30).

Schomburgk, Robert Hermann, Sir, *The History of Barbados* ... (London: Brown, Green & Longmans, 1848).

Sharpe, Horatio, *Correspondence of Governor Horatio Sharpe*, ed. William Hand Browne, 3 vols. (Baltimore: Maryland Historical Society [published as vols. 6, 9 and 14 of *Archives of Maryland*], 1888–95).

[Stephen, James?], *War in Disguise; or, the Frauds of the Neutral Flags* (London: C. Whittingham, 1805).

Stevens, B.F. (ed.), *Manuscripts of the Earl of Dartmouth*, 3 vols., Historical Manuscripts Commission (London: H. M. S. O., 1887–95).

Sugawara, Masae (ed.), *La deuda pública de España y la economía novohispana* (Mexico City: Instituto Nacional de Antropología e Historia, 1976).

Torre Villar, Ernesto de la, and Luis Chávez Orozco (eds.), *El contrabando y el comercio exterior en la Nueva España*, vol. 4 of *Colección de documentos para la historia del comercio exterior de México*, 2nd series (Mexico: Banco Nacional de Comercio Exterior, 1967).

Torres Ramírez, Bibiano, and Javier Ortiz de la Tabla Ducasse (eds.), *Reglamento y aranceles reales para el Comercio libre de España a Indias* (12 Oct. 1778; facsimile edn, Seville: Escuela de Estudios Hispano-Americanos, 1979).

Uring, Nathaniel, *A History of the Voyages and Travels of Capt. Nathaniel Uring* ..., 2nd edn (London: John Clarke, 1727).

[Walker, Alexander?], *Colombia. Relación geográfica, topográfica, agrícola, comercial y política de este país* ..., 2 vols. (London, 1822 [simultaneously in English and Spanish]; Bogotá: Banco de la República, 1973).

Walpole, Horace, *Memoirs of the Reign of George III*, 4 vols. (London: Richard Bentley, 1845).

Walton, William, *An Exposé on the Dissentions of Spanish America* ... (London: The Author, 1814).

Walton, William, *Present State of the Spanish Colonies; including a Particular Report of Hispaniola* ..., 2 vols. (London: Longman, Hurst, Rees, Orme & Brown, 1810).

Wellington, Arthur, Duke of, *Supplementary Despatches, Correspondence, and Memoranda of Field Marshal Arthur, Duke of Wellington, K.G.*, ed. Arthur, 2nd Duke of Wellington, 15 vols. (London: John Murray, 1858–72).

Whitworth, Charles, Sir, *State of the Trade of Great Britain in its Imports and Exports progressively from the year 1762* ..., 2 vols. (London, 1776).

Young, William, Bart., *The West-India Common-Place Book: compiled from Parliamentary and Official Documents, shewing the Interest of Great Britain in its Sugar Colonies, etc* (London: Richard Phillips, 1807).

Secondary Sources

Aiton, Arthur S., 'The Asiento Treaty as Reflected in the Papers of Lord Shelburne', *Hispanic American Historical Review*, 8:2 (May 1928), pp. 167–77.

Allen, Helen M., 'British Commercial Policy in the West Indies from 1783 to 1793' (unpublished PhD diss., University of London, 1928).

Allen, William Hervey, *Anthony Adverse* (New York: Farrar & Rinehart, 1933).

Alvarez, F., Mercedes, M., *Comercio y comerciantes y sus proyecciones en la independencia venezolana* (Caracas: Tip. Vargas, S.A., 1963).

Andrews, Kenneth Raymond, 'Beyond the Equinoctial: England and South America in the Sixteenth Century', *Journal of Imperial and Commonwealth History*, 10:1 (Oct. 1981), pp. 4–24.

Andrews, Kenneth Raymond, *The Spanish Caribbean: Trade and Plunder, 1530–1630* (New Haven: Yale University Press, 1978).

Arcila Farias, Eduardo, *Reformas económicas del siglo XVIII en Nueva España*, 2 vols. (Mexico: Secretaría de Educación Pública, 1974).

Armytage, Frances, *The Free Port System in the British West Indies: A Study in Commercial Policy, 1766–1822* (London: Longmans, Green & Co., 1953).

Arregui Martínez-Moya, Salvador, 'La instrucción de Guardacostas de 1803',

Anales de la Universidad de Murcia, 39:2–4 (1982), pp. 179–201.

Baeza Martín, Ascensión, 'La acusación contra el virrey Casafuerte en 1724', *Temas Americanistas* (Seville), 15 (2002), pp. 18–24.

Barba, Enrique M., 'Sobre el contrabando de la Colonia del Sacramento. (Siglo XVIII)', *Investigaciones y Ensayos* (Argentina), 28 (Jan.–June 1980), pp. 57–76.

Barbier, Jacques A., 'Anglo-American Investors and Payments on Spanish Imperial Treasuries, 1795–1808', in Jacques Barbier and Allan J. Kuethe (eds.), *The North American Role in the Spanish Imperial Economy, 1760–1819* (Manchester: Manchester University Press, 1984), pp. 134–41.

Barbier, Jacques A., 'Commercial Reform and *Comercio Neutral* in Cartagena de Indias, 1788–1808', in John R. Fisher, Allan J. Kuethe and Anthony McFarlane (eds.), *Reform and Insurrection in Bourbon New Granada and Peru* (Baton Rouge: Louisiana State University Press, 1990), pp. 96–120.

Barbier, Jacques A., 'Imperial Policy towards the Port of Veracruz, 1788–1808: The Struggle between Madrid, Cadiz and Havana Interests', in Nils Jacobsen and Hans-Jurgen Puhle (eds.), *The Economies of Mexico and Peru during the Late Colonial Period, 1760–1810* (Berlin: Colloquium Verlag, 1986), pp. 240–51.

Barbier, Jacques A., 'Peninsular Finance and Colonial Trade: The Dilemma of Charles IV's Spain', *Journal of Latin American Studies*, 12:1 (May 1980), pp. 21–37.

Barbier, Jacques A., 'Venezuelan "Libranzas", 1788–1807: From Economic Nostrum to Fiscal Imperative', *The Americas*, 37 (1981), pp. 457–78.

Barbier, Jacques A., and Allan J. Kuethe (eds.), *The North American Role in the Spanish Imperial Economy, 1760–1819* (Manchester: Manchester University Press, 1984).

Barras y Aragón, Francisco de las, 'Noticias y documentos de la expedición del Conde de Mompóx a la Isla de Cuba', *Anuario de Estudios Americanos*, 9 (1952), pp. 513–48.

Batcheler, L.E.M., 'The South Sea Company and the Assiento' (unpublished MA diss., University of London, 1924).

Becker, Jerónimo, *España e Inglaterra: Sus relaciones políticas desde las paces de Utrecht* (Madrid: Ambrosio Pérez, 1906).

Beckles, Hilary McD., 'The "Hub of Empire": The Caribbean and Britain in the Seventeenth Century', in *Oxford History of the British Empire*, vol. 1, *The Origins of Empire: British Overseas Enterprise to the Close of the Seventeenth Century*, ed. Nicholas Canny (Oxford and New York: Oxford University Press, 1998), pp. 218–40.

Beer, George Louis, *British Colonial Policy, 1754–1765* (New York: Macmillan Company, 1907).

Bell, Herbert C., 'British Commercial Policy in the West Indies, 1783–93', *English Historical Review*, 31:123 (July 1916), pp. 429–41.

Bonet de Sotillo, Dolores, *El tráfico ilegal en las colonias españolas* (Caracas: Editorial Sucre, 1955).

Born, John Dewey, Jr., 'British Trade in West Florida, 1763–1783' (unpublished

PhD diss., University of New Mexico, 1963).

Böttcher, Nikolaus, 'Casas de comercio británicas y sus intereses en América Latina, 1760–1860: estado y problemas de la investigación actual', *Ibero-Amerikanisches Archiv*, 22:1–2 (1996), pp. 191–241.

Böttcher, Nikolaus, 'Trade, War and Empire: British Merchants in Cuba, 1762–1796', in Nikolaus Böttcher and Bernd Hausberger (eds.), *Dinero y negocios en la historia de América Latina: Veinte ensayos dedicados a Reinhard Liehr* (Berlin: Iberoamericana, 2000), pp. 169–98.

Brading, David A., 'Bourbon Spain and Its American Empire', in Leslie Bethell (ed.), *Colonial Spanish America* (Cambridge: Cambridge University Press, 1987), pp. 112–62.

Brown, Vera Lee, 'Anglo-Spanish Relations in America in the Closing Years of the Colonial Era [1763–1774]', *Hispanic American Historical Review*, 5:3 (Aug. 1922), pp. 329–483.

Brown, Vera Lee, 'Contraband Trade: A Factor in the Decline of Spain's Empire in America', *Hispanic American Historical Review*, 8:2 (1928), pp. 178–89.

Brown, Vera Lee, 'The South Sea Company and Contraband Trade', *American Historical Review*, 31:4 (July 1926), pp. 662–78.

Bruchey, Stuart Weems, *Robert Oliver, Merchant of Baltimore, 1763–1819* (Baltimore: Johns Hopkins University Press, 1956).

Buist, Marten G., *At Spes Non Fracta: Hope and Co., 1770–1815; Merchant Bankers and Diplomats at Work* (The Hague: Martinus Nijhoff, 1974).

Bullion, John L., *A Great and Necessary Measure: George Grenville and the Genesis of the Stamp Act, 1763–1765* (Columbia and London: University of Missouri Press, 1982).

Burnard, T.G., '"Prodigious Riches": The Wealth of Jamaica before the American Revolution', *Economic History Review*, 2nd series, 54:3 (Aug. 2001), pp. 506–24.

Calderón Quijano, José Antonio (ed.), *Los virreyes de Nueva España en el reinado de Carlos IV*, 2 vols. (Seville: Escuela de Estudios Hispano-Americanos, 1972).

Canovas Botia, Antonio, 'La última crisis del comercio colonial mexicano, 1805–1808', in Juan Bautista Vilar (coord.), *Murcia y América. VII Curso de Aproximación a la España Contemporánea* (Murcia: Universidad de Murcia, 1992), pp. 225–37.

Carmichael, Gertrude, *The History of the West Indian Islands of Trinidad and Tobago, 1498–1900* (London: Alvin Redman, 1961).

Carter, Clarence E., 'Some Aspects of British Administration in West Florida', *Mississippi Valley Historical Review*, 1:3 (Dec. 1914), pp. 364–75.

Carter, Clarence E., 'The Beginnings of British West Florida', *Mississippi Valley Historical Review*, 4 (1917–18), pp. 314–41.

Caughey, John Walton, 'Bernardo de Gálvez and the English Smugglers on the Mississippi, 1777', *Hispanic American Historical Review*, 12:1 (Feb. 1932), pp. 46–58.

Caughey, John Walton, *Bernardo de Gálvez in Louisiana, 1776–1783* (Berkeley: University of California Press, 1934).

Christelow, Allan, 'Contraband Trade between Jamaica and the Spanish Main, and the Free Port Act of 1766', *Hispanic American Historical Review*, 22:2 (May 1942), pp. 309–43.

Christelow, Allan, 'Great Britain and the Trades from Cadiz and Lisbon to Spanish America and Brazil, 1759–1783', *Hispanic American Historical Review*, 27:1 (Feb. 1947), pp. 2–29.

Clark, G.N., *Guide to English Commercial Statistics, 1696–1782* (London: Royal Historical Society, 1938).

Claypole, W.A., and D.J. Buisseret, 'Trade Patterns in Early English Jamaica', *Jamaican Historical Review*, 5 (1972), pp. 1–19.

Coatsworth, John, 'American Trade with European Colonies in the Caribbean and South America, 1790–1812', *William and Mary Quarterly*, 24:3 (Apr. 1967), pp. 243–66.

Colmenares, Germán, *Historia económica y social de Colombia*, 5th edn ([Bogotá]: Tercer Mundo, 1997).

Connell-Smith, G., 'English Merchants Trading to the New World in the Early Sixteenth Century', *Bulletin of the Institute of Historical Research*, 23 (1950), pp. 53–67.

Costeloe, Michael P., 'Spain and the Latin American Wars of Independence: The Free Trade Controversy, 1810–1820', *Hispanic American Historical Review* 61:2 (May 1981), pp. 209–34.

Craton, Michael, *A History of the Bahamas* (London: Collins, 1962).

Crouzet, François, *L'Economie Britannique et le Blocus Continentale (1806–1813)*, 2 vols. (Paris: Presses Universitaires de France, 1958).

Cuenca Esteban, Javier, 'Statistics of Spain's Colonial Trade, 1792–1829: Consular Duties, Cargo Inventories, and Balances of Trade', *Hispanic American Historical Review* 61:3 (Aug. 1981), pp. 381–428.

Cuenca Esteban, Javier, 'Trends and Cycles in U.S. Trade with Spain and the Spanish Empire, 1790–1819', *Journal of Economic History*, 44:2 (June 1984), pp. 521–43.

Curtin, Philip D., *The Atlantic Slave Trade: A Census* (Madison: University of Wisconsin Press, 1969).

Dahlgren, E.W., *Les relations commerciales et maritimes entre la France et les côtes de l'océan Pacifique (commencement du XVIIIième siècle)*, vol. 1 (no further vols. published) (Paris: H. Champion, 1909).

Davies, K.G., *The Royal African Company* (New York: Atheneum Press, 1970).

Davis, Ralph, *The Industrial Revolution and British Overseas Trade* (Leicester: Leicester University Press, 1979).

Dawson, Frank Griffith, 'William Pitt's Settlement at Black River on the Mosquito Shore: A Challenge to Spain in Central America, 1732–87', *Hispanic American Historical Review*, 63:4 (1983), pp. 677–706.

Deagan, Kathleen, and José María Cruxent, *Columbus's Outpost among the Tainos: Spain and America at La Isabela, 1493–1498* (New Haven: Yale University Press, 2002).

Delgado, Jaime, 'El Conde de Ricla, capitán general de Cuba', *Revista de Historia de América*, 55–6 (Jan.–Dec. 1963), pp. 41–138.

Díaz-Trechuelo Spínola, Lourdes, Concepción Pajarón Parody and Adolfo Rubio Gil, 'El virrey Don Juan Vicente de Güemes Pacheco, segundo Conde de Revillagigedo [1789–94]', in *Los virreyes de Nueva España en el reinado de Carlos IV*, ed. José Antonio Calderón Quijano, 2 vols. (Seville: Escuela de Estudios Hispano-Americanos, 1972), 1:85–366.

Dookhan, Isaac, 'Viegques [*sic*] or Crab Island: Source of Anglo-Spanish Colonial Conflict', *Journal of Caribbean History*, 7 (Nov. 1973), pp. 1–22.

Dookhan, Isaac, *A History of the British Virgin Islands, 1672–1970* (Epping: Caribbean University Press, 1975).

Domínguez Ortiz, Antonio, *Sociedad y Estado en el siglo XVIII español* (Barcelona: Ariel, 1990).

Eltis, David, *The Rise of African Slavery in the Americas* (New York: Cambridge University Press, 2000).

Eltis, David, Stephen D. Behrendt, David Richardson, and Herbert S. Klein (eds.), *The Trans-Atlantic Slave Trade: A Database on CD-ROM* (Cambridge and New York: Cambridge University Press, 1999).

Fernández de Pinedo Echeverría, Nadia, 'Commercial Relations between [the] USA and Cuba in Times of Peace and War, 1803–1807', *Illes i Imperis*, 4 (Spring 2001), pp. 5–23.

Fernández Hernández, Bernabé, 'El contrabando británico en Honduras durante las guerras revolucionarias', in Antonio Gutiérrez Escudero (ed.), *Ciencia, economía y política en Hispanoamérica colonial* (Sevilla: Escuela de Estudios Hispano-Americanos, 2000), pp. 221–34.

Ferns, H.S., *Britain and Argentina in the Nineteenth Century* (Oxford: Clarendon Press, 1960).

Fisher, John Robert, 'Commerce and Imperial Decline: Spanish Trade with Spanish America, 1797–1820', *Journal of Latin American Studies*, 30 (1998), pp. 459–79.

Fisher, John Robert, *Commercial Relations between Spain and Spanish America in the Era of Free Trade, 1778–1796* (Liverpool: Liverpool University Press, 1985).

Fisher, John Robert, *The Economic Aspects of Spanish Imperialism in America, 1492–1810* (Liverpool: Liverpool University Press, 1997).

Fisher, John Robert, 'Imperial "Free Trade" and the Hispanic Economy, 1778–1796', *Journal of Latin American Studies*, 13 (1981), pp. 21–56.

Fisher, John Robert, 'The Imperial Response to "Free Trade": Spanish Imports from Spanish America, 1778–1796', *Journal of Latin American Studies*, 17 (1985), pp. 35–78.

Fisher, John Robert, *Trade, War and Revolution: Exports from Spain to Spanish America, 1797–1820* (Liverpool: Liverpool University Press, 1992).

Fisher, John Robert, Allan J. Kuethe and Anthony McFarlane (eds.), *Reform and Insurrection in Bourbon New Granada and Peru* (Baton Rouge: University of Louisiana Press, 1990).

Floyd, Troy S., *The Anglo-Spanish Struggle for Mosquitia* (Albuquerque:

University of New Mexico, 1967).

Fontana Lázaro, Josep, and Antonio Miguel Bernal (eds.), *El 'Comercio Libre' entre España y América (1765–1824)* (Madrid: Fundación Banco Exterior, 1987).

Fortune, Stephen A., *Merchants and Jews: The Struggle for British West Indian Commerce, 1650–1750* (Gainsville: University of Florida Press, 1984).

Frank, André Gunder, *ReOrient: Global Economy in the Asian Age* (Berkeley and Los Angeles: University of California Press, 1998).

Fraser, Lionel Mordaunt, *History of Trinidad*, 2 vols. (Port of Spain, Trinidad: Government Printing Office, 1891).

Fugier, André, *Napoléon et l'Espagne, 1799–1808*, 2 vols. (Paris: Librairie Félix Alcan, 1930).

Galbis Díez, María del Carmen, 'Miguel José de Azanza (1798–1800)', in *Los virreyes de Nueva España en el reinado de Carlos IV*, ed. José Antonio Calderón Quijano, 2 vols. (Seville: Escuela de Estudios Hispano-Americanos, 1972), 2:1–64.

García-Baquero González, Antonio, *Cádiz y el Atlántico (1717–1778). El comercio colonial español bajo el monopolio gaditano*, 2nd edn, 2 vols. (Cádiz, 1988).

García-Baquero González, Antonio, *Comercio colonial y guerras revolucionarias: La decadencia económica de Cádiz a raíz de la emancipación americana* (Seville: Escuela de Estudios Hispano-Americanos, 1972).

García-Baquero González, Antonio, *El comercio colonial en la época del absolutismo ilustrado: problemas y debates* (Granada: Editorial Universidad de Granada, 2003).

García-Baquero González, Antonio, 'Estados Unidos, Cuba y el comercio de "neutrales"', *Revista de la Universidad Complutense*, 26 (1977).

García Fernández, María Nélida, 'Negociando con el enemigo. El tráfico marítimo comercial Inglaterra – España y la colonia británica de Cádiz en el siglo XVIII' (unpublished PhD diss., Universidad de Cádiz, 2002).

García Fuentes, Lutgardo, *El comercio español con América, 1650–1700* (Seville: Escuela de Estudios Hispano-Americanos, 1980).

Gardner, W.J., *A History of Jamaica from its Discovery by Christopher Columbus to the Present Time* (London: Elliot Stock, 1873).

Gibbs, John Arthur, *The History of Antony and Dorothea Gibbs and of their Contemporary Relatives. Including the History of the Origin and Early Years of the House of Antony Gibbs and Sons* (London: Saint Catherine Press, 1922).

Gipson, Lawrence Henry, 'British Diplomacy in the Light of Anglo-Spanish New World Issues, 1750–1757', *American Historical Review*, 51:4 (July 1946), pp. 627–48.

Goebel, Dorothy Burne, 'British Trade to the Spanish Colonies, 1796–1823', *American Historical Review*, 43:3 (1938), pp. 288–320.

Gómez Gómez, Amalia, 'Nota sobre el contrabando gaditano a fines del siglo XVIII', in *La burguesía mercantil gaditana (1650–1868)*, ed. José Antonio Calderón Quijano (Cadiz: Instituto de Estudios Gaditanos, Excma. Diputación Provincial de Cádiz, 1976), pp. 237–45.

Gómez Molleda, María Dolores, 'El contrabando inglés en America. Correspondencia inédita de la factoría de Buenos Aires', *Hispania*, 10 (1950), pp. 336–69.

Gortari, Hira de, and Guillermo Palacios, 'El comercio novohispano a través de Veracruz (1802–1810)', *Historia Mexicana*, 17:67 (Jan.–Mar. 1968), pp. 427–54.

Graham, Gerald S., 'The Origin of Free Ports in British North America', *Canadian Historical Review*, 22:1 (Mar. 1941), pp. 25–34.

Grahn, Lance, 'An Irresoluble Dilemma: Smuggling in New Granada, 1713–1763', in John R. Fisher, Allan J. Kuethe and Anthony McFarlane (eds.), *Reform and Insurrection in Bourbon New Granada and Peru* (Baton Rouge: Louisiana State University Press, 1990), pp. 123–46.

Grahn, Lance, *The Political Economy of Smuggling: Regional Informal Economies in Early Bourbon New Granada* (Boulder: Westview Press, 1997).

Granda, Germán de, 'Una ruta marítima de contrabando de esclavos negros entre Panamá y Barbacoas durante el asiento inglés', *Revista de Indias*, 36:143–4 (Jan.–June 1976), pp. 123–46.

Grant, William L., 'Canada versus Guadeloupe, an Episode of the Seven Years' War', *American Historical Review*, 17:4 (July 1912), pp. 735–43.

Guiteras, Pedro José, *Historia de la Isla de Cuba*, 3 vols. (Havana: Cultural, 1927–28).

Hamnett, Brian R., 'The Appropriation of Mexican Church Wealth by the Spanish Bourbon Government – The "Consolidación de Vales Reales", 1805–180', *Journal of Latin American Studies*, 1:2 (1969), pp. 85–113.

Headlam, Cecil, 'International Relations in the Colonial Sphere, 1763–1783', *Cambridge History of the British Empire*, vol. 1 (Cambridge: Cambridge University Press, 1929), pp. 685–716.

Herrán Baquero, Mario, *El virrey Don Antonio Amar y Borbón: La crisis del regimen colonial en la Nueva Granada* (Bogotá: Banco de la República, 1988).

Heredia Herrera, Antonia, 'La presencia de extranjeros en el comercio gaditano en el siglo XVIII', *Homenaje al Dr Muro Orejón*, 2 vols. (Seville: Universidad de Sevilla, 1979), 1:233–43.

Hidy, Ralph Willard, *The House of Baring in American Trade and Finance: English Merchant Bankers at Work, 1763–1861* (Cambridge, MA: Harvard University Press, 1949).

Hildner, Ernest G., Jr., 'The Rôle of the South Sea Company in the Diplomacy Leading to the War of Jenkins' Ear, 1729–1739', *Hispanic American Historical Review*, 18:3 (Aug. 1938), pp. 322–41.

Holden, Furber, 'An Abortive Attempt at Anglo-Spanish Commercial Cooperation in the Far East in 1793', *Hispanic American Historical Review*, 15:4 (Nov. 1935), pp. 448–63.

Holland Rose, John, 'British West India Commerce as a Factor in the Napoleonic War', *Cambridge Historical Journal*, 3:1 (1929), pp. 34–46.

Horsfall, Lucy Frances, 'British Relations with the Spanish Colonies in the Caribbean, 1713–39' (unpublished MA diss., University of London, 1936).

Horsfall, Lucy Frances, 'The West Indian Trade', in Cyril Northcote Parkinson (ed.), *The Trade Winds. A Study of British Overseas Trade during the French Wars, 1793–1815* (London: Allen & Unwin, 1948), pp. 157–93.

Howard, Clinton Newton, 'Governor Johnstone in West Florida', *Florida Historical Quarterly*, 17:4 (Apr. 1939), pp. 281–303.

Howard, Clinton Newton, 'Some Economic Aspects of British West Florida, 1763–1768', *Journal of Southern History*, 6 (Feb.–Nov. 1940), pp. 201–21.

Howard, Clinton Newton, *The British Development of West Florida, 1763–1769* (Berkeley and Los Angeles: University of California Press, 1947).

Humphreys, Robin Arthur, 'Anglo-American Rivalries and Spanish-American Emancipation', *Transactions of the Royal Historical Society*, 5th series, 16 (1966), pp. 131–56.

Humphreys, Robin Arthur, 'British Merchants and South American Independence', *Proceedings of the British Academy*, 51 (1965), pp. 151–74.

Imlah, A.H., 'Real Values in British Foreign Trade, 1798–1853', *Journal of Economic History*, 8:2 (1948), pp. 133–52.

Inikori, Joseph E., *Africans and the Industrial Revolution in England: A Study in International Trade and Economic Development* (Cambridge: Cambridge University Press, 2002).

Izard, Miguel, 'Algunas notas sobre el comercio colonial atlántico: Los intercambios del Reino Unido con América, 1772–1808', *Revista de Indias*, 40:159–62 (Jan.–Dec. 1980), pp. 425–39.

Jackson, John Alexander, 'The Mexican Silver Schemes: Finance and Profiteering in the Napoleonic Era, 1796–1811' (unpublished PhD diss., University of Carolina, 1978).

Jacobsen, Nils, and Hans-Jurgen Puhle (eds.), *The Economies of Mexico and Peru during the Late Colonial Period (1760–1810)* (Berlin: Colloqium Verlag, 1986).

Jiménez Codinach, Guadalupe, 'An Atlantic Silver Entrepôt: Vera Cruz and the House of Gordon and Murphy', in Franklin W. Knight and Peggy K. Liss (eds.), *Atlantic Port Cities. Economy, Culture, and Society in the Atlantic World, 1650–1850)* (Knoxville: University of Tennessee Press, 1991), pp. 149–67.

Jiménez Codinach, Guadalupe, 'El comercio clandestino, 1797–1811', in Carmen Yuste López and Matilde Souto Mantecón (eds.), *El comercio exterior de México, 1713–1850: Entre la quiebra del sistema imperial y el surgimiento de una nación* (Mexico City: Instituto de Investigaciones Dr. José María Luis Mora / Instituto de Investigaciones Históricas – U.N.A.M. / Universidad Veracruzana, 2000), pp. 193–206.

Jiménez Codinach, Guadalupe, *La Gran Bretaña y la independencia de México, 1808–1821* (Mexico City: Fondo de Cultura Económica, 1991).

Johnson, Cecil, *British West Florida, 1763–1783* (New Haven: Yale University Press, 1943).

Jones, J. Stoddard, 'Historical Study of Anglo-Spanish American Trade, with Special Reference to the Period 1807–1825' (unpublished PhD diss., London School of Economics [in Senate House Library, University of London], 1934).

Kaufman, William W., *British Policy and the Independence of Latin America,*

1804–1828 (New Haven: Yale University Press, 1951).

Keeble, Thomas Whitfield, *Commercial Relations between British Overseas Territories and South America, 1806–1914* (London: Athlone Press, 1970).

Keith, Alice B., 'Relaxations in the British Restrictions on the American Trade with the British West Indies, 1783–1802', *Journal of Modern History*, 20:1 (Mar. 1948), pp. 1–18.

Kerr, Wilfred Brenton, *Bermuda and the American Revolution* (Princeton: Princeton University Press, 1936).

King, James Ferguson, 'Evolution of the Free Slave Trade Principle in Spanish Colonial Administration', *Hispanic American Historical Review*, 22:1 (Feb. 1942), pp. 34–56.

Klein, Herbert S., *The Atlantic Slave Trade* (Cambridge: Cambridge University Press, 1999).

Knight, Franklin W., and Peggy K. Liss (eds.), *Atlantic Port Cities: Economy, Culture, and Society in the Atlantic World, 1650–1850* (Knoxville: University of Tennessee Press, 1991).

Kuethe, Allan J., 'El fin del monopolio: los Borbones y el Consulado andaluz', in Carlos Alvarez Nogal *et al.* (eds.), *Relaciones de poder y comercio colonial: Nuevas perspectivas* (Seville: Escuela de Estudios Hispano-Americanos, 1999), pp. 35–66.

Kuethe, Allan J., 'Havana in the Eighteenth Century', in Franklin W. Knight and Peggy K. Liss (eds.), *Atlantic Port Cities. Economy, Culture, and Society in the Atlantic World, 1650–1850* (Knoxville: University of Tennessee Press, 1991), pp. 13–39.

Kup, A.P., 'Alexander Lindsay, 6th Earl of Balcarres, Lieutenant Governor of Jamaica 1794–1801', *Bulletin of the John Rylands University Library of Manchester*, 57 (1974–75), pp. 327–65.

Lang, J., *Conquest and Commerce: Spain and England in the Americas* (London: Academic Press, 1975).

Langford, Paul, *The First Rockingham Administration, 1765–1766* ([London]: Oxford University Press, 1973).

Langnas, Izaac Abram, 'Great Britain's Relations with Spanish America, 1808–1812' (unpublished PhD diss., University of London, 1938).

Lario de Oñate, María del Carmen, *La colonia mercantil británica e irlandesa en Cádiz a finales del siglo XVIII* (Cadiz: Universidad de Cádiz, 2000).

Lasky, Herbert, 'David Parish: A European in American Finance, 1806–1816' (unpublished PhD diss., Ann Arbor, Michigan, n.d.).

Laurence, K.O., *Tobago in Wartime, 1793–1815* (Barbados: University Press of the West Indies, 1995).

Lavrín, Asunción, 'The Execution of the Law of *Consolidación* in New Spain: Economic Aims and Results', *Hispanic American Historical Review*, 53:1 (Feb. 1973), pp. 27–49.

Le Riverend Brusone, Julio, 'Relaciones entre Nueva España y Cuba (1518–1820)', *Revista de Historia de América*, 37–38 (Jan.–Dec. 1954), pp. 45–108.

Lévy, Arthur, *Un gran profiteur de guerre sous la Révolution, l'Empire et la Restauration: G.J. Ouvrard* (Paris, 1929).

Lewis, James A., 'Anglo-American Entrepreneurs in Havana: The Background and Significance of the Expulsion of 1784–1785', in Jacques A. Barbier and Allan J. Kuethe (eds.), *The North American Role in the Spanish Imperial Economy, 1760–1819* (Manchester: Manchester University Press, 1984), pp. 112–26.

Liss, Peggy K., *Atlantic Empires: The Network of Trade and Revolution, 1713–1826* (Baltimore: John Hopkins University Press, 1983).

López Cantos, Angel, 'Contrabando, corso y situado en el siglo XVIII: Una economía subterránea', *Anales: Revista de Ciencias Sociales* (Universidad Interamericana de Puerto Rico, San Germán), new series, 1:2 (1985), pp. 31–62.

López Cantos, Angel, *Don Francisco de Saavedra, Segundo Intendente de Caracas* (Seville: Escuela de Estudios Hispano-Americanos, 1973).

López Cantos, Angel, 'El comercio legal de Puerto Rico con las colonias extranjeras de América (1700–1783)', *Revista de ciencias sociales* (Puerto Rico), 24:1–2 (Jan.–June 1985), pp. 201–27.

Lucena Salmoral, Manuel, *Características del comercio exterior de la provincia de Caracas durante el sexenio revolucionario (1807–1812)* (Madrid: Instituto de Cooperación Iberoamericana / Instituto de Estudios Fiscales, 1990).

Lucena Salmoral, Manuel, 'El comercio de los Estados Unidos con España e Hispanoamérica a comienzos de la presidencia de Madison', *Actas del Congreso de Historia de los Estados Unidos* (Madrid: Ministerio de Educación y Ciencia, 1978), pp. 171–241.

Lynch, John, *Bourbon Spain, 1700–1808* (Oxford: Basil Blackwell, 1989).

Lynch, John, 'British Policy and Spanish America, 1783–1808', *Journal of Latin American Studies*, 1:1 (1969), pp. 1–30.

Lynch, John, *The Hispanic World in Crisis and Change, 1598–1700* (Oxford: Basil Blackwell, 1992).

Malamud Rikles, Carlos Daniel, *Cádiz y Saint Malo en el comercio colonial peruano (1698–1725)* (Cadiz: Diputación Provincial de Cádiz,1986).

Manning, Helen Taft, *British Colonial Government after the American Revolution, 1782–1820* (1933; Hamden, CT: Archon Books, 1966).

Manning, William Ray, 'The Nootka Sound Controversy', American Historical Association, *Annual Report* (Washington: Government Printing Office, 1904), pp. 279–478.

Marichal, Carlos, 'El comercio neutral y los consorcios extranjeros en Veracruz, 1805–1808', in Carmen Yuste López and Matilde Souto Mantecón (eds.), *El comercio exterior de México, 1713–1850: Entre la quiebra del sistema imperial y el surgimiento de una nación* (Mexico City: Instituto de Investigaciones Dr. José María Luis Mora / Instituto de Investigaciones Históricas – U.N.A.M. / Universidad Veracruzana, 2000), pp. 163–92.

Marichal, Carlos, 'El tratado de subsidios con Napoleón y las finanzas novohispanas, 1803–1808', *A: Revista de ciencias sociales y humanidades*, 9:27 (1989), pp. 41–54.

Marichal, Carlos, *La bancarrota del virreinato. Nueva España y las finanzas del imperio español, 1780–1810* (Mexico City: El Colegio de México, 1999).

Marrero, Levi, *Cuba: Economía y sociedad*, 15 vols. (Madrid: Playor, D.L., 1972–92).

Mateu y Llopis, Felipe, 'Navíos ingleses en el puerto de Veracruz en 1763', *Revista de Indias*, 4:14 (Oct.–Dec. 1943), pp. 683–707.

McCusker, John J., 'Colonial Civil Servant and Counter-Revolutionary: Thomas Irving (1738?–1800) in Boston, Charleston, and London', in John J. McCusker, *Essays in the Economic History of the Atlantic World* (London and New York: Routledge, 1997), pp. 190–221.

McFarlane, Anthony, *Colombia before Independence. Economy, Society, and Politics under Bourbon Rule* (Cambridge: Cambridge University Press, 1993).

McFarlane, Anthony, 'El comercio exterior del Virreinato de la Nueva Granada: Conflictos en la política económica de los Borbones, 1783–1789', *Anuario Colombiano de Historia Social y de la Cultura*, 6–7 (1971–72), pp. 69–116.

McFarlane, Anthony, *The British in the Americas, 1480–1815* (London and New York: Longman, 1994).

McLachlan, Jean O., *Trade and Peace with Old Spain, 1667–1750* (Cambridge: Cambridge University Press, 1940).

Metcalf, George, *Royal Government and Political Conflict in Jamaica, 1729–1783* (London: Longmans, Green & Co., 1965).

Miller, Rory, *Britain and Latin America in the Nineteenth and Twentieth Centuries* (Harlow: Longman, 1993).

Mitchell, B.R., *British Historical Statistics* (Cambridge: Cambridge University Press, 1988).

Morales Carrión, Arturo, *Puerto Rico and the Non-Hispanic Caribbean: A Study in the Decline of Spanish Exclusivism* (Río Piedras: Universidad de Puerto Rico, 1952).

Morales Padrón, Francisco, 'México y la Independencia de Hispanoamérica en 1781, según un comisionado regio: Francisco de Saavedra', *Revista de Indias*, 29:115–18 (Jan.–Dec. 1969), pp. 335–58.

Moreno Fraginals, Manuel, *El Ingenio: Complejo económico social cubano del azúcar* (1978; Barcelona: Crítica, 2001).

Morgan, Edmund Sears, and Helen M. Sears, *The Stamp Act Crisis: Prologue to Revolution* (Chapel Hill, NC: University of North Carolina, 1953).

Mowat, Charles Loch, *East Florida as a British Province, 1763–1784* (Berkeley and Los Angeles: University of California Press, 1943).

Muller, Herman J., 'British Business and Spanish America, 1700–1800', *Mid-America*, 39:1 (new series 28) (1957), pp. 3–20.

Mullet, Charles F., 'British Schemes against Spanish America in 1806', *Hispanic American Historical Review*, 27:2 (May 1947), 269–78.

Nadal Farreras, Joaquín, *Comercio exterior y subdesarrollo: España y Gran Bretaña de 1772 a 1914: Política económica y relaciones comerciales* (Madrid: Instituto de Estudios Fiscales, 1978).

Nardin, Jean-Claude, *La mise en valeur de l'île de Tabago (1763–1783)* (Paris: Mouton & Co., 1969).

Navarro García, Luis, and María del Populo Antolín Espino, 'El virrey Marqués de Branciforte [1794–98]', in José Antonio Calderón Quijano (ed.), *Los virreyes de Nueva España en el reinado de Carlos IV*, 2 vols. (Seville: Escuela de Estudios Hispano-Americanos, 1972), 1:367–625.

Nelson, George H., 'Contraband Trade under the Asiento, 1730–1739', *American Historical Review*, 51:1 (Oct. 1945), pp. 55–67.

Nestares Pleguezuelo, María José, *El comercio exterior del Oriente venezolano en el siglo XVIII* (Almería: Universidad de Almería, 1992).

Nettels, Curtis, 'England and the Spanish American Trade, 1680–1715', *Journal of Modern History*, 3:1 (Mar. 1931), pp. 1–32.

Newson, Linda A., *Aboriginal and Spanish Colonial Trinidad: A Study in Culture Contact* (London: Academic Press, 1976).

Nichols, Roy F., 'Trade Relations and the Establishment of the United States Consulates in Spanish America, 1779–1809', *Hispanic American Historical Review*, 13:3 (Aug. 1933), pp. 289–313.

Novak, M.E., 'Colonel Jack's "Thieving Roguing" Trade to Mexico and Defoe's Attack on Economic Individualism', *Huntingdon Library Quarterly*, 24:4 (Aug. 1961), pp. 349–53.

Olmos Sánchez, Isabel, 'Contrabando y libre comercio en el Golfo de México y Mar del Sur', *Revista de Historia Naval* (Madrid), 4:22 (1988), pp. 83–104; also in *Estudios de Historia Social y Económica de América* (Alcalá de Henares), 6 (1990), pp. 55–64.

Olsen, James S., and Robert Shadle (eds.), *Historical Dictionary of the British Empire*, 2 vols. (Westport, CT: Greenwood Press, 1996).

Orbell, John, *A History of Baring Brothers to 1939* (London, 1985).

Ortiz de la Tabla Ducasse, Javier, *Comercio exterior de Veracruz, 1778–1821: Crisis de dependencia* (Seville: Escuela de Estudios Hispano-Americanos, 1978).

Osborne, F.J., 'James Castillo, Asiento Agent', *Jamaica Historical Review*, 8 (1971), pp. 9–18.

Palmer, Colin A., *Human Cargoes: The British Slave Trade to Spanish America, 1700–1739* (Urbana: University of Illinois Press, 1981).

Pantaleão, Olga, *A penetração comercial da Inglaterra na América espanhola (1713–1783)* (São Paulo: n.p., 1946).

Pares, Richard, *War and Trade in the West Indies, 1739–1763* (1936; London: Frank Cass & Co., 1963).

Parsons, James J., *San Andrés y Providencia. Una geografía histórica de las islas colombianas del Caribe*, 3rd Spanish edn (Bogotá: El Ancora Editores, 1985).

Payard, Maurice, *Le financier G.J. Ouvrard, 1770–1846 …* ([Reims]: Académie Nationale de Reims, 1958).

Pearce, Adrian J., 'British Trade with the Spanish Colonies, 1788–1795', *Bulletin of Latin American Research*, 20:2 (Apr. 2001), pp. 233–60.

Pearce, Adrian J., 'Early Bourbon Government in the Viceroyalty of Peru,

1700–1759' (unpublished PhD diss., University of Liverpool, 1998).

Pearce, Adrian J., '*Rescates* and Anglo-Spanish Trade in the Caribbean during the French Revolutionary Wars, ca. 1797–1804', *Journal of Latin American Studies*, 38:3 (Aug. 2006), pp. 607–24.

Penson, Lillian M., *The Colonial Agents of the British West Indies: A Study in Colonial Administration, Mainly in the Eighteenth Century* (London: University of London Press, 1924).

Penson, Lillian M., 'The West Indies and the Spanish-American Trade, 1713–1748', *Cambridge History of the British Empire*, vol. 1 (Cambridge: Cambridge University Press, 1929), pp. 330–45.

Pérez Herrero, Pedro, *Comercio y mercados en América Latina colonial* (Madrid: Editorial Mapfre S.A., 1992).

Pérez-Mallaina Bueno, Pablo Emilio, *Comercio y autonomía en la Intendencia de Yucatán (1797–1814)* (Seville: Escuela de Estudios Hispano-Americanos, 1978).

Pezuela, Jacobo de la, *Historia de la Isla de Cuba*, 4 vols. (Madrid: Carlos Bailly-Bailliere, 1868–78).

Pitman, Frank Wesley, *The Development of the British West Indies, 1700–1763* (New Haven: Yale University Press, 1917); reissued (New York: Anchor Books, 1967).

Platt, D.C.M., *Latin America and British Trade, 1806–1914* (London: Adam & Charles Black, 1972).

Potthast-Jutkeit, Barbara, 'Centroamérica y el contrabando por la Costa de Mosquitos en el siglo XVIII', *Mesoamérica*, 36 (Dec. 1998), pp. 499–516.

Prados de la Escosura, Leandro, 'El comercio hispano-británico durante los siglos XVIII y XIX', *Revista de historia económica*, 2:2 (1984), pp. 113–62.

Prados de la Escosura, Leandro, and S. Amaral (eds.), *La independencia americana: Consecuencias económicas* (Madrid: Alianza, 1993).

Pritchett, John Perry, 'Selkirk's Views on British Policy towards the Spanish Colonies, 1806', *Canadian Historical Review*, 24 (1943), pp. 381–96.

Pumar Martínez, Carmen, *Don Antonio Amar y Borbón, último virrey del Nuevo Reino de Granada* (Borja: Centro de Estudios Borjanos, Institución Fernando el Católico, 1991).

Radhay, Keith, 'Contraband between Eastern Venezuela and Trinidad, 1797–1802', *Revista / Review Interamericana* (Puerto Rico), 14 (1984), pp. 20–46.

Ragatz, Lowell Joseph, *Statistics for the Study of British Caribbean Economic History, 1766–1833* (London: Bryan Edwards Press, 1928).

Ragatz, Lowell Joseph, *The Fall of the Planter Class in the British Caribbean, 1763–1833* (New York and London: Century Co., 1928).

Ramos, Héctor R. Feliciano, *El contrabando inglés en el Caribe y el Golfo de México (1748–1778)* (Seville: Excma Diputación Provincial de Sevilla, 1990).

Real Díaz, José Joaquín, 'José de Iturrigaray (1803–1808)', in José Antonio Calderón Quijano (ed.), *Los virreyes de Nueva España en el reinado de Carlos IV*, vol. 2 (Seville: Escuela de Estudios Hispano-Americanos, 1972), pp.

181–331.

Redlich, Fritz, 'Payments between Nations in the Eighteenth and Early Nineteenth Centuries', *Quarterly Journal of Economics* (Cambridge, MA), 50 (1936), pp. 694–705.

Restrepo Tirado, Ernesto, *Historia de la provincia de Santa Marta en el Nuevo Reino de Granada*, 2 vols. (1929; Bogotá: Subdirección de Comunicaciones Culturales, 1975).

Robertson, William Spence, *The Life of Miranda*, 2nd edn, 2 vols. (New York: Cooper Square Publishers, 1969).

Rodríguez Baena, María Luisa, 'El virrey Don Manuel Antonio Flórez [1787–89]', in José Antonio Calderón Quijano (ed.), *Los virreyes de Nueva España en el reinado de Carlos IV*, 2 vols. (Seville: Escuela de Estudios Hispano-Americanos, 1972), 1:1–83.

Rodríguez Casado, Vicente, 'Comentarios al Decreto y Real Instrucción de 1765 regulando las relaciones comerciales de España e Indias', *Anuario de historia del derecho español*, 13 (1936–41), pp. 100–35.

Rodríguez del Valle, Mariana, 'Félix Berenguer de Marquina (1800–1803)', in José Antonio Calderón Quijano (ed.), *Los virreyes de Nueva España en el reinado de Carlos IV*, vol. 2 (Seville: Escuela de Estudios Hispano-Americanos, 1972), pp. 65–179.

Rodríguez Vicente, María Encarnación, 'El comercio cubano y la guerra de emancipación norte-americana', *Anuario de Estudios Americanos*, 11 (1954), pp. 61–106.

Romano, Ruggiero, *Moneda, seudomonedas y circulación monetaria en las economías de México* (Mexico City: El Colegio de México / Fonda de Cultura Económica, 1998).

Rydjord, John, *Foreign Interest in the Independence of New Spain* (Durham, NC: Duke University Press, 1935).

Rydjord, John, 'Napoleon and Mexican Silver', *Southwestern Social Sciences Quarterly*, 19 (1938), pp. 171–82.

Salvucci, Linda K., 'Anglo-American Merchants and Stratagems for Success in Spanish Imperial Markets, 1783–1807', in Jacques Barbier and Allan J. Kuethe (eds.), *The North American Role in the Spanish Imperial Economy, 1760–1819* (Manchester: Manchester University Press, 1984), pp. 127–33.

Sanders, G. Earl, 'Counter-Contraband in Spanish America: Handicaps of the Governors in the Indies', *The Americas*, 34:1 (1977), pp. 59–80.

Scelle, Georges, *La traite negrière aux Indes de Castille*, 2 vols. (Paris, 1906).

Schumpeter, E.B., *English Overseas Trade Statistics, 1697–1808* (Oxford: Clarendon Press, 1960).

Sevilla Soler, María del Rosario, *Inmigración y cambio socio-económico en Trinidad (1783–1797)* (Seville: Escuela de Estudios Hispano-Americanos, 1988).

Sevilla Soler, María del Rosario, *Santo Domingo, Tierra de Frontera (1750–1800)* (Seville: Escuela de Estudios Hispano-Americanos, 1980).

Smith, Robert Sidney, 'Shipping in the Port of Veracruz, 1790–1821', *Hispanic American Historical Review*, 23:1 (Feb. 1943), pp. 5–20.

Sonesson, Birgit, *Puerto Rico's Commerce, 1765–1865: From Regional to World-Wide Market Relations* (Los Angeles: U.C.L.A. Latin American Center Publications, 2000).

Sorsby, Victoria G., 'British Trade with Spanish America under the Asiento, 1713–1740' (unpublished PhD diss., University of London, 1975).

Souto Mantecón, Matilde, *Mar abierto. La política y el comercio del Consulado de Veracruz en el ocaso del sistema imperial* (Mexico City: Colegio de México / Instituto Mora, 2001).

Spindel, Donna J., 'The Stamp Act Crisis in the British West Indies', *Journal of American Studies*, 11:2 (1977), pp. 203–21.

Stein, Stanley J., 'Caribbean Counterpoint: Veracruz vs Havana. War and Neutral Trade, 1797–1799', in Jeanne Chase (ed.), *Geographie du capital marchand aux Amériques, 1760–1860* (Paris: Éditions de l'École des Hautes Études en Sciences Sociales, 1987), pp. 21–44.

Stein, Stanley J., and Barbara H. Stein, *Apogee of Empire: Spain and New Spain in the Age of Charles III, 1759–1789* (Baltimore and London: Johns Hopkins University Press, 2003).

Stein, Stanley J., and Barbara H. Stein, *Silver, Trade, and War: Spain and America in the Making of Early Modern Europe* (Baltimore and London: Johns Hopkins University Press, 2000).

Sutherland, L. Stuart, 'Edmund Burke and the First Rockingham Ministry', *English Historical Review*, 47:185 (Jan. 1932), pp. 46–72.

Tandrón, Humberto, *El comercio de Nueva España y la controversia sobre la libertad de comercio, 1796–1821* (Mexico City: Instituto Mexicano de Comercio Exterior, 1976).

Temperly, Harold W.V., 'The Causes of the War of Jenkins' Ear (1739)', *Transactions of the Royal Historical Society*, 3rd series, 3 (1909), pp. 197–236.

Temperly, Harold W.V., 'The Peace of Paris', *Cambridge History of the British Empire*, vol. 1 (Cambridge: Cambridge University Press, 1929), pp. 485–506.

Temperly, Harold W.V., 'The Relations of England with Spanish America, 1720–1744', American Historical Association, *Annual Report*, vol. 1 (Washington: Government Printing Office, 1911), pp. 229–37.

Thomas, Peter D.G., *British Politics and the Stamp Act Crisis: The First Phase of the American Revolution, 1763–1769* (Oxford: Clarendon Press, 1975).

Thornton, A.P., 'Spanish Slave-Ships in the English West Indies, 1660–85', *Hispanic American Historical Review*, 35 (1955), pp. 374–85.

Tjaerks, Germán O.E., and Alicia Vidaurreta de Tjaerks, *El comercio inglés y el contrabando. Nuevos aspectos en el estudio de la política económica en el Río de la Plata (1807–1810)* (Buenos Aires, 1962).

Torres Ramírez, Bibiano, *La isla de Puerto Rico (1765–1800)* (San Juan: Instituto de Cultura Puertorriqueña, 1968).

Torres Ramírez, Bibiano, 'La isla de Vieques', *Anuario de Estudios Americanos*, 12 (1955), pp. 449–66.

Trens, Manuel B., *Historia de Veracruz*, 6 vols. (Jalapa and Mexico City: Enríquez, 1947–50).

Villalobos R., Sergio, *Comercio y contrabando en el Río de la Plata y Chile, 1700–1811* (Buenos Aires: Editorial Universitaria, 1965).

Villalobos R., Sergio, 'Contrabando francés en el Pacífico, 1700–1724', *Revista de Historia de América* (Mexico), 51 (1961), pp. 49–80.

Villaurrutia, Marqués de, *Relaciones entre España e Inglaterra durante la guerra de la Independencia* (Madrid, 1911).

Walker, Geoffrey J., *Spanish Politics and Imperial Trade, 1700–1789* (London: Macmillan, 1979); in Spanish translation as *Política española y comercio colonial, 1700–1789* (Barcelona: Ariel, 1979).

Walters, Philip G., and Raymond Walters, 'The American Career of David Parish', *Journal of Economic History*, 4:2 (1944), pp. 149–66.

Ward, J.R., 'The British West Indies in the Age of Abolition, 1748–1815', in *Oxford History of the British Empire*, vol. 2, *The Eighteenth Century*, ed. P.J. Marshall (Oxford and New York: Oxford University Press, 1998), pp. 415–39.

Watson, J. Steven, *The Reign of George III, 1760–1815* (Oxford: Clarendon Press, 1960).

Westergaard, Waldemar, *The Danish West Indies under Company Rule (1671–1754)* (New York: Macmillan, 1917).

Whitaker, Arthur Preston, 'The Commerce of Louisiana and the Floridas at the End of the Eighteenth Century', *Hispanic American Historical Review*, 8:2 (Mar. 1928), pp. 190–203.

Whitaker, Arthur Preston, *The Spanish-American Frontier: 1783–1795. The Westward Movement and the Spanish Retreat in the Mississippi Valley* (Boston and New York: Houghton Mifflin Co., 1927).

Wilkinson, Henry C., *Bermuda in the Old Empire* (London: Oxford University Press, 1950).

Williams, Judith Blow, 'Mercados británicos en el Caribe y el Golfo de Méjico, 1750–1850', in *II Congreso Internacional de Historia de América, 1937*, 3 vols. (Buenos Aires: Academia Nacional de la Historia, 1938), 3:95–108.

Williams, Judith Blow, 'The Establishment of British Commerce with Argentina', *Hispanic American Historical Review*, 15:1 (Feb. 1934), pp. 43–64.

Wolf, Otto, *Ouvrard, Speculator of Genius, 1770–1846* ... (first published in German, 1932; London: Barrie & Rockliffe, 1962).

Wright, I.A., 'Rescates: With Special Reference to Cuba, 1599–1610', *Hispanic American Historical Review*, 3 (1920), pp. 333–61.

Zahedieh, Nuala, 'The Merchants of Port Royal, Jamaica, and the Spanish Contraband Trade, 1655–1692', *William and Mary Quarterly*, 3rd series, 43 (1986), pp. 570–93.

Zahedieh, Nuala, 'Trade, Plunder and Economic Development in Early English Jamaica, 1655–89', *Economic History Review*, 2nd series, 39:2 (1986), pp. 205–22.

Ziegler, Philip, *The Sixth Great Power: Barings, 1767–1929* (London: Collins, 1988).

Index